W9-DGF-965

CITIZEN, MOTHER, WORKER

CITIZEN

DEBATING PUBLIC RESPONSIBILITY FOR

MOTHER

CHILD CARE AFTER THE SECOND WORLD WAR

WORKER

Emilie Stoltzfus

The University of North Carolina Press

Chapel Hill and London

Designed by April Leidig-Higgins
Set in Electra by Copperline Book Services, Inc.
Manufactured in the United States of America

The paper in this book meets the guidelines for
permanence and durability of the Committee on
Production Guidelines for Book Longevity of
the Council on Library Resources.

Library of Congress Cataloging-in-Publication Data
Stoltzfus, Emilie.   Citizen, mother, worker: debating
public responsibility for child care after the Second World
War / by Emilie Stoltzfus.
p. cm. — (Gender and American culture)
Includes bibliographical references and index.
ISBN 0-8078-2812-2 (cloth: alk. paper)
ISBN 0-8078-5485-9 (pbk.: alk. paper)
1. Child care — Government policy — United States.
2. Federal aid to child welfare — United States.   3. Federal
aid to day care centers — United States.   4. Women —
Employment — United States.   5. Women — Government
policy — United States. 6. Work and family — United
States.   7. United States — History — 1945–   8. United
States — Social conditions — 1945–   9. United States —
Politics and government — 1945–1989.   I. Title.
II. Gender & American culture.
HQ778.63 .S76 2003
362.7'0973 — dc21   2003001849

cloth   07 06 05 04 03   5 4 3 2 1
paper   07 06 05 04 03   5 4 3 2 1

For Eugene and Gabriel,
who make me happy

CONTENTS

TABLES

ACKNOWLEDGMENTS

Many people enabled and encouraged me to write this book. Early in my research I had the good fortune to meet Belle Likover, a postwar day care activist in Cleveland. She hosted me on my first research trip there, led me to documents that she had wisely preserved, and shared with me her memories of the city's postwar day care battle. I could not have imagined a more encouraging beginning. I am deeply indebted also to Bernice Zahm, Ellen Andruzzi, Flora Calhoun, Constance Severn, and Frances Lomas Feldman, who each provided important insights into the postwar day care struggles waged in Cleveland, the District of Columbia, and California. I trust they will not be disappointed by how I have retold their stories.

I am grateful to Vicki Ruiz and Robert Dawidoff, first of all, for believing that I could be a historian. Aside from her loyalty and friendship, Vicki offered careful reading and useful criticisms of my work. Robert encouraged me to think broadly about the topic of child care and women and offered crucial publishing advice. Eileen Boris also provided essential encouragement for me to continue this project and the results of her thoughtful criticisms and suggestions are everywhere evident in this book. I am grateful as well to Sonya Michel and Elizabeth Rose, who both read all or parts of the manuscript and offered informed and useful criticisms. While the advice of each of these individuals has strengthened this book, any faults or misjudgments that remain I must claim alone.

Writing is lonely work, and I owe many people for their continued encouragement. My colleagues Karen Spar, Vee Burke, Gene Falk, Melinda Gish, and Shannon Harper have made me feel at home at the Congressional Research Service and continue to inspire me to write thoughtfully and clearly. My siblings and my friends, Rosanna Landis Weaver, Sarah Shaw, Ruth Ann Stoltzfus, Nathan Stoltzfus, Rhoda Kroeker, Nancy Steelberg, and Nelson Steelberg, have been endlessly patient with my writing preoccupation. This book is dedicated to my husband, Eugene Stevanus— because I could not have completed it without the daily care and support he continues to offer me—and to our son Gabriel; I never imagined how much fun it would be getting to know him. I am eager to spend less time at the computer and more time with both of them.

CITIZEN, MOTHER, WORKER

Women, just like men, have the role of voting, of thinking, of articulating—of taking a stand and expressing their beliefs. . . .

The broader sense of the concept of the role of women in the defense of democracy is that of the citizen doing her most for the preservation of democracy and peace. . . .

In the more narrow sense of the concept—the concept that makes a distinction on the basis of sex—the most important role of the woman in defense of democracy is her traditional role as homemaker. . . .

Since woman is the homemaker—the keeper of the home—she is the key individual of our democracy at the grassroots level. In that respect, woman is the primary and basic governor of our democracy for our governing starts right in the home. Woman molds the citizens of tomorrow in the rearing that she gives the children.

—Sen. Margaret Chase Smith, June 1953

INTRODUCTION

Citizenship and Child Care

Addressing graduates of Westbrook Junior College in Portland, Maine, Sen. Margaret Chase Smith (R-Maine) articulated two modes of civic participation for U.S. women in the middle of the twentieth century. The first pictured women as ungendered, voting citizens who were active in the debates and discussions of the public sphere. The second, explicitly gendered, saw them on the front lines of democracy as homemakers, and especially as mothers who "mold[ed] the citizens of tomorrow." When Sen. Smith gave this address, women's participation as voters in the public sphere had been sanctioned for little more than three decades, but the vision of mothers whose primary value to the state arose from their obligation to rear good citizens echoed rhetoric as old as the nation itself.

Citizen, Mother, Worker examines the way in which enduring gendered obligations of citizenship affected the possibilities for expanded social rights in post–World War II America. Recent scholarship explores the way social citizenship has been gendered and specifically the role that activist women played in describing rights and responsibilities of female citizens.[1] This book engages those discussions by uncovering the substantial efforts of working mothers to maintain public funding of child care services after the close of World War II and by examining the arguments that parents, primarily mothers, offered in defense of that funding. Within the context of postwar federal policy, it analyzes the debate concerning public versus private responsibility for child care provision and describes efforts to maintain public subsidy of child care in three locations: Cleveland, Ohio; the District of Columbia; and California.

Child care services subsidized with public tax dollars during World War II largely disappeared when the war ended. But this should not be understood as a postwar "natural" or uncontested resumption of traditional gender roles. Recognizing the importance of a child care service to their own self-interest and that of their families, many wage-earning mothers fought to retain public child care services. In doing so they forced public political debate and decision on this issue. With a few notable exceptions, however, their efforts to retain taxpayer-subsidized child care services were not permanently successful. A widespread reluctance to see mothers as citizens with an equal right to earn wages, as well as a failure to understand that childrearing and domestic duties were work that carried public economic value, constituted key parts of a postwar conservative gender ideology that was an important roadblock to continued public child care funding. Responsibility for child care in the postwar period continued to be understood as ideally a private matter—whether as a mother's obligation to her family or, increasingly, a market issue. At the same time, public financing for child care services came to be viewed predominantly as an alternative policy to existing cash aid for poor single mothers.

In looking at the ways in which motherhood, wage work, and citizenship interacted in the two decades from 1945 through the early 1960s, this book consciously discusses a traditional "women's issue" within the context of mainstream politics and social change. It takes the issue of child care as an important political matter and understands female workers and mothers as holding equivalent claims on the liberal democratic state as male workers and fathers.

Gendered Citizenship and Wage Work

Citizenship is an abstract concept that helps to define the relationship between a state and the individuals governed by that state. It suggests an equality of status, if not circumstances, among all who are full members of a political community. The ideal of the equal status of citizenship drew on Enlightenment notions of natural rights inherent in all humans and in a liberal state; it replaced the hierarchies of subjects within a monarchy.[2] Despite the universality of the concept of citizenship, its historical practice has been marked by exclusions and differences.[3] Of particular import to this study is that from the time of the nation's founding, ideal male and female citizenship carried distinct public obligations, and these ideals were further qualified by a citizen's race. The universal ideal of citizenship received early personification in a white man of independent means (a property owner) who participated in public political institutions by voting, serving on juries, and bearing arms in defense of the country. By contrast, female citizens, without the right or obligation to vote, serve on juries, or bear arms, were only indirectly connected to the public polity. At the same time, the concept of republican motherhood paradoxically linked white women to the public by the performance of a private, domestic duty—childrearing.[4]

As the nation grew and industrialization spread, the meaning of citizenship received further elaboration and redefinition. Significantly, in winning the right to universal white male suffrage in the first half of the nineteenth century, working-class men advanced a new understanding of wage labor as a laudable pursuit of an independent citizen—rather than a refuge for the landless and dependent. At the same time, the spread of a free market introduced new concerns about social order, and this trend both renewed and reinterpreted the public importance of white women's private domestic role. Nineteenth-century domestic ideology valorized white women as the guarantors of private familial ties and the salve against the crass self-interests of the economic world of men.[5]

Building on gendered ideals that tied women to the family (domestic) and men to the marketplace (economic), working-class men and women had begun to press both for shorter work hours and for a "family wage" in the early nineteenth century. The premise of the family wage was that a father, as the public head of an independent household, would be a family's sole financial support while his economically dependent wife would privately manage day-to-day household affairs and carry the responsibility of childrearing. In short, the ideal male citizen fulfilled his obligation to the public by acting as an economically independent wage earner; the ideal female citizen fulfilled her obligation to the public by attending to household and childrearing duties while remaining economically dependent on her husband.[6]

Nancy Folbre, an economist, asserts that the nineteenth-century "moral elevation of the home was accompanied by the economic devaluation of the work performed there." In this era, she observes, economists resolved an older dilemma about the productive value of "services" by treating unpaid household labor as moral and altruistic rather than economic and self-interested. Unlike the "unproductive" labor of a housewife, work done in return for wages was considered a part of the market economy and therefore "productive."[7] By the opening of the twentieth century this social science definition of work unequivocally linked "productive" wage-earning to the marketplace and unpaid, "unproductive" work to the family. Melded to the family wage ideal (now also embraced by middle-class reformers) that tied men to wage work and women to domestic labor, the definition bolstered distinct gendered meanings of work.

All women faced a devaluation of the substantial work that they did as mothers and housewives because this work did not accrue wages. For white women motherwork done for their own families did carry public moral acceptance, but the family work of African American women, who had long been expected to work as slaves or low-paid servants, did not carry this same public recognition. Domesticity was not an accepted option for black women. Faced with economic discrimination, even fewer African American men than white men were able to earn a family wage. Instead their wives, daughters, grandmothers, and friends were presumed available to make up the economic difference. This negated black women's role as child-rearers and keepers of their families' homes (without relieving these women of the public obligation to rear their children as acceptable citizens). At the same time, the wage work that these women did was frequently devalued as well. Agricultural work, frequently done by women of color, and domestic labor, an occupation in which African American women predominated well into the twentieth century, were among the lowest paid of all occupations and did not carry the same virtue of independence attached primarily to industrial wage work. Neither lauded for domesticity nor recognized for their wage work, women of color labored outside any conception of idealized citizenship.[8]

The idealized domesticity of white female citizens would be reimagined if not dethroned after the important achievement of female suffrage in 1920. The achievement of this quintessential political right at the crest of maternalist reform activism rested on a reinterpretation (rather than an uprooting) of older domestic ideology that tied women's public rights to her family obligations. The new interpretation enlarged women's responsibility for her family's general welfare to incorporate society at large — expanding her domestic sphere.[9] While white male suffrage had redefined ideal male citizenship by making wage earning an attribute of the independent individual, for a broad range of female suffrage advocates the value of women's direct public participation as voters rested on a presumed social altruism rather than a self-interested assertion of individual right. Newly enfranchised women were expected to broaden their "housekeeping" responsibilities and inculcate the electoral process with what maternalists understood as unique "female" values of nurturance and caring.[10]

Public Intervention in Private Institutions

In the Progressive and New Deal eras that roughly encompassed the half-century between 1890 and 1940, gendered citizenship would be redefined and reinvigorated through new state and federal social policy. Drawn from a maternalist vision of social policy, which closely linked the interests of mothers and children, as well as from working-class demands for new social rights tied to wage earning, the twentieth-century rise of the welfare state brought a wider acknowledgment of legitimate public interests in social obligations. Relying on older distinctions regarding work, gender, and race, reformers who called for new kinds of public provisions in the Progressive era and during the New Deal treated obligations that were keyed to the economy and wage laborers (understood primarily as white men) as distinct from obligations linked to the family (personified usually as white mothers and children). Significantly, the range of legitimate public interventions in the workplace expanded greatly as many workers gained the social rights of compensation in case of disability or death, collective bargaining, certain hour and wage protections in employment contracts, and old-age pensions. At the same time, issues tied to the family remained fully privatized for "normal" families, even as public policy formulated new kinds of intervention for "failed" or "dysfunctional" families. Keyed to a child's well-being, these ranged from mothers' pensions to juvenile courts and child support enforcement.[11]

In mid-twentieth century America the definitions of public interest and public responsibility, along with the kind of public intervention considered legitimate, hinged greatly on how a particular issue was tied to the now distinct institutions described as economic (i.e., the marketplace) or domestic (i.e., nuclear family). As the political theorist Nancy Fraser explains, both sets of institutions were considered private; this meant that they followed their own "natural" rules and, in theory, operated outside the realm of legitimate public political interventions.[12] Nonetheless, some justifiable public involvement in these central societal institutions had long since emerged.

Public interest in the private family came as early as the antebellum period, when courts identified a public responsibility to intervene in families where a child's welfare was considered endangered by neglect or other abuse. This limited public responsibility, which defined a state right to intervene in "failed" private families, stands in contrast with the broad state intervention in family life sanctioned by the contemporaneous common school movement. Identified as a public interest in the education of young children, public schooling eventually grew into a social right of all citizens.[13]

State intervention in the private marketplace developed in a separate trajectory. Allowing free private markets to grow up remained a defining feature of a liberal nation-state, and early calls for public interventions that stemmed from popular agrarian and antimonopoly movements had limited impact. Until the 1930s the private nature of the marketplace had not been substantially challenged. Importantly, the public interventions of the New Deal that imposed certain standards in labor contracts and guaranteed workers' right to collectively bargain with their employers came about not because certain private enterprises were seen as failures (which was the justification for intervening in the private institution of the family in the interest of child welfare) but rather as a general assertion of the social rights of wage-earning citizens.[14]

The new social rights of wage-earning citizens excluded many women, and men of color, and especially women of color who worked in low-paid service industries. When Progressive reformers succeeded in instituting protective labor legislation to set minimum wages, maximum hours, and other rules for women's employment and again when the New Deal instituted broader work rules for the marketplace, the protections yet excluded work done in canneries, on farms, and in private households (wage labor predominantly performed by women of color). Alternatively, when state and then federal policy instituted cash aid to poor mothers with children—thereby confirming a public interest in a mother's presence in the home despite a lack of adequate male income—administrative practice in many states reserved the limited aid available for white women. Black women's domestic labor as mothers of their own children received little or no help.[15]

When the nation emerged from the back-to-back crises of the Great Depression and World War II, women's and men's relation to the state remained distinct. Senator Margaret Chase Smith's characterization of women's civic roles in her 1953 address indicates that despite the important achievement of voting rights, the idealized female citizen—represented by the young, white, middle-class women Smith addressed—remained strongly lodged in the private domestic institution of the family. The idea that women served the public polity best by being in the home weakened considerably their claim to equal participation in the workforce. And because the most generous social rights of the new welfare state were expressly linked to wage work, arguing for the social provision of child care remained an uphill battle.

Since white mothers could not legitimately be seen as a part of this economic institution, public policy would be unlikely to foster social claims that bolstered equal participation in the workforce. Further, as long as women of color, "invisible wage-earners," made up a substantial proportion of women who worked outside the home, recognition of a public interest in child care would be hard to assert.

Postwar Child Care Activism

Despite significant barriers, the effort to retain publicly provided child care in early postwar America attracted a variety of supporters: wage-earning mothers of all colors, who wanted to combine wage work with childrearing, needed to do so, or both; social welfare groups, unions, and civic organizations, who asserted various societal benefits of a child care program; and early childhood educators and social workers, who envisioned distinct needs for and professional roles in publicly provided child care. Except for the organized opposition waged in some locations by the Catholic Church, public decision makers heard overwhelmingly positive assessments of the need for public subsidy of child care. That so few funding advocates won lasting public support of child care services is testament not only to lawmakers' fiscal concerns (which were perennial) but to an enduring conservative gender ideology that held a single vision of the ideal citizen mother as an unpaid childrearer.

Wage-earning mothers predominated among the parents who called for public provision of child care in the postwar era, because a gendered social division of labor ascribed the responsibility for child care to women. This gave them an evident class interest, as well as a self-interest, in publicly provided child care. Child care advocates did include some single fathers who used public child care services, and some married ones. But men, for whom the gendered social division of labor prescribed full-time breadwinning, were less likely to see the importance of a child care service. Like the much earlier male working-class call for a family wage, the postwar demand by wage-earning mothers for public support of child care might also be understood as an effort to reconcile individual experience and desire, cultural prescription, and family need.

Historians have offered both cautionary and celebratory stories of women's activism that drew on the public support of motherhood to demand everything from voting rights to a more peaceful world for their children.[16] Maternalist reformers of the Progressive era often organized their appeals around an idealized version of stay-at-home motherhood that presumed mothers' wage work to be undesirable, and they frequently advocated for government support and intervention on behalf of women and children who were poorer or in other ways different from themselves. Although they often appealed to policymakers from their position as mothers, postwar wage-earning mothers active in behalf of child care can be distinguished from earlier maternalists in several key ways. In the first place, the postwar activists organized their calls for public funding of child care services around their own concrete experience of motherhood—a motherhood that incorporated both childrearing and wage earning—and the demands they made were on their own behalf. Instead of shoring up an idealized female domesticity, their appeal for publicly supported child care called idealized female domesticity into question.

Child care advocates offered a broad range of arguments in favor of public financing. Immediately after the ceasefire that ended World War II in 1945, many people backed temporary continuation of wartime public child care centers until servicemen were safely home and employed. They concluded that with servicemen still overseas on active duty, many wives still needed to earn wages for family support and thus should continue to have access to publicly supported child care centers. This temporary rationale could not sustain a long-term program, however, and advocates of permanent public child care funding were fewer and faced greater skepticism.

Among the professionals interested in maintaining permanent child care services at the end of World War II, early childhood educators argued that *all* children could benefit from developmental training offered outside the home to improve social and other skills. By contrast, social workers argued that child care offered to *certain* families with professionally identified problems afforded the best chance of maintaining a healthy family unit and nurturing the child. (In the public financing debates that emerged in the 1960s the differences in these professional outlooks would be at least partially bridged by the rise of early childhood education theories that promoted "compensatory education" for the "culturally deprived.") At the same time, some civic organizations, in direct contradiction to many opponents of mothers' wage work, insisted that providing child care would reduce juvenile delinquency by ensuring adequate care for children at all times.

Working mothers drew on all these arguments and a range of others (which might in varying degrees be supported as well by educators, social workers, or civic and other interested groups). Many working mothers asserted their absolute need to earn wages in support of their family and the indispensability of child care to their ability to do so. This "necessity argument" had long been used in defense of women's wage earning, and it might sometimes be bolstered by an insistence that wage earning was superior (both morally and because it cost the treasury less money) to staying at home and receiving public cash assistance, commonly called welfare. Provision of child care, its advocates argued, allowed poor single mothers to maintain the dignity and independence associated with wage earning. With the exception of an infrequently made and roundly derided feminist assertion that women as individuals had a right to earn wages, the various rationales that mothers offered for public child care services in the first two decades after World War II were largely appeals to government that it should bolster women's efforts to aid their private families. In a unique argument, however, working mothers in California combined this more traditional call for aid to private need with an assertion of their own importance to the *public* economic good. Their "productive citizenship" rationale argued that child care centers were in the public interest not only because they allowed women to maintain their families but because the booming postwar (defense) economy needed their labor.[17]

In her history of child care, Elizabeth Rose studies the development and use of day care in Philadelphia. She argues that where day care had once been viewed solely as a private charity, in postwar America it emerged as a "socially legitimate need of 'normal' families, and even a potential responsibility of the state."[18] Focusing more completely on public child care provision in a variety of locations, *Citizen, Mother, Worker* tracks a different postwar redefinition of child care. Postwar working mothers did indeed understand their use of child care as "normal" and "socially legitimate," and this alone calls into question the absolute hold of domestic motherhood in this period. At the same time, wage-earning mothers were largely unable to convince lawmakers of these claims or to successfully insist on child care as a state responsibility in a broad sense. As a result public child care services, which had been a wartime public service for patriotic mothers, were primarily rationalized in postwar America as a public charity for the unfortunate poor.

Public Responsibility for Child Care Provision

As part of its effort to create jobs for out-of-work citizens, in 1933 the federal government made a sweeping entry into the field of preschool education by creating the Emergency Nursery School program. Committed to serving children from poor families, at its height the program operated in most states and had a capacity to serve 75,000 children. In 1942–43, facing now the crisis of war, the federal government initiated a new program for preschool children. This one focused exclusively on the children of working mothers. Borrowing the more educationally oriented administrative network of the Depression-era program, the wartime federally funded child care service eventually expanded to more than three thousand centers serving children in all but one state as well as in the District of Columbia. Congress members were reluctant to fund the program but acquiesced as program advocates emphasized the need for additional labor power to fuel war production and appealed to concerns about child neglect.[19]

At the war's end federal policymakers moved quickly to terminate the child care service, but they confronted a substantial and widespread protest from parents, primarily mothers, who relied on these centers to help them successfully fulfill both economic and domestic responsibilities for their families. Practicing "dissident citizenship," these women successfully politicized the issue of child care and placed it on the public agenda.[20] In her well-written account of U.S. child care policy and practice from colonial times to the present, Sonya Michel describes the rise of élite day care activism in the late 1950s and early 1960s.[21] *Citizen, Mother, Worker* focuses much more extensively on the broad grassroots activism that followed World War II and, especially in California, helped to bridge the gap between the end of wartime child care advocacy and the emergence of mostly eastern and élite day care activism.

The first chapter of *Citizen, Mother, Worker* looks at the broad context for this grassroots activism. It provides a brief history of child care in the United States and draws on popular and political debates about the meaning of "full employment," much desired in the postwar years, to examine the public meaning of motherhood and its relationship to wage work. Reviewing the position of mothers in the home and the workforce, this chapter gives special attention to how social expectation and early postwar public policy reinforced a gendered citizenship that insisted on female domesticity while granting women, at best, a secondary status in the paid workforce. I argue that women's ancillary position in the paid workforce was particularly damaging to their ability to claim child care as a right of social citizenship.

Further setting the stage for a closer look at postwar child care activism, chapter 1 outlines the three stages of public decision making that grassroots protesters faced in their efforts to retain broadly available, nonstigmatized, publicly subsidized child care centers: they had to secure a new funding source, undergo a redefinition of who would be eligible for public child care services, and establish a permanent justification for each public child care program. The child care struggles in Cleveland, the District of Columbia, and California, described in chapters 2, 3 and 4, show increasing success in negotiating each of these challenges. And by illuminating common ideological and institutional barriers to public funding of child care across the wide geographic, economic, civic, and governmental range that these three areas represent, each case study helps to construct a fuller understanding of the central issues surrounding public child care funding in postwar America.

Chapter 2 describes the activism of day care users in Cleveland within the national protest against the end of federal funding for child care, and their ultimately unsuccessful effort to achieve permanent local public funding. The protest by day care users in Cleveland and their many counterparts nationwide readily demonstrates how parents politicized the issue of child care and made an early and significant challenge to the postwar resurgence of domesticity. Working mothers sought to retain the better status they had achieved in the workforce during the war and understood that the social provision of child care would be crucial.

Contrary to a prevailing domestic ideology, Cleveland child care activists did not understand their wage work as being in conflict with their own or their family's best interests. Staging several public demonstrations to insist on public subsidy of child care, day care users argued for the right to recast motherhood in a way that incorporated both wage-work (economic) and family (domestic) responsibilities. By contrast, the city's professional and voluntary social workers, who also called for continued public funding of child care, clearly understood maternal employment as a problem to be solved and not a normal situation to be supported. Accordingly, as a group they offered a more limited defense of child care funding.

Opposition from prominent politicians as well as the Cleveland Catholic Diocese hamstrung the efforts of the city's day care activists and, despite broad civic support, the activists succeeded in extending the life of the wartime centers for only a few months. The short-term funding of the child care program initially won from the City Council promptly ceased once judgment rendered in a taxpayer lawsuit effectively barred the city from using its treasury to subsidize the child care centers. The arguments offered and decision delivered in this extraordinary lawsuit provide a compelling story and concrete description of the postwar belief that child care should remain a private family matter.

Day care activism in the District of Columbia is the subject of chapter 3. The unique governance structure of the District of Columbia—all city legislative and budget matters were handled by Congress—allows this local study to provide a window into the minds of national policymakers; the study also suggests that there was early potential political support for day care as an alternative to cash aid (welfare) for single mothers. Several factors combined to create an especially illiberal climate for the day care debate in the nation's capital. These included the complete lack of any elected political representation for District residents, the desire of the city's white élite to maintain the subordinate status of the city's many African American residents, and (as in other locations) a substantial will to conserve gender roles that tied men to economic duties and women to domestic responsibilities.

Despite these obstacles the dogged determination of D.C. day care activists won continued funding for child care services for five years after the war's end. At the same time, and with the encouragement of the city's highest appointees, federal congressional overseers severely restricted access and eligibility for child care, effectively reshaping the District's program from a wartime public service to a postwar public charity. Reluctance to understand women as ideally or properly a part of the wage workforce is clearly evidenced in the record of congressional hearings, testimony, debates, and funding actions related to the District's public child care program. Far from being able to assert their right to be in the paid workforce, mothers frequently found themselves constrained to defend publicly subsidized day care almost entirely by their desire to remain independent of the city's severely underfunded Aid to Dependent Children program. Contradictory American values, which on the one hand valorized the work ethic and independence, and on the other demanded economic dependence (for white women), competed for dominance throughout the child care debate.

An unwillingness to view wage-earning mothers as anything but unfortunate skewed program eligibility increasingly toward very low-income single mothers only. At the same time, the city's substantial population of poor African American residents qualified this tendency and helps to illustrate racialized gender constraints to public child care funding. The District child care program operated for five years without a permanent, agreed-upon justification for its existence, and federal lawmakers offered few explanations when they finally and abruptly halted all day care funding just before Christmas 1950.

Finally, chapter 3 also reviews federal debate around a second proposed wartime child care program—this time to meet needs created by the Korean War. Although lawmakers agreed in principle to such a program, they ultimately denied all funds for a child care service. Acting in a politically conservative climate, members of Congress were concerned with the potential for a "temporary" program to become permanent. Even in this new wartime environment, lawmakers who divvied up federal tax dollars held firm to their basic goal in the years following World War II: to expand the national economy through aid to private industry rather than subsidy of public services.

The largest federally supported day care program of the World War II era operated in California. Chapter 4 looks at the postwar success of California day care activists in turning this service into the only permanent statewide public child care program in the nation, and offers long overdue scholarly attention to this important part of U.S. child care history. After more than a decade of temporary program extensions, California day care activists won a permanently authorized, state-funded child care program in 1957.

The organized lobbying of wage-earning mothers on behalf of this state program was crucial to the continued program. Parents elsewhere had also shown persistence, but California activists enjoyed some critical advantages. A sympathetic governor combined with a wartime administrative role in the child care program for the State Education Department provided a central focus for advocates rather than dissipating the strength of their calls for a continuous service across many locations. At the same time, an expanding economy and a state political tradition conducive to pragmatic activism granted space for program advocates to present a range of rationales that appealed to state politicians across the ideological spectrum. Additionally, the call for continued child care centers received crucial organizational support from child care center teachers, who identified with the early childhood education profession and used the centers themselves as a base for activism on behalf of the program.[22]

Child care teachers' willingness to define the service that they provided as a potential benefit to *any* young child, a consequence of their professional understanding of child learning and development, contrasts sharply with the standard social welfare viewpoint (evidenced in California far less prominently than in other locations), which more readily understood child care as a stopgap program only for children whose families could not otherwise adequately care for them. Child care educators' support of California's program helped to ensure its continued administration in the State Education Department, provided a broad theoretical base on which to rest child care claims, and lent a prestige to the child care cause that was in other places lacking.

Finally, an ability to define maternal employment outside domestic or family need—to legitimate mothers' paid labor instead as a possible economic imperative—gave to California's day care activists a further critical advantage. In a state economy boosted by the defense industry, mothers described their ability to combine wage earning and childrearing as an indication of their "productive citizenship" and from this vantage point suggested that publicly subsidized child care was a social right.

For all of California's greater openness to maternal employment, however, an underlying view of public child care funding as an alternative policy to cash aid for poor single mothers remained of paramount importance in justifying the program's permanent existence. And this helps to explain actions of state lawmakers that increasingly constricted access to the child care centers for children from two-parent families. Further, California's precocious commercial child care industry laid claim to any potential child care client considered able to pay full cost for the service.

The book's final chapter brings the postwar public child care debate full circle; it returns to the nation's capital for a look at legislative child care debates during the 1950s and finally to the decision in 1962 to provide the first federal day care funds since the close of World War II. In that decision—as well as those of the decade leading to it—federal policymakers echoed earlier local and state debates on child care. Like their state and local counterparts, federal lawmakers were reluctant to take on the child care issue; when pressed, they generally favored limited policies intended to serve sole-support mothers. Indeed for much of the decade between the early 1950s and the early 1960s, child care operators and social welfare regulators shaped out-of-home child care provision largely without federal direction. In 1954 Congress enacted a tax code change providing a deduction for some child care expenses. The policy responded to calls for "tax fairness" for working mothers, and although limited in scope it advanced the notion of private, paid child care provision. Ultimately, with a steady rise in employment among mothers and little federal support for child care provision, the commercial child care industry grew more substantial and began to organize and advocate for its own place in the private market economy.

The federal day care funding agreed to in 1962 was enacted in the context of welfare reform. Federal policymakers envisioned day care as a necessary service to allow cash welfare families to "rehabilitate" themselves through training or work; separately, federal lawmakers made the provision of day care a function of child welfare services. In this context day care was intended to serve a limited number of families with working mothers whose children were deemed at risk of neglect. In either case an independent decision to seek child care services was not the key to obtaining publicly subsidized child care services. Instead access lay with social work professionals who identified a specific rehabilitation or child protection need within a family.

Finally, the book's epilogue briefly looks at the amount and kinds of federal public child care funds available today. Most programs that provide child care funds today are conflated with "welfare reform," and publicly subsidized child care is primarily understood as a cure for welfare dependency.

If our nation could rise to a higher standard of living with both husband and wife working, why not have nurseries in our school system. This would enable the entire family to work and our future generation might be greatly benefited mentally & physically. A child could not be harmed under the proper care of a school nursery and I feel sure that the love of the mother would not be one tiny speck less.

—Mrs. L. M. Stone, Dallas, Texas to President Franklin Roosevelt, ca. February 1945

ONE

Mothers and Work

The Federal Government, Women's Postwar Wage-Earning Status, and Child Care Provision

Even before their troops came home victorious, Americans began to imagine the shape of a postwar United States. Still haunted by the prewar Depression, many found their thoughts dominated by concerns about jobs and economic plenty. Responding to an inflammatory article predicting a postwar battle between the sexes for jobs and "personal ascendancy," Mrs. L. M. Stone wrote a worried letter to President Franklin Roosevelt. She proposed publicly supported nurseries for young children as a way to unite the nation's men and women, encourage families to have children, and thereby ensure the country's economic and social health for the future.[1]

By way of explaining her concern in this matter, Mrs. Stone enclosed with her letter to the president an article entitled "The Coming War on Women," which had been published in the February 18, 1945, edition of the national weekly newspaper insert *This Week*. Written by Willard Waller, an associate professor of sociology at Barnard College, the article predicted a multifront battle between the sexes in the postwar period. "May God help the men, the women and the United States of America if the men lose,"

Waller solemnly announced. A battle over jobs would soon ensue, and to grant returning veterans employment, Waller asserted, women would be "forced out of industry." Fewer women at work would be a first and necessary step toward winning a second battle, he continued, this one over the birthrate. The nation, he believed, would soon be a third-rate country if women didn't start producing more babies. "Other nations encourage reproduction by every device that the ingenuity of lawmakers can invent, but our country . . . continues to give every advantage and preferment to the unmarried and the childless. . . . If we are to have an adequate birth rate, we must hear less talk about women's rights and more about their duty to the race. The plain fact is that women do not produce children under the conditions of freedom and equality that have existed in the United States since the last war." Men had been called upon to sacrifice their bodies to the war, he noted; women had a comparable "obligation as the trustee of the race" to bear children. Ultimately, Waller concluded, both men and women would be emotionally happier if men defeated "petticoat domination."[2]

Mr. Waller and Mrs. Stone both sought a strong future for postwar America, but they proposed to get there in very different ways. Although Waller's rendition of the problem and the solution seem somewhat overwrought, he was certainly not alone in his fear of limited jobs and in his belief that in postwar America the "patriarchal family must be restored and strengthened. Women must bear and rear children; husbands must support them."[3] By contrast, Stone asked that government provide nursery schools so that men and women could both earn wages. This, she stated, would place childless women and mothers on the same footing and reduce tension between the sexes. She implicitly asked government to expand the economy to allow jobs for everyone. Waller believed that shoring up women's duties in and to the home would be essential for national survival and personal happiness; Stone believed that supporting women's efforts to leave the home would contribute to a rising economy and better families.

The future wasn't as neat as either writer imagined. The federal government's active pursuit of an expanding economy after World War II, aided by a Cold War arms buildup, soon brought on prominent discussion of the need for the increased use of "womanpower." Instead of leaving paid labor to their husbands, married women steadily entered the workforce, surpassing within a decade their wartime numbers. Simultaneously the country was awash in babies and young children, as both marriage and birth rates climbed dramatically. Nonetheless policymakers did not believe it a proper aim of the federal government to provide a social structure that explicitly recognized and supported paid employment for both husbands and wives.

Many continued to see the two-earner household—and specifically one with young children—as less desirable, even anathema to the preservation of the "American family."

Although not everyone used Waller's purple prose to denounce women's paid employment, the experts both inside and outside government agreed on the primary importance of in-the-home childrearing. When the White House forwarded Mrs. Stone's letter to the U.S. Children's Bureau for a response, a staff member replied briefly that some "social agencies" did concern themselves with the provision of day care for working mothers. But she explained at far greater length the importance that social workers and other professionals concerned with the well-being of children placed on "preserving the family home and providing for children in their own homes if possible." Finally, the letter confirmed that national policy actively supported this position, which required full-time stay-at-home motherhood: "The Federal Government has assisted in making it possible for children to remain in their own homes through the enactment of the section of the Social Security Act providing for [A]id to [D]ependent [C]hildren"[4]

But as the first postwar decade wore on, the federal government's primary preoccupation with an expanding economy threatened the demographic, if not the ideological, verity of the stay-at-home mom. Seeking a consumer-driven and growing economy, the federal government engineered a social structure that called on the individual family to purchase a private home, a car, household furnishings, appliances, and more. Fiscal policies aimed not to spend money on the public provision of a range of services and goods—child care among them—but rather on tax policies that would expand private enterprise, create jobs, increase the production of goods and services, and boost private purchasing power. In this context, two-earner families became increasingly commonplace and indeed did provide substantial fuel for the nation's rising standard of living in the two decades following the end of World War II. The responsibility for child care remained a private issue, but it began a modest shift from unpaid (and low-paid) work inside the home to low-paid work purchased from private entrepreneurs outside the home. Broadly available publicly subsidized child care facilities did not become a social fixture in the nation.

The lack of child care services had deep roots that left the call for their provision especially disadvantaged in an era dominated by postwar federal attention to fiscal policies aimed at expanding the official economy. Tightly bound together, the ideals of female citizenship, motherhood, and child care remained banished from this official economic world—the world of markets, paid workplaces, and private enterprises and corporations. As the response from the Children's Bureau's to Mrs. Stone suggests, social provisions guaranteed to mothers and children through the New Deal welfare state reinforced the import of this banishment by insisting on a single kind of full-time, in-the-home motherhood and expressly favoring male-headed, single-earner families. For publicly provided child care to be accepted, two preconditions would need to be met, and although there would be considerable movement neither would be fully achieved in the postwar era. First, women, and especially the mothers of young children, would need to be viewed as properly a part of the paid labor force and thus a normal part of the official "productive" economy. The second precondition was a corollary: a faith that young children could and would flourish in care and training situations not supervised by their own mothers.[5]

Women's paid employment grew impressively in the first two decades after World War II, but the "stay-at-home" mom remained in the majority. Both popular writers and historians of women have noted the substantial barriers in this period to the employment of women, especially mothers of young children. These included the dictates of popular culture, professional psychiatric, psychological, and social work wisdom, and cold war political goals.[6] At the same time, the perceived relationship of women's labor (paid and unpaid) to the official economy (privately run but publicly supported) provided an additional, powerful barrier to the employment of women and consequently to the goal of public spending on child care.[7]

Within the "official economy" a group or individual can be in one sense a private actor and in another public. While the meaning of public and private has frequently shifted, the insistence on distinguishing between things public and things private has been a staple of western political theory, and their definitions have shaped government's understanding of its responsibility to citizens. A difficulty for public funding of child care was that while a private father could easily be imagined as a worker in the public economy, a private mother could not be similarly viewed. Even though the proper raising of children—the nation's future citizens—was of preeminent public concern, the act of child care itself, because it was bound to the private mother, could not generally be seen as a public issue. As Linda Kerber observes, "political systems and systems of gender relations are reciprocal social constructions." In the postwar debates about public funding for child care, it is easy to spot the way social obligations of gender shaped government's expectations of its citizens and, in turn, its understanding of responsibility to its citizens.[8]

Women's proper relationship to paid labor played a critical part in debates about the public funding of child care, not simply because according to a mass of cultural and social mores women should stay at home, but because those mores and the public duties they inscribed were deeply bound up with the understanding of the federal government's responsibility to its citizens. Neither the labor liberals who initially sought a more explicit social policy role for the federal government after World War II, nor the conservatives who sought to roll back social policy expansion enacted during the New Deal and World War II, understood women—especially mothers of young children—as primarily connected to the productive economy.[9] Yet as early as 1946, the expansion of this economy emerged as a central purpose of postwar federal policies. Women's ancillary relationship to this economy proved a roadblock to the expansion of their social rights.

The Full Employment Act and Government's Role in Postwar America

The surge in female labor force participation during World War II drew wide notice, and many people worried about what this demographic change would mean for the postwar years. Taking up this concern, a symposium of business, labor, and women's representatives in 1944 examined exactly what women's role in "business and industry" should be after the war. Everyone agreed on the great wartime job that women were doing, and most acknowledged that some would remain in the paid workforce even after the needs of war production had abated. But should women expect to stay?[10]

For nearly every commentator at the symposium, the answer to this question depended on the quantity of available jobs after the war; the state of the job market would define the possibilities for women. Eric Johnston, president of the U.S. Chamber of Commerce, envisioned an exploding postwar economy in which women would remain essential producers of goods. The problem would not be one of "spreading employment to make available jobs go as far as possible but of expanding production to create more jobs," he optimistically asserted. His business colleague Frederick Crawford, chairman of the board of the National Association of Manufacturers, agreed that more jobs would be key but he showed less confidence that workers would be in demand. After praising the skills and adaptability of women workers at length and calling for every effort to expand the job market, Crawford offered a conservative finish. Employers, he argued, would need to formulate postwar employment policies that rationalized relative rights to the workplace. As he saw it, there were some easy calls: war widows had an undisputed claim, and those supporting disabled veterans "if they are skilled industrial workers, should virtually inherit their man's industrial priorities." By contrast, "married women whose husbands can support them should be the first to step aside in favor of any breadwinners during a shortage of jobs." Crawford continued, "The home is the basic American unit. Homemakers are essential to the morale and well-being of male workers, and also are the first line of prevention of juvenile delinquency. A woman who is away ten hours a day cannot do a full-time job of homemaking. . . . Young mothers, above all, are needed in the home." While he felt certain that most married women would quit paid labor voluntarily, Crawford did raise some gray areas. What about self-supporting women, he asked, or even the "leisure-class women" with coveted skills, professional training, and career ambition? Employers, he intimated, had the unenviable job of sorting out the "comparative rights of man over woman, woman over woman, and in some cases woman over man."[11]

As a spokesman for labor, Phillip Murray, president of the Congress of Industrial Organizations (CIO), viewed the job market from a decidedly different angle: yet women remained disadvantaged. The key to labor's postwar utopia lay in full employment coupled with expanded social protections including a solid minimum wage, guaranteed medical care, and better housing and community services. In this ideal economy mothers would not "have to take jobs because their husbands' earnings are meager. But women who need or wish to work should have the opportunity." In the workforce women would receive equal pay and opportunity for job advancement but also "special treatment adapted for women's special needs." This included machines to lift heavy weights and access to part-time work, "the only basis on which many wives can work outside the home without neglecting their households or overtaxing themselves."[12]

Crawford's explicit insistence that individual women exhibit circumstances entitling them to participate in paid labor, and Murray's suggestions that regardless of women's presence in the workplace they would always be homemakers first, confirmed that Dr. Minnie L. Maffett's pessimism was well-founded. The president of the National Federation of Business Women, a practicing surgeon, and an associate professor of gynecology, Maffett expressed her fears about postwar sex discrimination and noted the belief of some industrialists that women would simply return home. "I wish that I could honestly feel that the postwar economic, social and political horizons for women, as for men, might extend as far as the ideals of democracy guarantee to all the right to life and work, and happiness in this country but past experience hardly justifies this optimism." With reluctance, Maffett, like the representatives of organized business and labor, saw in an expanding economy the only prospect for more fair treatment of women.[13]

Mary Anderson, chief of the U.S. Women's Bureau, simply asserted both the need for full employment and women's right to work—although in her descriptions of working women she emphasized those who supported themselves and dependents.[14] So it would be up to Elizabeth Hawes to interrogate further the notion of full employment. A woman who chose a highly eclectic career, Hawes was a successful fashion designer and the author of several popular books who had also worked in an aircraft plant and turned this wartime experience into a best-seller, *Why Women Cry*. She was an organizer for the United Auto Workers (UAW) Education Department and a columnist for the *Detroit Free Press* when she made her comments about the postwar employment prospects for women. For Hawes the major issue of postwar planning would be ensuring that women truly had the right to decide if they wished to be in the workforce or not. She proposed, as a "minimal program for making women effective in their jobs," allowing men and women shorter work weeks so that both could combine household and work responsibilities, providing facilities for infant care and preschools, and improving public schools. Shops where prepared food could be purchased at a "fair price" and housing projects that incorporated community restaurants, laundries, and professionally staffed nurseries would be a further boon, she added.[15]

Significantly, for Hawes ensuring that women had the right to choose work did not translate to paying men more, granting better pension benefits to war widows, or any other plan calculated to reduce economic pressure on women to work—all measures that would have been consistent with the limited social welfare programs already functioning in the United States.[16] Instead, she approached the issue of combining household and wage labor without assuming that the current division of labor, by sex, necessarily needed to be a part of the future. At the same time, Hawes recognized that society clearly assigned to women the responsibility for housekeeping and childrearing and that these tasks were essential for society. To grant women entrance to the workforce as equals, she argued that society needed to make new plans for accomplishing these important domestic duties.[17]

While Crawford of the NAM clearly assigned unpaid home labor to women, Murray of the CIO waffled on this point. He proposed expanded community facilities to relieve "home drudgery" but was unwilling to fully envision community or family sharing of child care and household work. Instead, he believed that women should be helped to combine paid work and household responsibilities. For instance, he called for women's work hours to be "adapted to *women's* home responsibilities." Meanwhile, Hawes concluded that full employment would be important and even essential to postwar prosperity but said that additional social provisions would be needed "to allow women to work outside their homes to their full capacity."[18]

The popular and political buzz about a needed postwar employment plan received legislative form in January 1945, when Sen. James Murray (D.-Mont.) introduced the Full Employment Act.[19] Just how clearly the labor liberal authors of the bill presumed that a married woman's proper role should be that of unpaid housekeeper (outside the official economy) is easily deduced from the proposal's most controversial policy section. "All Americans able to work and seeking work have the right to useful, remunerative, regular, and full-time employment," the section began. But it then went on to significantly qualify the practical reach of this apparent "right" to employment. "It is the policy of the United States to assure the existence at all times of sufficient employment opportunities to enable all Americans, who have finished their schooling and *who do not have full-time housekeeping responsibilities*, freely to exercise this right [emphasis added]."[20] While this section of the proposed legislation received wide comment, in more than twelve hundred pages of Senate hearing records, very few men or women questioned the apparent placement of the majority of females outside the paid labor economy.[21]

During two days of preliminary hearings held in late July 1945, the primary sponsors and drafters of the bill had a chance to explain their goals and intentions for the legislation. Senator Robert Wagner (D-N.Y.), chairman of the subcommittee considering the legislation, opened with a sweeping statement about the right to paid work. He declared this right "synonymous with the inalienable right to live." Heading off criticism that the proposal gave the federal government job creation powers at the expense of private industry, Sen. Murray emphasized the importance of government promotion of free-enterprise capitalism in the full employment legislation. Senator Joseph O'Mahoney (D-Wyo.), aided by a small army of charts, sought to demonstrate that a plan for full employment was essential and that it could sustain economic growth through assuring broad purchasing power of goods produced.[22]

It would be Sen. Abe Murdock, a one-term Democrat from Utah, who questioned the exemption of housewives from the bill's declaration of policy on the right to paid work. Rereading the full section aloud, he commented that the exception seemed "hardly justified." As he read this part, it "impos[ed] an indignity . . . on what I consider one of the very fundamental labors of the Nation, and that is the housekeeping."[23] Murray, who had the floor when the question came up, responded as best he could.

Murray. Well, of course, it was not expected that this bill was intended to take the housewives out of the homes and put them into industry or other employment.

Murdock. Well, I do not want to do that, but I do not think that we should make an exception of any class. They are all entitled to the same opportunity. . . . If they are in the house today and want to get out tomorrow, in my opinion they should enjoy exactly the same opportunity as any other American.

Murray. I think that that provision can be construed to mean that. . . . But it seemed to me that we did not want to put ourselves in the position of advocating that everyone was going to work in American industry, because that would be impossible. We have to maintain—

Murdock. You do not want to exclude anyone from the opportunity.

Murray. No.

Murdock. You want to grant all Americans, as I understand it, under this bill, the right to work, if they are capable of working, able-bodied, and willing.[24]

At this point, Murray begged off the discussion. "The language was incorporated after very careful consideration," he stated, and "was suggested by the able Senator from Wyoming, who I am sure will be able, during the course of his explanation, to satisfy you that that language is appropriate."[25]

After lengthy discussion of other aspects of the bill, Sen. O'Mahoney turned to the proposed policy exception regarding housekeepers. His explanation emphasized that a mother's primary duty lay in the home. "The sponsors of the bill did not want to give rise to the inference that this measure was intended to maintain at Government expense employment for people who . . . *ought* to be at home helping to raise families, to make sure that we were not undertaking by a Government program to break up the family" [emphasis added]. The exemption became a part of the draft bill, he added, "largely for argumentative purposes" because the bill's sponsors were being accused of requiring the government to spend money on the employment of people who "need not be employed." Senator Murdock did not press the question further.[26]

The preliminary hearings closed on July 31, 1945, with testimony on the Full Employment Act slated to begin in earnest when Congress reconvened after the annual August recess. In less than a week, however, the United States dropped an atomic bomb on Hiroshima, and a few days later, Nagasaki. The war screeched to a halt, and on August 15, 1945, Americans celebrated V-J Day. Virtually simultaneously with the announcement of the Japanese surrender, the Federal Works Agency (FWA), which during the war had administered a nationwide publicly subsidized child care program for working mothers, put in motion orders to end it. Meanwhile, members of Congress hurried back from a much shortened recess and quickly took up important postwar legislation. So as groups of parents—mostly mothers—in cities and states across the country organized to call for continued public funding of child care, Congress returned to its debate on the right to paid work and the best plan to produce full employment in the new postwar America.

The presumption by some of the most liberal policymakers of the period that many women, in the words of Sen. O'Mahoney, "ought to be at home helping to raise families," echoed the adamant declaration of Crawford, chairman of the NAM, that "young mothers above all belong in the home" and underscores the stiff odds faced by day care activists who sought public funding in the immediate postwar era. Without an unqualified right to paid labor, how could working mothers insist on publicly subsidized child care as a social provision necessary to ensure their equal opportunity to paid work? While some child care provisions remained as reconversion measures, the focus quickly devolved on the economic need of some women to earn wages in support of their families, rather then their simple right to participate in the paid labor force. Instead of publicly supported child care in the postwar era as a means to greater equality of opportunity for women workers, called for by the UAW organizer Elizabeth Hawes and suggested as well by President Roosevelt's correspondent Mrs. Stone, tax-subsidized child care could rarely be justified as anything other than a quasi-public charity for otherwise needy families.

The record of hearings on the Full Employment Act in late August 1945 is replete with discussions of the right to paid work, but almost no one again asked why individuals with "fulltime housekeeping duties" should be excepted from this fundamental promise of the bill.[27] Representatives from women's groups frequently praised the proposal's promise of a right to paid work without commenting on this exemption.[28] When Mrs. J. B. Caulkins, president of the Young Women's Christian Association (YWCA), appeared before the Senate subcommittee holding hearings on the Full Employment Act, she insisted that women should not be treated as marginal workers and emphasized that they needed to earn wages in support of themselves and frequently their dependents. But she did not challenge the assumption that marriage and housekeeping would be the preferred situation for women: "It is undoubtedly true that most young women hope to marry, and that they hope their husbands will be able to support them. However, simple arithmetic shows that they cannot all have their wish. If every single male in the Nation marries there will still be 3,000,000 women left without any prospect of marriage." The failure to challenge the preeminence of housekeeping for women allowed the YWCA to quote the bill's policy regarding the right of "All Americans" to work without raising any objection to the housekeeping exemption.[29]

If the housekeeping exemption drew little comment, nearly everything else about the proposed Full Employment Act of 1945 provoked controversy, from its purported guarantee of a right to paid work to the methods that it set forth for implementing the guarantee. In the form in which the bill was introduced in 1945, efforts to stimulate private job growth were of primary importance, but the bill also called on the president to regularly forecast the nation's production needs and capabilities and compare them to the expected number of available workers. If a job gap appeared imminent, the president would propose public works projects or other federal spending measures to ensure full employment. Critics called this last aspect of the bill a "make work" proposal and believed that it would place publicly run industry into direct competition with private industry.[30]

By the time President Truman signed the act into law, however, any real or imagined threat of government competition had been removed. Substantially rewritten by committee conferees in early 1946 and renamed the "Employment Act of 1946," it declared simply that the federal government would "promote maximum employment, production, and purchasing power" through use of all "practicable means . . . in a manner calculated to foster and promote free competitive enterprise and the general welfare." The act reduced the significance of the president's economic report to an advisory one and omitted entirely the provisions for public works projects.[31]

The final wording of the government's policy commitment also eliminated the word "all" and promised only to "promote conditions" that allowed "those able, willing, and seeking to work" to find "useful employment."[32] The language adopted included no mention of the housekeeping exemption, which the legislative history suggests was deleted less because it offended legislators' sense of fairness than because it became unnecessary. Senator Murdock, who apparently had vigorously protested the exemption of housewives with "fulltime housekeeping duties," closed his early questions about this language by declaring "full agreement" with the legislative drafters' intent.[33] Further, the bill's opponents ceaselessly sought to weaken and generalize language that asserted *any* individual's federally guaranteed right to paid work. In the end, the compromise legislation that emerged redirected the emphasis of the government's responsibility from ensuring jobs for all Americans who were understood to be available for paid labor to the far more general goal of ensuring a growing economy.[34]

The rewriting of the Full Employment Act marked a telling defeat for postwar labor liberals. Their agenda—which included guaranteeing citizens' health care through an expansion of the Social Security Act and establishing permanent federal agencies to help set wages and control prices, combat employment discrimination, and assist in job placement—quickly lost out to conservatives and a less reformist liberalism in the immediate aftermath of World War II. The liberal rapprochement with conservatives centered on ensuring economic growth, not by changing social and economic structures but by shaping the existing system to promote substantial and sustained growth in businesses and the marketplace. For conservatives this translated primarily into advancing the cause of free (unregulated) enterprise; for liberals it meant advancing mass consumption as a way to ensure both a market for a high volume of goods and plentiful jobs. The Employment Act of 1946 had plenty of room for both liberals and conservatives to define government responsibility in postwar America.[35]

Women's Secondary Status as Wage Workers

Theoretically all Americans would compete fairly for the available jobs in this expanding economy. In practice women's marginal claim to labor force participation was already evident through the early postwar reassignment of women workers to lower status, less well-paid jobs and the reassertion of prewar female protective labor legislation. Women with children were additionally handicapped by a reduced number of child care options and community sentiment against employment of mothers.

As war contracts declined and then ended, factories laid off workers in large numbers—women as well as men. Between June and September 1945 one in four women factory workers lost her job.[36] Although factories began rehiring some workers as early as the end of 1945, women were less likely to be recalled. At General Motors women had represented 32 percent of the workforce in November 1943, but the proportion declined to just 16 percent two years later. At the rival automaker Ford, the proportion of women workers nose-dived from 22 percent in November 1943 to just 4 percent by January 1946. On the West Coast women shipyard workers faced a similar fate.[37]

MOTHERS AND WORK

Frieda Miller, who replaced Mary Anderson as chief of the U.S. Women's Bureau in 1944, commented that women were caught in a "back-to-the-home" campaign.[38]

Many women did not want to go home, or could not, and for them reassignment to lower paid "female" jobs was commonplace. Regardless of their skills, background, or training (wartime or otherwise), women were widely considered better in certain fields, including clerical work, some assembly jobs requiring attention to detail and repetition, and domestic work.[39] Job orders sent to the United States Employment Service (USES) routinely specified the sex of the worker (and sometimes the race as well), and placements were made to the employer's specifications.[40] In October 1946 the Women's Bureau reported that many jobs now available to women did "not fully use their best wartime skills" and paid "lower rates than their wartime jobs." An early postwar sample survey done by USES in Atlanta, Columbus, Ohio, and Trenton, New Jersey, found that 40 to 61 percent of openings for women were in clerical, sales, or service jobs, although only 15 to 18 percent of women making unemployment claims had last worked in these fields. [41]

"Women Want Jobs—but Not the Kind Offered by USES," the *Cleveland Press* reported in May 1946. Both women and employers were "fussier," according to the local USES office. Women disliked the low pay for office workers and "can't be induced to take typing and shorthand brush-up courses." At the same time employers were reluctant to hire women over thirty-five years of age but also sought the experienced women employee who had "a combination of skills" and could be a typist as well as a bookkeeper, or additionally operate calculating or billing machines.[42]

In October 1945 the *Cleveland Plain Dealer* noted an increase in available domestics since the war's end but added that "demand is still outrunning supply," wages were considered high, and increasingly applicants insisted on day rather than live-in work. The paper surmised, "Hundreds of women formerly in domestic service who worked in plants during the war will continue . . . to search for similar employment and will not seek domestic jobs until their unemployment benefits are exhausted or their claims are denied, and they discover that there is relatively no demand for women in industrial production."[43] Less than a year later, a news article in Cleveland reported that the first seventeen certificates would be awarded in a "household management" training program "as the result of an experimental community-wide project to relieve the city's domestic help shortage." The article pictured Mary Pinxone, eighteen, a former employee of General

Electric, and Annie Belle Ellis, twenty-four, a wartime welder, who were learning how to iron and prepare a formal table place setting.[44]

Reassignment to lesser status and lower-paid jobs demonstrates only one way that women remained marginalized as wage workers. Another was the reassertion of female protective labor laws after their widespread relaxation during wartime.[45] Primarily adopted during the first several decades of the twentieth century, these state labor laws regulated hours and wages, imposed other requirements such as rest periods and chairs, and prohibited women's employment in some jobs.[46] A review of why protective labor legislation was enacted and whom it was intended to "protect" helps to illuminate the specific ideal of motherhood that activists, policymakers, and judges sought to uphold in early-twentieth-century America; the reassertion of these laws provides a concrete example of how specific citizenship rights tied to wage work remained racialized and gendered in the postwar United States.

Campaigns for female protective labor legislation began in the nineteenth century but acquired great momentum after the landmark *Muller v. Oregon* decision delivered in 1908. In a unanimous opinion, the U.S. Supreme Court firmly grounded the rationale for female protective labor legislation in the presumed characteristics of Oregon women workers' potential motherhood rather than their status as workers.[47] The labor laws for women were a proper "object of public interest" because they aimed to preserve a woman's physical health and thereby the health of the future human race. According to the Court, a woman worker's "physical structure and a proper discharge of her maternal functions—having in view not merely her own health, but the well-being of the race—justify legislation to protect her. . . . The limitations which this statute places upon her contractual powers . . . are not imposed solely for her benefit but also largely for the benefit of all."[48] At the same time, protective labor laws enacted by state legislatures typically did not extend to workplaces dominated by women of color. Domestics, women who worked in the fields, and women in other kinds of service employment did not fit the dominant ideal of white motherhood and generally worked for wages without any specific protections or restrictions on their working conditions.

Finding a public interest in the need to protect women as potential (white) mothers rather than as workers allowed the U.S. Supreme Court to ratify state intervention in the employment contract. Although labor laws for women appeared to directly contradict the prevailing legal doctrine of "free contract," which figured the employment contract as a private agreement

MOTHERS AND WORK

between individual citizens and therefore not subject to state legislation or regulation, the Court in *Muller* specifically noted that it did not intend to overturn the free contract doctrine. Instead it argued that "legislation designed for [a woman's] protection may be sustained, when like legislation is not necessary for men, and could not be sustained."[49]

The Court's adamant continued support of the free contract doctrine severely limited the ability of male workers to seek state regulation of their workplaces, but some state protective labor laws, such as limited restrictions on hours of work and widespread worker's compensation, did come into place for male workers during roughly the same time that female protective labor legislation emerged. By the late 1930s the free contract doctrine had clearly been toppled. As part of the New Deal, an array of federal protective labor laws establishing a minimum wage, unemployment compensation, and maximum hours worked brought public regulation to the employment contract of many workers.[50]

Of necessity a different set of legal justifications underpinned this group of laws, applicable primarily to white male workers. Female protective labor legislation drew its constitutionality from a court-defined public responsibility to protect motherhood and by definition applied only to women; in the earliest decades labor laws that protected mostly male workers were ostensibly based on a public duty to ensure the physical health and well-being of citizens generally and extended to the (theoretically) ungendered category of "workers."[51] Created at a time of rising working-class militancy, New Deal protective laws applied on the basis of an individual's status as a wage worker rather than as a member of a particular sex or race. Further, the most important legal justification for the new intervention came through the interstate commerce clause of the U.S. Constitution, which was interpreted to allow the regulation of jobs that bore a connection to the national (and "official") economy.[52]

The peculiar problem faced by many women, regardless of race or ethnicity, was that the kind of work they engaged in did not afford them full worker status. For (white) women, the logic of protective labor legislation privileged their unwaged status as mothers and housekeepers rather than as wage earners; it tied their public or citizenship right to adequate wages and working conditions primarily to an idealized notion of the full-time stay-at-home mother rather than to an ungendered notion of the rights of any working person within the official economy. Placed outside the idealized notion of motherhood, most women of color were not covered by female protective labor legislation; neither did the kind of wage work they performed afford them the sort of full worker status that would have granted them protection based on their status as paid workers. Their invisibility as both "motherworkers" and wage workers confirmed the continuation of racialized and gendered rights in twentieth-century America.[53]

The use of a racialized sex distinction in labor legislation solidified the idea that white women were only secondarily wage earners and confirmed the invisibility of the wage and mother work done by women of color. The emphasis on motherhood or potential motherhood, and on duties of the household, explained everything from restrictions on working at night to limits on the amount of weight that any woman could legally lift on the job, and demonstrated that while women might be part of the paid workforce, their first and primary responsibility lay in childrearing and housekeeping.

Far from being a dead letter in the postwar period, state female protective labor legislation remained widespread. In 1951 the only states without some sex-specific protective labor laws in place were Mississippi and Florida. Hours limitations and wage minimums were among the most frequent protections afforded: in 1951 forty-one states had legal restrictions on women's hours of work and twenty-four states granted a minimum wage. That same year twenty-six states maintained "protective" laws that forbade women's employment in certain occupations, most frequently underground mining; a number of states also banned women in bartending or retail liquor sales. In other states a hodgepodge of occupations—from bellhop to crane operator, welder to golf caddie, blast furnace worker to meter reader, and many more—were declared off limits to women.[54]

While the legal theory behind these sex-specific labor laws clearly signaled women's continuing secondary workplace status, their everyday practical import for postwar women wage earners might be negative or positive. For instance, weight-lifting restrictions helped employers in manufacturing construct parallel "light" (female, less well-paid) and "heavy" (male, better-paid) job classifications even as they claimed to have done away with sex-based job descriptions.[55] And nightwork laws restricted a wife's option to earn wages during the hours when her husband would most likely be at home with the children. On the other hand, depending on the kind of work they did and other circumstances, women might derive more or less benefit from the legal protections granted. Female minimum wage and maximum hours laws were especially advantageous to women who worked in intrastate commerce jobs (frequently small, female-dominated workplaces), which were not covered by any federal wage or hours laws.[56]

Labor union women and their supporters in the U.S. Women's Bureau had been early and longtime supporters of protective labor legislation. In the postwar period as well, union women and their allies sought a new protection: equal pay for equal or comparable work. Generally written in sex-neutral language but primarily concerned with reducing a significant pay differential between men and women workers (which disfavored women), campaigns for this protection succeeded in fourteen states in the first decade following the end of World War II. By 1963, when activists won a long-fought battle for a federal equal pay law, twenty-two states had already enacted one.[57]

Where early-twentieth-century female reformers relied heavily on a politics of motherhood to enact female protective labor legislation, in the postwar era union women and their allies at the U.S. Women's Bureau and in civic and religious groups were much more likely to practice what historian Kathleen Laughlin has called a "politics of opportunity."[58] During the war and immediately afterward union women, supported by their elected leadership, did advocate for child care and other measures to ease women wage earners' domestic duties. But the attention that unions paid to such issues died rather quickly in the face of a conservative postwar backlash that gave greater prerogatives to male workers and, as the Cold War intensified, silenced the most progressive voices in the labor movement. With the limited exception of (largely unsuccessful) efforts to gain maternity leave guarantees, union women's postwar focus on workplace status tended to take their unpaid home duties for granted and highlighted instead the significance of their earnings to family well-being. Union women and the Women's Bureau sought to improve women's workplace status by combating sex-based job placement, working toward state minimum wage and hours laws for women not covered by federal law, and, in male-dominated workplaces, insisting on equal pay for their work.[59]

While the politics of motherhood helped to solidify the notion that a mother's first duty always lay in the home, the postwar politics of opportunity destabilized this notion without questioning women's socially assigned duty of homemaking and childrearing. Surveying the significant body of female protective labor legislation still on the books in 1968, legal scholar Susan Deller Ross observed that "while women are chivalrously allowed chairs for rest periods in 45 States, they are given job security for maternity leaves of absence in *no* State, and maternity benefits in only two."[60]

Aside from lower-wage, lesser-status jobs, and the reassertion of protective labor legislation, mothers who sought wage work in the postwar years also faced barriers to employment that stemmed explicitly from their perceived first responsibility as childrearers and homemakers. Some of the best evidence in this regard was compiled by the Women's Bureau in 1950 and 1951 when it sought to demonstrate the need for more child care services during the Korean War. In Hartford, Connecticut, the bureau's investigator found an employer that would consent to hire a mother with children under the age of six years only if the mother provided evidence that satisfactory care would be given to her children.[61] In Dallas, employers also checked on a mother's child care arrangements and were said to prefer care provided by relatives in or near the home to care in a center (because care by relatives made for fewer absences due to a sick child).[62] In South Bend, Indiana, "one of the largest plants ha[d] a general policy that their women employees will be only the single and widowed," who were thought to be more stable workers than married women.[63] A company in Dayton, Ohio, provided a child care center for its employees but allowed only one child per family to use it; any mother with more than one child would have to make other arrangements.[64]

Across the country, the investigation by the Women's Bureau suggested that women now had fewer child care options than during the World War II years, and that this caused employment difficulties. In New Haven, Connecticut, a "large aircraft-engine plant" reported that fifteen women had left employment in the first six months of 1951 because they could not get child care, and twenty-eight others had done so because of "home responsibilities."[65] Especially where industry did not see labor demands as pressing, the idea of providing child care so that mothers could work remained controversial. A surplus of unskilled and semiskilled workers in South Bend made an increased demand for women workers unlikely, according to the Women's Bureau, and "this is the basis for a strong opinion in the community that to provide child care arrangements might create more problems than it would solve."[66] In Gary, Indiana, the Women's Bureau investigator found that a "cleavage of opinion existed between those who for traditional or other reasons felt it unwise to do anything that might encourage mothers to work [i.e., establish more child care centers] and those who recognized the intensive economic pressures that impelled many mothers to work."[67] Additionally, the inflexible schedules of existing child care centers could also be prohibitive for those women who sought shift work at odd hours or at manufacturing plants where workers were routinely required to rotate the shift they worked.

Child Care, Protest, and Public Decision Making

Half a decade earlier, at the close of World War II, many women recognized the significance of public child care provision to their own access and opportunity in the workplace. These working women sought to retain a service to which many before the war had had no access (or perhaps had even been unaware of). Invariably they faced long odds. Even if they supported the idea of mothers working during the war, many citizens and policymakers believed that women should rightly return home in peacetime. Further, subsidizing day care appeared to be a costly drain on the public treasury; private voluntary agencies were similarly awed by the funding needs of day care and uncertain about its role. Schools, which housed many wartime child care centers and offered a natural location for both preschool and school-age programs, were in many cases already overcrowded and destined to become more so with the ensuing postwar baby boom. Postwar public child care advocates also confronted a long history of far more limited and resolutely private child care provisions.

Day nurseries for the care of wage-earning mothers emerged primarily in the middle to late nineteenth century as a private philanthropic venture of well-to-do women. The National Federation of Day Nurseries, founded in 1898, followed the lead of its conservative head Josephine (Mrs. Arthur) Jewell Dodge in steadfastly rejecting the notion of public support for day nurseries. With few exceptions private day nursery benefactors explained their work as a temporary charity, granting daytime care of children as a way to prevent "pauperization" and later to foster cultural assimilation. With the exception of some short-lived calls for regulation of commercial child care in the early twentieth century, the federation's partisans rejected any suggestion of public involvement. Dodge, as the head of the group, actively lobbied against efforts to establish publicly funded child care services during World War I.[68]

In a decision of great consequence for day nurseries and possible public support for day care, in the early years of the twentieth century child welfare reformers, led by settlement house workers and others who represented a rising professional class of social workers, came to doubt that day nurseries offered the appropriate aid to poor working mothers. Observing the difficult practical reality that many women faced in combining wage earning and childrearing, they questioned whether poor women should be in the workforce at all. Joining with maternalists across a wide political range, these reformers, including importantly the future leaders of the federal U.S. Children's Bureau, shifted their support from day nurseries to mother's pensions.[69]

The rise of the mother's pension—a state grant of money intended to allow a low-income mother to stay at home and raise her own children—threw the existence of day nurseries into question. Social workers, like earlier day nursery founders, argued that such a child care arrangement should be only temporarily available to certain families.[70] In the New Deal the idea of the mother's pension received federal sanction and funding through the Aid to Dependent Children program (later renamed Aid to Families with Dependent Children and commonly called "welfare"). Staff members of the Children's Bureau played a primary role in writing the new federal policy into the larger Social Security Act of 1935. Although mothers' pensions as they were put into practice had easily recognizable flaws, their legislative success at the state level and the federal blessing given to them in the New Deal helped to seal the private location of day nurseries and confirmed for many their inferiority.

As if to add an exclamation point, when the federal government during the Great Depression inaugurated its first program for children of preschool age, it turned for a model not to the day nursery but to the much newer nursery school. The nursery school movement drew primarily on studies of child development to argue that all preschoolers (primarily three- and four-year-olds) could benefit from out-of-home care. Privately funded through philanthropic grants and as demonstration projects in universities, nursery schools generally served middle- and upper-income families who could afford to pay a full-cost fee.[71]

The federal government's program for preschoolers during the Depression was in the first place a public jobs program for out-of-work teachers and support staff, and it served poor children primarily. By 1942, when the boom in war-related jobs made its job-creation purpose anachronistic, advocates of publicly supported care and education for preschoolers successfully lobbied for a wartime program that would serve the children of working mothers. With funding from the Federal Works Agency (FWA), the wartime child care program reached its high point in July 1944, when close to 130,000 children were enrolled in 3,102 centers nationwide. In the following year, with Allied victory in Europe recently achieved, the federal program had declined marginally to 2,792 centers that enrolled about 102,000 children.[72]

The child care program, which was allowed to receive funding under national defense-related public works legislation, popularly known as the Lanham Act (1941), grew smaller over this period for a number of reasons.[73] These included the general demise of many wartime programs due to postwar fears of big government, the absence of a bureaucratic child care infrastructure, and a widespread understanding that women's domestic and maternal duties were wholly private concerns.[74] Not least, however, the FWA itself became less inclined to renew funds for specific projects once war production needs appeared less pressing. Soon after the Allied victory in Europe, the agency reported to a congressional subcommittee on appropriations that it had reduced the estimated amount of federal funds sought by local child care administrators more than 40 percent because "the war need is coming down." An FWA spokesman added, "We have canceled in the last month about 50-child-care projects."[75] Furthermore, widespread layoffs that accompanied the cancellation of wartime contracts began well before a final ceasefire would be signed. Even though many parents who used the federally subsidized child care centers did not work in the direct production of essential military goods, the layoffs of women who did reduced the apparent need for a continued child care subsidy.[76]

Despite these cutbacks, the FWA's announcement in August 1945 that all federal funding of child care would cease no later than October 31 brought a torrent of protest. Even as the battle for an extension of federal funding intensified, the number of families who sent children to the publicly subsidized centers, or who had access to those centers, continued a steady decline. In the chaotic months following the war's end, no doubt many mothers did withdraw from the workforce (as federal lawmakers and local administrators believed they would). Some of these women left their jobs unwillingly in the large manufacturing layoffs that accompanied the war victory. Others, exhausted by the demands of the wartime six-day workweek combined with childrearing and housekeeping responsibilities, and constant concern for the safety of their husbands or other loved ones, gratefully withdrew from the workforce—even if temporarily. By February 1946, the final month of federal funding for the wartime child care centers, the program had shrunk to approximately 1,500 centers serving about 47,000 children.[77]

A little less than five years later, the only states that maintained public child care funding were California, where activists maintained support for a sizable state-funded program, and to a lesser extent Washington and Massachusetts. In a handful of major cities—Detroit, Philadelphia, the District of Columbia, New York, and Denver—publicly subsidized programs that served several hundred to several thousand children also survived.[78] But some of these programs would shortly be shut down, and by 1960 the number of publicly supported centers had declined even further. Philadelphia, New York City, and California were the only places where public centers that grew out of World War II programs still operated. Outside the 324 publicly supported centers operating in those locations, a report of the Children's Bureau in 1960 found just fifty-two centers nationwide that received at least partial public funding; more than half were in Texas.[79] It would miss significant social and political details, however, to conclude from these numbers that the need or desire for decent and affordable child care had substantially declined; or that the end of public funding was inevitable and that little discussion occurred on the issue; or that many women simply quietly and without much thought returned to their kitchens.

In the first place, between thirteen and fourteen million women worked before the war and planned to do so afterward. If they were returning anywhere, these women hoped that it would be to the better-paying jobs they had found during the war, and from which many were laid off at the onset of the postwar reconversion period. As activists repeatedly pointed out, the war did not create a need for day care services: it simply broadened that need.[80] Second, although the number and percentage of women in the workforce, as well as their proportion of the total labor force, did drop suddenly after the war, each of these indicators began a near immediate and steady rebound.

In the Eisenhower years, and just one decade after the war ended, women's labor force participation rate resembled the rate immediately before V-J Day. By 1955 the number of women working had climbed to 20.5 million, surpassing by more than 1 million their wartime high; the proportion of all women who were in the labor force stood at 35.7 percent (compared to 35.8 percent in 1945); and women accounted for 30.2 percent of the total workforce, compared to 29.2 percent in 1945.[81] The similar numbers of the two periods obscure significant differences, however—especially the rising percentage of married women who worked. By the middle 1950s, despite a prolonged and continuing surge in the birth rate, about 35 percent of married women who lived with their husbands and had school-age children were part of the paid labor force. That proportion roughly equaled the participation rate of all females—single, widowed, divorced, and married. Although the mothers of preschool-age children remained less likely to be in the paid workforce, their numbers were also rising. Thus, although mothers who were their children's sole support had much higher employment rates than mothers who lived with their husbands, the labor force participation rate of sole-support mothers remained fairly static, in sharp contrast to all others.[82]

Finally, and perhaps most important, to see the postwar end of most public funding for child care services as inevitable is to write the story based on a knowledge of its denouement, rather than by considering its possibilities. The resistance of parents—primarily mothers—to the cutting off of publicly provided child care represented an important early challenge to long-standing ideas about motherhood and the domestic ideal. This mostly female and largely grassroots protest made taxpayer funding of child care an issue that would have to be publicly decided rather than casually dismissed.[83] In the initial months after the Federal Works Agency announced the imminent withdrawal of federal support, thousands of people wrote letters, sent telegrams, and signed petitions calling for continued funding for child care centers. The national uproar forced the hand of members of Congress in Washington who were otherwise eager to cut back wartime spending wherever possible. Although the extension that they granted lasted only four months, it surely would not have happened at all without a tremendous and widespread outcry. Further, the extension allowed these same organizations and individuals a short but important time in which to call for public provisions in more local forums. A measure of the continuing and widespread protest is indicated by an FWA survey that found more than 77 percent of the former wartime centers continuing to operate one month after the withdrawal of federal money. Outside of New Mexico (which had never operated any wartime centers) and South Dakota, every state had at least one of the wartime centers operating on March 31, 1946. Nineteen states had twenty-one or more of the centers still open.[84]

Maintaining continued child care services after the withdrawal of federal subsidy, even for this short period, required a great deal of activist effort. Women across the country made insistent public demands for continued public funding of child care. They held mass meetings, picketed city halls, successfully requested public hearings, conducted letter-writing campaigns to newspapers and public officials, developed pro–day care radio spots, and lobbied decision makers. In their efforts to continue day care funding, working mothers found allies in civic and citizens' groups, social welfare agencies and their workers, child care committees set up during the war, and some early childhood educators. All this determined noise about day care demanded public attention, debate, and decision. Instead of allowing the issue to slide into oblivion, the activism of day care users and their supporters politicized the issue of child care and demanded a public response.[85]

Between 1945 and about 1951, when public calls for direct funding of child care services remained loudest, there were three relatively consistent stages of public decision making, each of which would need to be successfully negotiated if a given child care program was to be maintained. The first stage occurred in the months immediately after the war ended and primarily required finding a new source of subsidy. Activists sought state, city, and county sources of child care funding and turned as well to private social welfare agencies and a wide range of civic groups. The rationale of postwar reconversion need remained of crucial importance during this period and could secure a temporary continuation of a day care program. If they survived this initial hurdle, day care partisans would next need to weather a redefinition of their program—usually in 1947 and 1948. How would a postwar program

Table 1. Number of Federally Assisted Child Care Centers and Enrollment, Selected Months, 1943–1946

Month and Year	Number of Centers[a]	Enrollment
August 1943	1,726	49,194
January 1944	2,156	61,614
April 1944	2,495	84,075
July 1944	3,102	129,357
December 1944	2,827	99,287
February 1945	2,878	108,126
May 1945	3,013	111,094
July 1945	2,792	101,882
August 1945	2,665	91,270
December 1945	1,592	49,690
February 1946	1,504	46,566

All federal funding of child care programs ended on February 28, 1946.

Formerly federally subsidized centers

March 1946	1,147	Not available
July 1946	959[b]	Not available

Sources: California Legislature, *Technical Staff Report*, tables 44a, 44b; Mildred Arnold to Celvah Rosenthal, March 12, 1947, Records of the U.S. Children's Bureau, National Archives. (Both sources report data collected by the FWA and most data refer to the end of each month.)

[a] A center, designated a "unit" by the FWA survey, consists of a group of children under a head teacher.

[b] Number of centers operating may have been slightly higher, as the July 1946 survey excluded information from a limited number of areas.

(and now a largely post-reconversion program) justify a continuing use of public money? A widespread insistence on limiting any public child care services to families deemed financially needy (ideally families headed by sole-support mothers) meant that survivors of this second stage generally emerged with a newly minted or much more clearly defined financial means test to restrict access to programs. But even so, funding and authorization for child care programs generally continued only temporarily. By 1950 or 1951 a third requirement became permanent: day care supporters needed to justify a child care program's continued existence in the community.

MOTHERS AND WORK

The Federal Works Agency reported that 1,147 day care centers continued to provide services one month after the federal subsidy ceased, but it noted that "in many areas the existing financing and operating arrangements are temporary." Close to half of the centers still open were in Washington state, California, and New York, where legislators voted to temporarily grant them state funding. After state subsidy, the most common sources of funds were private social agencies and then "fees and contributions"; industry and municipal funding ranked a rather distant fourth and fifth.[86]

There were myriad barriers to achieving and sustaining funding for child care centers. Across the southeastern region, nearly all the centers listed as still being open remained so because of increased fees and private contributions. In Pascagoula, Mississippi, this strategy called for doubling fees; in Birmingham, Alabama, fees were raised to $10 a week.[87] Only a week after federal subsidies ended, a mother in Owensboro, Kentucky, sent a clear but distressed letter to the Children's Bureau. Her home town, a "semi-industrial city of 33,000," had housed four federally supported day care centers during the war, "two white and two colored." After two months of "concerted effort" to locate new funding, the "mothers of the largest white school" adopted a plan to save their center. With the blessing of the city commissioners, free space and equipment from the Board of Education, and the donation of their own time to manage the program, the mothers' group would be allowed to continue operation for a trial period of two months. The city council agreed to make up any operating deficit during that period, but if the trial showed that the operation could not be self-sustaining, the city would withdraw its support. "Our budget is based on an average attendance of 25 children per day and the fee raised from $3 to $5 per week. To reduce operating expenses, we have two teachers instead of three," the day care patron and activist explained. But "even with these economies," she continued, "it seems that we will need financial assistance since the enrollment has averaged only 20 for the first week. . . . When the fee was raised, approximately ⅓ of the enrollment was lost. The people who benefited by a nursery are low salaried, and they are the ones who had to take their children out of school." Convinced that some public support would be necessary to continue the program, she identified the U.S. Dept. of Agriculture's school lunch program as a possible source of funds and asked for suggestions of other possibilities.[88] A number of child care programs did initially rely on the Agriculture Department's subsidy of school food as a way to offset at least one relatively minor cost item. The National Committee on Group Day Care of Children, a temporary organization, recommended the school lunch subsidy to community and parents' groups seeking sources of funding.[89] But this proved a short-lived option. What had been a long-standing program funded year to year gained permanent status as the School Lunch Act in July 1946. When it made the law permanent, however, Congress specified that no school lunch money could support preschool programs.[90]

Finding or keeping facilities also proved difficult. A program in the Baltimore area that had survived in a child care facility constructed by the FWA on property of the Bethlehem Steel Co. found its facility threatened in 1947. After the steel company sold the entire property, the new owners notified the FWA that they wanted their land cleared of all buildings, and the FWA in turn notified the child care program that it must vacate the premises.[91] In Los Angeles, parents and civic groups organized to save several centers housed in FWA buildings that had been placed on the surplus property auction block and now appeared likely to fill the growing space needs of the city's grade-school population.[92]

By July 1, 1946, four months after the end of federal subsidies, a new survey by the FWA showed that the number of former wartime child care centers still operating had fallen below a thousand. In Chicago a combination of municipal funds carried nineteen centers through June 30, 1946, but no tax funds would be available in the new fiscal year. Two centers in Louisville, Kentucky, remained alive thanks to surplus money donated by the wartime Tire Ration Board, but this public subsidy was to run out by the end of July 1946. No doubt many of the programs that had initially continued by greatly increasing user fees had by now been forced to close. Meanwhile, those fortunate enough to have secured firm financing (and continued housing) carried on.[93]

In 1947 and 1948 the surviving programs would face the need to redefine their purpose. In both the District of Columbia and California this meant a newly defined and more restrictive financial means test. In New York, state funding did not survive, despite massive protests that included a motorcade that traveled to Governor Thomas Dewey's upstate home.[94] Although New York City agreed to pick up the slack left by the state's refusal to continue funding, a new financial means test combined with a more stringent casework evaluation of day care users effectively removed hundreds of families from the city's program.[95] In Massachusetts, where a statute enacted in 1945 permitted a very limited amount of money for child care centers that served "children of working mothers whose employment is essential to the welfare of the family," only two cities had such programs in place by 1948. A third, Springfield, had closed its last public center in 1947 after local groups could not agree on the purpose of the program: Should it serve economically needy families only, or be a part of the school and open to all? The local taxpayers' association complained about the cost of the program and "many people were much disturbed because they believe that the parents of a number of the children were in very comfortable financial circumstances."[96]

In 1950 and 1951 publicly supported day care programs faced the need to explain their increasingly permanent appearance. Curiously, this stage of public decision making occurred when American troops were again fighting overseas—this time on the Korean peninsula. But the war did not generate additional public funding. Washington state, which had continued a rather small program, decided in April 1951 to end all state funding. The legislators believed that there were too many "frills" in the state education program: child care, adult education, and even school lunches all came under fire.[97] The U.S. Congress, with little explanation, cut all funding for the Washington, D.C., program in late 1950. In Detroit publicly supported child care centers had dwindled from an initial postwar high of twenty or twenty-five to a total of five by 1950.[98] Public day care users in Philadelphia, however, seem to have successfully navigated each stage by this period, and in 1950 the program in fact added a center (bringing the total to thirteen). In California, lawmakers came within a hair's breadth of ending all funding before granting the statewide program its first two-year extension in 1951.[99]

While the practical considerations of money, facilities, and administrative jurisdiction were important in public decision making, the role of women in society—especially their duties as mothers of young children—constituted an important philosophical issue in these debates. Many people, even including a great many supporters of day care, held a view of motherhood that in the ideal world precluded women's participation in paid labor. Debates about women's access to wage work and the adamant reassertion of female protective labor legislation in the immediate aftermath of World War II reaffirmed the notion that mothers ideally belonged in the private home rather than the public marketplace. And the legislative compromises that secured the passage of the Employment Act of 1946 confirmed the importance that policymakers placed on fostering private markets to achieve public good (rather than the social provision of services). As long as policymakers were unwilling to redistribute social responsibility for child care, providing a social structure that supported mothers' ability to share domestic responsibilities with fathers and others, mothers would not have equal opportunity in the workplace.

The next three chapters look more closely at public child care activism in Cleveland, Washington, D.C., and California, where day care activists had increasing success in negotiating the funding, program redefinition, and permanent justification stages of postwar public child care decision making. Women's proper relationship to wage labor played an integral role in each of these locations and phases, as activists necessarily sought to explain women's presence in the workforce. In Cleveland, as the next chapter will discuss, working mothers who sought a publicly funded postwar child care service challenged the notion that women should remain solely private and domestic actors. They engaged in determined public actions to make their case for taxpayer funding of child care. Arguing for continued access to child care, they sought to recast motherhood in a way that adequately reflected both their economic and domestic responsibilities.

When a mother is obliged by hard necessity to assume the burden of family support, she has the right to look to society as her traditional ally in providing for the safety and well-being of her children.

—Cleveland Day Care Committee, ca. September 1945

Recasting Motherhood

The Early Postwar Battle for Publicly Funded Day Care in Cleveland

Day care users in Cleveland represent one group among many across the nation who organized to retain the fledgling publicly funded wartime day care service.[1] These mothers ceaselessly and unashamedly pressed their need to earn wages. Believing that broadly available, affordable day care of high quality was both a public need and a social right, they launched a series of letter-writing campaigns, open meetings, and public demonstrations that brought the issue of child care into general debate and forced official decision making.

The demand for continued public support for day care services came from women across the nation who sought to retain their wartime status in the workplace as wage-earning mothers. It represented a direct challenge to a reinvigorated, insistent domestic ideology according to which mothers in the postwar era always belonged at home. Organizing around a personal and family concern, these working women sought to recast motherhood in a way that more closely reflected their own lives. In short, they sought to ensure continued public provisions for child care to better enable themselves to combine wage-earning, household, and childrearing responsibilities.

The Struggle for Extension of Federal Funds

Months before the Japanese surrender that brought an end to World War II, the Federal Works Agency (FWA) had set in motion plans to withdraw funding from federally supported wartime day care centers. By January 1945 the agency began to warn state officials that federal dollars would expire with the war, and soon after the Allied victory in Europe in May the agency established a policy of renewing funding for the centers solely for the short term. On August 14, 1945, with Emperor Hirohito poised to announce that Japan would surrender, the FWA cranked its shutdown plans into their final phase. The agency sent notice to its field staff that all federal funds for day care centers would be withdrawn, at the very latest, by October 31, 1945.[2]

Federal money for the wartime child care program had been authorized through the emergency Lanham Act, a grab-bag measure that allowed federal public works funding for a variety of war-related reasons. At the program's height the funds helped to support more than 3,100 centers across all but one of the forty-eight states, as well as the District of Columbia and the territories of Alaska and Hawaii. Although the program never adequately met the tremendous need for child care, a great deal of which existed even before the war, it did represent a sizable federal expenditure and an unprecedented public policy concession to women as wage earners. The federal government eventually spent about $52 million on the program while local communities ponied up more than $26 million—the lion's share of which came from fees charged to parents who enrolled their children in centers.[3]

Located exclusively in areas formally designated as having a war-related need for child care services, the centers began to diminish in number after Allied victories in early 1945 lowered defense production needs. By the war's end, however, fully 2,650 centers remained in operation in close to 600 communities across the country. The city of Cleveland housed thirty-two of these federally subsidized child care centers, and for the nearly 900 mothers who used them the indescribably good news of the war victory arrived virtually simultaneously with the unsettling news that the child care services they relied on would soon be terminated.[4]

As in other locations, the announcement of imminent closings in Cleveland produced a great outpouring of support for continued public funding of day care from those who used the service. Mothers wasted no time in making clear both the value they placed on affordable, widely available day care and their intention to fight the closings. Within a few days of the announcement by the FWA wage-earning mothers organized committees at nearly every one of the forty centers, and then pooled those efforts to create a joint council named simply the Day Care Committee. Over the next several weeks, in an effort to rally support for a continued day care program, committee activists personally called on their county commissioners, members of the city Board of Education and City Council, the governor, the regional FWA representative, the entire Ohio congressional delegation, and other key members of the U.S. Congress. In addition to these visits, they wrote letters, made telephone calls, produced radio segments, and sent telegrams to publicize the situation and seek broad public support.[5]

Believing that others, once informed, would understand the gravity of their situation, the Day Care Committee sent air-mail, special-delivery letters to such well-known national commentators as Walter Winchell, Drew Pearson, Eleanor Roosevelt, and Lowell Thomas. Tying their concern to the war, they wrote: "Knowing of your interest in the serviceman and his problems, we are writing to you to enlist your aid in our cause. We are a group of mothers, mostly servicemen's wives and widows who have organized to keep the day care centers of the country open. We all have to work to either support our families entirely, or supplement the allotment [sic] we received from the government. These day care centers are the only reliable means we have of insuring the proper care of our children—children who by reason of the war are deprived of the care of their fathers. The F.W.A. has ordered that the funds for these centers be discontinued by October 31, 1945." In asking these public personalities to "acquaint the general public with this situation," the day care activists confidently concluded: "We are sure this publicity will do a great deal toward solving our problem."[6]

The Cleveland Day Care Committee represented only a small segment of what quickly emerged as a national protest against the proposed day care center closings. The movement for continued federal funding of day care services brought an avalanche of mail to the nation's capital. The fate of the day care centers became the hottest topic in the White House mailbag, and correspondence also crammed mailrooms on Capitol Hill and at federal agencies. "There are doubtless few members of the House who have not had a flood of letters and telegrams from working mothers desperate because care for their children during the working hours is shortly to be ended," commented Rep. Ned Healy (D-Calif.) during a September 1945 debate on the child care program in the House of Representatives. Major General Philip Fleming, administrator of the FWA, testified at an appropriations hearing that same month: "We get 400 or 500 communications a day from people protesting against withdrawal [of child care funding]."[7] Indeed, just one month after announcing that the centers' federal funding would end, a tally by the FWA showed that close to six thousand individuals and groups from at least twenty-six states and the District of Columbia had signed petitions or sent letters, wires, and postcards to request that the subsidy be continued. The agency also duly noted receiving a total of six letters approving the immediate closing of the child care centers.[8]

The widespread nature of the protest should not come as a surprise. Historians of women have sometimes noted the inadequacy of the federal government's wartime day care program. Relying on local initiative and administration, the service clearly did not meet all of the need, but the centers were widely distributed throughout the country and no doubt provided the best day care option that many of their patrons had ever been offered. During the war working women in particular had experienced greater job opportunities and much better pay. The child care program was virtually the only concession made to the necessity for many women to combine six-day paid workweeks with multiple and time-consuming household responsibilities.[9]

The rationale for this wartime federal spending had been the need to free mothers from child care responsibility so that they could boost war production. In their letter to national commentators, the Cleveland Day Care Committee zeroed in on a separate war-related argument for the extension of federal funding for day care—an argument repeated across the United States. The new line of reasoning stressed that the war emergency continued for wives whose servicemen husbands were not expected home for many months and who still needed to financially provide for their families on an inadequate government allotment. One mother in Cleveland who wrote to the Children's Bureau quickly summarized this appeal: "My daughter, Georgia age 3 is at present in a Day Nursery. Since my husband is in the service, in the Pacific, where he will be for some time to come, it is imperative that I work to maintain my home & feed and clothe my child and I. Since the news of V-J day, the Nursery is scheduled to close. Where am I to place my child?"[10] Basing the argument for public funding on the peculiar needs of servicemen's wives avoided discussion of a permanent plan and implied that only those considered the most deserving would need a temporary extension of help. The focus on a temporary extension of funding, however, did not obscure the call for permanent public provision of child care. Beyond the continued need for child care experienced by servicemen's wives, the FWA cited "the need of mothers who are sole support of their children," and "a lack or inadequacy of other forms of satisfactory care in the community" as the two most common reasons given for requesting extended federal funding of the day care program. Letters received at the White House after the FWA survey of responses confirmed the existence of many longer-standing concerns unrelated to the war.[11]

One mother who appended the notation "(colored)" to her signature pleaded with President Truman to recognize her continued need for day care: "Im mother of two little boys. I have a one hundren per cent know good man[.] If the nurserys dont open Ive got to ask for help for I havent made enought to save any and my little boys got to eat. President you don't realize how much you are hurting mother of the world[.] Yes it some realy dont have to work but just think of poor me who got to take care of two boys and half the time dont know where father is[.] I know Im not the best Writer but I do hope you understand me and let me be one of the mothers that get some consideration please."[12] Other writers also described their own situations in calling for continuation of the child care program. A mother from Oakland noted that she had been divorced against her wishes and asked the president, "Please help me and the other working mothers to keep our Babies happy and healthy." And from the District of Columbia, another mother wrote that she and her husband were not financially able to live on one income and therefore needed access to affordable day care.[13]

A number of letter writers described the child care program as a boon to themselves, their children, and the public. From Ogden, Utah, a mother warned of the national problem of child delinquency and informed the president that day care had not only benefited her child but also enabled her to do a better job at work. Signing "a proud Democrat" beside her name, a mother from Chicago insisted that she had to work to support her family of six and that the day care centers were the only safe place to leave children. Besides, she wrote, without them she would have to go on relief, whereas by working she could "less[en] the tax payers burden."[14]

Also from Chicago, the father of a four-and-a-half-year-old boy appealed for extended federal funding on his own family's behalf, as well as that of many other middle-income families. Writing of a "serious desire for a continuation of war nurseries," he urged President Truman to consider that living costs were up, that private nurseries were expensive and often inadequate, and that women might choose to work: "My wife wants to contribute towards the household expenses and other needs of the family and at the same time, achieve a certain degree of independence. As a psychiatrist, I have to recognize this need in her as well as in millions of other American women." But in the end appeals that looked beyond wartime concerns and called for continued federal day care funding—whether to prevent economic want, or to help secure greater economic or personal independence —went largely uheard.[15]

The federal government had specifically justified its expenditure for the operation of day care centers as a war measure. "Our national policy in peacetime is that mothers of small children may best serve the nation by remaining at home and giving personal attention to the rearing of their children," stated Florence Kerr, who directed the FWA's department in charge of the program for most of the war. The wartime program existed, Kerr explained, because "mothers were working whether anybody liked it or not. We had to protect the home, not by keeping mothers in the home with their children but by putting mothers in the war industries wherever necessary to hasten defeat of the enemy and thus save the American home."[16]

This patriotic rationale for child care centers was politically expedient. An educator who was previously a part of the Emergency Nursery School program, a federal effort that originated in the Depression, Florence Kerr may have seen longer-term needs for child care. Still the political constraints —even within her own agency—were real.[17] Under questioning about the day care program, General Fleming never missed a chance to cite the end of war production as the rationale for the abrupt end of day care funding. In fact, soon after the Allies declared victory in Europe in May 1945, the FWA brokered a "gentlemen's agreement" with several House committees and a few key senators that promised to stop day care funding as soon as war ended. The FWA entered this agreement because, General Fleming wrote, "we realized that the need for women in war production was tapering off, and that the funds appropriated to us would not carry the program for a whole year." The plight of servicemen's wives struck Fleming as a "welfare need" rather than a war issue.[18]

Virtually overnight the public provision of public child care changed (in the minds of many) from a legitimate war-related service to a "welfare need." The evidently mutable meaning of public child care provision derived from its relationship to mothers and wage work. During the war citizen mothers who worked to increase war production were seen as acting in the public economy and for the public good; accordingly they had been granted some access to child care services. But citizen mothers who sought to continue wage earning after the war ended were no longer viewed as assets to the public economy and so could not assume the same access to child care. At best, mothers in the postwar period might be considered worthy of publicly subsidized child care if they could show a private family obligation that necessitated wage earning (and especially if the need could be called war re-

RECASTING MOTHERHOOD

lated). In short, postwar motherhood was expected to resume its exclusive devotion to the private family; paradoxically this made private childrearing a mother's foremost peacetime public obligation.

If the valorization of stay-at-home motherhood limited day care advocates' ability to provide a postwar rationale for a continued public child care service, their efforts to retain the service also suffered from the wartime program's weak institutional hold in government. Although the federal day care program had a strong constituent base in many communities across the country, it held only a shaky bureaucratic place in Washington and displayed very limited staying power at the state level. Agency infighting between the Children's Bureau and the FWA had plagued the child care program from the beginning of the war. Heavily invested in the Social Security Act's Aid to Dependent Children program (as a superior alternative to mother's work outside the home), the Children's Bureau hesitated in its support for public child care even in wartime. Ultimately the bureau did back the idea of federally supported wartime child care centers, but it lost the battle for program definition.[19]

The wartime jockeying for position between the federal agencies had important consequences for the child care program. The FWA's victory left the wartime program laden with far fewer professional social work criteria than the kind of service that the Children's Bureau envisioned—either as a war expedient or as a permanent measure. The FWA approached day care pragmatically, as a service that the country needed to boost production and win the war. Toward this end the agency gave direct grants to local education and civic groups that sought to establish and operate day care programs. Beyond evidence that an area needed women workers to boost war production, the funding basis largely precluded investigating a mother's family situation or finances to certify her eligibility for the service. This approach helped to broaden the use of day care, a service previously associated almost exclusively with very poor or dysfunctional families.[20]

Specifically, the program administered by the FWA did not fund casework consulting and foster home day care, both programs that the Children's Bureau saw as essential to any comprehensive child care program. By the 1920s child welfare workers had come to understand day care as an available "therapy" for families that regrettably could not financially manage without a mother's wages, or in which other troubles made the home an uncertain place for children to grow up. Even once war exigencies finally forced the bureau to concede that a greater number of mothers could legitimately be in the workforce, it still understood a mother's wage work as a fundamental threat to her children's healthy development. Accordingly it offered support late and continued to bemoan what it saw as a day care service exclusively based on the needs of war production rather than those of children.[21]

In short, the FWA administration of the wartime program meant that parents had a brief but important opportunity to understand day care as a public service for "normal" families. At the same time, the narrow focus on a war rationale for the program, combined with the FWA's practice of giving direct grants to local communities, made the program a kind of hothouse flower. Without so much as a bureaucratic toehold in most states—only four state governments contributed tax dollars to wartime child care services—complete withdrawal of federal funds left the program acutely vulnerable.[22] In Ohio the state's only involvement in the wartime program was to channel a nominal amount of federal Children's Bureau money through the state Department of Welfare. The Greater Cleveland program used this money to fund case work consultants at its centers. Ohio itself did not provide a penny for the program—neither did Cuyahoga County, where Cleveland was located.[23]

The absence of a state or county bureaucratic stake was compounded by the missing, or at best anemic, federal support for publicly provided child care in the postwar period. Although they vigorously sought full control of the wartime program, FWA administrators showed virtually no interest in a peacetime day care service. General Fleming himself repeated a criticism of the FWA many times spoken by supporters of the Children's Bureau, when he told a senator's aide in mid-September 1945, "Just between you and me, we did it during the war because we had the funds and we had the authority. We are, of course, a construction agency and not a welfare agency."[24] As plans to shut down the program proceeded, the Children's Bureau did suggest the need for some continued public support, but the bureau's political power had been waning for several decades. Seeking a sharply redefined child care program, it asked that money be channeled from its own budget, through state agencies, and finally to local groups who would provide a range of child welfare programs, possibly including day care. Day care programs funded in this way would be expected to incorporate casework counseling in their admissions process—that is, to provide an intake social worker who could counsel a mother regarding whether wage earning represented the best decision for her family. Again the bureau sought to define any government-supported day care program not as a permanent service to families with working parents but as a specialized program that could temporarily serve selected economically or otherwise "needy" families.[25]

Along with the Children's Bureau, several national, nongovernmental child welfare and education organizations envisioned a permanent day care service and sought an extension of federal funding for day care services. These included the American Home Economics Association, the Child Welfare League of America (CWLA), the National Congress of Parents and Teachers, the National Education Association, and the Association for Childhood Education. A dozen representatives of these groups arranged to meet with President Truman on September 21, 1945, to urge an extension of the wartime day care program.[26] The CWLA took a lead role in this effort. It advocated a temporary extension of the current federal program, with a longer-term restructuring of the federal bureaucracy that would institutionalize a program along the lines envisioned by the Children's Bureau. A survey by the CWLA, conducted in forty-four communities after the announcement that the wartime child care centers would soon close, concluded that the program should continue to operate because large numbers of women needed to work in the postwar period. The survey found that many of the children in day care still had fathers in the service and also suggested that working mothers often needed a day care service whether or not their husbands were service men. If federal funding continued through the 1945–46 school year, the CWLA argued, the extension would allow communities time to determine the level of peacetime need for day care and to make arrangements accordingly. Failure to make public provisions for day care, the league reported, "will require mothers to use unsupervised day care services, will encourage the development of commercial child care facilities with exorbitant rates which most mothers cannot afford and lead to neglect and resulting delinquency for children who get no care at all."[27]

But like the letters from constituents, appeals by governmental and non-governmental agencies that identified a permanent need for some publicly funded day care were generally met with indifference, or hostility. Lawmakers now railed against what they viewed as a bloated wartime government, and the day care program looked like an easy place to start cutting back. Wage-earning mothers, previously pictured as wartime patriots "manning" assembly lines, were now more readily seen as absentees from their peacetime jobs at home, and as impediments to the civilian job placement of returning veterans. To buy time and ensure uninterrupted public funding for child care, a new rationale was needed, and a war-related rationale seemed most logical.

Grassroots activists explicitly recognized the political expediency of a rationale for day care that was premised on the needs of servicemen's wives, as is clear from a letter sent by a group of District of Columbia day care users to their counterparts in Cleveland. Regardless of how much the women sought a permanent program of publicly funded day care centers, the D.C. group cautioned that the current rationale had to be that the war emergency remained. "If we stress the permanent need, the Lanham Committee will blandly recommend that we try to make permanent arrangements before October 31, 1945, through local facilities and not count on Federal funds. You can guess how long that may take, and you will agree that any cessation of the program will retard progress in establishing child care centers."[28]

Indeed the plight of war widows, and of wives whose husbands had not yet been demobilized, had as early as August 24 prompted a White House communication with the FWA that stated the president's opposition to an abrupt ending of the centers. Truman instead favored a "taper[ing] off" of funds to keep the program operating specifically for servicemen's wives and widows, and he instructed Fleming to seek the consent of the appropriate congressional committees for this action. Toward this end, the FWA conducted a new survey of the day care centers to determine as of August 31, 1945, the number of servicemen's wives and widows who used the day care program. The proportion in each state varied from a low near 30 percent to a high around 70 percent. In Ohio, where 3,700 women sent their children to the federally subsidized wartime centers, the proportion of servicemen's wives and widows stood at about 40 percent—close to the median among all states of approximately 41 percent.[29]

The Cleveland Day Care Committee took its calls for continued federal funding of day care directly to Washington, D.C. It sent two members to lobby Congress and establish ties with working mothers in the District, who had also organized to save the child care program. Belle Likover, one of the Cleveland activists who made the trip, remembered it as a "very jam-packed day." She recalled visiting each member of the Ohio congressional delegation as well as members of the critical Lanham Committee. Likover recalled the day as discouraging. While a few members of Congress supported the call for extended funding, most wouldn't make a commitment and others patronized the women. "The last person that we went to see that day was Congresswoman Frances Payne Bolton, who was my Congresswoman." She was "a very proper Republican woman and when we walked into her office," Likover recalled, "she said, 'I have been following your progress all day. I know every place you've been and everyone you have talked to and I must tell you that you have behaved like ladies and I'm proud of you.'" While she endorsed their "ladylike" behavior, Bolton did little to support the women's request for continued federal funding of day care centers.[30]

Back in Cleveland, however, many of Bolton's constituents accepted the argument that federal funding of the day care program should be extended for the sake of servicemen's wives and widows. An editorial in the *Cleveland Press* urged that federal funding be continued up to six months longer. Although the editors commented that because some mothers would always need to work the question of permanent funding required "thoughtful answering," they insisted that at the moment the issue was simple: "37 per cent of the 1550 [children in day care centers] involved in Cleveland are those of wives of servicemen who are working to add enough to allotment payments to meet the family bills. That's a war problem as long as it exists, one for which no federal agency should abruptly terminate responsibility in the name of hasty reconversion."[31] In September the Cleveland City Council made its first public statement on the issue when it unanimously passed a resolution asking Congress to appropriate sufficient funds to continue the day care centers. The resolution noted that "continued operation of Child Day Care Centers [is] an essential part of the program of orderly reconversion as well as an obligation to the men in the Armed Forces." Citing the large proportion of servicemen's wives and widows, and "wives of the incapacitated," who were using the centers, the City Council noted that as chief wage earners these mothers would need permanent day care centers during 1945 and 1946. Apparently taking their cue directly from the Day Care Committee, the council members also asserted: "When a mother is obliged by hard necessity to assume the burden of family support, she has the right to look to society as her traditional ally in providing for the safety and well-being of her children."[32]

To capitalize on growing local support, the Day Care Committee called a mass public meeting to push for an extension of public funding for day care centers. With the meeting set for early October, committee members wrote letters to potential speakers and supporters, wired each state legislator in Ohio asking for support, and sent a telegram to the Children's Bureau requesting a list of day care committees at federally supported centers across the country. Despite running out of time before they could organize the national attendance they had hoped for, members of the Day Care Committee could only have been heartened by the success of the October 4 meeting.[33] Five to seven hundred people gathered in a high school auditorium to hear a litany of strong endorsements for the extension of federally funded day care centers and support for the Day Care Committee. Cleveland Mayor Thomas Burke topped the speaker's list and pledged the city's support. Representative Clyde Doyle (D-Calif.), a strong supporter of day care funding on Capitol Hill, gave the keynote address, and Ohio State Sen. James Metzenbaum suggested that state revenues could support day care centers.

Other speakers lending support included local representatives of the Congress of Industrial Organizations (CIO) and the American Federation of Labor (AFL), a juvenile court judge, the dean of social work at Western Reserve University, and a chaplain from a veterans' hospital.[34]

The program handout included a statement of principles reiterating the earlier City Council resolution to Congress. It called for emergency federal and state funds to prevent the closing of the day care centers and sought assurance of adequate permanent funding of day care through passage of pending federal legislation. Reflecting the careful advance work of the committee, more than fifty individuals and groups signed the Day Care Committee's statement of principles and were listed as sponsors. These included community, church, and synagogue leaders, social welfare organizations, civic groups, labor federations, two of the three members of Congress from the Cleveland area, industry representatives, a coalition of veterans' groups, three state senators, and nine state representatives.[35]

Prominently absent from the lineup of supporters was Governor Frank Lausche of Ohio and Father Albert J. Murphy of the Catholic Charities of Cleveland. Both men represented key political bases that the Day Care Committee hoped to secure for their cause. As governor, Lausche, a former mayor of Cleveland, essentially had the ability to put child care funding on the state agenda. But as with earlier attempts to win his approval of continued public funding for the child care program, Lausche remained intractable. Although asked, he apparently chose not to sign the Day Care Committee's statement of principles, speak at their October meeting, or send a representative (or message) in his stead.[36] Father Murphy also declined a request to offer his support. Sending the Day Care Committee's regrets that he could not accept their invitation to speak, the program chair, Bernice Zahm, asked simply for the father's support of the committee's statement of principles—or, if he could not support all the points, a statement indicating the extent of his support. Zahm noted: "Your opinion would have much weight in our community . . . a good percentage of our mothers are Catholic and are very much concerned with what you have to say." Father Murphy's unwillingness to lend his voice to the call for continued public funding suggested that the sizable and politically important Cleveland Catholic diocese, which had a large presence in the city's private child welfare establishment, did not support continued public funding of child care.[37]

Although the participants at the Cleveland meeting could not know it at the time, President Truman made a second and more decisive move in favor of continued federal funding of day care late on the day of their mass gathering. On October 4 the president called on Congress to reduce planned postwar budget cuts at the FWA by $7 million and thus allow the child care program to operate until March 1, 1946.[38] The president's statement gave important clout to advocates of extended federal funding, but congressional appropriators still needed to lend their approval. Soon after Truman's announcement a House of Representatives appropriations subcommittee heard testimony in support of continued funding of the day care program from the District of Columbia Parents' Committee for Child Care and a long list of representatives from California (who were under strong pressure from their constituents to ensure that public day care services remained available). Mary Hunt, spokesperson for the D.C. day care committee, said that the group spoke for many working women who, like the committee members themselves, sought continued day care services. She added that mothers' groups in Cleveland, Alexandria, Virginia, and Greenbelt, Maryland, had specifically asked them to represent their desires for extended federal funding before Congress. "We have also been in touch with mothers in nine other States, including Detroit, Chicago, and Philadelphia," Hunt continued, "[and] although we cannot say that we represent them, our conditions seem to be similar."[39] This testimony supported what California legislators had sought to impress on the committee the previous day: that the call for continued day care funding was a national one.[40]

Nonetheless, with the deadline of October 31 approaching, the appropriations subcommittee seemed reluctant to allow the funding. Its chairman, Clarence Cannon (D-Mo.), insisted for the record that "No one can take care of a child like its mother," and in a private memo Fleming of the FWA expressed a great deal of skepticism about receiving congressional approval for extending the federal commitment to day care. Congress did, however, ultimately accede to both popular pressure and Truman's request. Assured that the necessary dollars would remain in their budget, the FWA approved another round of child care funding in late October 1945.[41]

Despite what had been an immediate outcry by mothers against abruptly closing down the child care centers, the delayed approval of funds by the president and Congress had already dealt a severe blow to the national program. Close to 40 percent of the federally subsidized day care centers still operating in August had closed their doors by the time new funds were granted in October. Although some families may have voluntarily withdrawn their children from centers, undoubtedly many found themselves suddenly without necessary child care arrangements. In Cleveland, where a great many of the centers set up during wartime remained open, Day

Care Committee mothers greeted the news of the temporary extension of federal funding with relief. They now set about regrouping for their next struggle: a permanent program of publicly funded day care.[42]

Searching for a Permanent Public Funding Source

That working mothers from Cleveland helped to secure an important extension of federal funds for day care services represented a surprising victory; in the words of an employee of the Children's Bureau, it showed "what can happen when mothers become organized and have leadership."[43] The vigorous struggle by wage-earning mothers for public day care services came at a time when wage-earning people in general showed a remarkable willingness to collectively take their demands for increased wages and benefits to the streets. More specifically, the struggle fits within the context of working women's postwar efforts to consolidate gains they had made during the war in the workplace and in their social status.[44]

Encouraged by the popular image of women confined to a domestic role in the 1950s, conventional history suggests that women, overcome by a strongly resurgent current of domestic ideology, quickly and quietly returned to the kitchen at the end of World War II.[45] In a much cited study of female war workers' job intentions, however, the Women's Bureau found that as many as 75 percent of the thirteen thousand women whom it surveyed in 1944 and 1945 intended to stay on the job even after the war ended. Three-quarters of the surveyed women war workers had between two and ten years of wage-earning experience before the United States became involved in World War II. During the war they found much better work opportunities, and many were reluctant to lose the better wages and status they had achieved.[46] Women in the automotive, electrical, and meatpacking industries, for instance, took on both management and (in some cases) union leaders, insisting on their right to remain in positions that before the war had been classified as "male."[47] That despite these protests women in large part lost their foothold in "nontraditional" jobs does not necessarily mean that they simply returned home. As Ruth Milkman observes: "For women who worked for pay, whether by choice or necessity, exclusion from 'men's jobs' did not mean the housewifery first celebrated and later decried as the 'feminine mystique.' Instead, it meant employment in low-wage 'female' jobs, especially clerical, sales, and service work—all of which expanded enormously in the postwar decades."[48]

As it did throughout the nation, in Cleveland the labor force participation rate of women declined only briefly after the war ended and then began a steady and long-term rise, rebounding as early as January 1947.[49] Within this demographic shift, the difficult struggle by working mothers to maintain widely accessible day care demonstrates the powerful sway of the postwar domestic ideology—yet it also forcefully illustrates the way women's social role remained open for redefinition. The activism by working mothers in behalf of day care and their related effort to recast motherhood argues first against the belief that the social order resumed a "natural" hierarchy in the postwar period, and second against the assumption that all women understood (or experienced) motherhood in the same way.

Working mothers in Cleveland expressed a desire for day care services as part of their effort to define motherhood in a way that reconciled their social and economic responsibilities: wage earning, childrearing, and housekeeping. Reorganized in October as the Parents Day Care Association (PDCA), the Cleveland group now sought to move beyond the war emergency to justify its call for a permanent plan of public funding for day care services. Having earlier fallen short of its goal of organizing a national conference of mothers, the Cleveland group nonetheless remained in contact with other mothers who had organized day care committees in Chicago, Detroit, Philadelphia, Richmond, Washington, D.C., and a number of cities in Ohio. The PDCA intended to establish a speaker's bureau and to continue running radio spots in support of day care as a way to educate the public to the benefits of day care, and committee members maintained the relationship built with the city's professional and volunteer social workers during the federal funding campaign.[50]

While the plight of servicemen's wives received primary attention in the struggle for extending federal day care funding, the PDCA now sought to build support for permanent and universal access to publicly funded day care. Economic necessity, a key aspect of the rationale that day care was primarily a means of supporting servicemen's wives, remained high on the list of justifications for a public program. Mothers needed day care because they worked to support their families, the PDCA argued. They might be widowed, divorced, or separated from their husbands, their husbands might be disabled, or their husbands' wages might not be sufficient to support the family, but in all cases (and, they added, without regard to income level) the wives should be granted access to day care.[51]

Among the women war workers surveyed by the Women's Bureau, 84 percent reported earning wages to support themselves or others. The remainder sought to continue working so that their families could buy homes or send their children to school, and a few volunteered that they liked to work and have their own money.[52] To suggest that the great majority of these women, like working mothers in Cleveland, placed family needs at the center of their justification for work does not imply, however, that women held no individual aspirations or that they saw their needs as entirely synonymous with those of the family. Historians have frequently found that working women developed a consciousness and activism around family and community connections. This might indicate the conservative nature of a protest but often strengthened the calls for reform or change.[53]

In justifying their need for permanent public funding of day care, members of PDCA went beyond stating how their families would benefit economically. They pointed out how they stood to gain as individuals when they stressed that providing mothers with a subsidy for child care exemplified the "American way." It kept mothers off relief and allowed them to remain self-supporting and self-respecting. Day care of high quality, they further reasoned, could only be assured with the standards attached to public funding. They added that failure to spend money for day care would inevitably lead to greater levels of juvenile delinquency, thus harming the community. With these rationales, working mothers in Cleveland expressed a desire to adhere to the American ideal of independence and individual success, and they linked childrearing to the larger community good. In this light, the provision of child care became an important public service for a government to provide to its citizens.

For working mothers these pragmatic rationales constituted "common sense" about public responsibility. At the same time, each of these frequently invoked justifications for public funding of child care—economic necessity for mothers who wished to work, a desire to remain off "relief" and to prevent juvenile delinquency—might also limit an understanding of the public responsibility to subsidize day care. The PDCA sought broad access to publicly supported child care; it explicitly rejected economic limits. Yet a primary focus on financial need as the reason for public funding of child care encouraged the idea that public interest in funding this service stopped with a woman's domestic obligation to work (family need) rather than her autonomous decision to enter the paid workforce. Public references to maintaining independence through wage work successfully countered conservative gender ideals that assumed the economic dependency of women. At the same time, they might also reinscribe negative ideas about the people who accepted "relief" and again suggest that only the most desperately needy women should have access to child care (as an alternative to public relief). Finally, public attention to the issue of juvenile delinquency made calls for its prevention through support of child care centers both timely and politically expedient. But where mothers felt understandable concern about their children's safety and activities while they worked, the logic of the juvenile delinquency rationale might lead some people to conclude that wage-earning mothers themselves were the root cause of delinquency and thus bind women even tighter to the full-time duty of childrearing.[54]

Other arguments for a public interest in funding day care services—ones that more explicitly stressed women's equality, and tied this as well to the interests of family and children—were available but much less frequently cited. The women who organized St. John's Day Care center in Cleveland developed a strong statement, first circulated in August 1945, that clearly showed their desire to define motherhood in a way that combined concern for their children, their families, and their own individual achievement. The statement spoke of financial necessity that forced many women to work but went beyond this to stress the advantages of preschool education for children and to appeal to women's equality. The women wrote, "We believe that a democracy which professes no discrimination because of race, sex, or creed and in which co-education is prevalent has a responsibility to provide the service women need to enable them to express themselves in the way for which their talents, education and skills enable them, especially when this service contributes positively to the development of their children." This statement directly challenged a traditional and resurgent concept of motherhood as an all-encompassing occupation. It granted women, as individuals in a democratic society, both independence and the ability to choose their vocation. Some users of day care centers may have found this language of entitlement too strong, and the Cleveland Day Care Committee chose not to adopt the St. John's language as the official statement of the full group. The Cleveland group continued to place its primary emphasis on mothers' economic need to work, although it also touched on concerns about juvenile delinquency and the desire to remain off relief rolls.[55]

Although vulnerable to other uses, in the hands of wage-earning mothers the financial-need justification for public funding of child care didn't rule out individual autonomy for citizens in a democracy. Writing for the Children's Bureau's monthly publication *The Child*, Glenna Johnson (a professional who had been director of social work for the Welfare Federation in Cleveland during World War II and was a supporter of progressive causes) describes a lively discussion among Day Care Committee members concerning their rights:[56] "'Certainly servicemen's wives need this,' says one mother, 'but some of the rest of us have needed a service like this, too.' She is questioned by a mother who is not sure that they have a right to ask for a public child-care service for any child. Shouldn't it be for just those who need it? Promptly the questions pour in on this doubting mother: 'But how do you decide who needs it?' From the heated discussion that follows, it is clear the majority believes that in a democracy the parent is the one to determine her own need and that of her child, and to decide the best way to meet such needs."[57] This exchange demonstrates how members of the PDCA could move from a rationale of financial need to one of personal choice. The decision about access to day care, they argued, rested with the individual mother. By implication, it remained the public's responsibility to grant mothers the opportunity to make the choice that would best serve themselves, their families, and their children. In this way, members sought to transform the financial-need rationale—what the political theorist Nancy Fraser describes as a "needs claim"—into a more powerful call for publicly subsidized day care as a "social right" of citizenship.[58]

Members of the PDCA apparently recognized that as working mothers who regularly relied on day care they held a unique vision of a permanent program and needed an independent voice in the day care debate. A provision of the group's new constitution allowed associate membership to individuals who agreed with the goals of the group, but granted a vote only to active members who sent their children to day care centers or were on a center waiting list.[59] "We find these mothers to be amazingly clear as to their own needs and the value of day care in meetings these needs," Glenna Johnson wrote. "They see sometimes more clearly than some of the social workers the place of the social worker in such a program to meet their needs. We have therefore found ourselves in partnership with them in an attempt to assure a future program," she concluded.[60]

Although their language at times overlapped, the PDCA's use of financial need as a justification for public funding of day care differed from the official rationale offered by professional and volunteer social workers in Cleveland who also continued the fight for permanent day care facilities. During the war many of these activists, both men and women, served on or supported the wartime Emergency Child Care Committee (ECCC). The ECCC released its "Report on Future Program for Day Care of Children" around the time when congressional approval of funding assured continuation of the public day care program at least through February 1946. Although the report acknowledged that some women would always work and stated that a need for day care sufficiently justified the expenditure of public funds, it rationalized this call for day care funding by giving lengthy attention to the therapeutic benefits that professional social workers could bring to children, parents, and families as a whole. Like the Children's Bureau, the ECCC of the postwar understood mothers' wage work as a problem to be solved, not a normal practice to support. In this way of thinking, publicly funded day care should be carefully doled out by professional social workers as a prescribed "treatment" for dysfunctional families.[61]

Stressing that staying at home remained both the ideal for women and their duty, the ECCC Day Care report declared emphatically "that the community should make every effort to see that mothers of young children have the opportunity to *fulfill their obligation* to remain in the home and provide proper care for their children" (emphasis added). To this end it suggested that higher payments under the Aid to Dependent Children program might allow more women to be stay-at-home mothers. Thus while the ECCC granted that a number of mothers would always work for wages, it also made clear that a woman's true place lay in the home. Having defined a mother's highest interest as being a homemaker, it then made this role synonymous with the best interest of families and children.[62]

Still, the ECCC's acceptance of the need for any public funding of day care set it well apart from the most vocal organized opponent of publicly funded day care, the Cleveland Catholic Diocese. Although the diocese left no record of statements to city and county officials concerning its opposition to a permanent plan for day care, a Catholic parishioner in Cleveland would have been hard pressed to miss the message. In the highly regarded *Catholic Universe Bulletin*, received weekly by more than fifty thousand parishioners in the Cleveland area, the church loudly and consistently preached the divine order of the male-headed family.[63] Immediately after the Allied victory in the Pacific, the newspaper launched a front-page series under the subtitle "America's No. 1 Social Problem—Women in Industry." Although it acknowledged that some women worked to help support their families, the newspaper decried this as a tragedy and repeatedly asserted the need for a "family wage" so that men could support their wives and children. If men earned enough to adequately provide for their wives and children, backers of the family wage urged, there would be no need for female employment.[64] Long advocated by labor unions, the family-wage ideal represented a consolidation of middle-class gender ideals for working-class families. In the name of protecting and glorifying women, it insisted that they stay at home.[65]

A woman's highest calling, the *Bulletin* frequently reiterated, was to bear and rear children within a male-headed household. By performing their private duties at home, women served society socially and economically, the *Bulletin* reported. As mothers, they were primarily responsible for rearing children who were law-abiding and responsible citizens. Economically, the paper reported, society lost productivity when women did wage work, because one mother performed such a variety and number of home tasks that a whole of host of other workers needed to be hired to fill her place.[66]

Indeed, in his call in October for what the *Bulletin* described as a "woman's crusade to restore the home, the family, and an orderly human society," Pope Pius XII spoke at length on woman's special sphere: "Now the sphere of woman, her manner of life, her native bent, is motherhood. Every woman is made to be a mother: a mother in the physical meaning of the word or in the more spiritual and exalted but no less real sense. For this purpose the Creator organized the whole characteristic make-up of woman, her organic construction, but even more her spirit, and above all her delicate sensitiveness. Thus it is that a woman who is a real woman can see all the problems of human life only in the perspective of the family. . . . Your day is here, Catholic women and girls. Public life needs you."[67] The call to public duty by retreat to private home could not have been made more clearly.

The conservative gender ideology espoused by the Cleveland Catholic Diocese mattered a great deal to the city's day care debate. Many Catholic women used the day care centers, and for them the church gave important spiritual leadership. Even more important, the diocese represented a significant institutional power in Cleveland and held a strong political position on the day care issue by virtue of its long-term role in encouraging and providing a variety of social services in greater Cleveland. The Catholic Church consistently called on members to donate their support to its several orphanages, foster-care programs, and even day care centers, which were among the child welfare institutions that it ran for those deemed needy and deserving. Church leaders regularly called on their parishioners to support the yearly Community Fund drives and encouraged their voting support of ballot items that funded many community services.[68] Finally, in immediate postwar Cleveland a number of prominent city leaders, including Mayor Thomas Burke; the law director, Lee Howley; and the finance director, Joseph T. Sweeny (each of whom would play a key role in the battle for permanent day care funding), were themselves Catholic parishioners. Correspondence between Father Albert J. Murphy of Catholic Charities and social workers at other Catholic agencies indicates a desire for both more public attention and funding for child welfare and a simultaneous distrust of the publicly funded programs' presumed secularism.[69]

With the notable exception of the Cleveland Catholic Diocese, organized day care users' focus on financial necessity as a rationale for public funding of day care succeeded in aligning a wide coalition of support behind their cause. Civic groups in Cleveland and many churches backed their call for some kind of plan granting permanent taxpayer subsidy to day care services. Among the prominent supporters of the plan was the Welfare

Federation. A local backer of the wartime day care program, and the central body used to distribute Community Fund dollars, the federation had for many years been a major source of financing for the privately run Day Nursery Association. Significantly, the federation now saw expanded day care as an important goal for the Cleveland area. It set out to achieve a permanent program by appointing a Long Range Planning Committee for Day Care. (The Planning Committee would largely adopt the limited rationale for day care laid out by the professional and voluntary social workers of the ECCC.) Convinced of the importance of more day care and the need for public funds to allow for it, both the Parents Day Care Association and the Planning Committee still faced the necessity of locating a specific source of taxpayer dollars.

Members of the PDCA knew that war-related federal funding would soon expire and hoped to ensure a new source of federal funds through their support of the Maternal and Child Welfare Act. Encouraged in their support for the legislation by their close relationship with the professional social work community, this proposed federal legislation would have dedicated unprecedented federal sums to a broad program of maternal and child welfare. Its structure reflected the philosophy of child welfare held by the federal Children's Bureau: state welfare agencies would receive money to design and administer their own programs, to benefit children and their mothers. The PDCA correctly assumed that money from these federal grants could be used to provide day care, but precisely how the money would have been used remains unclear. The legislation did not specifically dedicate funding for day care and, although it had liberal authors, it embodied a definition of child welfare services quite compatible with a long-standing philosophy that viewed these services as available only to children deemed "dependent, neglected, or delinquent."[70] In this view child welfare services were a justifiable, if unfortunate, public intervention that protected children from "failed" families. In short, while the money attached to the proposed Maternal and Child Welfare Act would certainly have encouraged a greater number of state child welfare programs, precisely who might have been served and for what purposes remains unclear. A narrow, but clearly plausible reading of the legislation would have bound any newly created day care program to serve a much more limited clientele than what the PDCA sought.[71]

Along with other labor-liberal measures of the immediate postwar era, the Maternal and Child Welfare Act failed to garner enough political support to become law. Members of the Welfare Federation's Planning Committee (like the PDCA) supported the idea of federal funding for child welfare services. However, long before the proposed legislation was finally defeated, they were skeptical that any federal money would be forthcoming. "Everywhere there is evident a reversal and denial of responsibility on the part of the federal and state governments for maintaining local services," noted the minutes of the Planning Committee's meeting of November 29, 1945. Searching for other sources of public funds for day care, committee members suggested that cities and counties could possibly handle the funding—or that the public school system might be expanded to incorporate a day care program.[72]

The Cleveland Board of Education had been the nominal home of the wartime child care program, but there is no indication that it sought to continue this role. Bernice Zahm, a member and organizer of the Day Care Committee, believed that the board never wanted responsibility for the program in the first place, and that it sought to derail its postwar continuance. And she publicly charged the board's business manager with bias against the Day Care Committee in regard to scheduling the use of a school auditorium for the October rally in support of day care. Finally the president of the board, Norma Wulff, made clear her opinion that the public child care service should remain a wartime anomaly.[73]

State and county officials appeared no more ready to back a postwar day care program. They had been the weak links in the fight for extended federal funding of the Cleveland day care centers. Although the county commissioners and the state legislators had passed resolutions asking Congress to continue federal support of the emergency wartime program, they showed little willingness to do more. At the beginning of the struggle, Governor Lausche flatly told a delegation of mothers from Cleveland that the state had no money for day care. Although news reports suggest that he later waffled slightly on this point, by the end of 1945 Lausche again firmly insisted that no state finances could be used to continue the wartime day care centers. Assessing the state funding option, the Planning Committee noted that "the Governor is known to be against the idea of mothers working outside the home. He would have to be sold on the extenuating circumstances that forces so many to work." Additionally, the committee pointed out that "the state is more interested in full-time care and in institutional care."[74]

Continuing the committee's review of public funding options, its chair, Leyton Carter, stated that "the county is not in a financial position to undertake it, however, well fitted it may be by any tradition and in administrative experience." Cuyahoga County's inability to fund at least some day care centers is debatable. In each year from 1943 to 1946 it maintained a strong budget surplus. As Carter noted, the county also had experience in administering what were standard child welfare programs for children at the time. It handled Aid to Dependent Children cases, maintained a detention home as a temporary shelter for children awaiting placement, and through its Child Welfare Board directed the placement of dependent and neglected children in foster and adoptive homes.[75]

That the county commissioners lacked enthusiasm for a day care program, despite appeals from the PDCA, the Planning Committee, and several municipalities for assistance, would become more apparent in the coming months as the commissioners mulled over Ohio's recently adopted Child Welfare Act. Designed to "supplement, expand, modernize and integrate child welfare services," the act became state law on January 1, 1946, and included language that authorized county commissioners to levy necessary taxes to provide child welfare services, including "day nurseries." These services were to be coordinated through each county's Child Welfare Board, although the state itself provided no funds for them and no absolute mandates about specific services needed. The counties would have full discretion.[76]

Responding to questions raised about county responsibility for day care funding in suburban Cuyahoga County, the county commissioners requested an interpretation of this new law from state Attorney General Hugh Jenkins. In early March 1946 Jenkins replied that the act granted the county authority both to operate day care centers and to levy taxes for their support. Despite having requested the ruling, the county commissioners—and especially its Child Welfare Board with which, according to the attorney general's reading, the operating authority rested—did not begin an investigation into even the most limited support for day care centers, nor did they propose taking over the still functioning wartime day care centers.[77]

If federal, state, and county money was not forthcoming, the city of Cleveland alone would be left as a possible public funding source. The war years breathed life back into a depression-ravaged city economy. The year 1946 marked the sesquicentennial celebration of the town's founding by a small band of New England settlers. By 1940 Cleveland had grown to be the sixth-largest city in the nation on the strength of its industrial pursuits, and although it now contained a racially and ethnically diverse population, a strong Yankee tradition of local know-how and local government prevailed. In what David Van Tassel and John Grabowski have called "a tradition of reform," Clevelanders had long sized up specific problems and devised what they believed to be the most efficient and orderly approach to solving them.[78]

Clearly on the public agenda, the effort to find public funds for a day care service resulted in a series of meetings in late 1945 and early 1946 between Mayor Thomas Burke, the city's finance director Joseph T. Sweeny, and representatives of the PDCA and the Welfare Federation's Planning Committee. Initially, both Burke and Sweeny seemed genuinely interested in a continued day care plan, but the apparent goodwill began to evaporate as the late February 1946 deadline for final withdrawal of federal funds drew closer. At a meeting in mid-February involving the school board, welfare leaders, and the Parents Day Care Association, Sweeny, the mayor's point man on the day care issue, protested that other agencies had reneged on their roles in the program and that the city was left holding the bag. Indeed the school board, which still provided housing for many of the wartime centers, insisted that because state law prohibited it from funding services to preschoolers it might have to stop giving facility space to the program. The leaders of the Welfare Federation said that a multitude of postwar needs made on the Community Fund prevented them from continuing the same level of financial support that they had offered during the war. Meanwhile county officials, including Sweeny, who was himself the chair and a founding member of the Child Welfare Board, said that they were waiting for the attorney general's opinion (not released until March) before they would act.[79]

Day care advocates kept up the pressure. Sweeny responded by organizing another round of meetings between city officials and the center supporters. Hewing to a conservative interpretation of child welfare provision, he argued that the city could not do more than provide relief funds to needy families. According to his estimate, about a quarter of the women using the centers would be eligible for relief support. The continuing wartime day care program, he implied, served too broad a clientele and cost too much money. While the number of public day care centers operating in Cleveland had fallen from thirty-two to nineteen, Sweeny calculated that the city would still have to come up with more than a quarter-million dollars a year to keep them running. In the end, he thought, a day care program didn't make good economic sense. It cost $500 a year to provide one child with daytime care five days a week, he reasoned, compared to only $450 a year to pay foster parents for care round the clock, seven days a week.[80]

Practicing "Dissident Citizenship"

Cleveland mothers weren't looking for foster-care homes, however; they remained determined to keep day care as an available public service. Having exhausted more formal and deliberative methods of securing funding, the PDCA now turned to public dissent. Practicing what the political scientist Holloway Sparks has called "dissident citizenship," day care users refused to allow their calls for continued child care to be marginalized by the city's most powerful politicians.[81] On February 21, 1946, only days before the scheduled shutdown of the centers, approximately 150 PDCA members held a dramatic all-day sit-in at City Hall. Refusing to leave until they were given a definite plan for the continued operation of the public day care centers, in their physical intransigence they pushed city officials into a scramble of impromptu meetings that culminated in a late-afternoon announcement granting a new reprieve to the city's public day care centers.[82]

The female demonstrators were unimpressed when early in the day the city's law director, Lee Howley, announced that the mayor had called a special meeting with the board of control to discuss the day care centers. Bella Tracht, president of the PDCA, told Howley: "We have been given the runaround for three months. We will stay here until we know what is going to happen to our youngsters." When Mayor Burke appeared to give his personal assurance that the day care centers would not close in two days, he found the protesting mothers just as unwilling to be placated. They wanted specifics about how the program would be continued—something he couldn't supply. A report in the *Cleveland Press* described Mayor Burke as "flushed" when he left the room.[83]

The women continued to wait. Rather than risk a second appearance before the group, the mayor now sent Howley out again. This time Howley informed the group that Mayor Burke planned to ask the City Council to appropriate funds to keep the centers open for the next thirty days. The women cheered this announcement. But leaving nothing to chance, they refused to go home without an assurance that the school board had been consulted and that it had agreed to continue making available its facilities for the day care program. While the city's law director dutifully went about arranging an afternoon meeting with school board officials, the mothers' group settled into the City Council chambers for the day, eating lunch and relaxing on the chairs and tables. Finally, as the workday came to a close, the PDCA members received word of the school board's cooperation and their daylong vigil ended. Four days after the demonstration, in receipt themselves of more than a score of telegrams urging continued funding, and with many members of the PDCA looking on, the City Council appropriated $20,000 for the continued operation of the day care centers.[84]

The council's ordinance repeatedly stressed that the funds could not be used beyond March 31, 1946, and an effort to consolidate the service meant that the number of centers in operation soon declined from nineteen to seventeen. Further, although the centers had been nominally administered through the city's Board of Education during the war, the funding ordinance now designated the division of relief (within the city's Public Health and Welfare Department) as the home of the day care program. City offi-

At a sit-in at City Hall in February 1946, Bella Tracht (standing) and other members of the Cleveland Day Care Committee call on city officials to fund continued operation of the child care centers established during wartime. Cleveland Press Collection, Cleveland State University Library.

cials, working with the Welfare Federation's Planning Committee, also instigated a survey to determine eligibility and need for city-subsidized day care, and they planned to institute a sliding scale of fees for the service. Finally, and arguably most significant, city administrators immediately began to deny all new enrollment in the publicly subsidized centers.[85]

The City Hall sit-in won Cleveland mothers a new reprieve from what had appeared to be the certain end of public funding for day care, and the action injected momentum into an issue that city and county officials had seemed content to let die even as community support remained strong.[86] Immediately after the demonstration, several labor and civic groups addressed resolutions and letters to the council members and other city officials, demanding that they fund centers on a longer-term plan and prevent a second closing crisis on March 31.[87] Additionally, the Welfare Federation's Planning Committee continued to press forward, and a separate base of support appeared in early April when the Citizens Committee for Day Care was formed. Led by Leonard Mayo, the nationally respected dean of social work at Western Reserve University, the committee produced a four-point resolu-

Mothers from the Cleveland Day Care Committee cheer the promise of city funding to continue operation of the child care centers set up during wartime (February 1946). Cleveland Press Collection, Cleveland State University Library.

tion, signed by "the social register of Cleveland's clergy, civic leaders, educators, social workers, and labor." The resolution urged permanent maintenance of day care centers as a *public* obligation. It called for reopening enrollment at the public centers and insisted that city financing of the program needed to continue until the county or some other governmental agency could take over.[88]

Despite this encouraging development and the continued efforts of the Parents Day Care Association and the Planning Committee, a permanent program for day care remained elusive. In the meantime, more interim steps were taken to keep the centers alive. In late March the City Council extended beyond March 31 the final deadline for use of the funds it had already appropriated. In early April it approved an additional $20,000 to carry the centers through another month, and on April 29 a third appropriation of $10,000, this time unanimously, to maintain the centers through May.[89]

The continued incremental funding of the centers, along with the failure to arrive at a permanent plan for the day care program, suggests that city leaders could not find a way to say no to a vocal group of organized mothers who were demanding a broad-based program of day care—especially while community members backed up their demands. Recalling the community reaction to the public demonstration by the PDCA, Belle Likover commented: "It was for [the city leaders] a public disaster in that they weren't being sympathetic to mothers with little children. I think that in large part helped us be successful, at least for a short period of time."[90] Immediately after the demonstration at City Hall by the PDCA, the Cleveland Industrial Union Council (a CIO group) declared it "the shame" of the city that mothers had "to leave their work and their children to spend eight hours at the City Hall in a desperate effort to get some action from the city administration to assure the care of their children while they worked."[91]

While the public activism of PDCA members on behalf of their own cause did elicit continued support for day care, it also called into question their status as private and "proper" mothers. The *Cleveland Press* supported the outcome of the February sit-in, but it objected to Bella Tracht's remark after the demonstration that the PDCA would "move City Hall," if officials failed to produce an entire year of day care funding. "We don't like to hear the chairman of the mothers issuing an ultimatum to the city," the editors wrote. "As one who has gone along with the mothers so far this newspaper counsels that it will not be persuaded further by any pressure tactics."[92]

The sort of motherhood explicitly claimed by the activists—one that combined childrearing and wage earning—severely challenged an older ideal of motherhood, which stressed full-time care of children in the home and assumed female altruism, not self-interest. Writing to the *Cleveland Press*, one woman could not bring herself to use the word "mother" to describe the women who left their children in the care of "paid political attendants." She derisively called them "individuals."[93]

The members of the PDCA claimed the right to public funding of child care based on their own and their children's interests; the committee never denied that its members were wage earners. Still, PDCA members could not always escape a more traditional frame of reference, even had they wanted to. For instance, working mothers in Cleveland never used the word "mother" in the names of their organizations. They initially chose the generic title Day Care Committee, and followed this with the Parents Day Care Association. Still, newspaper reports frequently skipped the official name of the group entirely and simply referred to its members as "mothers" or "day care center mothers." A report in the *Cleveland Plain Dealer* on an early meeting of the Day Care Committee—at which the group produced a long list of decisive steps that they intended to take to keep the day care program open— began with this unmistakably domestic-bound language: "Wrathful women, angered by the Federal Works Agency . . . last night set numerous pots boiling in hope of steaming loose funds to aid their children's care."[94]

Because the obligations of traditional motherhood always required that women stay at home, they weighed heavily against public funding for day care. Explaining his reluctance to consider the use of state funds for day care centers, Governor Lausche stated: "Basically, I do not believe encouragement should be given mothers to place their children in nurseries rather than to give them maternal care at home."[95] Insisting that working mothers simply sought to shirk their duties at home, advocates of traditional motherhood frequently denied the economic significance of wage-earning women to their family incomes. Mothers worked merely for "pin money," they asserted—to purchase inconsequential items. Echoing this belief, the Cleveland Board of Education president Norma Wulff complained: "Those centers were set up originally by the government to help women take war jobs while their husbands were in service. They were not set up as a convenience for women who want to make a little extra money."[96]

While traditional motherhood insisted on housekeeping and childrearing as the identical vocation of all women, traditional fatherhood prescribed to men the duty of providing for their family's economic well-being. At the same time, this prescription might allow some room for expected variations between men. Speaking at the Diocesan Institute on Catholic Family Life, Edward Crawley, a prominent lay Catholic and the chief probation officer of Cleveland's municipal court, asserted: "A man has a bounden duty to provide for all the material needs of his family to the best of his ability. But in the providing process, his everyday job, he should not be expected to ignore his talents, his inclinations, the job where he is happiest solely that he may become a mere producing machine." A wife, he noted, should be content with whatever the wages her husband's "inclinations" provide, because too often marital difficulties arose when a woman insisted that her husband "bring in as much money as her neighbor's wife has."[97]

The conservative gender ideology espoused by the governor, school board president, and a prominent Catholic layperson, each of whom represented a significant base of institutional power in Cleveland, goes a long way toward explaining why no permanent plan for a publicly subsidized child care center had yet been reached. By May, municipal funds continued to keep seventeen day care centers in operation, but the program remained on a decidedly contingent basis. Perhaps the most troubling aspect of the city administration's policy had been its refusal to allow new enrollment at the centers. Coupled with a policy that placed women who wanted access to the service on a formal waiting list, this had produced a list of some three hundred mothers, while the number of children attending the city centers had dwindled from about seven hundred in March to four hundred in May.[98]

It's not clear how much, if any, of this reduction in enrollment may have resulted from the city's promised investigations of women's need to work. Bella Likover described the high turnover as normal in a day care program: "Children grow beyond the age at which they require day care, or become ill and have to be withdrawn, or mothers find, for any of a number of reasons, that they no longer need to work." In any case, the reduced number of children represented an equally weakened membership base for the PDCA. Although its constitution allowed mothers whose children were on the day care centers' waiting list to be active members, the PDCA's leadership no doubt began to feel its reduced numbers and recognized that the city, rather than kill the centers outright, had set a course that would slowly suffocate the program.[99]

Seeking to address this decline and to jump-start long-term planning for the day care service, in mid-May 1946 members of the PDCA staged a second demonstration at City Hall. The women continued to flaunt both their wage-earning and their childrearing responsibilities. A few demonstrators brought their children to the protest. "About 15 children romped about City Hall lobby," the Cleveland Press reported, "munched peanut butter sandwiches and cried when they got tired, to prove their mothers' point that they needed a place to stay while there was no one at home to care for them."[100]

But the PDCA members brought more than their children to explain their latest action. Distributing a printed flier titled "We Can't Even Tell It to Sweeny," they protested that the city's finance director had refused to meet or even confer by telephone with them and that their request to meet with Mayor Burke had also been ignored. The heart of the leaflet charged that Sweeny had closed intake at the centers "with little explanation" and in spite of the mothers' desire to stay off the city relief rolls. It also suggested that as chairman of the county child welfare board Sweeny should by now have assumed legal responsibility for operating the centers with county funds. Finally, it contrasted his apparent intransigence with the full support that mothers had received from members of the City Council. Day care centers for children of working mothers, the leaflet concluded, are "the city's best insurance against juvenile delinquency." One of the demonstrators recalled that Sweeny was "apoplectic" after reading the handout.[101]

No doubt wishing to avoid the public embarrassment of the February sit-in, city officials this time arranged to meet with a committee of four demonstrators rather than the whole group. The women reasserted the need to open intake at the city-run centers and suggested that a committee—of which

Cleveland mothers and children again bring their call for continued city funding of child care centers to the steps of City Hall (May 1946). Cleveland Press Collection, Cleveland State University Library.

Children lobby City Hall in Cleveland for child care funding (May 1946). Cleveland Press Collection, Cleveland State University Library.

they asked to be a part—should study keeping the centers open permanently. Lee Howley responded by stating that city financing of the day care centers might not be legal, and in a surprise second announcement Sweeny disclosed that he had resigned as head of the county's Child Welfare Board. The women stuck to their demands, but Mayor Burke foreclosed further debate by giving them an ultimatum: leave now and he would think about their requests and get back to them, or stay and the day care centers would be closed, period.[102]

It was by now late spring, and as the war emergency receded in people's minds, community support for the centers became more mixed. The head of the Citizens Committee for Day Care, Dean Leonard Mayo, responded to the latest PDCA demonstration by calling on the city, county, Welfare Federation, and school board to "stop passing the buck" and work out shared responsibility for a permanent program.[103] For its part, the Welfare Federation produced a press release stating that the "need for tax support to supplement Community Fund contributions in providing day care for children was emphasized by the 'march' on City Hall by mothers and children today."[104] By contrast, an editorial in the Cleveland Plain Dealer defended the city's decision to keep intake at the centers closed. The city had kept the day care service running "under the pressure of public opinion," the editors wrote. To disallow new applications, they continued, made sense "on the theory that these did not represent cases growing out of the war." To be consistent, the editors concluded, the city should screen current users of the system to ensure that all of them did so on the basis of war necessity.[105]

With the day care centers' future again at center stage, the Cleveland News featured the question "Should we have publicly supported child day care centers?" in its regular column "Saturday Town Meeting." As was customary, the newspaper ran a positive and a negative opinion on the question and then provided a mail-in ballot for readers to check "yes" or "no."[106] On the pro side, Bella Likover, herself a recently remarried war widow and the mother of a toddler, argued that day care services in Cleveland had been woefully inadequate before the war and that the wartime program simply showed the great need for an expanded permanent child care service. After reciting a long list of situations in which women worked by economic necessity, she responded directly to the pervasive message that since the war had been won, women should return to the kitchen: "It has been said that the woman's place is in the home and that such centers only encourage mothers to shirk their responsibilities. Such an argument is not realistic and fails to face facts. Mothers using Day Care Centers must work." Briefly addressing the specific needs of children, she noted that because of current shortages some families lived in too-crowded housing, and suggested that their children would be better off in a day care center. Others, she insisted, would be saved from juvenile delinquency by the centers. Besides, Likover argued, day care centers cost the city less than relief and allowed mothers to maintain self-respect. Mothers weren't asking for free care but rather proposed a sliding fee scale ranging from twenty-five cents to $2 a day. Finally Likover supported the use of public funds for day care centers because, she insisted, independent centers could not be run as profit-making institutions and at the same time meet the needs of working mothers. Private institutions failed to stay open the necessary hours, and the standards for health and personnel in public centers could not be rivaled. She urged the city, school board, county, and Welfare Federation to work together to create a permanent day care program.[107]

Writing against public funding for day care centers was Edward Crawley, whose comments just a few days earlier at the Cleveland Diocesan Institute on Catholic Family Life indicated his strong disapproval of wage-earning mothers. Crawley stressed that while recently the best thing for children had been to win the war—meaning that some children were cared for outside the home while their patriotic mothers bent their efforts toward war production—now that the war had ended the best interest of children would be served by mothers "return[ing] to their homes and tak[ing] up their war-interrupted responsibility of raising their children."[108] Two groups of mothers continued to work, however: the first because of family needs; the second, "merely to keep their family income on a higher level." With the postwar standard and cost of living on the rise, two-income families would become increasingly prevalent.[109] Yet Crawley insisted that only the first group of women justifiably worked outside the home and deservedly sought help from the public community. For these mothers, he continued, the community had responded by providing Aid to Dependent Children. If the payments were insufficient, he added, this was an administrative issue to be dealt with, but the form of public obligation had already been decided. (In the few cases where day care outside the home was needed, he believed that private charity services were already adequate.) By contrast, he wrote, mothers who worked simply to raise the family income had "no just claim to the taxpayers funds to provide for the care of their children which is a matter of parental responsibility and obligation."[110]

Crawley feared that the centers, rather then being a "panacea" for social problems, could instead contribute to them by becoming acceptable substitutes to the home. In language steeped in the emerging cold-war rhetoric, he asserted: "This is a dangerous fallacy—one that can set tides of erosion sweeping against the structure of the home itself which is the basic cell, or unit of our free American society."[111] Additionally, Crawley felt that the centers would allow bad mothers to produce bad children: "If mothers should come to feel that there must be such centers where they are privileged to drop their children because they have a desire to work, it does not take deep study to foresee the results—maladjusted personalities, fertile grounds for delinquencies, or at best, children whose earliest and hence most lasting impressions of behavior were gained through a pattern of regimentation. Didn't Hitler and Mussolini foster and promulgate that same pattern," he asked.[112]

Five days later the *News* published the ballot results. It did not give the total number of respondents but reported that 52.8 percent agreed with Likover and 47.2 percent with Crawley. The newspaper also published letters that respondents included with their ballots. While the typical letter opposing public funding was brief and read something like "mothers should stay in the home," advocates of public funding added their own stories and arguments to the record. A Mrs. W. K. Northrup wrote perceptively that the argument between Likover and Crawley seemed less about whether there should be day care centers than about who should be able to use them. She especially took exception to what she characterized as Crawley's suggestion that day care centers were a necessary evil and a last resort for mothers who had exhausted all other charity. Private charity would never be sufficient, she argued, and by using a sliding scale, the public would give financial aid only to those families that needed it. Answering Crawley's suggestion that the centers produced fascistic tendencies in children and could lead to increased juvenile delinquency, she observed that her son, despite having received almost two years of care at a day care center, displayed no such tendencies. "The regimentation Mr. Crawley seems to fear so greatly consists of the children learning to dress and undress themselves, wash their own faces, care for their own clothing, and feed themselves properly. Horrifying isn't it," she concluded sarcastically.[113]

Ruling against "Public Funds for a Private Purpose"

While city officials continued to stall, the question of permanent public funding for day care had been brought to a new decision-rendering forum: the county courthouse. Two days after the May demonstration at City Hall, Parker Fulton, an attorney, sought an injunction to prohibit the city from spending more taxpayer funds on the day care centers. The legal action was brought in the name of a widower and a retired city fire warden, Patrick T.

Ferrie, and named as its defendants Sweeny and the head of the city's Public Health and Welfare Department, Edward Worthington. Fulton's petition argued, among other things, that the war emergency no longer existed, and that in any case the city could only use its funds to give temporary relief to the poor. City day care centers, he charged "do not render any service of charity but only a service of convenience to their patrons."[114]

What prompted Patrick Ferrie to file this lawsuit? The most straightforward answer comes from Belle Likover, who asserts that the city law department and the Catholic Diocese simply used Ferrie to bring the lawsuit and thus rid themselves of the day care program and the politically hot issue of permanent funding. "Augustus Parker, who was my city councilman, told me in the privacy of his office that that taxpayer's suit originated with the Catholic Diocese—and that the Catholic Diocese was anxious to get women out of the workplace and back into the home were they belonged," Likover recalled. Further, Councilman Parker told Likover "that there was collusion between the Catholic Diocese and Lee Howley who was the law director of the City of Cleveland at the time; and that the planning for the lawsuit actually took place in Lee Howley's office."[115]

While I could find no documents specifically indicating the city law department's complicity or the Catholic Diocese's urging of the lawsuit, it would have been indeed unusual to find this kind of discussion on paper. Evidence does suggest that Patrick Ferrie had little reason to feel he was an aggrieved taxpayer. By the early 1940s Ferrie had retired from his job as a fire warden. A Catholic parishioner and the owner of a modest home on the city's west side, Ferrie saw his property taxes decline slightly in 1944 and 1945, making him liable for $59.60 in each of those years compared to $63.47 in 1943. Just a few days after *Ferrie v. Sweeny* came to trial, the *Cleveland News*, citing the "financial ingenuity" of Sweeny, noted an impressive decline in the city tax rate. The decreases came, the story continued, "despite increased operating costs throughout the city service." This record doesn't support the idea that Ferrie acted because of financial hardship brought about by his taxes.[116]

But the use of a taxpayer lawsuit to contest how the city spent its money wouldn't necessarily arise out of financial aggrievement. A lawyer searching for a way to challenge the actions of a city body, in this case the City Council, might have discovered the case history of an earlier local taxpayer's lawsuit. In 1916 suffragists in Ohio successfully brought such a lawsuit against the East Cleveland Board of Elections after it refused to put in practice the women's suffrage language previously adopted by city voters. Such a sophisticated approach to litigation would suggests a calculated strategy by an organized group rather than the kind of legal work that a civil service retiree could expect to buy.[117]

As the legal action against the city proceeded, Mayor Burke announced that unless an injunction was ordered, he would support a permanent day care program that relied on joint financing between the city, county, the Welfare Federation, and the school board. But most of these parties continued to plead their inability to provide money for day care, and a legal cloud now hung over the city's involvement. Given these facts it is not clear if Mayor Burke intended his joint-financing plan as anything more than window dressing. While the *Cleveland Press* detailed his proposal in news reports, the more patrician *Cleveland Plain Dealer* didn't bother. Instead it reported on the filing of the lawsuit and commented that while Mayor Burke had formally under consideration a request from the PDCA that city centers reopen enrollment, "even before the threat of legal action he had shown signs of winding up the program as rapidly as possible."[118]

On June 3, 1946, with the centers now operating under a recently approved fourth extension of temporary funds, the case of *Ferrie v. Sweeny* went to trial. The plaintiff's brief asserted that the day care centers were not charity institutions while the city's authority to use taxpayer funds to operate them was limited to temporary charity; and that even if the day care centers did serve only the poor and needy, the city still didn't have the legal right to appropriate the money for them because state law expressly granted to the county the authority to do this.[119] In his opening remarks, Parker Fulton stressed that by operating the day care centers the city put itself in direct competition with private industry. He insisted that the city was spending public money for what were private purposes when it appeared that there were adequate private funds to run the necessary day care centers. Calling Sweeny to the witness stand, Fulton elicited his opinion that the day care centers, which had been established to help women take employment in war industries, were now simply a "convenience" rather then a necessity.[120]

The weak defense, as prepared by the city's law department, supports the idea that the city did not want to win the case. In responding to the injunction against its operation of the centers, city lawyers earlier had narrowly argued for the council's right to appropriate funds for day care on a temporary and emergency basis (rather than a permanent one). They now added a heavy reliance on the Ohio constitution's "home rule" provisions. But rather than discuss the finer points of home rule themselves, the city lawyers deferred at length to a recent decision of the state attorney general that dealt with the home rule provision, devoting some two-thirds of the brief to a line-by-line reprinting of the decision. (The decision recognized local funding authority for postwar housing.) The remainder of the defendants' perfunctory brief depended more on rhetoric than on legal analysis or precedent to counter the plaintiff's claims against city operation of the day care program.[121] Calling Sweeny to testify in his own defense, the city's attorney asked whether public hearings had been held before to the City Council acted in support of the day care centers. Sweeny said that hearings had not been held in the customary manner and that no hearings had been held before the council's most recent extension of funds. This line of questions and answers could hardly have been calculated to improve the city's position on its right to fund the day care centers.[122]

In contrast to this tepid defense, an *amicus curiae* brief filed on behalf of Bella Likover and the Parents Day Care Association, by Howard Metzenbaum, an attorney and state representative from Cleveland, took up and refuted the plaintiff's case point by point. Although the judge denied Metzenbaum's request that the Parents Day Care Association be made a defendant in the case, Metzenbaum was allowed to deliver oral argument. Metzenbaum, who would later serve as a distinguished U.S. senator from Ohio, offered a legal analysis that allowed broad eligibility for permanent public day care services. He located authority to appropriate city funds for day care centers in the Ohio constitution, state law, and the city charter. As part of his oral presentation Metzenbaum introduced evidence that the city, apparently without legal repercussion, had operated a day care center from 1936 to 1942. Although Sweeny protested that he did not know about this center because it preceded his tenure at City Hall and had not been itemized in the city's annual budget, his failure to be aware of the city-funded program is difficult to understand. Sweeny began financial directorship of the city early in 1942. Further, he had been the chair of the county's Child Welfare Board since its founding in 1930. By virtue of this and his other work in the field of child welfare, he might have been expected to be acquainted with the city's expenditures on facilities for children.[123]

While the judge had these arguments under consideration, Malcolm Vilas, now the acting chair of the Child Welfare Board, brought a proposed plan for a continued day care program to the attention of Sweeny. With the apparent support of various groups, including the Citizens Committee on Day Care and all parties to the plan except the city, the new plan called on the county to provide case work services for the program, asked the Welfare Federation and the School Board to make continuing contributions of equipment, space, and services, and sought to establish a revolving operating fund, with initial $25,000 to come from the city. Sweeny assailed the plan as "dump[ing] all the responsibility in the city's lap." He said he would ask the City Council to continue funding the day care program "until July 30 when something else 'will have to happen.'"[124]

In what had by now become an end-of-the-month ritual, the City Council on June 25 appropriated $10,000 for the operation of the centers throughout the entire month of July.[125] A day later, however, "something else" happened and the city effectively rid itself of the day care funding issue. Judge Charles McNamee of the Court of Common Pleas issued his decision in favor of Ferrie. The city, he said, did not have the legal authority to use its funds on the day care program, and the terms of the city funding "contraven[ed] the provisions" of and were "repugnant to the spirit and purpose" of Ohio's new Child Welfare Act. He ordered the city to stop paying for the centers' operation. Having noted that more than half the children at the city day care centers were from families with incomes of more than $200 a month, and repeating the plaintiff's allegation that the centers were not "charity institutions," Judge McNamee wrote: "The bestowal of care at public expense to children of those whose financial condition does not require it, is *an expenditure of public funds for a private purpose*" (emphasis added). Although he dutifully praised as a mark of enlightened civilization the trend in government toward expanded social services, the judge added that taxpayers "for the most part are citizens of modest means" and had to be thought of first. "To the extent that the taxpayer is relegated to the status of the 'forgotten man' the ability of government to fulfill its essential functions, including relief and care of the needy, is diminished correspondingly."[126]

Judge McNamee defined the provision of day care services as being outside the scope of city funding in part because he believed the care of children to be the sole responsibility of private families. Subscribing to the view that the public interest was affected only where children were neglected or in abject need, he effectively ruled against the use of public funds for any broadly accessible day care program open to the majority of the city's families. In an inconsistency that only Metzenbaum's brief would touch on, no one doubted the legal right of the city to fund recreation programs for children of all income levels. Although that expenditure was decried as far too small for a "progressive, intelligent community," Cleveland budgeted well over half a million dollars for recreation programs in 1946. The reasons advanced in the appeal for public funds to ensure superior recreation and playgrounds paralleled some of those offered for day care. Good playgrounds were thought to decrease juvenile delinquency and to benefit children. Noticeably missing, however, was any argument stemming from women's presence in the workforce—a crucial part of the public day care debate. In contrast to the more than half a million dollars spent on recreation, Cleveland spent only $50,000 on day care in 1946 before the legal challenge shut the service down.[127]

Despite being on the losing side of *Ferrie v. Sweeny*, it's difficult to believe that Sweeny was anything but relieved when he announced that the centers would finally and abruptly close in less than a week. The city was now simply obligated to pay a few hundred dollars in attorney fees for the plaintiff and it had gained an apparently airtight defense against calls for it to continue funding of the day care program. City and county officials had little advice for mothers who suddenly found themselves without the day care service that they relied on. Sweeny assured mothers that if they had an "actual need," the city could use relief funds to help mothers stay at home and take care of their children. Malcolm Vilas proved no more encouraging. Protesting that a lack of funds prevented the county from doing more, he suggested that some PDCA mothers might be able to use the county's small foster-home-for-a day program. But even he admitted that most of these homes were too far away from the areas where mothers needed day care and that the program was small.[128]

Again the county's announced funding difficulties remained debatable. At a private meeting in early June the county budget commissioner had promised Vilas that with a recommendation to do so from the Child Welfare Board, he could possibly find $60,000 to help fund day care centers for the rest of 1946. There is no indication that Vilas had yet made this recommendation. Unconvinced by the county's assertion that it had no excess funds, members of the PDCA went looking for money themselves. They pointed out that the county each year gave surplus dog license money to the Animal Protective League and asked why this money couldn't be spent on children rather than animals. In 1945 the county gave nearly $48,000 to the league from its Dog and Kennel Fund and transferred approximately another $5,500 in surplus income from the same account to its general fund. Although Vilas responded by saying he hadn't thought of using these excess funds—and implied they could possibly be used for the centers—nothing seems to have come from this suggestion.[129]

Clearly on their own, the PDCA mothers organized alternative day care. They brought fifty to eighty children down to the public lawn outside City Hall, where volunteer day care providers looked after them during the day. The children played near posters left on the grassy mall reading: "We must work to support our children. They are here because there are no day care centers," "Cuyahoga county will spend $1,000,000 for dogs and cats but not a penny for day care," and "Curb juvenile delinquency. Open day care centers to all who need them." On the first day PDCA mothers received support

With a crowd of former public day care users looking on, (seated right to left) Edward Worthington, director of Public Health and Welfare in Cleveland, Bella Likover, chair of the Parents Day Care Association, and Lee Howley, law director for Cleveland, review the city's agreement to determine mothers' need for public assistance. Cleveland Public Library.

from the CIO, which at lunchtime delivered milk for the children. But the July sun proved too much for the youngsters, whose tiredness and sunburns prompted PDCA mothers to withdraw from the plan after two days.[130]

With the centers no longer operating, the group soon lost its organizational base. While the PDCA sought to rally its members to a new fight, and continued to press city and county officials for support, the resolution of the lawsuit in favor of Ferrie dealt a near fatal blow to the mothers' group.[131] In mid-July the PDCA mailed a letter to members, applauding them for their efforts to date, and insisting on the importance of an organized call for day care. Urging members to attend a meeting concerning the organization's future, the letter noted: "We're tired of fighting—yes. However, if we give up it will only mean that each mother fights a battle alone trying to solve her problems. If we all pull together with one idea in mind, we'll have good day care centers for our children instead of makeshift arrangements that depend upon the whim of individual, and cause us more wear and tear in the long run." Despite this appeal, only a few members found the energy to continue the struggle for publicly funded day care.[132] For a period the Parents Day Care Association incorporated with the soon to be defunct Citizens Day Care Committee in an effort to privately raise funds and establish day care centers, but this effort appears to have failed as well. Still, even as the civic groups involved in the struggle disbanded, a few members of the PDCA kept the organization and the fight for day care alive.[133]

At the conclusion of the lawsuit day care advocates, including the Welfare Federation's Planning Committee, the Citizens Committee for Day Care, and the PDCA, unanimously believed that the responsibility for implementing a program of public day care lay strongest with the county and its Child Welfare Board. But the county remained sluggish at best in its support of day care centers. In early September the County Commissioners finally accepted the resignation of Joseph Sweeny from the Child Welfare Board. Sweeny had announced his resignation four months earlier when the efforts by PDCA mothers to achieve a permanent, publicly funded day care program had reached an earlier crisis point. The failure to replace Sweeny undoubtedly left the board somewhat adrift at precisely the moment when day care advocates needed its forceful administration. In what can only be read as a continued antipathy toward public day care services, the county commissioners now selected Edward Crawley to fill Sweeny's unexpired term on the Child Welfare Board. Crawley had loudly decried day care centers in a feature in the *Cleveland News* in May, and in other public pronouncements as well he had shown remarkable hostility both to day care centers and to wage-earning mothers.[134]

While the lawsuit was under way, the Child Welfare Board had resisted calls that it take over the program, by protesting its inability to administer the day care program as it stood. Because the city service extended to some children whose families would not have been eligible for public assistance, the Child Welfare Board claimed to lack the authority to operate the program. The PDCA and its supporters insisted that if the payment for day care services would be established on a sliding scale, public funds would only be supporting actual financial need. The county officials had remained unconvinced, and in his decision in *Ferrie v. Sweeny* Judge McNamee appeared to take their side. Despite investigators' findings in March 1946 that only 2.5 percent of the families using the city's day care centers could afford to pay the full daily cost of $2, and that more than 60 percent could not even pay as much as $1.25, McNamee cited income levels of the families at the city-run day care centers as proof that children being cared for were not needy. Like the county, the judge justified his point of view that only very poor or neglected children were eligible for publicly funded day care by referring to the opinion rendered by the state attorney general on March 2, 1946, regarding the state's new Child Welfare Act.[135]

Indicating that the emphasis by the PDCA and its supporters on the merits of a sliding-scale system might have convinced some, a division of the Ohio Public Welfare Department now appealed to the attorney general for a clarification of his earlier decision. Did he in fact mean to prohibit the use of a sliding payment scale in all cases? In his response in January 1947, the attorney general liberalized slightly his reading of Ohio's Child Welfare Act and gave the green light for county Child Welfare Boards to operate day care centers with a sliding scale of payment. At the same time, however, he signaled that the state would continue to take a generally conservative approach to public funding of day care. He maintained that only children who upon investigation were found to be "needy" in either a "social or economic" way might have access to these centers, and he described government intervention in these cases as "public charity." This reading of the law maintained the division between families professionally diagnosed as "dysfunctional," the only group for which there was some public responsibility in the field of child welfare, and those diagnosed as "normal."[136]

After this opinion, the Ohio Public Welfare Department assigned a consultant to assist the Cuyahoga County Child Welfare Board in surveying need for public day care services, developing those services, and providing casework for programs established. The Child Welfare Board itself appointed an Advisory Committee on Day Care. While the PDCA had representation on the committee, the board named Edward Crawley as its chair. Crawley's handling of the Advisory Committee apparently prompted members of the PDCA to send a letter of complaint to Katherine Lenroot at the federal Children's Bureau. The women by this point were openly airing their belief that the Catholic Church impeded their achievement of publicly subsidized day care centers. They were immediately suspicious of the state's designated worker, Daniel Sullivan, because of his Catholicism. They also viewed the latest survey as redundant and a stalling tactic.[137]

In October 1947 the Advisory Committee presented its survey of day care needs in Cuyahoga County to the full Child Welfare Board. The report cited the high cost of living and large number of available job opportunities as two major causes behind a steady increase in the county's number of wage-earning women. Accordingly it suggested a need for increased day care services and indicated that even children from families with incomes above the eligibility limit for public assistance might be best served by a day care program. But in the end the report gave no recommendations for establishing a day care program, and as with earlier and similar efforts, nothing came of this documenting of day care need in Cuyahoga County.[138]

In mid-1945, with the federal Lanham Act providing two-thirds of the needed funding, mothers in Cuyahoga County had access to forty day care centers, in addition to eleven privately run programs. In 1949 only the Jewish Day Nursery, the West Side Community Center, and the Day Nursery Association—which operated eight centers—continued to sponsor day care centers in Cleveland. By 1951 Ohio delegates to the White House Conference on Children reported that the state had no publicly funded day care centers and that only forty-four private day care centers existed in all of Ohio.[139]

The adamant postwar call around the country for publicly funded day care centers signaled working mothers' desire to reconcile their responsibilities as wage earners and as childrearers. The culture of female homemaking would receive great sanction in the postwar period, yet for a variety of reasons wage-earning women sought public accommodation and acknowledgment of their work outside the home. Organizing around a family need, they sought to recast motherhood in a way that more closely reflected their own lives.

In Cleveland, mothers who used publicly subsidized day care centers emphasized that they needed to combine wage earning with childrearing. A public day care service not only enabled them to do this, they argued, but also served their own best interests and those of their children, their families, and the community as a whole. Despite gaining impressive community support for their cause, and apparently winning a majority of City Council members to their side, the Parents Day Care Association lost out to a conservative gender ideology that was powerfully advocated by the Cleveland Catholic Diocese and several prominent state, city, and county politicians. Ultimately a court decision effectively ruled away their ability to demand continued support of day care from their city leaders.

Both the court decision in June 1946 and the legal opinions of Ohio's attorney general reaffirmed a long-standing vision that stigmatized public child care services by granting them only to families found to be in professional need of assistance. Even if the county officials or state lawmakers had decided to grant funding for a day care program in Cleveland, these controlling legal interpretations of such a program would have restricted individual parents' ability to enroll their children in the program as they chose. In contrast to a program defined as limited in service scope, the members of the Parents Day Care Association had sought broad access to publicly subsidized child care as part of what they believed to be their social right as citizens. Where Ohio officials saw day care as a public charity, these wage-earning mothers understood it as a valuable public service.

The failure of Cleveland's working mothers to achieve a permanent, broad-based program for day care cannot simply be dismissed as predetermined—the result of a purported postwar retreat to domesticity on the part of women, or on any single pervasive cultural or political ideology. Instead the demise of funding for public day care in Cleveland has a specific social and political history. The day care struggle in Cleveland occurred in the earliest postwar months, when the narrowing of political and social possibilities eventually effected by the Cold War had not yet been completely realized. The institutional opposition that Cleveland day care activists faced, however, fully anticipated the coming chill.[140] Mothers in Cleveland faced substantial roadblocks in the form of the Cleveland Catholic Diocese, the local judiciary, and many prominent politicians. Even while their practice of dissident citizenship initially compelled support for continued public child care funding, they could not finally overcome the formidable institutional opposition to their cause. In other cities and states around the country parents (mostly mothers) with varying degrees of success pressed government leaders to develop policy that recognized a public interest in day care services.

The next chapter studies the experience of women in the District of Columbia. Confronting much of the same conservative gender ideology, but a far more convoluted and diffuse institutional opposition, white and African American women in the nation's capital persisted against very long odds, and they succeeded in keeping a postwar public day care program alive for five years. At the same time, because lawmakers and city officials granted only an extremely narrow definition of who could be served by public child care, the District parents confronted the day care program's full redefinition from a wartime public service to a peacetime public charity.

We pray that you will do all in your power to help us to help ourselves and our children.
—Mrs. D. L. J., Washington, D.C., to the U.S. Senate District Committee
March 27, 1947

Determining the Deserving

Day Care as a Public Charity in the
District of Columbia, 1945–1950

Many of the arguments that were made in Cleveland both for and against the continued provision of day care also appeared in the five-year battle over public funding in the District of Columbia. Through the genuinely herculean efforts of parents, sympathetic members of Congress, and a handful of civic leaders, a public program remained alive in the nation's capital until December 1950. Although the day care program did not become a permanent institution, D.C. day care activists did successfully negotiate the first two stages of public decision making: they won new public funding for their program and subsequently underwent a redefinition of whom the program would serve.

Because of the District's peculiar system of governance, which provided for full control of its affairs by the U.S. Congress, this local case study also provides a unique opportunity to view the ideology of national lawmakers regarding child care in the postwar period. The postwar policy debate regarding potential eligibility for publicly subsidized child care and the development of local administrative rules in the nation's capital illuminate racialized and gendered divisions in thought and policy. In short, there was a social expectation that (white) women had a right to be privately supported by a man and that (especially white) men had a right to maternal care for their children.

During World War II eligibility for publicly funded day care had been conditioned solely on the employment status of mothers. A wage-earning mother presumably performed a public duty in the wartime economy; thus any working mother could avail herself of public child care.[1] After the war, however, lawmakers and many community members viewed (white) wage-earning mothers as derelict from their primary duty as full-time, in-the-home childrearers. Accordingly the child care program in the District of Columbia underwent a redefinition. What had been a wartime public service became a peacetime public charity. To avail herself of the child care program, a working mother now needed to prove that inescapable financial need drove her into the workplace. In a prosperous postwar era marked by rising standards of living, locating the dividing point between those women who needed to earn wages and those who merely chose to do so proved difficult.

The determination of postwar eligibility for public child care was also clouded by race. Economic discrimination in the capital wholly limited its substantial number of African American residents to the most menial and low-paid jobs. This made wage earning essential (and expected) for many black mothers. That many low-income black mothers were wage earners raised few, if any, concerns for decision makers who approved of the District's entrenched racial hierarchy. At the same time, the existence of these workers complicated the creation of an eligibility mechanism based on financial need. White conservatives could easily construe a public child care service—especially one carefully restricted to the most financially needy—as a benefit largely to the District's black community and thus a threat to the racial order. Thus a desire on the part of some decision makers to preserve a racially discriminatory system lessened the chances that advocates of public day care funding in the District of Columbia could secure a permanent system of publicly funded child care.

The District's unique municipal structure further complicated the debate. Residents of the nation's capital, although citizens, did not have the right to vote. The District of Columbia's highest officials were appointed and all local affairs were overseen by the U.S. Congress (in which the city's residents also had no elected representation). Despite determined opposition from the District's appointed and staunchly conservative leadership, the day care program remained alive as federal lawmakers benevolently acceded to residents' repeated calls for postwar public funding. This context for continuation of the public program tended to confirm the idea that day care was a charity granted to the needy rather than a service available to independent citizens.

The limited federal acquiescence to demands by District residents for publicly funded child care ended, ironically, just as a wartime rationale for its existence reemerged. Soon after federal budget appropriators forbade District tax revenues to be spent on the public child care funding, they also denied federal funding of a national child care program (which had been authorized by the whole Congress as a part of prosecuting the Korean War). Members of Congress who held the federal purse strings grappled with the idea of permanent versus temporary (war-related) funding of services even as the ensuing Cold War stretched ahead indeterminately. They feared an indefinite "defense-related" rationale for services and chose to dedicate federal war-related domestic spending almost exclusively to housing mortgage insurance and other programs designed to spur the private construction industry. Believing that in contrast to funding of public services this use of tax dollars would boost the nation's long-term economic growth, they rejected most of the relatively limited public spending for community services that had been approved during World War II.

Keeping the Day Care Program Alive

For eleven months, from the announcement in August 1945 by the Federal Works Agency (FWA) that federal funding for day care centers would abruptly end, to the assumption in July 1946 of the District's program under its Board of Public Welfare, the day care program operated on the brink of extinction. Program attendance plunged more than 50 percent in those months as the number of centers declined from twenty-two to twelve. Given the day care program's precarious existence and decidedly uncertain future, that several hundred parents continued to rely on it remains strong testament to their belief in its merits, as well as their inability to find decent alternative care for their children.

The news in August 1945 that federal funding of more than twenty day care centers set up during wartime would end by October came as a surprise blow to the nearly six hundred parents who used the centers for daytime child care.[2] "We feel that the bottom has dropped out of things," one woman wrote to a local newspaper.[3] Calling attention to the unique and dominant industry of the District—government—she protested that women employed there were not a part of actual war processing and so could not expect immediate release from their work with war's end.[4] Other District day care users and supporters echoed arguments made in Cleveland and across the nation, insisting that the centers should stay open because the war emergency had not ended for many women whose husbands remained in the service. "Will you assure us that our husbands will be home from overseas by October 31?" one group of mothers asked.[5]

Just two days after initial word of the day care program's apparent demise appeared in the local newspapers, seventeen mothers and one father met in a downtown living room to organize their protests. Within days the group added a representative from each of the District's twenty-two day care centers and formed an ad hoc Parents' Committee for Child Care Centers; a few weeks later the group formalized its status and elected a first set of officers. To secure continued day care funding the committee conducted a letter-writing campaign and petition drive directed at official policymakers, and members visited federal administrators and congressional representatives; October found them giving testimony in Congress in behalf of continued national support for child care. To shore up their efforts the members of the Parents' Committee solicited assistance from community groups and sought other local backing by organizing a radio broadcast sympathetic to the day care cause, holding several well-attended open meetings to discuss the need for a continued child care service, and mailing their opinions about the program to local newspapers.[6] These efforts yielded promises from some thirty-eight community groups for active help and guidance, and out of these commitments grew the Citizens Committee for Child Care. Prominent members of this new coalition included the Washington Federation of Churches (an interracial group of Protestant churches) and the Council of Social Agencies (the District's major private welfare planning body). Other civic and church groups also joined, as did the local American Legion and the Washington Industrial Union Council (a CIO group). Day care advocates also sought to broaden their base of support by reaching out to suburban parents and others across the country who were waging campaigns to save public funding of day care.[7]

Strong local support emerged even though of the District's four daily newspapers, only the *Washington Post* (still trying to climb out of relative obscurity) gave unabashed editorial support to the day care center cause. Calling the action to shut down the day care centers "overhasty," the *Post* editorial writers countered: "It seems to us that the FWA has unfortunately confused the end of the shooting in Japan with the end of the war emergency."[8] In other newspapers, the day care program fared less well. Paradoxically, the centers were labeled both a "charity" and a "luxury," and from the beginning of their struggle, the Parents' Committee adamantly denied charges that its members simply wanted a government handout. Responding to this impression, committee members pointed out that fees paid by parents who used the day care centers in July and August 1945 had virtually equaled the subsidy provided by the federal government.[9]

Despite this the *Washington Daily News* contributed an op-ed piece to the day care debate that strongly objected to "the mothers who have become accustomed to this practically free baby-checking service and want to keep on working." The columnist posed the funding question as "whether your Uncle Samuel should continue to mind the baby" and answered it with a resounding no. Confidently he wrote that with the war now won, "many mothers will soon be quitting their jobs and going back to housekeeping" and "there should be other solutions" for wives of servicemen and widows with dependents to support.[10]

The District's oldest and most respected paper, the *Washington Evening Star*, made an early negative assessment of continued day care before moderating this view temporarily. Wearing their local budget concerns on their sleeve, the paper's editors opined: "It is difficult, once the element of essential war work is eliminated, to regard the centers as a necessary public service." Instead, the centers fell "into a category of a luxury when the service they perform is compared with many other unmet needs of the community." But just a week later, once arguments about the federal obligation to servicemen's wives had begun broader circulation, and it became clear that money might be forthcoming from the *federal* budget, the editors appeared to reverse course. The FWA's announced plan to end the subsidy for day care centers, they now wrote, brought "too abrupt an end" to the wartime service.[11]

The number of servicemen's wives and widows who used the publicly funded day care centers remained a popular index of continued war-related (read most legitimate) need in the weeks and months immediately following the end of World War II. At a little more than 36 percent, the proportion of District public day care users who were the wives and widows of servicemen fell below the median among all states of 41 percent. In its letter-writing campaigns, petitions, and congressional testimony, the D.C. group sought to expand the "legitimate need" category by emphasizing that a majority of the District's day care center parents were either servicemen's wives *or* women still engaged in "essential war work."[12] While the Parents' Committee clearly sought a permanent publicly subsidized day care service for any working parent, after meeting with officials at the FWA, its leaders quickly understood the political power of the war-rationale argument.[13]

By October 1945 the FWA had received the congressional go-ahead to provide funds for continued operation of the nation's wartime child care centers until March 1, 1946. But the weeks and months that followed this reprieve continued to be filled with uncertainty for the District's public day care users. Congressional lawmakers and the FWA stressed that the day care service had been temporarily continued to allow communities and states time to consider supporting local programs on their own (or, in the event that this didn't occur, to give parents a chance to find alternative care).[14] With this in mind, Clevelanders had pressed their elected state, county, and city officials for support of a permanent day care program; they ultimately turned to direct action as a means of securing municipal funding. District of Columbia residents, however, had no elected officials to whom they could turn.

As the seat of the federal government, the District of Columbia had a unique and constitutionally described relationship to the U.S. Congress and a distinct city government. The law that established the District's governance in 1878 allowed residents no right to direct elected representation at the local or federal level. Rather, three presidential appointees served as city commissioners, the District's top officials. They were assisted by locally appointed volunteer heads of agencies whose paid staffs were expected to administer day-to-day affairs; full congressional approval of all municipal actions was required. This unique situation meant that the Parents' Committee now faced the daunting task of both securing the endorsement of unelected local leaders and winning support for a day care program from a federal Congress that remained largely uninterested in (or hostile to) the District's affairs, and in which they also had no elected advocates.[15]

Journalist David Brinkley, recollecting life in Washington, D.C., during World War II, wrote that its municipal government was "more joke than government." The commissioners "were usually aging hacks . . . and they had so little power they could do little more than fill potholes and replace burned-out street lights without asking Congress for approval." The president of the Board of Commissioners, Brinkley continued, "could often be found conducting municipal business in the Mayflower Hotel bar, there usually being little business to conduct."[16] Indeed all municipal matters affecting District residents—from each budget line item to the city speed limit—had to pass through committees in the House and Senate, be voted on by the entire Congress, and, if successful, go to the president for final approval. In effect, the U.S. Congress was a city council with more than five hundred members, although most members seemed indifferent to the duty.[17]

Brinkley's characterization may accurately describe how the D.C. commissioners appeared, but it also discounts their important ability to conserve the status quo. In the District of Columbia the status quo meant that racial segregation and discrimination remained firmly entrenched, a low tax base ensured few community services, and both factors worked to the advantage of the local white business élite. In a revealing statement about the absence of the political right of representation for residents of the nation's capital, an observer in 1946 understood the commissioners' "main job" as "maintain-[ing] a balance between the complaints of residents and the pressure of inconvenienced congressmen."[18] An early postwar exchange of letters between a member of Congress and the head city commissioner, John Russell Young, illustrates this dynamic at work in the day care debate. "Dear Rus," began Rep. George Mahon (D-Tex.), "A lady has just called me on the telephone and advised me that a big letter-writing pressure campaign is in progress, the purpose of which is to secure continuation of the Day Care Centers in the public schools. I was asked to write you a letter and urge you to do everything in your power to secure funds. I don't know whether the program is a good one or a bad one and I haven't the time to investigate but did want you to know of the nature of the campaign being conducted." Brushing aside the letter-writing effort without an apparent thought to its aim, Commissioner Young responded: "Letter-writing pressure campaigns give us a headache but it seems that there is nothing we can do about them." He included some pleasantries about Texans and closed eagerly with, "I hope to have the opportunity of seeing you again real soon."[19] Although the commissioners could not initiate or finally execute an action they could nevertheless severely damage its prospects; during the day care struggle the commissioners would prove their mettle. In a prescient statement after a meeting in early September with the city commissioner Guy Mason, delegates from the Parents' Committee reported that Mason, who oversaw the District's health, education, and welfare agencies, was "indifferent and most uncooperative."[20]

High-level local opposition, combined with a complex government structure, required that the Parents' Committee flawlessly navigate a confusing maze of municipal rules and legislative details if they hoped to see public day care continue beyond the now firm scheduled date for federal withdrawal of funds. Both the appointed District officials as well as their congressional overseers had roles in enacting and funding local programs. Each year the appointed commissioners considered program and funding recommendations of all District departments and proposed an annual budget. The proposal drew primarily on funds generated by local taxpayers, but members of Congress who served on committees that authorized District programs, and on separate committees that determined their level of funding, could choose to accept as much or as little of the proposal as they liked. To make their strongest case for continued District funding, day care activists would ideally receive program support through a budget line item in the commissioners' proposed plan. Even so, activists would further need to gain the approval of both District authorization and appropriations committees in the Senate and House, all of which had substantial power to sink the day care program (either by failing to authorize the program's existence, or, once authorized, by denying funds during the appropriations process).

With federal support scheduled to expire at the end of February 1946, four months before the end of the government's fiscal year, the Parents' Committee faced the headache of somehow getting special congressional approval for the District to add money for day care spending to the current year's budget. (In the congressional lingo of the time, they needed a "deficiency appropriation.") At the same time, they needed to make sure that District leaders put day care funds in their regular budget requests for the forthcoming fiscal year (1946–47). Both the "deficiency" appeals and the regular District budget requests were necessary to gain approval from Congress to spend local tax dollars; they were not requests for federal funds.

The details of this twofold struggle, developing through much of the first seven months of 1946, read like a bureaucratic nightmare. When federal funding stopped, the Parents' Committee cobbled together a temporary, voluntary agreement with staff to keep twenty-one centers operating by using increased parents' fees and contributions. But District leaders immediately announced they were not willing to ask Congress for the $50,000 deficiency appropriation needed to subsidize the program through June 30, 1946.[21] Following the commissioners' lead, the D.C. school board compounded the activists' troubles when it completely barred the day care centers from operation on school property. (The board cited concerns about insurance liability among its reasons for its decision to evict all day care centers.) The decision by the school board left fourteen of the more than twenty former wartime centers without housing. The Parents' Committee arranged makeshift quarters in four church basements and two personal living rooms, but these donated quarters proved grossly inadequate. They often lacked even the bare necessities, such as a place to cook a hot meal for the children's lunch or a good spot for them to rest. Newspapers showed photos of children napping on church benches and living room floors, and ran stories about their having to drink milk at lunch counters. Critics decried potential health hazards.[22]

The crippling lack of facilities prompted some members of the Parents' Committee to threaten a downtown demonstration in front of the District's elegant red-brick school administration building. While this threat did not materialize, about a dozen committee members did launch a protest on April 11, 1946, at the home of a key member of the school board, C. Melvin Sharpe. The women gathered several blocks from Sharpe's house in the upper northwest part of the District. Arriving together at his doorstep, they demanded a meeting to explain why the school board continued to lock out their children. In the two-hour discussion that followed, Sharpe promised quick action, but he could not deliver. By this point, only approval of the day care program by the commissioners would give the school board the green light to rehouse the day care centers.[23]

Having decided against seeking necessary congressional support for a deficiency appropriation, the commissioners maintained a studied indifference to the day care program's difficulties. Instead they announced what would remain their long-standing preference for private rather than public day care funding. In keeping with this preference, the commissioners suggested that parents themselves should come up with the necessary funds to operate the centers.[24] Although they still hoped to gain public funding for the new fiscal year beginning July 1, 1946, the Parents' Committee responded to this latest setback by organizing an extensive fund-raising appeal and making plans to form a corporation—a necessary legal step toward administering an interim, privately funded day care program. The Washington Federation of Churches donated the full-time efforts of a senior staff member to lead the cause and a variety of religious and civic groups joined the parents in helping to solicit funds. A local attorney, Harry Wender, volunteered his legal services to the Parents' Committee and drew up a corporation plan for Child Day Care Centers, Inc. (CDCC). The lightning speed of this response, made within the first week of March, contrasts sharply with the glacial response of the commissioners. The commissioners announced first that they would need time to get a legal analysis of the corporation plan (which ran for approximately one page); later they explained that they were unable to process the corporation plan, because of the greater urgency of congressional budget hearings.[25]

Pushing ahead despite this official intransigence, the Parents' Committee finally caught a break when the Community War Fund agreed to grant the would-be corporation up to $40,000 in operating funds. War Fund administrators stressed that the money constituted a one-time only, short-term grant designed to carry the program until funds could be appropriated from the District budget. Harry Wender, attorney for the Parents' Committee, immediately notified the commissioners that the CDCC was "ready, willing and financially able" to operate the centers. But the commissioners continued to stall, running every issue through a frustratingly long and circuitous gauntlet of approval steps. When the delays finally ended in approval on April 25, 1946, nearly two full months after approval was first sought, enrollment at the centers, both those located in schools and those not, had dropped by nearly half to around 350 children. Increased fees had forced some parents to withdraw, while others, likely thinking that any child care arrangement they could make would be better than the uncertainty of the public day care program, made different plans. Although the CDCC had been authorized to run twenty centers, no more than fourteen centers would reopen.[26]

A Racially Divided City

That these centers remained at all shows just how tenacious the Parents' Committee and other day care advocates remained in the face of official indifference and hostility. At the heart of the bureaucratic foot dragging and apparent disdain for day care activism lay the District leadership's resolutely conservative politics. A publicly funded program not only upset the traditional gender ideology of the District's leadership but required certain gestures—however tiny—toward racial equality. A privately funded day care program would necessarily remain small and almost certainly under the direct control of the District's white social élite. For the District's leadership, such an arrangement posed the least threat to the gender and racial hierarchies that marked the social order.

When they initially declined a request by the Parents' Committee to seek needed funding to carry the day care program forward, the commissioners argued that the question wasn't whether the money could be found but rather the "principle" of the day care program. Holding firm to the ideal of the male breadwinner and female homemaker, they argued that the District government shouldn't even try to subsidize a program that handed out money to working mothers without at least checking if their husbands were working or if the family income level required their wages. Commissioner Guy Mason had worried during wartime that the child care centers might "be breaking up homes by making it too easy for mothers to work" and in the postwar debate he showed no sign of losing this concern.[27]

More than a conservative gender ideology animated this thinking: racial politics also played a central role in the District's decided tendency to stay the course in formulating social policy. Assisted by numerous southern senators and representatives, the District had evolved a highly segregated society that reserved ultimate advantage to a powerful white élite.[28] Its relatively stingy social welfare provisions shared a heritage with the racial politics that underlay many of the state's rights arguments made by southern politicians, which helped to maintain tiny benefit levels in their home states. In the early postwar years, the District's rate of General Assistance (local aid usually for the poor and unemployed) fell under that of forty-five of the forty-eight states and stood at four times below the national average. Children in the District of Columbia were also less likely to be aided. Nationally one in every thirty-five children received Aid to Dependent Children benefits; in the District of Columbia only one in fifty children received these benefits.[29]

As in many southern states, relatively low government expenditures on education and social welfare measures conserved the status quo. Poor whites tended to remain poor, but the population that most suffered from the exceedingly miserly social provisions were African Americans who were pushed by discriminatory hiring practices to the economic margins of society. A report in 1948 on segregation in the District details the appalling housing conditions and job segregation endured by many of its African American residents. According to the 1950 census, the median annual household income of blacks in the District of Columbia fell below $2,200, or less then two-thirds of the median income for white households.[30]

Blatant discrimination fueled this substantial differential in living standards along the color line. Before World War I, the administration of President Woodrow Wilson formally instituted job segregation in the city's primary employer, the federal government. By the period following World War II, notable improvements appeared but a number of federal departments continued to show strong bias against hiring African Americans; significantly, blacks continued to occupy the lowest levels of government employment, often working as charwomen or laborers.[31] "The Federal Government still discriminates although it piously protests that it doesn't and the District Government discriminates and makes no bones about it," a lengthy bulletin on job discrimination from the local NAACP reported. Some blacks held city jobs as laborers and custodial workers, but anything above the most menial of tasks was reserved for white workers. White-collar government jobs in the District were absolutely off limits to the more than one-third of the city's residents who were African American, with the exception that black teachers were needed in the segregated school system and in a handful of other social service positions.[32]

The situation in the private sector offered no relief. For instance, during the war the privately owned Capital Transit Company chose to advertise for white employees in other cities and curtailed its operations during the peak war demand rather than hire local blacks. Additionally local labor unions in the District tended to be associated with the more conservative American

Federation of Labor (AFL) rather than the rival, and more racially open, Congress of Industrial Organizations (CIO).[33] Unions in the building trades, dominated by the AFL, were especially egregious discriminators. Many of these unions prevented any blacks from joining and barred their entrance to apprentice schools. Others maintained segregated locals, or allowed only a few black members, who were assigned the smallest and least skilled jobs.[34] Wage differentials and job segregation held true among women as well as men. The District of Columbia represented the postwar future for women workers across the country. Instead of riveting, the prototypical female war worker typed. The job color line, however, meant that some 59 percent of the city's employed white women earned their wages in clerical and related jobs compared to just over 21 percent of the city's black women workers. The largest number of African American women, some 56 percent, performed domestic or service work (see table 2).[35] Among District of Columbia public day care users who worked in the private sector in 1950, close to 62 percent of black women gave their occupation as "domestic" compared to 3 percent of their white counterparts.[36]

Within this conservative and racially discriminatory system, the District maintained segregated and highly inadequate public welfare institutions for children in the immediate postwar period; the racially divided school system was the keystone of the city's racial order.[37] The city's wartime day care centers, like the schools and housing projects in which they were located, were segregated by race. Grants that the FWA made to local administrators of the wartime day care centers across the country came with relatively few federal strings attached. Indeed, given that some 95 percent of the wartime child care programs nationwide were administered through school systems, many of which were legally (or de facto) segregated, the District's racially split day care program was likely not unusual.[38] Both during and after the war the city operated roughly equal numbers of day care centers for "white" and "colored" children. The "equal" treatment in a severely discriminatory city resulted by 1949 in a waiting list of financially eligible families at black day care centers that was more than six times as long as the waiting list at white centers.[39]

Like the city's public schools, housing projects, and recreation facilities, District civic groups were commonly divided along racial lines as well. The Parents' Committee apparently originated as a group of parents from the whites-only centers but soon elected delegates from all of the wartime centers. Mass meetings in support of day care, fundraising, and securing of makeshift centers occurred within the African American and white communities, and the day care advocates found some of their strongest commu-

Table 2. Percentage Distribution of District Workers within Major Occupation Groups, by Race and Sex, 1950[a]

Black women[b]	Black men[b]	White women	White men
Operatives and kindred workers; service workers; laborers; private household workers			
68.8	65.9	11.1	18.0
Clerical and kindred workers; sales workers			
22.5	17.0	66.2	25.5
Professional, technical, and kindred workers; managers, officials and proprietors; craftsmen, foremen, and kindred workers			
7.6	15.6	21.2	54.8

Source: U.S. Bureau of the Census, *Census of Population, 1950*, vol. 2: *Characteristics of the Population*, part 9: *District of Columbia*. Washington: Government Printing Office, 1952. Adapted from table 28a.

[a] Columns do not sum to 100 percent because table excludes workers whose occupations were "not reported" and a very few farm-related workers.

[b] The 1950 Census reported the percentage distribution of jobs by "whites" and "nonwhites." Because all but about 1 percent of the non-white residents in the District were classified as Negro, in this table "black" is substituted for "non-white."

nity support from civic groups with integrated or black memberships. Still, they did not appear to directly challenge the racial segregation of the centers.[40] In an interview in 1997, Flora Calhoun, an African American widow whose son began attending a public center after the war ended, stated simply that "the schools were segregated so [discussion about integrated centers] didn't come into the picture."[41] Ellen Andruzzi, a white activist member of the Parents' Committee, echoed this recollection. She remembered that even the hospital where she worked had been segregated. "Segregation was the way things were done then," she recalled.[42]

Working Women as Adult Delinquents or Deserving Mothers

Instead of racially integrated day care, the progressive vision of the District group in its early days was a system that granted access to day care without regard to income. No one had more at stake in this argument then Mary Hunt, president of the Parents' Committee and its spokesperson. A white mother who worked at the Library of Congress while her young son stayed a few blocks away at the D Street Center, Hunt had a high profile in the local day care debate. Newspaper reporters regularly quoted her, and her lobbying efforts in behalf of a federal extension of day care funding had culminated in October 1945 in her testimony before a congressional committee on the issue. She had also appeared before the District commissioners and the Board of Education to demand local continuation of the centers. After local officials refused to help, Hunt led a delegation of one hundred day care supporters to the office of Rep. John McMillan (D-S.C.), chair of the House District Committee, which prompted him to review the issue.[43]

By the time she led off testimony at the resulting hearing before the U.S. House District Committee, Mary Hunt knew her subject well. Clearly seeking to move beyond temporary and war-related rationales for continued public funding, she began her testimony by recounting the benefits that organized day care offered to children. "It is a traditional principle of American life that our children are always of concern to the community," she testified. Citing taxpayer funding of public schools and recreation areas for the benefit of all children, she insisted that day care centers simply offered a comparable public service, this one "custom-built for working mothers and especially adapted to the particular needs of children of these mothers."[44]

Hunt followed this broad rationale for public funding of child care with more specific arguments that she believed both justified a public day care service and indicated its general acceptance. The District of Columbia had an unusually large number of working mothers, she noted, and many of the District's day care users were sole-support parents. She dismissed private nurseries in the District as too expensive for many families or too crowded to enroll new children. Just as quickly she rejected the idea that mothers should expect public support for staying at home to care for their children. This, she argued, would be "a psychological disaster to the family" and economically more costly to the community. In closing her prepared statement, Hunt confidently reviewed the substantial community support for day care, ticked off a list of places nationwide where public funding for day care continued or was being considered, and—for the fiscally conscious members of Congress—described how parents who sent their children to day care centers were ready to shoulder a greater part of the postwar operating cost.[45]

When her prepared statement ended Hunt easily fielded a number of questions regarding the center's operation, but the discussion shifted rapidly to more personal ground. Are you a working mother?, Rep. Everett Dirksen (R-Ill.) asked plainly. Hunt replied that she worked at the Library of Congress but quickly added that she had submitted her resignation. In what seems unusual, Commissioner Guy Mason, by now the arch-nemesis of the Parents' Committee, requested and received permission from the committee to question Hunt himself. Reviewing facts that he likely knew well, Mason established for the record that Hunt was the wife of Clyde Hunt, a chief engineer for CBS in New York, and he asserted that together the Hunts earned about $12,000 a year. This amount of money placed the Hunts' annual household income well within the top 7 percent of all families in the District. Commissioner Mason himself earned just $10,000 annually. Meanwhile, for whites in this period the median family income in the District stood at around $3,400 while the comparable figure for black families was below $2,200.[46]

Now on the defensive, Hunt began to explain: Her son attended day care because she worked at the Library of Congress during the war. (She had in fact spent fifteen years there before the birth of her child.) Noting the express mission of the Library of Congress to serve the needs of members of Congress, she continued, "I asked that they relieve me, but so far they haven't been able to get some one to take my place in the Library, where we try to give you gentlemen the best possible service during the war and we have been terribly understaffed; I stayed on at the Library because they asked me to do it and I thought I could contribute to the war effort." Hunt defended her family arrangements and choice of day care, noting that she lived within a block of the library and had arranged her schedule to leave her home at the last possible moment, to return to it for lunch, and to leave work as early as permitted. No fewer than fifteen nursemaids had proved unsatisfactory, she added, and while she wanted her son to play with other children, none lived on the block. The nearby D Street day care center solved both concerns, and her child had "benefited greatly." Emphasizing her willingness to pay more, and noting, "if the program continues or not, I will be home as soon as my boss relieves me," she now argued that she was not speaking for herself but rather for many other mothers, "most of whom are in desperate need of this service." Commissioner Mason remained unimpressed. "I would just like to have the record to show who is agitating this," he responded.[47]

Mary Hunt's testimony began by emphasizing the community responsibility and legitimate concern for its children; she did not highlight any personal need to work. This sets her testimony apart from that of a number of parents who also spoke that morning, and indeed from nearly every piece of testimony given by the Parents' Committee and its members in the years to come. Hunt reported matter-of-factly that many mothers in the District earned wages outside the home, although she found it difficult to justify her own work. Instead, she suggested that those who used the public day care centers were predominantly mothers providing sole support for their children, the wives of veterans, and the wives of husbands still in the service. In questions that followed her testimony she sought to at least partially expand the group of women who might receive congressional approval for their work when she noted that several mothers with children in the centers were registered nurses, and that one was a doctor. The community badly needed these trained professionals; how could these women resign? Hunt's defense of her own work followed the same logic, according to which some women's work was a societal necessity, but relied most heavily on her intention to leave the paid workforce at the earliest opportunity.

In short, Hunt first tied public provision of day care to children because she did not know how to defend her own employment. Not unreasonably, her argument likened day care to a number of public services considered universally available, such as recreational areas and schools. But she also linked day care to the reality of working mothers; indeed members of Congress could not see children in day care centers without at the same time seeing their mothers out of the house. Even if they had been willing to condone or perhaps even encourage some mothers' employment during the war, most legislators were not at all inclined to do so after its end.

When Hunt appeared before a U.S. House Appropriations subcommittee a few weeks later, she gave a virtually identical prepared statement, but her answers to questions from committee members showed that she had done more thinking about whom day care centers should serve. Presenting a universal day care program as fiscally appealing, she argued that a program open to working mothers of all incomes would be less costly to taxpayers because high-wage-earners paid full cost and thereby helped to subsidize program overhead for all others. It was true, she added, that these parents "could go on and have small nurseries themselves and exclude all the others. That is what we did not want to do."[48]

Hunt's fiscal appeal and even responses to the committee's questions appear to have provoked the members' thinking but in the end made no headway in shifting the rationale for public day care onto the universal terrain of schools and recreation. One member of the committee, Rep. Karl Stefan (R-Neb.), at one moment expressed nothing but scorn for mothers who "farmed out [their children] to strangers" but at another commented that many mothers would be willing to pay full cost for a good day care service and that even his daughter might benefit from access to such a program.

The following exchange captures his vacillation, Hunt's even-toned responses, and the central concerns of day care opponents about wage-earning mothers:

> *Stefan.* The finest thing would be to let the mothers go home and take care of their own children. That is the trouble with America today.
>
> *Hunt.* You could tell her that and exclude her from the program. It would cost the taxpayers more money.
>
> *Stefan.* Let me tell you something: If you have a father and mother both working and receiving $8,000 a year you send that mother home to take care of her own children.
>
> *Hunt.* We cannot tell her. I do not know who can.
>
> *Stefan.* I would not appropriate anything to promote adult delinquency. That is what that represents. If that mother is not home taking care of her children she is committing a crime against that child, because her place is in the home when her husband can earn enough money for her and her husband.
>
> *Hunt* [recalling that high-income parents paid the full cost of care]. You would not be appropriating money for her.
>
> *Stefan* [changing the subject]. I wish my daughter, who has two children, could find a place like that to send her children so she can go downtown and shop once in a while. She cannot find anybody to take care of the children.
>
> *Hunt.* Many people are in the same boat.[49]

Although conflicted, Rep. Stefan's comments combined the desire to preserve women's primary duty as stay-at-home mothers with the suggestion that not all mothers had equal claims to the public purse.[50]

After a hearing of the school board in January 1946, one member, Dr. James Gannon, expressed similar concerns when he stated his "wish to . . . have mama discard her overalls and her stenographic notebooks and go back home to the nursery and the kitchen." Gannon explicitly tied this desire for a renewal of stay-at-home motherhood to his definition of who might be eligible for public day care services: "I would be very sympathetic with the movement to prolong the life of the day nurseries if I could be assured that each case would be investigated thoroughly and that it could be ascertained that the mother was retaining her job because it was necessary and not because she thereby could get out of her home duties or have money for luxuries such as fur coats."[51] Gannon's comments summed up a popular postwar sentiment: many people distrusted women's work motives and emphatically believed that mothers belonged at home. In this way of thinking, wage-earning mothers were always guilty of (in Rep. Stefan's words) "adult delinquency" and "a crime against the child" until they were proven innocent by certifying inescapable family financial need.

According to this logic, Mary Hunt had no reason to leave her house for her office desk, much less to use a public day care center—under any fee structure. Her careful emphasis on the public responsibility to children got her nowhere without an adequate defense of her own right to earn wages. Any child, it was argued, would be better off at home with his or her mother. Public money, this reasoning continued, should only involve itself in the private matter of childrearing as a last resort. Members of Congress suspected that too generous public provision of day care might allow "undeserving" mothers to earn wages.[52]

Hunt's own conflicted views also appear in her testimony. Although she gave agile arguments in defense of a program of day care available to families of all incomes, and even briefly suggested that women had an individual right to choose to be in the labor force (when she told Rep. Stefan that she knew of no one who could tell a woman to "go home"), Hunt at other times failed to defend her own right, and that of other mothers in high-income families, to earn wages. No doubt reading the political realities at hand and wishing to preserve at least some part of the public day care service, she suggested that the Parents' Committee would encourage mothers in higher-income households to quit work if Congress made day care funding for others available. As a statement of good faith, she added: "I, myself, already am resigned to stay home from my job. I have been at the library only because of the war."[53]

Although clearly not all women bought into the postwar domestic prescription, to argue for the right to work as an issue of self-fulfillment rather than financial need, or even improved family status, would have required a strong measure of independent thinking. It required a feminist argument, and specifically a willingness to claim self-interest in a day care program that catered to all classes. Hunt did not make this claim and no one from the era's moribund feminist movement rose to her aid. Although she remained an active day care proponent, by July 1946 a roster of the CDCC officers listed her occupation as "housewife."[54]

Even if the postwar prescriptions for female domesticity reached the ears of working-class and lower-middle-class mothers in the District of Columbia, economic realities meant that they could not choose to heed them. In February 1946 about half of the 572 households relying on the public day care centers were headed by single parents or wives whose husbands were still in the armed services. The median income of the entire group of day care users remained moderate.[55] Outside the public centers there were limited options. Private nurseries were expensive for preschoolers and nonexistent for school-age children who often needed supervision before and after school, as well as summer care; nonprofit nurseries were also few and largely without vacancies.[56] No doubt some women would look for private help in their homes, but this could also be costly, and with the war giving unprecedented opportunity for domestic workers to take better-paid and better-respected jobs in government agencies, private household workers were both more expensive and scarce.[57]

In short, without the day care centers the hard-earned economic independence of families who used them might give way to economic dependency or even force the separation of some mothers from their children. A widow, Gertrude Tucker, told a congressional committee in February 1946 that her need to work was a "permanent thing" and that without public day care centers the cost of child care would be prohibitive: "For over four years I had to keep [my son] in an orphanage because I did not make enough to maintain a place for him and get private help." The fate of the centers, she stated, would "determine as to whether or not I will be able to keep my son with me or have to put him back into an orphanage or institution."[58]

Gertrude Tucker's direct appeal to preserve her ability to live with her son undoubtedly struck congressional members as a more appropriate display of motherhood than Mary Hunt's attention to the social and other benefits that her child received from group day care. Tucker's situation epitomized the highly successful argument made by early-twentieth-century promoters of mothers' pensions. She was a young white widow whose son had spent much of his early years in an institution simply because his mother could not afford to raise him. But where Tucker apparently found day care a good option, Progressive Era activists who pushed for the passage of mothers' pension laws sought this reform precisely because they believed the opposite. In the words of Jane Addams, founder of Hull House, day nurseries "tempt[ed mothers] to attempt the impossible"—that is, to try to combine childrearing and wage earning.[59]

Addams, and many other activists who fought for mothers' pensions, viewed the cash benefits that they advocated for needy mothers as an earned and deserved pension. Nevertheless the sentimental appeal to motherhood that helped to enact these state programs—combined with widespread discriminatory administrative practices and a tight grasp on program purse strings by state lawmakers—meant that they were bestowed, at best, as a gesture of benevolent relief to a chosen few. The federalization of the program through the Aid to Dependent Children program in 1935 pointedly preserved state and local control of eligibility determination and benefit levels and did little (if anything) to equalize treatment.[60]

It's unlikely that even with her "ideal" case history Gertrude Tucker could have met the tight eligibility requirements of the District's severely under-funded Aid to Dependent Children program. In any case, the response to Commissioner Guy Mason's suggestion in February 1946 that sole-support mothers could apply for Aid to Dependent Children and thus alleviate any need for public day care demonstrates why she likely had no intention of applying.[61] At $67 the District's average monthly ADC grant fell well below the cost of living. To put the figure in perspective: When the wives of ser-vicemen had insisted that it would be impossible to live on a monthly allot-ment of $100 — a sum nearly half again as great — no one had suggested that these women just needed to budget better. Mothers who received ADC benefits in the District of Columbia, like their counterparts in many other localities, would need to find some kind of work to supplement the meager aid offered.[62] The Parents' Committee sent a telegram to administrators in the District building to "repudiate the frightful suggestion of Commissioner Guy Mason that they can quit their jobs and go on relief." In a separate let-ter to the commissioners, Mary Hunt wrote that "widows can not bring up their families on $67 a month. It would mean moving to tenements and a host of horrible conditions. You can't seriously propose such a plan when mothers are able to work and willing to pay all they can for efficient, kindly supervision and training in a well-run child care center."[63] A mother who provided the sole support for her two children wrote to the Star to repudiate the idea that women should quit their jobs and "accept charity," which she believed was not the "American way." Signing as "Desperate Mother," she asserted: "We do not want charity — we want a chance to work and pay our own expenses, which we can do if there are suitable places to leave our chil-dren while we are at work."[64]

The political scientist Virginia Sapiro has convincingly argued that the gendered goals of American social policy did not support economic inde-pendence for women. But the appeal to independence as a universal "Amer-ican way" had a strong rhetorical power for public day care advocates in a postwar era that held contradictory beliefs about women's proper role in so-ciety in general and their degree of economic independence in particular.[65] Several community members' protests centered prominently on the viola-tion of American ideals represented by Commissioner Mason's suggestion that day care users could quit wage earning and accept ADC benefits instead. "Self dependence is our American heritage," asserted Colonel William Tufts, head of the local Community Chest budget committee; "to expect people who are able and willing to work to apply for assistance would be destructive to self-dependence."[66] A private citizen, Dr. Thomas F. Mattingly, wrote in another letter printed by the *Star* that he "question[ed] the essential wisdom of an administrative policy which would rebuke working mothers who aspire to a living standard above the indigency level and which cruelly discourages and handicaps the working mother who is enough of a rugged individualist to insist upon working out her own economic survival rather than predicate it on the precarious makeshift of an unpredictable subsidy." Shutting down day care centers and offering ADC as an alternative would not make the "selfish or delinquent mother" dedicate more time to the kitchen and her children, Mattingly continued, but would "penalize the *truly deserving* working mothers heroically striving to achieve their own economic stability and independence" (emphasis added).[67]

In a study conducted in 1946, social worker Patricia Bledsoe found the amount of money that poor, single day care users could expect to receive from ADC to "represent [an] intolerable decline in family living standards" for many. She argued that if the community hadn't held to its responsibility in providing adequate ADC grants, it should "at least respect the rights of mothers who wish more for their children."[68] In the contradictory currents of popular thinking, deserving working mothers were to be congratulated for their efforts at economic independence and encouraged to continue earning wages, while undeserving working mothers—those whose husbands' wages could at least minimally support the family—were castigated for doing the very same thing.

Rather than accept Aid to Dependent Children, Mary Hunt most likely resorted to the kind of economic dependency generally approved of for women when she left the workforce: she relied on her well-compensated husband. Letters and testimony directed to members of Congress by a number of day care users in the District verify that working-class women might also aspire to this ideal of playing female housekeeper and childrearer to a male breadwinner. Verone Moreno, who told her story both to the *Washington Post* and to congressional committees, vividly illustrates a working-class woman's wish to be a part of this kind of "family wage" household.

A divorced mother who received no child support, Moreno had come to Washington from Oklahoma in 1944. By 1946 she had worked her way up the government pink-collar ladder from yearly earnings of $1,440 to a little over $2,000. On these wages she supported herself and her four-year-old son (who attended the same day care center that Mary Hunt had used to care for her boy) and assisted in the support of her out-of-state, elderly, and disabled uncle. What Moreno wanted, as the *Post* reported on the front page of its hometown section, was a husband; ideally he would be tall, blond, and a "rhumba enthusiast":[69]

> The call—labeled 'desperate'—was issued yesterday by a glamorous black-haired secretary at the marketing facilities branch of the Agriculture Department.
>
> Chief reason: Closing of the District's child care centers. . . .
>
> Mrs. Verone Moreno, a 29 year old divorcee, explained her plight. 'I don't know what I'll do when Johnny can't go to the center anymore,' said the frail, 89-pound woman. 'It's just about impossible to find an opening in a private school—even If I could afford it and I can't.'
>
> Her hope is that a suitable man will marry her and thus make it possible for her to stay home and care for her son. . . .
>
> Not retiring, Mrs. Moreno listed her own qualifications to be a good wife, 'I have a wonderful disposition . . . and lots of experience in cooking, cleaning, washing and ironing. My son is handsome and lovable too.'[70]

Moreno wasn't looking for a quick trip to easy street. She ruled high-earning men out of her ideal husband category because "when a man gets so he's making lots of money he's usually old too." The *Post* followed this high-profile personal story with a report that the story (and accompanying photo) had resulted in seventy phone calls. Although the six suitors whom Moreno chose for an initial group date all apparently stood her up, she had a reserve six in mind and insisted that she was "not disheartened."[71]

The *Post* dropped this personal saga after two days, but a little more than a week later Verone Moreno, apparently still without good prospects for a husband, appeared before the House District Committee to plead for continuation of the centers. Now focused on her need to support herself, she met a relatively unfriendly committee. "You find it absolutely necessary to work?" asked Rep. John McMillan, the committee's southern Democratic chair. "Yes, it is absolutely necessary," replied Moreno. "If I quit there would be no money coming in from any place." After Moreno had been further quizzed on her marital status, where she lived before moving to D.C., and where the disabled uncle she helped to support lived, Rep. Thomas Abernethy (D-Miss.) still sought to uncover any undisclosed source of aid that might lessen her financial responsibilities. "I do not mean to be too inquisitive," he pushed, "but what other members of the family are contributing to your uncle's support?"[72]

More than a year later, with the public day care centers' future once more in jeopardy, Moreno would again testify in her own behalf. Still earn-

Verone Moreno and her son, Johnny, February 1946.
© 1946, The Washington Post. Reprinted with permission.

ing just over $2,000 a year, she paid $5 of her $40 weekly wages for day care.
The renewed threat of the centers' closing now caused her to dream not
hopefully of a husband but fearfully of losing her child: "I have been having
horrible dreams that I would have to let somebody take my little boy." Imag-
ining visits after this separation, she continued, "You know, he is nice to me
but he wants to run to somebody else." Now that Moreno had apparently
lost her bid to acquire appropriate economic dependency—marriage to a

male wage earner—her fears of separation from her son tugged at the heart and drew on an equally approved set of values for motherhood.[73]

As many women whose children attended the day care centers could have told Moreno, having a husband might increase one's chances of retiring from wage earning, but it was no guarantee of being able to give full-time, in-the-home care to one's children. A survey of day care users in early 1946 showed that slightly more than half the households that sent children to the day care centers had two wage earners; many of these families were not in the upper income brackets. Instead two incomes, especially among African Americans who found themselves relegated to the lowest-paid work in the District's job market, were frequently necessary to support the family.[74]

"Excepting some clergymen, professional and businessmen, there are few other men among our people who are fully able to provide for their families," Rosina Tucker explained at a hearing in June 1946 on the fate of the District's public day care centers. A veteran labor union organizer with the Brotherhood of Sleeping Car Porters, founding member of the union's important Ladies Auxiliary, and a longtime African American civic activist, Tucker spoke on this occasion as a representative of the District's black Federation of Civic Associations.[75] "Being members of a minority group," she continued, "[black men] are restricted to certain jobs, usually menial and the salaries of many are as low as $35 a week." Black mothers worked, she pointed out, because they had to help pay the rent and buy food and clothing. Their work enabled a family to stay together and build a good future. "The mothers of my group have ambitions for their children," she added. The alternatives to working would be institutionalizing the children or public assistance. Neither seemed an attractive option. Institutionalization would be a "costly expenditure to the Government" and would "deny to these mothers the comforting presence of these children," Tucker noted. Public assistance she dismissed as "certainly not a morale builder—or, worse it will mean a larger number of penal institutions."[76]

After multiple hearings and some floor debate, Congress eventually approved continuation of a limited public day care program in the District of Columbia. Presumed war-related family disruptions remained a key rationale for many legislators. Consequently, the original legislation supported by the Parents' Committee, which established a permanent program open to any working mother and administered by the city's education department, underwent dramatic changes to gain full congressional approval. To ensure enough votes for passage in the full House of Representatives, the proposal was amended to require an investigation of a mother's *need* to work and to include an annual budget cap—ensuring the program's limited growth. A Senate committee moved day care administration from education to the city welfare department, and in the most restrictive amendment to date, the senators limited the program to a one-year continuation only.[77]

Once all these changes were incorporated, Congress voted approval of the program in principle. But continuation of even this limited day care program remained in doubt, because of the initial failure of budget appropriators to grant (out of the District treasury) any money to run the service. The indefatigable Parents' Committee responded with personal visits to key senators' offices. At the eleventh hour, after an unusual Senate floor fight on an appropriation line item, the program received the necessary funds. When President Truman formally signed the funding bill on July 23, 1946, the District Public Welfare Department inherited the program along with $250,000 to operate the centers for one year.[78]

Finding a Postwar Rationale for Publicly Supported Day Care

In the first year after the war ended, day care advocates in the District had survived a lengthy, demanding campaign that ultimately secured continuation of the public day care program through mid-1947. After a scant few months of rest they began a new push for program permanency. Predictably, local leaders immediately announced their opposition to any continued public support for day care. Day care activists persevered. Bypassing official local opposition, they won the independent backing of two senators who introduced legislation calling for a second one-year continuation of the day program. In the ensuing debate, members of Congress, District officials, and day care users would renegotiate the boundaries of public responsibility for a day care program. Each of the parties struggled to move the program closer to its own views of why a day care service should (or should not) be continued; financial necessity for a mother's employment quickly emerged as essential.

By far the most conservative voices in the discussion remained the city's unelected officials.[79] Not placated by the program's many new limits, the commissioners had unsuccessfully called for a presidential veto of the day care legislation enacted in 1946. The city's commissioners also early sought to undermine any argument based on financial necessity with a thinly veiled racist argument. "Assuming a figure around what is considered the minimum standard of decent living, it would probably be found that there are many thousands of working mothers who would qualify, notably among the colored population," a Board of Commissioners' postwar planning report noted. Based on this blunt assessment of poverty in the District, the report argued that a financial means test could result in a program expansion entailing "millions of dollars in capital construction and more millions of dollars in annual costs," and it pointedly gave notice that such an income-restricted program would certainly benefit a substantial number of the city's African American residents.[80]

Commissioner Guy Mason introduced related arguments to weaken the viability of a financial-necessity rationale for public child care. He sought to derail the program both by proposing a highly restrictive definition of financial need and by highlighting the practical policy difficulties inherent in dividing mothers who "need" to earn wages from those who "choose" to work outside the home. Under pressure Mason reluctantly conceded that a day care service might be a good thing if it served only the neediest families. But he sought to limit this concession by defining "needy" as synonymous with "indigent." The city day care program was "just another form of financial aid to indigents," he testified, adding, "We have a certain element we have to take care of." At a subsequent congressional hearing, Commissioner Mason expanded on what he meant by "indigency" and the difficulty of establishing a limit on public responsibility for day care. "We know that there are thousands upon thousands of families in the District of Columbia living on $3,000 a year or less and taking care of their own children; if [day care] became a public need, it should be restricted to indigent, that is those folks who could not do it on actual showing and the children would be on the [city welfare] Department. . . . Personally I can say that the low income group should be helped, no doubt, as you express it, but it is quite a problem to administer and eliminate chiselers."[81] Commissioner Mason raised a difficult question. If financial need represented a legitimate claim to public resources, what constituted financial need? At bottom, he also revealed the mismatch between the city's minimal public social service assistance and the more liberal support granted to day care users in the earliest years of postwar operation.

A study by the Bureau of Labor Statistics (BLS) in 1947 found the District of Columbia to have the highest cost of living among thirty-four cities it surveyed. The agency calculated that the city's average working family of four would need almost $3,500 to reach an "adequate standard of living"; using this same model, a family of two or three would need an income of between $2,250 and $2,900 a year.[82] In comparison to these numbers the city's level of public assistance remained absurdly low, while the day care program that it now administered might grant an "adequate" standard of living to those whom it served.

By the time the debate unfolded in 1947, the average day care family (of any size) earned an annual income of $2,400. Meanwhile, the city's Aid to Dependent Children program did not even consider granting benefits unless annual household income fell below half that level; in the event that a family was found eligible for ADC, the city's radically low monthly grants meant that a family of four could expect to receive a total of about $850 a year. Access to even this paltry sum was automatically denied to any mother who could in some way arrange daytime care for her children while she worked. A report in 1950 commented that the District's ADC eligibility requirements "continued to tend to force mothers of young children to go to work."[83] Commissioner Mason's argument for "indigency" as a standard of eligibility in fact pressed public day care toward extinction. Given the limited assistance available to poor women and children, and the way that assistance was administered in the District, an indigency standard amounted to obligating poor mothers to work for the lowest of low wages or withdrew day care support entirely.

Senator John Cooper, a freshman Republican from Kentucky who presided over a series of day care hearings in mid-1947, expressed concern about too liberal access to public day care, but he could not go along with Commissioner Mason's indigency standard. The program's purpose, he countered, was "to provide [day] care for families in order to keep them employed." But the senator's understanding of public responsibility for day care differed from Commissioner Mason's in degree more than substance. The record suggests that both men rationalized a public day care service as an alternative to cash relief for nonworking mothers. Senator Cooper, like several members of Congress who joined the day care debate, drew a distinction between working and nonworking poor mothers. The working poor conceivably needed access to day care services to prevent them from lapsing into the less favored nonworking group. By contrast, Commissioner Mason saw a single group of poor people who, because of personal or familial failure, relied on public handouts.

Many mothers who wrote letters to members of Congress pleading for the day care program's continuation highlighted their economic need to work, and some also spoke of their desire to avoid public relief. But the day care users might also have understood their presence in the work force in far more expansive ways than either Commissioner Mason or Sen. Cooper, and they imagined broader rationales for a public day care service.[84] When she joined the effort to keep the District day care program afloat, Ellen Andruzzi, an activist belonging to the Parents' Committee, was already more than a decade into a lifelong career in nursing and about to embark on graduate studies in nursing administration. Explaining in an interview in 1997 her decision to combine motherhood, graduate studies, and a career, she simply responded, "Well I was intensely interested in what I was doing. And there was advanced education available with some federal funds to defray the cost of tuition [for nursing careers]. . . . And we needed the money. As a police officer my husband wasn't making enough money to support the style of living that we desired—I mean all we could afford was a one-bedroom apartment with two kids. It was mostly, you know, a practical consideration."[85]

At the same time, Andruzzi fully understood that the "the basic attitude of most members of Congress at that time was that a mother's place is in the home." This meant that unlike other members of the Parents' Committee she rarely if ever discussed her personal situation as a mother who found day care a good option. While she wrote letters, visited members of Congress, and submitted testimony as the legislative chairman for the Parents' Committee, Andruzzi never appeared on the public record discussing her own use of the day care centers. Her statement to the Senate subcommittee considering the day care program in May 1947, for instance, drew on her experience as a public health nurse and her husband's work as a police officer to explain the health and delinquency problems associated with the lack of adequate day care for low-income families. "Usually we would put [Marguerite] Grey forward since she was employed as a telephone operator and her income was lower than some of the rest of us," Andruzzi recalled. "We thought she'd make a better spokesperson."[86]

Marguerite Grey came to head the Parents' Committee after the resignation of Mary Hunt. As a single, white mother raising her children alone Grey approximated the postwar ideal that members of Congress apparently envisioned for public day care users. Grey was a sole-support mother, and no one could say that she worked simply for luxuries. Without the money she earned from her work at the telephone company there would be no money to pay for the one-room apartment with kitchenette and bath that she and her two children shared, no one to put clothes on their backs and food on the table.[87] Grey easily spoke of her use of the day care program, and like Andruzzi she understood how Congress expected a public day care program to be defended. No doubt she tailored her presentation accordingly. "As chairman of the Parents' Committee," Grey told a Senate subcommittee, "I would like to tell you of my own case, as I feel it is one which applies to so many of our mothers." She continued:

> I have two children, and am their sole support. It is not a matter of choice whether I work or not. I must work. I have no one to leave my

children with as both of my parents are dead. I cannot afford a maid or a private school if there were vacancies, as my income is not sufficient.

In the centers the children are well cared for, and have good supervision. I am able to do my work better, knowing that they are safe. I want to keep my children together, even though we do have a long day as it is necessary to get them up at six a.m. [to] give them breakfast, get them dressed, and take them to the center.

It is late when we return, and the washing and ironing for them has to be done at night. If the centers close, we will have . . . 320 broken homes as well as 400 children with no place to stay.[88]

In this story, Grey stressed her own need to work, the lack of child care alternatives, and her ability to keep her family together. In subsequent years she would continue to emphasize these same points before congressional committees and introduce other day care users who had similar stories with "certifiable" needs to work. Grey also sought to alleviate the concerns among members of Congress about lax enrollment policy, when she testified at a hearing in July 1947 on day care funding that the public welfare department "thoroughly screen[s] each family. I know that I was thoroughly screened by a social worker, and I feel sure that everyone was done the same way."[89]

Yet despite her obvious need to work, and her convincing testimony about the difficulty of being a single working parent with children, everything about Grey's history suggests that even if she did not develop a professional career in the same way that Andruzzi did she found earning wages more than just a way to pay the bills. When she retired from AT&T after forty-one years of service, she had worked her way from the bottom rung to a position in the engineering department that involved sales preparation. According to her daughter, Constance Severn, Marguerite Grey never stopped working after her marriage or the subsequent birth of her children. "My mother didn't marry until she was in her thirties . . . so I think she developed a very strong personage," Severn commented. "It's terrible to say 'women's lib.' . . . She was very independent, I guess is the best way to put it." Whatever may have been her desire to work, Grey could truthfully testify about her absolute need to work as well as the difficulties of raising young children as a single parent. Both she and Andruzzi understood how much this mattered in the District's postwar political debate on day care.[90]

The hearings of 1947 are the last ones in which Mary Hunt testified, and her comments show how far the program had moved from the idea of a public service patterned after recreation and schools. As she began her statement, Rep. A. L. Miller (R-Neb.) interrupted to question her directly about the administrative difficulty of separating those parents who "need" a service from those who might "want" it. "There are two distinct individuals?" he queried. Hunt, testifying now as a member of the Advisory Committee on Child Day Care Centers, responded, "Yes . . . We accept the premise that it must be on a basis of need—I think everyone concerned with it— those are the people who are in desperate circumstances and who must have help. The others, with more economic latitude," she continued, "have the opportunity to look around and make the best of whatever facilities they may find."[91]

Administering a Public Charity

The fate of the District day care legislation in 1946 and 1947 revealed the crucial importance of the financial-need argument for most policymakers and pointedly suggested the principle of publicly subsidized day care as a policy alternative to the Aid to Dependent Children program. Federal lawmakers relocated the postwar District program from education to welfare administration and by 1947 limited access exclusively to financially needy families and their children. Many advocates of publicly funded day care emphasized that the program encouraged a self-supporting citizenry; at the same time, a day care program explicitly serving only the neediest could be argued in more conservative terms as a way to limit or even replace public relief expenditures for poor women and children.

Compared to other city welfare programs, the District day care program provided a high standard of service on a marginal budget. Despite its administrative relocation, the program maintained a strong education component and a reasonably well-trained staff. Lucille Lewis, the superintendent of the city program, had studied at the Merrill-Palmer Institute in Detroit. The institute was among the first in the country to begin advocating nursery school education and the training of teachers when it opened its doors in 1922.[92] Andruzzi recalled that the program had "developmentally sound principles" and "pretty well-prepared teachers." As soon as her youngest son turned two—the minimum age for a child admitted to the public centers— she took her children out of a day nursery operated by the Daughters of Charity. The staff at the philanthropic nursery, she recalled, were "good-hearted," but "they just didn't know much about the normal development of young children." A widow, Flora Calhoun, found that the all-black Mott day care center not only cost less than other options but gave her son more advantages. "It was a teaching atmosphere," she said in 1997, "rather than in a private home where the only thing they did was either slept or eat or sit up. They had things to do."[93] Mothers' positive experience of the centers aside, a day care program justified as serving only the financially destitute implied that publicly supported day care was less than the ideal for children. The logic behind limiting access to the financially needy closely matched an older rationale for public child welfare provisions generally and philanthropic day nurseries in particular. This justification granted the right and responsibility of government involvement in what was deemed the wholly private responsibility of childrearing only when judicial or other professional opinion found that a child would otherwise be harmed.[94]

The day care program that Congress initially enacted for the District in 1946 suggested the need for this kind of professional judgment by specifying that the program was available only to parents who "are employed and are financially unable otherwise to provide for the day care of their children or who are so handicapped that they cannot otherwise provide." Responsibility for interpreting this eligibility clause fell to the District welfare board. Relying on the past practice at the centers and the proffered expertise of private welfare advocates, the board defined "handicapped" so as to allow significant room for a social worker to assert nonfinancial needs for day care. Aside from several war-related exemptions, however, these needs revolved around a popular, as well as a professional, notion of the family that assigned economic responsibility to men and insisted on the superiority of full-time homemaking and childrearing for women.[95]

In this schema, the failure or inability of the father to provide the household finances triggered a "legitimate" right for a woman to work and gave her children access to public day care. Accordingly, families in which the fathers were "alcoholic or for other reason incapable of sustaining full-time employment" qualified for publicly supported day care. A father who did work might also expect support. A separate provision granted access to day care where "the father works at night and has to sleep during the day so that the children have to be kept too quiet for their own good, and even then the father's rest is broke[n]."[96]

Two provisions allowed single-parent households, regardless of income, to use the public day care centers, and their different language strikingly underlines the gender roles that social workers expected to prevail in a family that was not "handicapped." These exemptions read: "Mothers who are the sole support of their children" and "Fathers who are deprived of a mother's care for their children by reason of illness, death, divorce or separation." The exemption for female-headed households centers on a mother's obligation to be the breadwinner and leaves implicit her inability to provide full-time, at-home child care; the exemption for a male-headed household stresses the absence of maternal care and, in turn, leaves unstated a father's need to work.[97]

The postwar policy debate over eligibility for publicly subsidized day care, along with local agency development of eligibility rules, reveals the gendered nature of mid-twentieth-century social expectations and rights. In short, there was a social expectation that women (especially white women) had a right to be privately supported by a man—and, as the case of Verone Moreno illustrated, they were encouraged to seek out this support. By the same token, social expectation granted men (especially white men) the right to the "maternal care of their children." Mary Hunt violated this right of a man when she "deprived" her son of full-time care and chose to work despite adequate financial provision by her husband. The day care program conformed to these popular expectations by granting access to publicly subsidized child care on these gendered terms.

The handicaps outlined by the board were one important eligibility criterion, but financial need remained central. When it took over the program in July 1946 the Board of Public Welfare established an income eligibility benchmark of $3,000 for a single parent (or a two-earner family) with a single child. By basing this annual income limit on take-home pay and allowing higher incomes for some families with two or more children, however, the agency set a reasonably relaxed standard. This did not last long.[98] By 1947 Congress was keenly concerned that the day care program too generously assisted families. At three separate hearings on the day care legislation in 1947, Sen. Cooper pored closely over the details of day care users' financial and marital status provided to him by the District's welfare department. He questioned especially the provision of day care to families who for any reason were exempted from the congressionally mandated financial means test. In a House hearing on the public day care program, Representatives A. L. Miller and James Auchincloss (D-N.J.) sought personally to verify the legitimacy of program access for each witness. Few members of the Parents' Committee spoke much beyond giving their name and the number of children they had before the members of Congress launched into questions. At bottom, they sought to learn the marital status of the witnesses—where was the male provider?—and to determine any available alternatives to public day care: Could the mothers pay for private care? Did they have relatives in the area? Were they getting pension or alimony money that they hadn't reported?[99]

In the end, choosing a middle ground between District officials' obvious distaste for any public day care program and District residents' call for continuing an important service, Congress granted another year of life to the program but added significant new eligibility restrictions. It eliminated all exemptions to the financial means test and instituted a flat $2,600 limit on the gross annual income for families (of all sizes) who used the public day care service. Congress also reduced program funding by 40 percent. The new rules effectively excluded about one-third of the households (107 families) previously using the service, and reduced funding forced half the centers that were operating to close. The dramatic changes in eligibility criteria and resulting reduction in the day care service—only six centers remained, with a capacity to serve 270 children—fully confirmed that day care in the District of Columbia was now a matter of public charity.[100]

The group of families most affected by the new income limits were those with two earners. In a study of families disqualified by the new restriction, based on a random sample of about a quarter of the total, close to two-thirds had been families with two wage earners. Although the income limitation would be revised somewhat in subsequent years, single-earner families, nearly all headed by women, would account for more than 90 percent of the District day care users throughout the remaining life of the program (see table 3).[101]

Again, the focus on serving sole-support mothers emphasized that the day care program was an alternative public policy to the older Aid to Dependent Children program. Although the District's position on access to the public centers appears extreme, administrators of publicly subsidized day care programs in other locations as well apparently viewed sole-support mothers as ideal recipients. In the postwar debate in the decidedly more liberal state of California, for instance, day care activists found that the broadest political acceptance of public day care coalesced around mothers who necessarily reared and supported their children alone.[102]

In 1948 attendance at the District's centers dropped below capacity to 222 children. Day care administrators blamed the reduced enrollment on the exceedingly low income ceiling that Congress had imposed. The District's public welfare department estimated that of some seven hundred denials of requests for day care, about 59 percent had been made on the basis of income. Additionally the welfare department noted that despite a dramatic reduction in service occasioned by the reduced appropriation, the District's taxpayers had spent close to the same amount of money as in the previous year because of substantially reduced income from parent fees.[103] This curious outcome—a "cost-saving" gesture resulting in substantially less service at the same expense to taxpayers—occurred because the day care program was now restricted to parents able to pay at most a token fee. The result was a plunge in the proportion of operating costs offset by parents and a com-

Table 3. Single Wage-Earner Households as Number and Percentage of Total District of Columbia Public Day Care Households

Date	Total Number of Households	Number of Single Wage-Earner Households	Single Wage-Earner Households as Percentage of Total
February 1946	572	284[a]	49.7
December 1946	300	177	59.0
March 1948	162	156	96.3
March 1949	204	188	92.2
December 1950	224	202	90.2

Sources: U.S. Congress, House, Committee on the District of Columbia, *Child Care Centers*, 1946, 31; Board of Public Welfare, "Some Statistics about the Child Day Care Centers," Tray 80A-F6 118, Committee on the District, Records of the U.S. Senate, National Archives; U.S. Congress, House, Committee on the District of Columbia, *Child Day Care Centers*, 1948, 7; "Day Care, Dec. 1950," folder s. 3258, box 14, SEN 81A-E5, Committee on the District, Records of the U.S. Senate, National Archives; U.S. Congress, Senate, *Continuing a System of Nurseries and Nursery Schools*, Senate Report 364, 81st Cong., 1st sess., May 1949, 4.

[a] Includes wives of servicemen still active in the armed forces.

mensurately increased per capita cost to taxpayers. Immediately after the war, when some D.C. day care users could legitimately be classified as middle- and upper-income earners and the program suffered through a period of virtually no public or philanthropic backing, fees paid by parents somewhat unrealistically covered close to 50 percent of the program cost. Once the Board of Public Welfare began to administer the program and removed the highest income earners from it, the proportion of parents' contributions to program costs leveled off at just below one-third. The annual income ceiling of $2,600 instituted in 1947 sent that figure plummeting to less than 14 percent. Even after the most stringent restrictions on income were lifted in 1948, the proportion of operating costs paid by parents never exceeded about one-quarter of program expenses throughout the remaining life of the program.[104]

The relative increase in single-earner families among all day care users, and the stringent income limits that radically lowered the amount of operating costs covered by parents' fees and also reduced attendance below capacity, showed the extent to which the District's public day care program had been successfully redefined: from a public service to patriotic working mothers during wartime to a public charity for unfortunate women during peacetime. In March 1948, out of 162 families using day care, only 6 had two earners. The average annual (gross) family income had dipped again, to around $1,800, and more than 90 percent of the women and men using the day care service were employed as clerical workers, private domestics, laborers, sales clerks, or laundry and food workers. When the centers closed in 1950 the cost of living had been climbing steadily, yet the average gross annual income stood at $2,034 and the occupational status of most parents also remained unchanged.[105]

The Final Push for a Permanent Program

Despite the strong antipathy of District officials and numerous lawmakers, the public day care program in the capital hung onto life through 1947 and gained a third one-year renewal in 1948. The skillful lobbying and tenacity of the Parents' Committee and community groups provide the only explanation for the program's life. Each year committee leaders persuaded a core group in Congress to introduce legislation to continue the program and then guide the bill through hearings and floor votes and on to final enactment. Minimizing the crucial efforts in behalf of day care that she and other members of the Parents' Committee members had made, Ellen Andruzzi commented: "There are a lot of parliamentary ways to get legislation through the Congress and sometimes what [Congress members who supported day care] did was introduce it on a day when a bill could be voted up or down without any debate—or with other District of Columbia bills. They used various parliamentary strategies to get it through."[106]

In 1948 Congress, over the repeated objections of District officials, agreed to extend the program for an additional year. Members seemed surprised that administrators had managed to maintain a strong program despite a limited budget. Rep. A. L. Miller, who visited some of the centers as part of his committee's investigation into their renewal, remarked on the "excellent care" the children received and pronounced the centers' equipment "far better" than he had expected.[107] In this round of program renewal, Congress grew suspicious that there were too many administrators and teachers for each pupil. While it continued to seek an end to the program, the D.C. public welfare department nonetheless steadfastly denied that the program could be run with fewer personnel. The department insisted that if the income ceiling were lifted the same staff could serve a larger number of children and a greater share of costs would be recaptured by parents' fees. Congress responded by allowing the income ceiling to expire, but it maintained minimal funding and thus guaranteed that the program would remain limited.[108]

After the program was renewed relatively easily in 1948, a strong drive to make the centers permanent began in 1949 and 1950. Led on Capitol Hill by Sen. Margaret Chase Smith (R-Maine), the effort nearly succeeded. A former member of the U.S. House of Representatives newly elected to the Senate, Smith had given committed backing to the wartime child care program. She opened hearings on the District's day care program in May 1949. Instead of questioning if women truly "needed" to be working, or seeking to pare costs by reducing staffing or otherwise compromising the quality of the program—strategies that had helped her forerunners define the program—Smith focused single-mindedly on child welfare. What would happen to the children, our "future citizens," she prodded the District's legal counsel Vernon West, if the day care centers were closed? West, who found himself fielding difficult questions for the absent District commissioners, tried to avoid answering but ultimately conceded, "I think in some of the cases the parents can make other arrangements to take care of [their children]. But I think certainly there are some cases where parents could not."[109] For Smith this was "reason enough to continue the day centers until we find a place for those children," and the effort to keep the day care program operating was off and running. Over two days of hearings Smith and her committee heard a stream of testimony in praise of the centers. As is clear from the tenor of the testimony by both day care users and community activists (especially on the second day), once supporters realized that Smith was on their side, and specifically that she viewed child welfare as the preeminent rationale for day care, testimony shifted a bit from explicating dire financial need to suggesting positive objectives for the program.

If West had been uncertain what would happen to children once the day care centers closed, mothers who used the centers were not. They related any number of child care arrangements that they had previously used, ranging from inadequate to appalling, that included hired maids, full-time foster care, supervision by a neighbor, and even private nursery care. Marguerite Grey recalled: "I attempted to have a maid, and as you probably know, at that time [pre-war] you could get a maid much cheaper than you can today. . . . The first I had, I was left with a little baby in the house alone, 14 months old, and I was called by the druggist on the corner to get my little girl, who was left on the corner at the drugstore."[110] One day care user, Helen Simborski, gave equally damning testimony concerning her use of a maid. "When I had a maid to take care of [my son], many times I would have to come home during the day to check up on the child. Lots of times I came home in the evening when the child was actually shaking, when I gave him a glass of milk."[111]

In some measure these white members of the Parents' Committee defended public day care centers by denigrating the quality of what members of Congress undoubtedly understood to be black domestic help. Neither Grey nor Simborski could afford to pay anything close to decent wages, and they therefore could only have hired the District's most economically marginalized workers: black females, likely young and inexperienced. To recognize the racial subtext of these stories is not to deny that the women experienced poor caregiving; neither does it follow that they consciously sought to enhance their call for day care with a bigoted argument. At the same time, white women's expectation that black women or girls would, for very low wages, willingly and conscientiously perform the household and child rearing work that the mothers themselves had left behind reflected their own devaluation of home labor.[112]

Devaluation of domestic work and its association with the economically marginalized could also mean that even those financially able to pay adequate wages might not be inclined to do so. As the first president of the Parents' Committee, Mary Hunt had a family income that placed her among the District's wealthiest residents and should have given her significantly more ability to pay for adequate domestic help. Yet even she had earlier testified that no fewer than fifteen household workers proved unsatisfactory caregivers for her son. Paradoxically, if the racial undertones of the argument helped to secure some sympathy for white day care users, they also stiffened the chances of achieving adequate public day care funding, or any at all. Why should public dollars be spent on childrearing if it was so obviously not an economically valued commodity?

Kathryn Meese, a single mother with a four-year-old, offered the most expansive argument of day care's benefits for lower-income mothers. Arguing that whether a working mother could somehow manage financially without a public day care service was beside the point, she stressed the important personal margin of security and independence that the centers granted to lower-income women: "I don't gamble my money away, nor do I drink, but before I entered my child in the Child Day Care Center, I spent every cent I made for living. I was unable to put anything aside for that rainy day. Where is the incentive for living, day after day, under such conditions? . . . I believe that any working mother is entitled to at least two new dresses a year, to be able to buy a new pair of hose when the last pair runs without having to wait until the next payday to do so. Is this too much for us mothers to expect?"[113] This argument—that access to day care gave women greater security and independence—strayed a long way from the understanding that District officials and members of Congress had of day care as a public charity, or as an alternative to Aid to Dependent Children.[114]

Having opened the door for broader rationales in support of the program, Sen. Smith no doubt kept her focus on the program's value as a child welfare measure when she lobbied her colleagues for continued program support. Smith persuaded her fellow members of the Senate District Committee to call on the District of Columbia commissioners to support the day care program or propose some alternative method of care for the children it served. In May 1949 the Senate committee wrote to the District commissioners requesting that a study be made and a report of its findings be sent to the Senate by November 1, 1949. Moving at their usual pace, the commissioners swung into action in mid-October, five months after receiving the request. Ignoring the specific request of the Senate committee that day care users and community day care advocates be involved, the District's officials appointed a handful of upper managers from its legal, budget, education, and welfare departments to study the matter. In a decision that likely surprised the commissioners, the task force, which included several members who had previously been unfriendly to the day care centers, voted to recommend that the program be made permanent.[115]

The task force appears to have made the recommendation in spite of itself. Its report observed that the day care service was established as a temporary measure, that it was a "specialized service" reaching only a small segment of the total District population, that operation of the centers took the District government into an area of service formerly reserved for private charity and commercial nurseries, and finally, that the purpose of the day care program overlapped with the longer-established and permanent policy of providing Aid to Dependent Children. Having said all that, however, the task force found no better solution to care for the children of working mothers than the day care program. It noted that the program "relieved pressure" on the District's severely underfunded ADC program and added: "There is also a rehabilitative factor that should not be overlooked. The recipient of this service will be gainfully employed and contributing materially to the support of her family. She will not lapse into hopeless apathy apparent in the majority of cases entirely dependent upon charity and the opportunity is always present for the person to improve her financial status and completely support her family."[116]

Confronted with this positive recommendation, the commissioners delayed. First they shuffled the report off to the Board of Public Welfare, which insisted that it should not be asked to administer the program and recommended that perhaps local churches could run the program as a private responsibility. Once the Washington Federation of Churches made clear that it did not have the resources to take on this project, the commissioners recognized the need to send their final recommendation to the committee.[117] Contradicting their task force, they expressed "their considered opinion that day care centers should not be established as a municipal function of the District of Columbia."[118]

One thing missing from the letter was an alternative recommendation for the care of children of working mothers—something insisted on by the Senate District Committee, especially Sen. Smith.[119] But by now it was March 1950, and despite the commissioners' stalling tactics, legislation to continue the program had again been introduced. At Sen. Smith's insistence, the proposal was amended by her committee from a fifth one-year continuation to establishment of a permanent program. By mid-May the bill to make day care in the District of Columbia permanent passed the full Senate. Opposition to the program remained more firm in the House, where representatives threatened to kill the program before ultimately agreeing to a fourth one-year continuation.[120] To reconcile this separate legislation, the two chambers compromised and agreed to grant the day care program an unprecedented three-year extension.[121]

The elation of day care center users and supporters soon diminished, however, as Congress failed to include any money for the program in the District appropriations bill. Just as in the first year of its postwar life, the day care program had gained congressional authorization only to face near-extinction when no appropriations were initially granted to the program. Now Congress gave its longest authorization of the program yet—a three-year extension—but threatened to kill the program by refusing to allow any of the District's funds to operate it. Initial fiscal year appropriation bills simply set aside the politically charged issue of day care funding. In late September 1950, after employees had been operating the program as volunteers for nearly three months, President Truman signed a $17 billion "supplemental supply bill"—a catch-all piece of legislation designed to fund hundreds of projects. The bill dedicated $50,000 from the District treasury for the day care centers but stipulated that the program had to be "liquidat[ed]" no later than December 31, 1950.[122] The Parents' Committee refused to accept this death notice without a fight. The centers closed their doors just three days before Christmas 1950. One day after Christmas a group of some thirty mothers and sixty children gathered at the District building to insist that the commissioners fight to reinstate funding for the centers. Additional pressure on the commissioners came from members of Congress including Sen. Smith, who no doubt was alluding to the Korean War when she pronounced herself "greatly disturbed" at the centers' closing given the "world situation."[123]

Although the commissioners formally announced now that they would seek to restore funding, given their long history of hostility it is difficult to believe that they put their backs into the task. The new chair of the Parents' Committee, Irene Raine, led a twenty-five-woman delegation to a House appropriations hearing in February 1951 and asked that money be reinstated. A few days later, apparently confident that the appropriations committee would ignore their request for day care funding although it had not yet acted, District officials began dismantling the centers and removing equipment to storage.[124] Ultimately the day care center funding did not find its way back into the District budget. In testimony in April 1951 that the *Star* reported as a "key" part of the appropriations committee decision not to reinstate funding, a city welfare administrator testified that the number of Aid to Dependent Children cases had not climbed appreciably since the closing of the centers. Only four families had been referred to the department, he reported, and of those one was accepted while the other three had not pursued their applications. Explaining its failure to approve day care center funding, the appropriations committee reported only: "Such centers are in conflict with the regular programs of the Board of Public Welfare. The responsibility of caring for dependent children beyond the scope of these programs is not the responsibility of the District Government."[125]

Federal Postscript: Defaulting on a Second Wartime Child Care Program

The program that some opponents had railed against as just another "wartime measure" that didn't go away was shut down by the appropriations committee precisely when U.S. troops were once again engaged in combat. Fighting on the Korean peninsula broke out in June 1950; by July President Truman had committed ground troops. Federal legislators came to view this latest overseas deployment as part of a larger and long-standing semipermanent defense stance, however, and they were consequently less willing to suspend standard operating rules to prosecute the war. Further, the political climate had grown considerably more conservative since the years immediately following World War II, and this strongly limited the notion of a role for the federal government in providing any public services to citizens.

As if to accentuate the irony of its timing, the same legislation that ordered the liquidation of the District day care centers appropriated $3 million to "provide extra office space for additional defense employees."[126] The centers' closing clearly worked a hardship on those parents who had relied on them. At the same time, day care activists with less immediate needs may have taken some comfort in a newly proposed federal wartime child care program. Already in January 1951 Congress began debating a new measure to provide housing and other community facilities and services in areas affected by the war. The "Maybank bill" served as the Korean War equivalent of the Lanham Act in World War II, but unlike its predecessor it specifically called for funding day care as part of more general community assistance proposals.

Throughout the program debate, funding for services in communities affected by war remained the stepchild of the Maybank bill. Hearing records and congressional floor debates on the bill are dominated by discussion of government housing policy. In a sign that even in wartime lawmakers preferred supporting private industry to meet the preeminent postwar goal of boosting long-term national economic growth, the final bill authorized $1.6 billion for government-backed housing mortgage insurance; less than one-twenty-fifth that amount, $60 million, was set aside for all other community facilities and services in areas affected by the war—including hospitals, schools, recreation, water and sewer works, and a child care program.[127]

Unsuccessful in gaining administrative control during World War II, the Federal Security Agency this time won the right to administer community programs. But because almost none of the $60 million authorized for them would actually be appropriated, this appeared to be a hollow victory. For the FSA, however, a major concern in the Maybank hearings was to ensure that a series of separate, recently won legislative victories granting it broad funding authority in health and education matters would not be supplanted by temporary wartime legislation. FSA administers argued that they could supplement existing programs to meet wartime needs.[128] Of course no national child care service remained to be supplemented, but day care figured as a minor concern (at most) of the FSA officials who testified on the Maybank bill. Some mothers would necessarily be working because of the military action and thus child care provisions would have to be made, they argued. "Such care is basically a local responsibility," the agency's administrator, Oscar Ewing, asserted without further explanation, "but Federal consultation and limited aid may be needed."[129]

In contrast to the years immediately following World War II, in 1951 a more constrained view prevailed of what social programs the federal government should provide. At the end of World War II, conservatives had been eager to rein in what they saw as excessive government activism and spending. While they failed to roll back the substantial changes wrought by the New Deal, they did halt efforts to create new guarantees for citizens, for instance health care. At the same time, the political chill brought on by fear of domestic communism worked to quiet popular calls for broader social services and to shift the national debate rightward. In this context there were few people willing or able to make day care funding a priority.

Within the federal government, the Children's Bureau and Women's Bureau expressed some interest in a federal child care program, but both agencies were experiencing declining political power. The Women's Bureau sent field investigators to areas affected by the Korean War. They documented considerable need for child care, but the agency could do little more than publish the data.[130] In a sign of its declining political fortunes, the Children's Bureau in 1946 had been transferred out of a cabinet agency, the Department of Labor, and was now placed under the Social Security Administration of the Federal Security Agency. The move meant that Children's Bureau officials were now several layers removed from their previous status of directly reporting to a cabinet officer.[131]

In January 1951 the Children's Bureau and its FSA education counterpart, the Office of Education, held a two-day joint conference, "Day Care of Children of Employed Mothers in Areas Affected by Defense Mobilization." The conference brought together thirty-six educators and social workers representing public agencies in eight states and twelve cities, as well as several national organizations.[132] But neither the Office of Education nor the Children's Bureau apparently made clear to legislators on Capitol Hill their desire to administer child care funding. An administrator from the Office of Education, testifying at a congressional hearing on the second day of the conference, made no mention of the day care planning conference when questioned about the Maybank bill's day care provision. Further, although both education and health officials from the FSA spoke about the community facilities provisions in the Maybank bill, no representatives from the Children's Bureau would similarly testify in behalf of day care.[133] The most spirited defense of federal funding for child care at the Maybank hearings came from Catherine Fahy of the American Parents Committee, a relatively new organization led by George Hecht, publisher of *Parents* magazine.[134] Fahy argued that despite the "ongoing need" for good child care, federal funds had been withdrawn after World War II, and state and local governments had "been very disorganized about providing for day care." Relying on an official economic explanation for women's employment, she cited the labor needs of the defense industry to explain why many women now earned wages and why more women would soon need to do the same. Given the high rates of marriages and births, she continued, certainly some of these women would be the mothers of young children. The upsurge in employment related to the Korean War, she explained, had personally left her in need of a new child care arrangement: "Two days before New Year's my housekeeper was offered two government jobs in one day. They are that short of 'womanpower' in the Government here. So I called five different agencies in town and I got not one response, which means that there are no interested workers to be had. What I need is a day care center."[135]

Fahy's testimony about the shortage of "womanpower" in the government underscores how unfortunate it was for congressional appropriators to end all public funding for day care in the District of Columbia, and also demonstrates how class (and no doubt race as well) positioned women to understand "womanpower" differently. For Fahy's housekeeper the increased demand for women workers meant simply better job options. If she had child care arrangements of her own to make, this apparently did not dampen her enthusiasm to leave household work for a higher-paying job that accrued more respect. For Fahy herself, a tighter female job market translated into a lesser ability to obtain in-the-home child care and a consequently greater awareness of the need for social services.

Although argued in the context of war, Fahy's reference to "ongoing need" and her statement that "day care centers are difficult to discuss in relation only to this bill because the need for them is constant" accented permanent needs as well.[136] The idea of permanent government-supported child care is precisely what concerned the politically important Catholic spokesman Monsignor O'Grady of the National Conference of Catholic Charities. He saw day care as one of the "most highly debatable programs envisaged under community facilities and services in the [Maybank bill]." The World War II program, he believed, had been of questionable need and had quickly ended not only because of its cost but because "the American people were not and are not sold on the idea of encouraging mothers with young children to go to work and turn their children over to a center operated by a governmental agency." Centers under "private auspices" existed and apparently were used to a much greater extent, he continued. Whereas day care advocates took the presence of many women in the work force as an indication of the need for federal funding, O'Grady went to the heart of the debate over permanent versus temporary wartime child care when he drew the opposite conclusion. "It certainly cannot be said at the present time that this is a war need," he asserted. "We have no evidence as yet that the need for day-care centers arises from the need for women workers in war industries."[137]

For day care, as with the Maybank bill in general, the new war rationale for additional public support proved difficult to disentangle from the emerging semi-permanent defense rationale. Controversy over the bill's necessity kept the proposal tied up in Congress until late summer, and by the time President Truman signed it into law, U.S. troops had been fighting in Korea for more than a year. To follow the money is to watch a declining possibility for a new broad-based federally supported child care program. Senator Maybank had begun by calling for $3 billion to fund housing (primarily) and community facilities. Congress cut this amount nearly in half, authorizing $1.6 billion (over two years), of which only $60 million could be used for community facilities. The FSA, granted the right to operate most of the community facilities, sought $44 million for these programs in the first year. But the administration's Bureau of Budget limited its request for the agency to $25.5 million; out of this money the FSA proposed to spend about $1.3 million on child care. Congress in the end reduced the total money granted to the FSA for all of its community facilities work to about $4 million, and none of this money was to be spent on day care.[138] In the House Report accompanying the funding legislation in 1951 appropriations committee members stated: "No funds have been allowed . . . for construction, operation, development, or administration of day-care facilities or programs. The committee is definitely not convinced, all things considered, that we have yet reached the point in the mobilization effort that would justify inauguration of a Federally assisted program of this kind."[139]

Although absent from the earlier congressional debates on authorizing day care funding, the Children's Bureau had testified at the appropriations hearings in fall 1951. Dr. Martha Eliot, who had replaced Katherine Lenroot as head of the agency earlier that year, testified before an openly skeptical House subcommittee on the need for day care funding. To the insistence that the defense industry needed more workers, and that the employment of women helped to minimize housing needs caused by migrations of labor, Rep. John Fogarty (D-R.I.), the committee chair, responded that there were plenty of out-of-work textile and jewelry workers in his state; he thought the government should be more selective about where it created defense facilities.[140] Rep. Winfield Denton (D-Ind.) found the current situation different from that which prevailed in World War II ("not an all-out mobilization"), and he too questioned the need for federal child care funding. "Is it good policy for the Government to go in and try to encourage women to work when their husbands are making good money?" he asked.[141] In the end the appropriations subcommittee finessed the issue of denying all day care funding by insisting that proper surveys of need had not yet been conducted and, ignoring the World War II experience, that there was no established procedure for distributing funds.[142]

In 1951 the FSA had proposed a modest child care program that emphasized using existing private and public facilities. The chief of the Children's Bureau, Martha Eliot, estimated that the program would directly accommodate only about 4,500 children around the country.[143] Failing to gain even this tiny toehold of federal child care funding, in 1952 the bureau changed its tack and asked merely for a grant of about $40,000 to cover the next sixteen months. The money would be used to pay three professional staff members and two clerical workers who would "work with State departments of health and welfare in developing improved day-care." "They are asking for this kind of help in increasing the work in the day-care field," explained Neota Larson, assistant chief of the bureau. "They are wanting what they call program materials." She added: "There are services that are needed in order that these centers will be a good place for children to use."[144] Federal appropriators did not grant even this limited request.[145]

It is revealing that both an approved extension of the District of Columbia's public day care program and an authorized federal wartime program met their death through a lack of appropriations. Their failure suggests both a strong distaste for day care programs among some members of Congress (who happened to serve on the powerful appropriations committee) and, as the Cold War deepened, a decreased base of support for publicly financed social provisions of any kind. In 1946, when the Senate appropriations committee had balked at allowing local tax dollars to be spent on child care, concerted lobbying by District day care activists (within the context of calls for continued public funding of child care nationally) had provoked an unusual challenge of the appropriations committee. After a contentious floor debate, the full Senate successfully reinstated child care funding in the District. By the time of the Korean War, federally financed wartime child care was a distant or nonexistent memory for most working parents across the country, and legislators mustered little opposition to proposals to eliminate child care services locally and nationally.[146]

By 1950 the District of Columbia program had reached a critical juncture. Having survived an initial funding crisis and undergone a redefinition from public service to public charity, it now needed to justify its existence as a permanent public program. Senator Margaret Chase Smith sought to promote the welfare of children as a program rationale. Others, such as the District task force that recommended a continued child care program, favored child care over the Aid to Dependent Children program as a policy that offered "rehabilitative" potential to poor women and children. Although these arguments proved persuasive enough to allow the full Congress to approve a continued program, the service ran aground with congressional appropriators. Acting in their capacity as local legislators, the members of the appropriations committees simply dismissed these arguments when they ruled that a child care service was not a municipal responsibility.

A study in 1951 found that most former users of the District's public day care program continued to work for wages but that few had been able to secure comparable care for their children. Another survey, in 1955, found only seven private day care centers in the District that used a sliding scale to charge fees based on what a family could realistically afford. The average flat fee at the still relatively scarce commercial centers ran to $12.50 per preschooler per week—a cost prohibitively high for most if not all of the families that had used the public day care center. Little after-school and summer vacation supervision was available for school-age children.[147]

The postwar District of Columbia day care debate took place in a highly illiberal political context. To begin with, District residents had no leaders, local or federal, who were directly accountable to them through the ballot box. The lack of voting rights did not prevent day care activists from seeking action on their behalf, but it significantly affected how their request fared. At bottom District residents had to trust in the good graces of those appointed to represent them rather than press those leaders to remain accountable or face rejection at the polls. Day care advocates sought, and found, a number of benevolent congressional patrons to foil the adamant conservative opposition of their unelected local officials. But this necessary maneuver only underscored the idea that the public day care program could only be granted as a charity for dependent residents rather than a service for independent citizens.

The debate over public funding of day care in the nation's capital was also limited by a broad consensus that mothers ideally belonged in the home and not the workplace. At bottom, having a day care program meant that some mothers were working and thus not giving full-time care to their children at home. Mothers could not claim a social right to day care because they could not assert their own right as individuals to choose an occupation separate from full-time, stay-at-home motherhood. Even day care programs offered on the basis of child welfare protection or family preservation still had to negotiate the question of what circumstances guaranteed the legitimacy of a woman's decision to earn wages. The economic prosperity of the postwar era brought new expectations about decent standards of living, and this both fueled the decision of an increasing number of women to work and made it more difficult for policymakers to find the exact point at which a financially needy and thus deserving mother turned into an undeserving chiseler.

In addition to the limitations imposed on the D.C. day care debate by a widely shared conservative gender ideology, some members of Congress and nearly all local officials were eager to preserve the city's racial status quo. Within a job market segmented into "appropriate" male and female occupations, whites received the best opportunities while blacks were strictly segregated into the least desirable and lowest-paid wage work. Awareness of the city's substantial number of low-income African Americans had long contributed to a preference for private social programs and stingy levels of public benefits. In the particular instance of day care, even if a conservative gender ideology limited public responsibility to only "desperate" mothers, racially conservative whites might resent this as a potential boon to the city's African American community.

In this conservative political context, the day care program that survived for an unlikely five years was rationalized as a public charity. Many policymakers explicitly understood the day care program as a policy alternative to the longer-standing Aid to Dependent Children program, and day care users found themselves constrained to argue for the program primarily on the ground that it would prevent them being reduced to relief recipients. As the next chapter will show, day care activists in California made this same argument. At the same time, the state's neo-Progressive politics, along with an early childhood education framework for the child care program, allowed day care users to shape this justification of public support for day care into a more powerful form. California parents stressed that publicly subsidized day care allowed them to engage in "productive citizenship" and thereby enhance the state's economic growth.

Further, led by the aerospace industry, California's superheated postwar economy contributed to both the demand for services and the apparent ease with which those demands could be fulfilled. Between 1940 and 1950 the state's population grew more than 53 percent—from under 7 million inhabitants to more than 10.5 million—with much of the increase due to migration brought on by the state's plentiful jobs. During the 1950s the state's growth continued to outpace the rest of the nation and by 1960 its population stood at 15.7 million. Where Cleveland and District of Columbia officials were struggling to find ways to meet the fiscal needs of war-bloated populations, California, despite its own burgeoning population, rode through the war on an immense wave of federal wartime spending and growing tax revenues. California emerged from the war with a budget surplus, and in the postwar years federal spending to wage the Cold War arms race continued to disproportionately benefit California's economy. In this period, Governor Earl Warren presided over a budget surplus so mammoth that he could grant an immediate short-term reduction in taxes even as he oversaw increased state services.[6]

Finally, as one sorts through letters, articles, and other documents from this period, it is impossible to miss a pervasive positive attitude held by Californians about their future. In the midst of Cold War hysteria and nuclear war anxieties, Californians embraced societal change and sought to bend it toward their own image of a positive future. In Los Angeles County, where the largest wartime program of Child Care Centers had existed and where by 1950 more than half the families who sent their children to public Child Care Centers lived, a seemingly permanent defense industry boom and postwar suburbanization brought the good life to many white Angelenos. Not immune to this rising economic tide, Los Angeles County's Latino, African American, and Asian-origin communities organized to try to shape their postwar futures even as they continued to face stiff housing and job discrimination.[7]

For the child care debate, a postwar change of particularly key import would be the swelling number of women in the state's paid labor force. The state's war industries employed an unprecedented number of women. Still, less than a decade after the fighting ended, the wartime record had been surpassed. California's dramatic population growth accounted for only part of the tripling in the number of women workers between 1940 and 1960. Women's total share of the labor force grew from 24.8 percent in 1940 to 31.7 percent in 1960; in the state's urban areas women occupied a full third of the labor force. Tacit acceptance by many residents that women's changing employment status represented an inevitable factor in their state's growing economy and contributed to it would be a crucial argument for California's day care supporters. Rather than a mortal threat to the social order, the state's politicians began to observe this change in women's workforce participation as a "neutral fact" that required a pragmatic response.[8]

Because the use of child care is often intimately tied to the employment of mothers, even subtle changes in attitudes toward women's wage earning can affect the public policy debate on child care. As women's employment in California began to gain status as a part of what the political theorist Nancy Fraser calls "official-economic institutions," politicians could more easily justify action to provide child care. Characterized by markets, paid workplaces, and 'private' enterprises and corporations, official-economic status, Fraser writes, "depoliticizes certain matters by economizing them; the issues in question here are cast as impersonal market imperatives or as a 'private' ownership prerogative or as technical problems for managers and planners, all in contradistinction to political matters."[9] Within this logic, if women's wage earning was essential to the state's economic success (as it had been during the war), public child care represented simply a necessary service rather than a debatable political action. At the same time, the act of childrearing itself remained firmly lodged in what Fraser calls "domestic institutions." Domestic institutions are characterized by the male-headed nuclear family; they depoliticize an issue by making it personal or familial. In short, they take an issue off the active public agenda. The understood private, familial nature of childrearing worked to limit the day care program developed in California so that it was available primarily to low-income mothers who provided the sole economic support for their children.[10]

Neither the unique rationales offered nor the social, economic, and political contexts of the state could have allowed this child care program to continue without remarkable grassroots lobbying by the California Parents' Association for Child Care Centers and the substantial and long-term efforts on behalf of the program by educators in the state's child care program. Parents' groups in both Cleveland and the District of Columbia received their greatest community and organizational support from social welfare agencies. In California some social welfare support was important, but over the longer term the most critical and consistent aid came from the workers who were daily associated with the Child Care Centers as teachers, center directors, and supervisors. Claiming their identity as education professionals, this group of day care partisans helped to frame the child care debate in more universal terms than was generally offered by social welfare advocates. Additionally, in a state where legislators and many citizens took great pride in the first-rate quality of the public education system, the education context better allowed the statewide Parents' Association to define itself and the child care program as being outside public charity.

Compared to the program's detractors, supporters of state-subsidized child care were extremely well organized. Nonetheless, the substantial difficulties that advocates in California encountered in enacting a permanent day care program illustrate the staying power of a conservative gender ideology in postwar America, as well as the way this ideology remained closely bound to an understanding of private and public responsibilities. The sustained and largely unique emphasis on education and the distinct rationale of "productive citizenship" did not prevent a great number of California legislators from understanding the state child care program as a latter-day version of the nineteenth-century day nursery: a program that gave aid to the deserving poor. The legislature enacted a financial "means test" to determine eligibility for the service and (with some notable exceptions) allowed only lower-income families access to publicly subsidized child care. Even as they enacted a permanent program, California lawmakers remained deeply suspicious of non-maternal care for young children.

California's Role in the Extension of Federal Funding

Insistently prodded to act by their constituents back home, California's elected officials played an outsized and effective role in the effort to achieve extended federal funding for the wartime child care program. Grassroots activism compelled a variety of elected California officials across a range of political viewpoints to take up the cause of continued child care funding. Members of the state's congressional delegation raised the issue of continued child care funding frequently and with a noticeable effect on Capitol Hill. State legislators promptly held hearings that called for continuation of the centers and, in a move that apparently impressed members of Congress who held the program's purse strings, indicated that they simply sought time to fashion a state solution to the child care issue. Finally, Governor Earl Warren wrote to President Truman urging some continuation of federal funding for child care centers. Warren's early and sustained openness to the child care program stands in sharp contrast to the adamant opposition of Governor Frank Lausche of Ohio and was a key ingredient in the success of child care advocacy in California.

California had by far the largest wartime child care constituency: more than 21,000 children attended the centers at the end of August 1945, about four times as many as the next-largest state, Washington. At the close of the war, well over one in five of all children who remained enrolled in the federally sponsored child care program lived in California, and close to half the mothers of these children were the wives and widows of servicemen.[11] Letters from California constituents, which began to blanket federal and state offices after the centers' imminent closing was announced in mid-August 1945, not surprisingly emphasized the needs of servicemen's wives.[12] One month after it had announced that the federal subsidy for child care would soon end, the Federal Works Agency reported receiving protests from more than 2,300 Californians, most of whom sent letters or postcards.[13] Additional letters arrived in the mailboxes of state and federal representatives. "True the shooting is over, but what about the fathers that will be in service for a long while yet?" queried a mother of two preschoolers from Los Angeles in a letter to Rep. Helen Gahagan Douglas (D-Calif.) in August. "We must still carry on until our husbands are discharged," another day care user added. "To my child," a third wrote, the war "won't be over until his daddy is home. Now, why should he be subjected to indifferent care when his father is still serving his country?"[14]

Representative Douglas received only a small fraction of the mail. Her southern California colleague Rep. Ned Healy (D) testified that he had received "literally hundreds of letters from mothers" who were concerned about the planned closing of the wartime child care program. From the northern part of the state, Rep. Frank Havenner (D) commented on the House floor: "I have had scores of letters from mothers in San Francisco saying that they would not know how to get along, how to keep their families decently, unless this service should be continued." Finally, Rep. Clyde Doyle (D-Calif.) told his colleagues that mass meetings regarding the impending day care center closings had been called in his home county of Los Angeles and added, "I have received more letters on this subject in the last two weeks than on any other subject."[15]

Prodded by a large and vocal day care constituency in their home state, California's members of Congress became important, recognized leaders in the fight for continued child care nationally. When the General Fleming of the FWA indicated that separate legislation might be needed to ensure even a temporary continuation of the wartime program, Rep. Doyle, in his first term representing the Long Beach area of Los Angeles County, which had been heavily affected by the war, introduced just such a measure.[16] California representatives, led frequently by Doyle, brought the child care funding issue to the House floor with far more regularity than any other state delegation.[17] And concern about the fate of their state's centers led the California representatives to hold a special conference with the FWA. Finally, in October seven members of California's House delegation testified before an appropriations subcommittee that was to decide on an extension of Lanham Act funding for child care.[18]

In the early postwar months child care advocates might attract supporters across a broad political spectrum. This was true not only of politically active organizations but of individual politicians as well. Representative Doyle's subsequent career in the House of Representatives as a staunch "anti-red" activist and avid supporter of the arch-conservative House Un-American Activities Committee seemingly makes him an unlikely child care advocate. By contrast to Doyle, Rep. Helen Gahagan Douglas was a liberal and progressive politician who would be severely red-baited in her unsuccessful Senate campaign in 1950. Especially by insisting that the FWA catalogue the vast number of communications it had received regarding the child care service, and then by placing that information on the public record, Douglas played a significant role in bringing attention to the nationwide call for continued child care funding. Doyle and Douglas both had a high enough profile on the child care issue that when the Cleveland Day Care Committee sought a speaker for its mass meeting in October 1945 it successively invited Douglas, who was unable to attend, and then Doyle. Douglas was also invited to address a public meeting on child care called by D.C. parents in March 1946.[19]

Other California politicians, importantly including the Republican governor, Earl Warren, also responded to day care activists' letters by calling for continued federal support of the wartime child care program. In mid-September 1945 Governor Warren wrote to President Truman that the end of federal funding for the child care program posed a "serious situation" for his state and observed, "to close the centers abruptly would cause a great wrench in our community life." He stressed the size of the California program, noted that federal war jobs had spurred a great population migration to California, and implied that many of the newcomers lacked family or community ties that would enable them to privately handle child care. Importantly, he also emphasized the number of war service families who relied on the child care program. Finally, and significantly, he suggested that the state itself would be willing to develop a child care funding strategy if given adequate time to act.[20]

War-related arguments aside, the suggestion that California sought continued federal support only until it could devise a child care solution itself played well with congressional appropriators eager to reduce federal budget commitments. The House appropriations subcommittee considering an extension of funding seemed impressed by the latter argument. Chairman Clarence Cannon (D-Mo.) anticipated a promise from Governor Warren that child care would be included in an expected special postwar session of the state legislature, and a member of the California state Assembly, Gardiner Johnson (R-Berkeley), entered a statement with Rep. Cannon's committee that implied broad support for child care in the California legislature. He reported that after holding a daylong hearing on the issue the Assembly's Interim Committee on Education had unanimously asked Governor Warren to place child care on the legislative agenda and that it had urged federal legislators, the FWA, and President Truman to support California's child care centers "until the full effect of the war has terminated." A further sign of broad interest among state legislators was a separate daylong hearing on continued child care services held by the Interim Committee on State Training Schools for Boys and Girls of the state Senate. The committee called for continued federal child care funding until "such time when it can be definitely assured the whole country has in fact returned to a peacetime normalcy."[21]

The FWA initially responded to the call for more time to plan for postwar child care services by asserting that every state had been given ample warning that child care funds would be discontinued with the end of the war. California politicians countered that the fighting had ended abruptly, and noted that state law forbade the appropriation of state tax revenues for support of the child care program. Other states may have had similar laws in place, and state legislatures generally met only one or two months annually or biennially. Thus even if a state sought to carry a program forward, child care advocates argued, there would need to be time for a legislative session to convene, study the issue, and act.[22] The large number of servicemen's wives in California whose need for child care could be explicitly tied to the war, combined with the promise of significant state action, were no doubt key to President Truman's request for extended funding and the eventual agreement by Congress to allow the program to continue, with federal subsidy, until the end of February 1946.

Arguing for Child Care in Sacramento

Despite widespread support for publicly provided child care, the struggle in California's state capital to ensure a continued program appeared no less daunting than it had been in the nation's capital. Much of the high-powered political advocacy for the child care program focused on immediate war-related reconversion concerns and gave little, if any, attention to what permanent needs or rationales might exist for publicly subsidized child care. Even the effort to allow state and local administration of federal money for the wartime child care program had been controversial in Sacramento. Fearing that the program would outlive the war and might require other public funds, California legislators had enacted specific prohibitions against the use of state and local funds for child care. Wartime opponents of child care, like those of the postwar period, argued that the centers would destroy the family; some labeled the program communistic and others considered it too costly.[23]

Some of the most enthusiastic wartime backers of the California centers were war industrialists. Company officials raised concerns about labor shortages, turnover, and absenteeism among women workers (attributed to child care problems) as reason enough to establish child care centers. Eventually the war-related, "patriotic" rationale for public child care forced grudging accommodation, and in 1943 the state legislature formally gave school districts the right to solicit federal Lanham Act funds to operate child care facilities. A few districts had gone ahead without explicit approval, but the new law opened the way for an explosion of subsidized child care across California. Just twenty-nine federally funded centers operated across California in March 1943; three months later 167 were running. By June 1945 a cumulative total of 536 child care centers had been established statewide.[24]

Promoters of publicly subsidized wartime day care in California did not become quiescent once the first centers arrived. Social welfare advocates, labor unions, and war production contractors called on Congress to expand and continue money for wartime child care services. Pragmatically they campaigned to promote the funding of a child care service by first establishing its importance to essential war production and only secondarily mentioning the welfare of children.[25] Nationally, the Children's Bureau decried the focus on war production as a rationale for child care. In California, by contrast, the state wartime Child Care Coordinating Committee was led by southern Californians, including those with strong ties to both business and social welfare agencies, who embraced the wartime rationale apparently without reservation. The Child Care Coordinating Committee's executive secretary, George D. Nickel, was a social worker trained at the University of Southern California who had been a field worker in California's State Relief Administration during the Depression. By wartime Nickel had moved on to become a lobbyist and regional representative for a consumer finance corporation. His secretary and business office (in the Los Angeles Chamber of Commerce Building) served as the Child Care Coordinating Committee's staff and headquarters.[26]

With the war ended, the urgency brought to the argument for child care services by employers disappeared as quickly as the lucrative federal war

production contracts that fueled the need for increased wartime employment of women, though for a time the Child Care Coordinating Committee, especially through Nickel and its social welfare connections, continued
to lobby for publicly funded child care. But a potent new source of postwar
child care advocacy emerged among parents who used the service. Group
child care, long stigmatized as a charity for the poor (compounded in wartime by fears of childrearing by the government), had not always received
support from parents. Lois Meek Stolz, a well-placed state employee and
early childhood educator, recalled that during his last two years in office
(1940–42) Governor Culbert Olson was "besieged" by mothers who peti-
tioned for child care provisions. But a report in 1945 from the state Department of Education noted that when the child care program began "mothers were inclined to view with suspicion the government suggestion that
Child Care Centers could be satisfactory for their children."[27] To counter
any skepticism, in southern California the wartime Citizens' Manpower
Committee planned to sponsor billboards, posters, radio announcements,
press attention, window displays, and motion pictures that would advertise
the availability of child care and encourage mothers to use it. Ultimately
the avid postwar support of child care by parents who used the centers is testament to the high esteem in which they held the centers and their confidence in the care their children received. Day care users emerged as a
forceful and significant bloc among the activists who launched what the
Education Department called "vociferous and unrelenting" protests to the
proposed closing of the centers.[28]

A statewide parents' committee would not emerge for several years, but
in the meantime more local groups organized across the state on behalf of
publicly subsidized child care. Acting within two weeks of the closing announcement and no doubt aided by community activists, parents at each
child care center in Los Angeles organized and appointed representatives to
attend an early evening meeting dedicated to preserving a child care service. At the meeting, on August 28, 1945, a crowd of approximately four
hundred spilled outdoors and into the hallways at the Van Ness Avenue
School.[29] The meeting included educators and featured speeches from two
local members of the state Assembly, Ernest Debs (D-R) and Augustus
Hawkins (D-R). Both legislators gave strong support to the child care service
and in the legislative session that opened in January 1945 had sought, unsuccessfully, to win supplemental state funding for the wartime program.[30]
Parents in northern California organized similarly, and by late August 1945
anyone could see that the California wartime child care program would not
simply fade away.[31] Dispatched to attend the child care meeting in Los An-

geles on August 28, a representative of the governor's office relayed notice that attendees had agreed on a letter-writing campaign directed at the governor and aimed at securing child care as an agenda item for the state legislature's upcoming special session. (The governor had the sole power to set the legislative agenda in this instance.) Noting that plans were made for an even larger child care meeting to be held downtown in the upcoming week, the aide suggested that if Governor Warren intended to allow the child care program to be debated at the next legislative session, "it would relieve a great deal of emotional steam . . . to so announce at or before this meeting. This would transfer the emotional pressure from you to the Federal administration and to the Legislature."[32]

A meeting in downtown Los Angeles in early September drew a crowd of twelve hundred and extended the letter-writing campaign in support of the child care service to include state legislators, but Governor Warren deferred any announcement. These early meetings and letter-writing campaigns likely received major impetus from social welfare activists, educators, and sympathetic legislators, but parents quickly raised their own voice.[33] "Today [September 17, 1945] representatives of the parents and children of 90 nursery schools formed a parents council for the purpose of marshaling all community forces to work for the continuation of the child-care center program," wrote the executive secretary of the Los Angeles group, Marjorie Rowe. Members of the Parents Council worked with child care center personnel to determine tactics and strategies in their campaign for a continued child care program. At the state level they visited key state legislators to urge their support and to invite them to visit a child care center in their district, so that they could see firsthand the kind of work being done. Some parents traveled to Sacramento to lobby in person.[34]

According to the Los Angeles Times, the Parents Council secured the conditional support of Sen. Jack Tenney (R-Los Angeles). Tenney served for most of the 1940s as the zealous head of California's Un-American Activities Committee, and during the most recent legislative session he had branded as "communistic" a measure permitting California schools to operate nursery schools. The chair of the Parents Council, Mrs. Marian Grenier, reported that after meeting with her Tenney had agreed to support the child care service, on the condition that the centers exclusively serve children of working mothers, that a minimum fee be charged, and that "at least 3,000 mothers will qualify to avail themselves of these schools."[35]

Removing Tenney's almost certain opposition to the bill was a crucial step, but the child care program won a true advocate in the statehouse after a first-term Assembly member, Ernest Geddes (R-D–Pomona), received an invitation to speak at a parents' meeting, at the Baldwin Park center in his district. The meeting was dedicated to keeping the centers open in peacetime. "I told them as an economy-minded Republican I couldn't do anything about it," Geddes remembered several years later. Curious about the program, however, he decided to investigate the work of the centers himself. "The next morning I snuck over to the center anonymously to take an honest look. I watched the children play, heard them say Grace before their meals. Something happened inside of me and I haven't been the same since!" A Republican who rarely faced Democratic opposition during his fifteen years in the Assembly, Geddes backed moderate child care legislation and was well positioned—and inclined—to bring together the array of conservative and liberal forces within the coalition of child care advocates. Although his district on the outer eastern edge of Los Angeles County included only one child care center, Geddes adopted the program as his "contribution to social welfare in our State," and he worked closely with child care workers and parents to keep the program alive through its long temporary status. Reflecting on his career many years after his retirement, he named permanent Child Care Centers as among his proudest accomplishments.[36]

Until state support for the child care service could be enacted, the Parents Council had called for an extension of federal funds to ensure the "welfare of the children and the economic stability of the parents and the community."[37] Although the stated concern for "stability" could be read as a reference to war reconversion, the group did not specifically mention a wartime rationale in this early letter, and a large portion of California's grassroots day care promoters seemed interested in a permanent program from the start of their postwar activism. A reporter for the *Los Angeles Times* described "overwhelming sentiment favoring continuation of war established Child Care Centers" among the "audience of about 200 persons, mostly women" at a state Assembly committee hearing on September 25: "A luckless witness who suggested putting the brakes on, that we have gone far enough in socializing the family and the individual and that 'schools are to train and educate children and not to wipe their noses' was met with feminine boos, hisses and other exclamations of disapproval." A nursery school professional laughingly rejoined that the child care centers aimed through their health programs to make wiping children's noses unnecessary, and her comment brought applause from the audience. Witnesses who advocated a permanent program at this hearing ranged from those who called for the state to help "parents in distress cases—mothers without husbands or fathers without wives, or similar cases" to union supporters who proposed a pro-

Ernest Debs (left) and Ernest Geddes (right), members of the California Assembly, visit a state Child Care Center (undated). Courtesy of Virginia Geddes Dukes.

gram open to any working mother, to child care workers who "stressed the value" of preschool education "to the child, the parents and society."[38]

Like the mothers in the District of Columbia and Cleveland, California women cited their absolute need to work as a rationale for a permanent day care program, but given a different political context (and perhaps encouraged by organizers of letter-writing campaigns) they seemed more free to rest their call for a publicly funded child care service on appeals to personal satisfaction or references to their "rights" as citizens and taxpayers. "My whole future depends on the decision," one mother from Los Angeles wrote as she urged Governor Warren to take action in support of the child care centers. Noting the sense of accomplishment she felt as a single mother who maintained the family expenses and sought to offer her eight-year-old son a "balanced life," she added: "Personal satisfaction should score somewhat too. Parents of the children who stay at Child Care Centers are busy people. We work all day—then hurry home to take care of our family. I often thank God that my little family is healthy and happy and that I have this reason to hurry home."[39]

In a "Readers Editorial" in the *Los Angeles Times* in early September

1945, one woman whose preschoolers attended the child care program described the service as a "vast-boon to mothers." Many mothers and young parents, she continued, wanted the program to be a "permanent institution." The program served the needs of children and their parents. Mothers were assured that their children received good food and constant, trained supervision in the secure environs of the public school ground; at the same time children happily found "congenial playmates." Displaying confidence in the importance of expert knowledge for childrearing, she added that "the average housewife or business-woman cannot properly and efficiently entertain busy young hands hour after hour as well as the thoroughly trained teachers in this group of selected folk can do."[40] In a neatly typed, lengthy letter, a mother from Hollywood, writing as one who "votes to put our Legislatures into office and pays my quota to the maintenance of our institutions," described the child care service as an essential builder of strong citizens in a country full of crowded city streets and limited housing. "Quite apart . . . from my [need to support family] and personal interest in having the Nursery Schools continued," she wrote, "it seems to me to be eminently desirable that this be done, nay a national necessity."[41]

The Welfare Council of Los Angeles also offered economic and social service reasons for a permanent program. A precursor to the United Way of Los Angeles, the Welfare Council sought foremost to promote sound social welfare planning in the region. The Emergency Child Care Committee (ECCC), funded by the council during wartime, drew from a spectrum of community interests. In the early postwar debate the committee duly noted that many women supported their families, but it went on to assert that the working mothers who used the day care centers were "essential to the peacetime economy." As many as 75 percent, the committee reported, held "normal peacetime occupations." In addition, the ECCC noted that some of these working mothers served important community needs as registered nurses and public schoolteachers. Both occupations were presumed female and experienced severe labor shortages in the early postwar period.[42]

By late November 1945 Governor Warren had received requests for well over 150 separate items to be included in the agenda for the upcoming special session of the state legislature, but "the largest volume of correspondence" concerned the child care program. Women, many of them working mothers, were the most frequent correspondents on this issue and represented a critical and substantial pressure group.[43] Ultimately, Governor Warren selected fifty-three items for the special session's postwar agenda—including specifically the child care program, along with housing, urban redevelopment, agricultural research, race relations, veterans services, and other issues. Taking a cautious approach, in his announcement of the post-war agenda in January 1946 Governor Warren highlighted the continued need of servicemen's families to use the centers and called it "imperative that the Legislature determine immediately what should be done as long as this condition exists." But he also left open the door for a non-emergency rationale for the centers when he asked the politicians to decide "what the permanent policy of the State towards these institutions is to be."[44]

Recommending that he sign the initial legislation passed to continue the wartime centers temporarily, Governor Warren's legislative secretary noted that no objections had been received and that "a large volume of correspondence favoring provision of Child Care Centers has arrived in the office." A moderate Republican who "insisted that rapid wartime and postwar growth necessitated the expansion of a host of state services," Governor Warren signed the child care bill on February 20, 1946. Muting the legislature's call for a program with access limited by financial need, Governor Warren released a statement essentially asking the State Department of Education not to enact too strict an eligibility test. "We should take a liberal attitude when applying laws that deal with human needs," he asserted.[45]

Framing the Public's Interest in Child Care

In both Cleveland and the District of Columbia the end of the war brought a reassignment of publicly subsidized day care from education to welfare supervision and administration. This change did not occur in California. The state's child care program became linked both administratively and in the minds of parents and other advocates with the state's prized public school system. The administrative location of the program had important consequences for how California parents could frame the public's interest in day care. Within a public welfare framework, the child welfare rationale suggested that day care would be limited to families with some special need; within an education framework, theoretically any family and child could benefit from the service. Professional social workers and educators made arguments for day care within these frameworks and the prominent role of educators in the California debate gave California's day care users an indispensable boost.

Both social workers and nursery school educators believed that a child care program should be child-centered and should seek to foster the physical, social, and emotional development of young children. And by World War II, both groups of professionals understood their service as a "supplement" and not a "substitute" to the home. But the views of social workers and educators on the importance of a child care program diverged precisely along their distinct lines of professional learning. Social workers drew on their clinical understanding of the family and their training in casework management to insist that only certain children might need a supplement to full-time maternal care. They argued that with their expert abilities and knowledge, and through "counseling" of mothers who sought to enroll their children in a center, they could identify which families needed supplemental care. By contrast, nursery school educators, steeped in child development theory, emphasized that every parent could be taught better child-rearing skills and that every child could benefit from some expert, nonmaternal care. If the early childhood educators' assertion of the value of group experience and out-of-the home learning for young children sounded novel in 1945, social workers' contention that full-time maternal care nearly always served children's best interests reconfirmed long-held societal values about motherhood and family life.[46] Paradoxically, while both social workers and early childhood educators made claims on the administration and definition of California's child care program, unanimous agreement about the importance or meaning of this service did not exist in either profession. The lukewarm attitude toward the centers by both the state's Education and Social Welfare departments demonstrated considerable ambivalence toward child care in both fields. While some professionals within the state agencies had feuded over who exercised administrative control of the program during the war, interest in the program appears to have been driven by individual educators and welfare workers rather than the bureaucracies as a whole.[47]

The Welfare Council of Metropolitan Los Angeles, along with the San Francisco Community Chest, was among the social welfare groups calling for continued operation of California's Child Care Center program in the immediate postwar period.[48] And at legislative fact-finding hearings held across the state in 1946, 1950, and 1954, various private welfare groups sought to include funding for counseling and casework in the state's child care program (whether as part of the Education Department or the Social Welfare Department). But enthusiasm for publicly supported child care from these private welfare groups and workers does not appear to have caught on with the State Department of Social Welfare (SDSW). At repeated public hearings on the program, the SDSW did not seek the right to administer the child care program, or even to speak for or against its existence. In 1948 the department's director, Charles Wollenberg, wrote a letter to Governor Warren that stopped just short of recommending that the governor veto legislation to continue the child care program. "At the present moment we are confronted with increased unemployment in the industrial centers as well as in the agricultural centers," Wollenberg noted. "This bill in many instances will prevent employment of bread winners who should be supporting a family because the fact that a wife whose husband is employed will be able to park her child at partial expense of the state while she occupies a position that might be filled by someone in need."[49] Wollenberg's obvious hostility to women's wage earning and preference for male breadwinners sounds anachronistic for a public agency in forward-thinking California, but it rang true to the official, Progressive-era state policy regarding women and children.[50] The SDSW after all administered California's Aid to Dependent Children (ADC) program, which provided government pensions to poor mothers and their children in the absence of male economic support.[51]

As Sonya Michel has argued, by enshrining ADC as the single public policy toward poor mothers and their children, policymakers foreclosed the option of tax-supported child care services without ever truly discussing them. Certainly opponents of public day care in both Cleveland and the District of Columbia had offered the ADC program as proof that public policy toward poor women and their children dictated full-time motherhood and not support of childrearing and wage earning through subsidized day care. (The most conservative voices in California would repeat this same argument.) As the administrator of federal and state pensions to dependent mothers with children, California's SDSW bureaucrats could easily see the state child care program as a competing and less legitimate form of aid.[52]

Although the question of administration never disappeared completely, for much of the first fifteen years following the war the State Department of Social Welfare limited its involvement with day care administration to its long-established function as a licensing authority for a variety of child welfare institutions. Apparently ceding control of the public child care program to the Education Department, in November 1945 the SDSW claimed licensing jurisdiction over any private group care facility that enrolled children under the age of kindergarten admittance. A court challenge brought by an independent preschool operator in 1950 confirmed the SDSW's regulatory assertion, and many privately run, part-day programs that viewed their work as expressly educational continued to chafe under the imprimatur of a "welfare" agency for decades to come. As if rubbing salt in this wound, the public child care service, increasingly designed to serve low-income families in full-day programs, did not fall under the welfare agency's licensing authority.[53]

Like the State Department of Social Welfare, California's Education Department showed less interest in the child care program than did individual education advocates; unlike the SDSW, the department could not avoid a high profile in the postwar debate because the legislature had created a state administrative role for it in the wartime child care program. Rather than simply allow local school districts to use federal money to operate a child care service, state lawmakers required the Education Department to grant permits to child care workers and set general standards across all school districts. The decision gave California's child care program a considerably stronger bureaucratic beachhead in the postwar public education system than similar programs had in either Cleveland or the District of Columbia.[54] At the same time, many of the local school districts where the centers operated showed apprehension about the program. The California education bureaucracy shared the fear, also voiced by education officials in the District of Columbia, that a program for preschool children would ultimately drain revenue away from grade-school education, and they similarly doubted that the wartime centers truly served an educational purpose. Speaking at 1946 hearings on preschool policy in California, state education officials supported greater public funding of kindergarten and nursery schools but reserved final judgment on the child care program. Child care centers, they believed, met particular rather than general needs and were thus "essentially different in character" from nursery schools.[55]

The field of early childhood education grew up independently of much of the established public education system. Apart from kindergartens, which had been advocated for nearly seventy-five years in the United States, the public schools largely ignored the early childhood field. Nursery schools, which were associated with demonstration research on early childhood development and catered to younger children than kindergartens, generally did not open in the United States until the 1920s. In mid-1946 the National Education Association conducted a survey of attitudes toward including preschool programs in the public school system: among thirty-three state education departments surveyed, public kindergartens were supported by more than 80 percent of respondents but nursery schools by only 50 percent and child care programs by only a third. At the local level the survey found even less support for preschool programs. Among 203 city education boards surveyed, kindergartens were supported by a large majority of respondents but nursery schools by only a quarter and child care programs by only 17 percent.[56]

As the survey made clear child care centers maintained the most precarious position in the preschool hierarchy. When the District of Columbia's public school superintendent declared in 1946 that child care programs did not have educational value and thus could only be understood as "social welfare projects" he evidently stated a relatively common understanding among his colleagues.[57] Despite the involvement in child care of public schools administrators and facilities, the California Public School Superintendents' Association did not define the state's Child Care Centers as an educational program that incidentally gave children care and supervision but rather as one "primarily designed for the custody and physical care of the children."[58]

The reason why child care was seen as a social welfare rather than an educational concern stemmed from a view that it properly served only a selected group of families. As a spokesperson for California's State Department of Education testified in 1946, "the criterion [for Child Care Centers] is the necessity that parents be away from their children." This brought a class distinction to peacetime public support for child care that had not existed during the war. Although the wartime program only served children of working mothers, the meaning of this limitation changed as public support for female employment declined. In peacetime it was initially understood that only mothers from very low-income families would (or should) continue to seek work outside the home; this in turn meant that only the working poor would need a subsidized full-day child care service. A program premised on the needs of employed mothers could not be understood as an educational program available to all.[59]

California's public child care service operated year-round, five or six days a week, and centers were open ten or eleven hours a day. Some staff members were poorly trained, but a substantial minority had kindergarten, elementary school, or higher teaching credentials and for many years would battle the notion among their colleagues that they were simply "baby-sitters" masquerading as educators. Although the treatment accorded to Child Care Center workers no doubt varied by school district, two workers with long careers in early childhood education recalled being barred from teachers' restrooms because the principal insisted that they weren't teachers. Furthermore, when they participated in school district meetings, elementary school representatives were identified as teachers while all Child Care Center representatives were simply "ladies."[60]

Not only did child care teachers encounter hostility from elementary school educators for decades, they also found an uneasy acceptance among some of their apparent allies in the field of early childhood education. For these educators the notion of day care, with a prototypically low-income clientele, seemed to jeopardize their claims to be professionals who applied "pure" child development research to educate and enrich young children. The prototypical nursery school would be operated by all professional educators, stay open for only part of the day, and remain closed during the summer. Although the child development theory that provided a rationale for nursery school education applied to all children, privately run programs effectively excluded the children of low-income families where a mother worked: many of the programs necessarily charged high fees to maintain their operations, and their part-day schedule presumed that someone would be available to pick up a child from the nursery school in midday. These differences caused some early childhood education professionals to draw a strong distinction between the program intent and activities of a part-day nursery school and the intent and activities of a full-day child care program.[61]

As relative newcomers to the education fraternity, nursery school educators sought to shore up the public's understanding of what they did as purely educational. At a legislative hearing on preschool programs in 1946, an official of the Association for Childhood Education (ACE) dismissed the state's Child Care Centers as not a part of the education system. The program's "set up indicates child care, not teaching," she explained. The ACE feared that too rapid an expansion of preschool programs would sacrifice the quality of the program for the needed quantity of teachers. While the ACE supported nursery schools, it recommended against establishing a statewide program until many more trained teachers were available.[62] More than a decade later, tension continued between part-day and full-day early childhood educators. When the National Association for Nursery Education (NANE), one of the oldest professional associations for early childhood educators, held a symposium on day care in 1957, the well-attended proceeding remained an "unofficial" part of the group's biennial conference. One observer noted: "An interesting demonstration of feeling boiled out at the conclusion of this session in which the full day care people present expressed considerable feeling that the executive board of NANE was not giving them program representation, and that the full day care members were not being given due recognition." He continued, "There was feeling expressed that the nursery school group does not understand the day care program," and child care workers said "they wished 'integration' with NANE, not 'segregation.'"[63]

Owing in no small part to their facilities, locations, and administrative capabilities, schools had been the natural and legislatively prescribed location for all but a handful of the wartime child care centers. In the postwar period, despite the misgivings of some educators, a number of factors continued to favor the placement of California's Child Care Center program within the State Department of Education.[64] Undoubtedly a most decisive issue was that a core group of state child care workers, who identified themselves as education professionals, organized themselves to retain the public program and to upgrade its status and their own. Cooperating with and enlisting parents who used the centers, these workers provided an important network of support for the program. In daily contact with each parent using the centers, they were in the best position to organize meetings at centers and to help coordinate letter-writing campaigns.[65]

Another significant and unique advantage for Californians who sought to cast the child care service as an education program was the relative dearth of private charitable day nurseries in the state. This was especially true in southern California, where the largest wartime program emerged. By 1940 the entire county of Los Angeles, with a total population of nearly 2.8 million, housed only nine licensed nonprofit and commercial day nurseries. Los Angeles had no strong history or presence of charitable day nurseries, in part because when concerns about burgeoning "unassimilated" immigrant populations in the late nineteenth century first prompted a great expansion of philanthropic day nurseries in the east (and in San Francisco), southern California was just emerging as a destination for white, Protestant, middle-class residents from other states. The growth of a large white, Protestant population did not, however, submerge the Catholic influence developed during the long history of Spanish and Mexican rule in the region. Many of the oldest social welfare advocates were agencies associated with the Los Angeles Catholic Archdiocese, which operated a very small number of day nurseries. Except in wartime, the Catholic Church believed that this limited kind of day care was as it should be; as they had in Cleveland, Catholic Church leaders in California emerged as early opponents of public funding for child care.[66]

California's public education administrators and practitioners, again especially in the south, appear to have entered the war with a much stronger connection to services for children of preschool age than their counterparts in Cleveland and the District of Columbia. In the Los Angeles school district a small number of day care centers emerged as part of the school program soon after the state's Compulsory Education Law of 1910 began to be enforced. The program, operated in part by volunteers and funded by parents' fees and school district money, was designed to relieve school-age children of the responsibility to care for younger siblings—thus allowing them to escape a truancy charge. Initiated by a local Parent Teacher Association, the program received formal support and supervision from the local school board in 1917 and a decade later had grown to twenty centers that enrolled about fourteen hundred children. The Los Angeles school board also experimented with support for demonstration nursery schools in the late 1920s—rationalized by the need to provide training for current and future parents—and during the Great Depression housed the state's greatest concentration of federally supported nursery schools for children in low-income families. Through a number of key professionals, a significant line of continuity ran from the nursery schools of the 1920s and 1930s to the postwar Child Care Center program. Elizabeth Woods, Theresa Mahler, and Rosalie Blau were among the early childhood educators who established their careers in the Los Angeles public programs, and all three would become key activists for California's postwar statewide child care program.[67]

Significantly as well, California's education system had long received the attention of reformers who sought to make it a model public system. California's women Progressives had been among the nation's earliest, most successful advocates of extending school services downward through the creation of public kindergartens. A little more than a decade after the initial establishment of a kindergarten training school in Los Angeles, a revision of the city charter in 1889 granted to the Los Angeles Board of Education the authority to establish public kindergartens. The kindergarten movement also developed a strong presence in San Francisco, and as early as 1913 the state legislature required establishment of kindergartens by local school districts if a specified number of parents with five-year-olds requested this. Finally in November 1946, in the midst of a renewing Child Care Center debate, California voters overwhelmingly approved a ballot initiative that for the first time provided state funds for kindergartens and thus made them a full-fledged component of the state's general education program.[68]

The momentum and relative status enjoyed by early childhood education in postwar California can also be seen in the actions of the state legislature. Despite formally limiting the child care program to a one-year extension based on the reconversion "emergency," legislators accentuated their permanent potential by grouping Child Care Centers, nursery schools, and kindergartens under a single preschool policy umbrella when it commissioned a legislative committee to study these different programs. The resulting *Technical Staff Report*, prepared for the state legislative session of 1947 and released in January, summarizes committee research into laws, regulations, and opinions about the various programs. The full report, with extensive appendices and tables, ran to 449 printed pages and epitomized the "fact-finding" impulse of California's neo-Progressive political style.[69] It gave legislators ample room to justify a state-subsidized child care program administered by the State Education Department, and noted that any review of the necessity for a child care service should begin by examining the welfare of children, including the program's "educative effect." The report expressed the view that final justification for such a program rested with the state's own need for educated citizens. By raising the question of whether such a large program, one admittedly not entirely about education, should be given to schools to administer, the report removed the professional interests of early childhood educators and social workers from the debate framework and condensed to its most pragmatic level the argument over welfare versus education. The line between education and social welfare had already blurred, it argued—noting the education system's involvement with the school lunch program, vocational guidance, and the administration of some work permits. When choosing between social welfare and education for administrative purposes, the committee concluded that the basic question for legislators should be which group has the best resources to handle the program. "If public schools are best equipped to administer the program this could be decisive."[70]

Pragmatism aside, many state policymakers remained unsure about the need for any child care program in the postwar period. Permanently keeping the service alive necessitated developing a new consensus on why such a program warranted substantial state funding. Advocates of the state Child Care Centers struggled for more than a decade to develop political agreement on permanency. Compared to their opponents, supporters of publicly supported child care centers organized themselves prodigiously and quickly. Parents' groups, civic and social welfare groups, and early childhood educators organized immediately after the war to save the centers from otherwise certain closure. In 1947, after their first legislative victories, these groups formed a loose coalition, the California Committee for Child Care. By 1948 parents' groups created their own statewide body, the California Parents Association for Child Care Centers. A dues-paying organization, the CPACCC sent lobbyists to Sacramento each legislative session and held an annual convention at which they elected regional and statewide representatives to promote their efforts to save the centers. Working primarily through the northern and southern branches of the California Association for Nursery Education, child care workers created a formidable bloc of support for continuing the program, and a Child Care Centers Directors and Supervisors Association eventually grew out of program conferences sponsored by the State Department of Education.[71]

Natalie Fousekis convincingly argues that the parent and child care worker activists drew strength from these largely female networks "while simultaneously collaborating and strategizing with some of California's most powerful men." Assiduously courted by child care workers and parent leaders, these day care advocates included experienced and influential lobbyists (Lawrence Arnstein and George Nickel), officials at the state Department of Education (including John Weber and Frank Wright), and legislators (most significantly Ernest Geddes). Finally, while child care parents and workers made continuing a state program their central mission, support for the Child Care Centers—varying substantially in degree, kind, and persistence—also came from labor unions, veterans' groups, the League of Women Voters, the state Parents and Teachers Association, and the California Communist Party.[72]

In strong contrast to this virtual menagerie of pro–child care organizations, in the last half of the 1940s the Catholic Church stood virtually alone as a well-organized lobbying opponent. By the mid- to late 1950s official Catholic opposition had largely disappeared, but operators of private child care and preschool centers emerged as new opponents. Also, throughout the struggle to maintain California's unique program, advocates faced formidable ideological opposition to state support of day care, as well as fiscal and political opposition from some state legislators—especially those representing rural areas where almost no centers were located.[73]

The Family under Siege and a Necessary Answer to Why Mothers Work

Advocates and opponents of Child Care Centers shared a belief in the centrality of the family unit to the health of American society. Yet everywhere around them they saw real or imagined threats to traditional families. An unprecedented number of women, and especially married women, were leaving their homes to work for wages. Massive wartime mobility separated immediate from extended families and, in the case of servicemen, even husbands from wives, and fathers from their children. Through divorce, separation, and desertion more marriages seemed to be ending than ever before, and juvenile delinquency appeared on the upswing. Depending on one's view, publicly subsidized child care either represented a needed and important salve for all this apparent disintegration or greatly exacerbated the problems.

Advocates for Child Care Centers, importantly including parents who used their services, argued that in the face of all these continuing changes a child care program allowed family members simply to remain together and ensured that others could establish themselves in the traditional American fashion. Further, they asserted that Child Care Centers both curbed juvenile delinquency and reduced its potential by training young children in the duties and values of democratic citizenship. Opponents countered that the centers had exactly the opposite effect. The centers had been a wartime contingency only; in peacetime they needlessly broke up families by encouraging women to seek employment rather than attend to household duties. Thus to provide child care for families was to weaken them by removing the function of childrearing from the home, and enabling high levels of divorce and desertion. Finally, in the minds of some, the child care program represented a direct assertion of state rather than family responsibility for childrearing; this aspect of the program made it "communistic" and certainly, opponents argued, incapable of instilling democratic citizenship values in children.

Parents clearly saw a continuing need for child care unrelated to the demands of war. In letters, testimony, and lobbying, they explained why the state should maintain support of the Child Care Centers. "Child care is not an emergency provision for women required to work as a result of the war but as a matter of fact is a necessary social development, here to stay, and inevitably tied in with our peacetime economy," declared the Parents Council for Child Care Centers in Los Angeles.[74] Stating that the war had only led government to recognize the need for child care services by magnifying the problem, the Federation of Parents for Child Care Centers attributed the postwar growth in women's employment to a rapidly rising cost of living and an increasing number of "broken homes."[75] A mother from Los Angeles struck a more dire warning note in her letter to the governor in December 1946, but she also suggested that Child Care Centers could save the day: "Face it Governor; Face it America, the American home is broken. War casualties and emotional maladjustments and economic conditions, forces many a mother to get out and make the living for her family. You *can't* desert *future* America! The Child Care Centers are aware of their great task. Its teachers are trained to mold their impressionable young charges into socialby [*sic*] desirable and trustworthy citizens."[76]

The idea that young children were taught citizenship values in a public, state-sponsored setting, rather than in the home, led opponents to charge that the centers were communistic. Parents countered this charge directly, stating instead that their children learned valuable lessons in democratic citizenship at the centers. "Now I understand, these Child Care Centers are being threatened and worse, being called 'communistic centers'!" one war widow wrote. "If you could see some of them the term 'communistic' would be blasted completely. If these centers do close [I] will again have to lose all contact with my child except to pay for the various bills that boarding out involves. You're not a mother to your child—you're just a pleasant visitor who brings goodies and toys. I can't face that situation again."[77] Like this widow, other mothers argued that affordable and reliable child care preserved rather than weakened or destroyed their families, by permitting them to raise their own children. Parents also remained convinced that their children gained educational and developmental benefits and that this alone justified continuing the program. A mother from Reseda who had been "somewhat amazed" by the progress of her own children after she enrolled them at a public center wrote that Child Care Centers helped young children to gain a "head start toward becoming good, useful citizens." Declaring further that "our social ills can be cured only by education, and education must start very early if it is to have the desired effect," she concluded, "I do not see how a forward looking State like California can afford not be [sic] provide PERMANENT Child Care."[78]

Arguments about educational and developmental benefits to children mattered a great deal more to supporters than opponents, for whom, although the prevention of juvenile delinquency seemed undisputedly good, the whole question of children's best interests could be answered simply by insisting that mothers make childrearing and homemaking their sole vocations. Early critics of the public child care program called on state government to affirm, even reassert, that the proper place for women should be in the home. A prominent social welfare official in the politically important Los Angeles Catholic Archdiocese, Monsignor Thomas J. O'Dwyer, argued that "with the return of peacetime conditions the reintegration of the home should be one of our primary concerns."[79] O'Dwyer and his fellow Catholic social welfare leaders insisted that "everything should be done to enable the mother to retain the child in the home so that she can fulfill her noble responsibility of parent and educator. Day care service should not be extended in conflict with the Aid to [Dependent] Children Program, a liberalization of which would enable more mothers and children to remain at home."[80] Mayor Harley E. Knox of San Diego acknowledged the personal financial necessity of some families for a child care service but strenuously opposed using public money for a child care program. "No encouragement should be given to both parents working and leaving the children in some institution. While it upgrades the standard of [living for] the family," he argued, "it degrades the welfare of the child."[81]

The debate raged for more than a decade, but advocates of permanent publicly supported child care eventually won because most legislators became convinced that the societal changes affecting the family were irreversible. The best way to head off negative consequences, day care advocates successfully argued, would be to forge a new response to the changes. Of critical importance to this argument would be finding a more positive way to understand wage earning by mothers. Two documents from this period are especially clear in indicating how advocates helped to edge public and legislative opinion toward the conclusion that women's wage earning was essential, unavoidable, nonthreatening, and of positive public value. The *Technical Staff Report*, published in January 1947 for the benefit of the legislators considering long-term policy toward preschool children, laid important groundwork. Nearly two years later, with the legislature's continued reliance on the disruptions created by war providing an increasingly anachronistic explanation for continuing the program, educators and parents' groups produced a lengthy pamphlet, *A Brief Inquiry into the Need for a Child Care Program in California*; in it they provided a historical context and explanation for women's wage earning.

The *Technical Staff Report* first attempted to set parameters for thinking about a permanent child care policy. It declared that child care, in contrast to nursery school programs designed for all children, "concerns only the children of mothers who are employed." Importantly, it added that government policy should be "based on conditions as they exist" and that while "policy might be affected by changes in social order it is the effect more than the cause of these changes." Legislators needed only to turn to the detailed summary of findings for an explanation of the "conditions as they exist": "Child care centers exist mainly because of the employment of women in business and industry, either because they have no other source of support, or to augment family income." Although granting women autonomy to maintain a job, the report largely absolved working mothers of young children from the decision to work. Some women took jobs during the war when their employment was encouraged and they simply never left paid work, it explained, and others remained in the workforce because a rapidly advancing cost of living made their earnings necessary for the family. Obliquely referring to a preference for low-wage employees, the report stated that a third factor in women's postwar employment was that the lower wages they earned (compared to men) "affects the labor market for women." And finally, the report noted that "some women prefer to work," before adding reassuringly, "it is evident that whenever women have both economic support and young children, the likelihood of their working fulltime is only 1 to 10."[82]

In contrast to the unwillingness of most politicians in Cleveland and the District of Columbia (and many day care advocates) to think beyond the logic of a private family necessity for women's employment, the *Technical Staff Report* opened up several lines of reasoning for women's peacetime employment based on the strength of society-wide economic forces that brought women into the workforce. Neither women nor their families, in this view, could be blamed for the preference of businesses for lower-waged employees or for the rising cost of living. These rationalizations tended to "depoliticize" the issue of mothers doing paid work by making it a part of what the political theorist Nancy Fraser calls the "official-economic system." While the *deus ex machina* of the economy brought women into the workforce, the report reassured its readers that the social order had not been completely usurped; given an economic choice, mothers of young children apparently didn't want to work. In this way of reasoning the Child Care Centers became a pragmatic public policy response to a relatively small and unthreatening change in the social order.[83]

Early childhood educators exercised chief responsibility for conceiving and drafting *A Brief Inquiry into the Need for a Child Care Program* in 1948, and their roots in the nursery school movement are strongly evident in the pamphlet's section on "Historical Background." The family's growing inability to provide optimal childrearing had been an early conviction of the nursery school movement. Increased urbanization deprived many young children of environmental stimulants that older generations had enjoyed, these pioneers believed, and parents (especially mothers) lacked both the knowledge of child development and the necessary play equipment to compensate for the changed circumstances.[84]

A Brief Inquiry began by asserting that the need for Child Care Centers grew out of the "unprecedented change in our manner of living brought about by the 'industrial revolution' and the consequent growth of urban population." It painted an idyllic past, when a husband, wife, and children harmoniously produced the total needs of their family within a stable rural community—complete with "husking bees, house-raisings, community socials, and community religious services." In this setting, the report continued, a woman's "production of goods by spinning, weaving, sewing, preparing and preserving foods, and by the manufacture of certain articles, was quite comparable, in economic return to the husband's work." Further, the report added, "the education of children took place in a home functional environment, replete with work projects that directly prepared children for their future life on a farm." The industrial revolution had changed all this by removing most economic production from the home to the factory, and crowding together diverse groups of people who lived anonymously in apartment housing. "Where formerly the wife could '*earn*' *and supervise* her family, she must now work *away* from the family if she is to aid in the maintenance of family health and family living standards." The alarming rate of divorce, "which has at times recently reached a ratio of one to one with our marriages," along with "desertions, mental breakdown" and "various forms of crime or sabotage," resulted from the great strains of city living, the argument continued. And what would answer at least some of these "social problems" created by these "largely man-made" urban conditions? "The group issuing this pamphlet believes that Child Care, properly conceived and administered, will constitute **one democratically acceptable means** of reducing the pressure on city people and of preserving and strengthening the city family and its constituent members" (boldface emphasis in original).[85]

As the decade progressed, Californians would develop additional "official-economic" reasons for women's employment. By insisting that women workers represented a necessary resource to win the Cold War—thereby requiring women to leave their homes for the defense plant—California's mammoth defense production sector turned the postwar notion of female "domestic containment" on its head.[86] The general call for "womanpower" to stoke the state's expanding economy and staff defense industries (not referred to, significantly, as war industries) proved important to the child care debate. These nondomestic reasons for women's presence in the workforce encouraged a pragmatic public policy response to the needs created by the employment of mothers with young children. A consensus developed that for a variety of reasons, a significant number of mothers needed to earn wages and therefore the state had an interest in the welfare of those women's children. The growing acceptance of female employment, however, did not lead state lawmakers to support a widely accessible child care program. Instead, this acknowledgment of change simply coexisted with an older conviction that all families should be able to earn sufficient income for full-time, in-home maternal care (still viewed by most as the highest ideal of child welfare) or in some way to make other *private* care arrangements.

Finding the Right Admission Calculus

In early 1946 state legislators had continued the Child Care Centers as a temporary measure during the reconversion to peace. Many certainly assumed that a limited number of mothers might need short-term assistance, but that with the return of servicemen and reestablishment of "normal" peacetime living, demand for publicly provided child care would decline. Within a few months, state education officials administering the funds for the program realized that demand had been miscalculated. Instead of coasting downward, enrollment jumped nearly 16.5 percent and by September approached sixteen thousand.[87]

Employment of women in California decreased immediately after V-J Day but did not decline to prewar levels as many had expected. One indication of women's postwar job intentions and employment is a finding of the Los Angeles Welfare Council that twice as many Child Care Center mothers had sought work in September 1945, immediately after the shutdown of many war industries, as in January 1946. The largest single group of mothers with children enrolled in the Los Angeles Child Care Centers (just under one-quarter) worked in "peacetime" occupations, as secretaries and office clerks. While this had also been true immediately after the war, the survey did report a slight increase in the proportion of mothers who worked as domestics and unskilled laborers, and it noted a comparable decline in the proportion employed as foremen and technicians.[88]

The growing number of children attending the publicly subsidized centers, combined with postwar inflation and less user-fee income than expected, forced state Child Care Center administrators to project a serious shortfall in funds designated for the program. Seeking to avoid shutting down earlier than planned, in September 1946 the State Department of Education instructed local school districts to dramatically raise fees for the child care service and practice other economy measures. Because most school districts continued the wartime practice of charging a flat rate for child care (meaning that regardless of family income, parents paid the same amount of money for the same service), the hike in fees fell hardest on the poorest families. The Los Angeles Parents' Council protested that the rate change priced the child care program out of reach for the most needy families. Approximately one month after the fees were increased, the Council reported "a steady stream of withdrawals from the Child Care Centers, literally by the hundreds, until at present 300 children have left Extended Day services, and we don't know how many from the nursery age centers." The parents' group added that only in "rare instances" had alternative care been found. "In most cases our children are now 'on the streets.'"[89]

If school administrators had hoped that their economy measures would defray costs by stopping the expansion of the program, they were in fact rewarded with an immediate slump in child care enrollments.[90] Shortly, however, officials noted that while "many patrons in the lower economic brackets found it necessary to withdraw their children their places were soon taken by families better able to pay the increased fees because of higher incomes." Rather than reduce the size of the program, the fee change simply made it more middle class. At the same time, higher-income families could not completely replace poorer ones because child care centers served income-stratified neighborhoods. Again, Los Angeles provides an example. A report in early 1946 found 1,547 children on waiting lists for centers in Los Angeles, of whom half lived in the city's better-off Wilshire and Hollywood districts.[91]

The 1947 legislative session opened with continuing protests by day care users that the hike in fees made centers inaccessible to those who most needed them. While legislators voted to extend the public child care program, they worked quickly to reverse the trend in service toward middle-income families. State lawmakers had expressly stipulated that financial need be a condition of access to the public child care service when they began funding the program a year earlier, but they had deferred the specifics to education administrators. Now the legislature took more definite action and wrote into state law income levels above which families would not be eligible to use public child care. Assemblyman Ernest Geddes crafted the bill that included the first maximum income levels. This foray into writing child care legislation marked the beginning of more than a decade of consistent efforts in behalf of the program's continuance; many years later, a retired Geddes explained how his years as a management official in a laundry in southern California prepared him to understand women's presence in the workforce. The majority of a laundry's employees were women, he noted, and "every woman who stands up all day long on a cement floor with her head in the steam and her feet on a floor where it is either very hot or very cold, and always very hard, has to have a job or she wouldn't have that kind of job if she had any choice." This "understanding of the position of those people who worked for one primary reason, which was that they had to live" both confirmed for Geddes the need for publicly provided child care and suited him perfectly to steer the politically moderate (even somewhat conservative) course that proved essential for its survival.[92]

The legislature's enactment of a specific income test in 1947, along with its adoption of the principle of fees charged on a sliding scale, capped a yearlong debate about how best to determine eligibility for public child care. Parents, social workers, and educators brought separate opinions to this public discussion. Their arguments demonstrate the difficulty of defining need and also illustrate how the professional interests of educators and social workers differed. Social workers disputed the legislators' presumption that a family's income level should be the primary basis for determining eligibility. Instead, they argued that a properly targeted program, one that ensured both private family health and accumulated public social and economic benefits, could best be obtained through a system of casework and counseling. "If the admission of the applicant is without a prior careful scientific social study, the real needs of the children and families will not be met and a great part of the value of the Child Care Centers will be lost," one social work partisan explained.[93]

Social workers' advocacy of casework and counseling could also be argued as a way to bring greater precision to the problem of both directing the service toward families with "real" need and obtaining the highest public cost savings (through prevention of juvenile delinquency or other social problems). Explaining this sorting process before a California legislative committee, one social worker, Joseph Andriola, described his experience in a mid-sized town in Michigan, where public demand for child care at first suggested a need for four centers. Through casework and counseling, however, community leaders determined that only one center should be supported. "We found only a small percentage of the initial requests really involved placing children in the centers," Andriola explained. "Inquiry by our staff of social workers found that sometimes the mother wanted to leave her husband and get a job to be independent. Another mother of four—two to nine years—with a husband in service, really wanted to be home, so she supplemented her allotment with neighborhood jobs. Others wanted to pay off a mortgage or pay doctor's bills but often the clothes, transportation, and expenses incidental to working and placing the children in a center were nearly equal to the additional income." By contrast to these families, deemed not well served by group day care, Andriola went on to cite several instances involving the emotional health of the mother or the social development of a specific child, where a child care service could be beneficial.[94]

California educators and parents strongly objected to this kind of scrutiny for Child Care Center applicants. "The autonomy of the home, so greatly prized by Americans, would be invaded were it necessary for eligibility to be established through the judgment of individual case workers," they insisted. "Most families who have sought Child Care service have found it a major factor in the **solution** of their home problems" (boldface emphasis in original). Family autonomy aside, the cost of setting up a statewide service to provide casework and counseling—estimated by some at $650,000 annually —likely provided the strongest inoculation against the prospect that the legislature would approve a program administered by social workers.[95]

Drawing from their conviction of education's universal value, educators were reluctant to identify any particular subset of families as being especially in need of child care. Doing so, they believed, undercut their argument that the program served educational rather than social welfare concerns. They took pride in the service they could offer. Had there been no requirement that a mother be employed, one early childhood educator proudly insisted, California's wartime centers, instead of peaking at around 25,000 children, would have enrolled as many as 100,000.[96]

Thus the state legislative stipulation in February 1946 that child care services be available only to those parents who were working and "financially unable to provide otherwise" for their children's care introduced unwelcome new duties for child care directors. Forced to formulate admission standards, they turned to a standard budget as a general indicator of eligibility. Some child care educators, however, believed that these numbers should serve only as a benchmark, not an absolute cutoff; even after the legislature enacted explicit and much more restrictive maximum wage levels in 1947, some child care workers pointedly refused to investigate the income claims made by applicants or, as one administrator put it, "get into Social Welfare work."[97]

The legislature in 1946 had passed final admission authority to local school districts, but it expected the State Department of Education to provide guidance. The recommendations released by the department suggested that education officials had taken to heart Governor Warren's admonition to "show a liberal attitude." State lawmakers had granted a specific across-the-board exemption from the financial means test to any family connected to the armed services; the Education Department embroidered its own "exempt" class into the Child Care Center program by recommending that many parents should have unrestricted access to the centers based on their *kind* of employment. Citing the statute's intended purpose "to prevent the . . . disruption of the economic life of the State by the immediate withdrawal from essential industry and services of persons charged with the care of minor children," state education officials recommended that parents who were teachers, nurses, or in "other industr[ies] or occupation[s] essential to the public welfare or in the public interest" should not be subject to the financial means test.[98] A survey of admission standards in 1946 shows that many California centers did indeed make exceptions for teachers, nurses, and others in "essential industry." Other center administrators cited extenuating circumstances, such as "large doctor's bills, debts, [and] loans," as part of their admission criteria. The San Francisco school district, which admitted "veterans with new jobs and debts" and "families conducting joint businesses," appeared to be among the most expansive in its admission practices. By contrast, centers in Santa Barbara and rural Porterville reported limiting attendance to families with maximum income levels well below the guidelines suggested by their fellow educators in 1946 and even below the much more restrictive limits established by the legislature in 1947.[99]

In short, while the written admission practices recommended by the Education Department and local school districts remained liberal, criteria for access to public child care also drew from local and sometimes more conservative community mores. The ideal of universal access to public education had frequently fractured along racial and ethnic fault lines. Child Care Centers in California were not an exception. Although segregation was not legislated by the state, neither was it prohibited, and public Child Care Centers, like the school systems with which they were associated, might effectively separate groups of children through administrative exclusion.[100]

California's public child care program in general admitted children from a wide range of racial and ethnic backgrounds. A survey of attendance in Los Angeles city public Child Care Centers in 1949 found that close to one-third of the children enrolled were "Negro, Mexican, or Oriental."[101] Immediately after the war a serviceman's wife had approvingly noted the "policy of nondiscrimination so adequately and smoothly enforced" at the center her child attended.[102] A year later a veteran's wife from Los Angeles praised the "racial tolerance" that her son learned at the public center he attended.[103] And in 1951 a mother from Millbrae wrote: "At the care center, my child learns to get along with children of all races and religions, which is the American way of life that we are striving for in Korea, and which men died for in the last war."[104]

This kind of racial openness undoubtedly did not greet all parents who sought access to the state child care service. Tse Hua Chang, a Chinese graduate student in southern California, visited some of the public centers in Los Angeles in 1949 and reported both positive "intercultural aspects" and "racial prejudice." Observing that children seemed eager to play with each other regardless of race or ethnicity, Chang identified the head teacher —the top staff member who handled admissions and day-to-day supervision at a given center—as key to setting the center atmosphere. She noted approvingly that head teachers were both African American and white, and that they were assisted by Mexican Americans, Japanese Americans, and other blacks and whites. She regretted, however, that not all centers had integrated staffs, which she felt would have produced a more positive racial attitude, and she added that although the standard application form did not require a photo or any mention of national origin or race, some of the public centers were considered solely "Caucasian." Chang cited one head teacher who told her, "'My children are almost all Anglo-Americans, but I have two Japanese-Americans. Even though some families of Mexican backgrounds live in the neighborhood, still I don't think their children can come to my center because they are so dirty and cannot follow my regulations.' She said this with a very disagreeable expression," Chang added. "It was realized that she felt racial prejudice and did not want to talk to a Chinese [person]."[105] Chang's experience suggests that head teachers might have considerable leeway to deny public child care to applicants, even if those applicants met the legislated means test and other eligibility standards. Apart from a long history of segregation in California's education system, discrimination in admittance to private and commercial child care services remained commonplace in postwar California. The California State Department of Social Welfare issued a first directive barring discrimination at state-licensed day care and other child welfare facilities in August 1963.[106]

Regardless of their race, ethnicity, or economic class, parents saw themselves as the most accurate judges of their own need for publicly subsidized child care. They sought the freedom to use public day care as they chose, or at the very least to help shape the rules of access. Indeed as it became clear that legislators and education officials were making decisions sharply affecting who could use the Child Care Centers, parents protested loudly. Parents in Los Angeles met to "voic[e] their alarm" after the Education Department's directive in summer 1946 increased their user fees by as much as 100 percent. In a detailed letter to Roy Simpson, California's superintendent of public instruction, the group strenuously protested the Education Department's assertion that the steep fee increase was the "least objectionable alternative" for dealing with a projected income deficit for the centers. "We know of nothing more objectionable than taking a program that our legislative representatives recognized as necessary and voted on for our use, and making it inaccessible by settling on a fee impossible for us to pay," the group wrote. "This least objectionable alternative was chosen without any consultation with those most affected and without any adequate hearing where we might present our case." The Parents Council requested a return to prior fee levels until a new solution to the deficit could be found. Finally, because of the city's substantial number of Child Care Center users, the group called for "open hearings in Los Angeles where people can express themselves on the fees."[107]

Declaring that the standards for economic eligibility being prepared by the State Department of Education in 1946 were "undesirable" and "unnecessary," the San Francisco Child Care Council, composed of both parents and child care workers, voiced equally strong opinions about the right of parents to determine their own access to the program. "[The standards] would assume for the State the right of determining what shall be an adequate standard of living, and in effect dictates to specific families what their income shall be. This is a measure of interference in family affairs grossly at variance, we believe, with the principles of our government . . . since an accurate determination of financial necessity for use of the Child Care facilities can only be made by the parents themselves. They are the persons best informed and best qualified to make this determination." To comply with the letter and spirit of the law the group suggested that each parent sign a simple statement attesting to his or her financial need of publicly subsidized child care, and like the Los Angeles group, San Francisco parents insisted on consultation: "We should like to be advised of public hearings on this issue in order that we may present further testimony in support of our position."[108]

Parents frequently understood "financial need" in different and more expansive ways than legislators and administrators did. Letter writers described child care as giving their families a deserved and necessary hand up, rather than a handout. A war veteran's wife from Los Angeles wrote to decry the fee increase and assert the importance of child care to her family's future: "The present increase [in fees] presents a great hardship to parents like ourselves (veteran going to school and mother working) who are trying to keep our home functioning on $33 a week. [High child care fees] means we must sacrifice food and clothing necessities if we're to keep any degree of pride. Our roof leaks and we can't afford to have a new one or even to have this one patched. We haven't a washing machine or refrigerator or any rugs on the floors, but we don't need those things; all we need is a chance to keep our heads above water until Dwight finishes school."[109] Following the popular practice of conflating certain tax-supported social welfare programs with charity, day care users emphatically denied that they sought a public handout. "We don't want charity. We ask only the opportunity to work and maintain our homes, to meet our problems with independence," a representative of the Federation of Parents for Child Care Centers wrote in early 1947.[110]

In 1950 a recently remarried mother wrote at length to Governor Warren, "[on] behalf of myself and other families in the middle-income bracket"; she urged him to support greater access to the state's child care service. As a divorced mother she had been relieved to find the public child care service, and her daughter, "after two years of being shifted here and there and becoming so insecure as to be almost neurotic," was both "happy and settled." Since her remarriage, however, her new family income level exceeded the legislated maximum for the child care program and her own as well as her daughter's newfound security was threatened. Middle-income families would largely pay for the expanded program, she argued, and less restricted access would also be more equitable.[111] Like this mother, some child care advocates and a minority of state legislators continued to press for a broadly accessible program, but these supporters could not finally redefine the program as a service that any parent could decide to use.[112] With a few notable exceptions such as nurses and teachers, the 1947 law set the maximum annual income for access to the Child Care Centers at $2,700 (for a single parent providing for one or two children) and $3,300 (for two parents providing for one or two children).[113] As points of reference, the Education Department guidelines in 1946 had permitted a single parent with two children to earn as much as $4,140 annually, and by 1949 the median income for families of all sizes in urban California would stand at $3,705.[114]

In 1948 educators and parents declared that any admission calculus would discriminate against some individuals, but they made peace with the new eligibility standards by arguing that a standard scale adopted by the legislature was fairer and easier to administer and thus preferable to giving admission decisions to a trained caseworker. Having an elected legislature determine the specific eligibility rules, they implied, at least gave parents the right to together insist on uniform changes, while the case-by-case expert decisions of a social work professional could not be challenged this way.[115] But while legislative review gave to child care parents a greater degree of collective oversight, parents had correctly observed that any admission calculus might have discriminatory effects. In the first place, standard eligibility rules might be applied discriminatorily by local administrators—a practice that at the very least restricted child care access for some Mexican American families.[116] Aside from discriminatory application along racial and ethnic lines, even a standard income scale employed with complete evenhandedness could act to limit class mobility and confirm specific gender mores. Most uniform income scales drew on "standard budgets" designed by experts who both consciously and unconsciously confirmed specific ideas about class and gender. The Heller Committee guidelines on which educators based their unofficial income scales in 1946 created four standard budgets, with increasing levels of income for families categorized as "relief," "wage-earner," "white-collar," and "executive." This meant substantial differences in "necessary" income. As of March 1945, the committee calculated a monthly "relief budget" for a family of four at $127.41 and a "wage-earner budget" for four of $259.92.[117]

As wage levels increased in tandem with steady and at times steep rises in postwar living costs, parents and other child care advocates found it difficult to gain the legislature's approval for similar increases in the means test. Efforts as early as 1949 to gain an automatic cost-of-living adjustment for the income scale did not succeed. The first modest increases were achieved in 1951. Subsequent hikes in allowable income levels were similarly modest, and the means test did not keep up with California's racing economy or rising consumer expectations.[118]

The Effect of the Means Test

When the first legislated scale of income eligibility became effective in July 1947, nurses, teachers, and a few other groups of parents remained "exempt" from the financial means test. At the same time, "many parents with higher incomes were required to withdraw their children from Child Care Centers." Enrollment initially dropped by several thousand children before restabilizing at previous levels.[119] In the first half of the 1950s some Child Care Centers continued to maintain waiting lists of eligible low-income parents, but overall the means test severely hampered program enrollment. The first upward adjustment of the income maximum came in 1951, but it failed to arrest declining enrollment numbers. A report in March 1952 concluded, "the operation of this means test during a period of rising wages has resulted in a decrease in enrollment and the rendering ineligible of families for service." In about half a year the report found that 4,080 families had been denied initial access to the child care service or had been dropped from enrollment at a center because of their income; about 60 percent of these families exceeded the prescribed income maximum by $50 or less.[120]

The report also noted a "definite increase" in the use of centers by single-parent families and a "decrease in two-parent families." In 1946 two-parent households represented 63 percent of all families using the state child care program. By the early 1950s two-parent households were a minority, and a decade later they represented only about 22 percent of all public child care households. In the District of Columbia an insistence on desperate financial need as a condition of eligibility and the notion that day care was a public policy alternative to the ADC program had created a picture of the "ideal" public day care user as a mother who provided the sole support for her family. Even in the considerably more liberal political environment of California these rationales for public child care and the notion of the "ideal" day care mother remained important.[121] Accordingly, families with both a working mother and a working father were the most suspect class of public child care users. Although a public opinion survey across a diverse group of Californians in 1949 found a majority willing to pay taxes in support of a child care program for low-income single- and two-parent households, support was much greater for single-parent (84.7 percent) than two-parent households (59.0 percent). Most respondents who opposed having tax dollars spent on two-parent households simply asserted that the combined income of two parents would be sufficient to arrange necessary child care privately.[122]

Whether given at home, in a child care center, or by another arrangement, child care was understood as a mother's duty. (In contrast, a father bore the economic responsibility for enabling the "ideal" child care arrangement: in-the-home rearing by a mother.) Thus despite the relatively high number of working fathers who had children enrolled in public centers, as evidenced by the number of two-parent households sending children to the program, fathers were not generally seen as served by the program. The legislated means test proved an effective way to direct the program away from the suspect category, two-parent households, and toward the ideal day care users, sole-support mothers. The conflict between wage increases granted to meet higher living costs and a relatively static means test was compounded in two-earner households. A statewide survey of applicants for the child care service in 1954 found that the proportion of two-parent families applying for child care was double the proportion of two-parent families with children actually enrolled in the centers. And in a sample survey of some twelve hundred rejected applications, the largest group, close to 40 percent, had been submitted by two-parent families unable to qualify under the means test.[123]

The number of two-parent household using the public child care service would have fallen even lower had certain families not been exempt from the financial means test. In 1954 two-parent families accounted for about 77 percent of all exempt families using child care, compared with about 29 percent of all Child Care Center families.[124] Exemptions were granted for three reasons: (1) because of war service or (after June 1951) work in an "essential industry," (2) because a parent worked as a public schoolteacher or nurse, and (3) because the family helped to harvest or can crops. The first exemption was created for patriotic reasons while the last, which as one observer noted rarely applied to any families with incomes exceeding the means test, appears to have been designed to placate rural legislators who were perennial foes of the child care program. The second exemption, for nurses and teachers, was created both because the tremendous population expansion caused by the baby boom made nursing and teaching increasingly in demand, and because they were considered "female" occupations. Both the Welfare Council in Los Angeles and the State Education Department early asserted that eligibility for public child care should be granted to these public servants. Politicians continued to grant access to the centers to these exempted workers, even if at times grudgingly, throughout the 1950s.[125]

The legislated means test restricting access to Child Care Centers for low-income families suggested a public interest in ameliorating the effects of poverty. At the same time continued exemptions, especially for workers deemed essential to the economy, provided a potentially much broader base for understanding public responsibility for a permanent child care service. As the 1940s drew to a close the child care service had the look of a perma-

Table 4. Single-Parent and Two-Parent Households as Percentage of Total Families Enrolling Children in California Child Care Centers[a]

Date[b]	Total Number of Families	Single-Parent Families, in Percent	Two-Parent Families, in Percent
August 1946	11,972	37.2	62.8
1947	n/a	43.8	55.2
October 1949	11,548	54.6	43.9
Early 1952	n/a	59.9	39.0
Early 1953	10,742	62.1	36.9
Aug.–Nov. 1954	9,194	70.7	29.3
June 1962	8,959	77.6	22.4
November 1966	10,632	82.3	17.3

Sources: California Legislature, *Technical Staff Report*, table 72; California Legislature, *Child Care Center Operations under Geddes-Kraft*, 15; California Legislature, Assembly, 1951 Session, "First Preliminary Report by the Assembly Interim Committee on Social Welfare on the Child Care Center Program," in *Assembly Journal*, January 1951, 115; California Legislature, "The Child Care Center Program: State of California," Legislative Analyst, 16–17 (figures extrapolated), Papers of Theresa S. Mahler, Archives of the Pacific Oaks College, Pasadena, Calif.; Ronald Cox, State Department of Education, to Hon. Carlos Bee, appendix C, table I, California State Library, Sacramento; Summary of Survey on Children's Centers, November 14–18, 1966, folder DC/PS, box 3, Anne Ostomel papers, California Social Welfare Archives, University of Southern California, Los Angeles; "Child Care Center Questionnaire," March 1953, F3752:1562, State Department of Education, California State Archives, Sacramento.

n/a = not available

[a] Some rows do not sum to 100 percent because a small number of children were living with guardians other than parents.

[b] Dates approximate the period when data were collected.

nent program—it remained popular with state taxpayers, consistently enrolled between twelve and thirteen thousand children, and had the backing of all the state's major political parties—without the reality of a formal, legislated reason for its long-term existence.[126] Although the reasoning increasingly stretched credibility, each year state lawmakers continued to justify the public child care program as a temporary measure enacted to enable smooth reconversion from wartime activities. The repeated failure to legislate a permanent rationale for the program's existence left the state child care service vulnerable to attack.

Challenged by a Rural-Urban Political Faultline

An important political faultline for the program's support ran between the state's rural and urban legislators. Very few state-subsidized child care centers operated in rural areas during the war, and this only became more true after the war ended. By 1949 Los Angeles County alone enrolled 52 percent of all the children attending the state program. Although Child Care Centers operated in twenty-one counties across the state that year, California's four most populous counties—Los Angeles, Alameda, San Francisco and San Diego—together housed more than 85 percent of the state-subsidized centers.[127]

For program advocates, the geographic distribution of the child care centers spelled the biggest trouble in the state Senate, where electoral representation roughly corresponded to county lines (as opposed to the Assembly, where it was based on population). For instance, by 1950 about 40 percent of the state's population lived in Los Angeles County, which meant that Los Angeles sent more than thirty Assembly members to Sacramento. In the state Senate, however, no county could have more than one senator, and no senator could represent more than three counties. Los Angeles County, with more than four million residents, and Imperial County, with about 63,000, each had one state senator.[128]

In the Child Care Center debate, senators such as Ben Hulse (a rancher from Imperial County) argued that their constituents were being asked to subsidize an urban problem more properly dealt with by urban communities. In 1949, after the full state Assembly passed legislation that removed the war-related rationale and would have made the Child Care Centers permanent, Hulse and his colleagues on the state Senate Finance committee (virtually all rurally based) effectively killed the plan. The initial Assembly legislation contained language justifying the program's permanent status based on the "demonstrated need" for a child care service, "so that parents who are engaged or hereafter engage in work may have assurance of proper care of children." In response, Hulse's committee engineered an "eleventh hour and 59th minute" maneuver that reasserted the program's connection to the "emergency" employment of mothers (because of reconversion needs) and further insisted that because any war-connected need was obviously disappearing, no state money would be available for child care after June 30, 1950. Among the eleven members on the Senate committee responsible for these changes only one represented a large urban county (Alameda) with a significant number of child care centers. The remaining ten had a total of seven child care centers among themselves.

Child Care Center supporters in the Assembly were reluctant to support the now severely restricted measure but resigned themselves to casting a yes vote for fear that the program would otherwise be killed outright.[129]

The concentration of available jobs and people in urban places by definition meant that metropolitan areas would always have more centers, but a need for public child care also existed in rural areas. Child care supporters responded to the rural critique by pointing out that urban taxpayers also helped to support rural programs, and that overall the four most urban counties provided about two-thirds of the state's general fund tax revenues. At a child care hearing in 1946 a representative of the San Diego Parent's Council did call for a child care program that served "urban or rural areas," but this testimony appears as the exception. Most Child Care Center supporters seemed most interested in finding rural constituents who could influence their elected rural representatives to vote for a program largely serving urban areas. Suggesting that the child care program should be expanded to new areas meant sounding like a spendthrift and risked political criticism. For this reason, and likely because of their own blindness to the needs of rural workers, especially farm workers, child care supporters did not early or often suggest that rural families could benefit from access to publicly subsidized child care.[130]

Neither, despite evident need, did rural state senators appear to have sought funding for their communities as a way to offset urban dominance in the Child Care Center program. A report in 1951 found that in Fresno, Kern, Madera, Merced, and Tulare counties the peak seasonal population at migrant farm labor camps alone ran as high as 49,500. Children under fourteen accounted for about 26 percent of the migrant families, the report continued: "Among this group there would thus be a large number of very young children requiring care and supervision while parents are engaged in agricultural work."[131] A report from Tulare County added, "It is a common sight to see pre-school age children left in the automobile while their parents toil in the fields. School age children remain at home to mind the younger children. . . . There is a great need in the county for child care centers."[132] But child care advocates had specifically explained the need for child care as a consequence of urbanization, most recently in their extensively circulated *A Brief Inquiry into the Need for a Child Care Program in California*. This rural need undercut that reasoning.

The implication by child care advocates that rural California women, unlike their urban counterparts, could simultaneously "earn" and "supervise" their children was belied by the realities of California agriculture. Rural California farm workers, many of whom were Mexican Americans, were a part of massive agribusiness operations that Carey McWilliams earlier described as "factories in the fields." Some families followed the planting, tending, and harvesting cycle of different crops by moving from location to location; others lived permanently in a region. The only part of the rural idyll experienced by many Mexican American farm workers' children was that they learned the skills of their destiny: farm labor.[133]

Just as advocates of the state child care program explained the need of urban women to earn wages as part of an "official-economic" system, the Tulare Board of Supervisors explained that "due to economic pressure, the mother in the agricultural family has been forced to join her husband in the role of breadwinner."[134] According to child care advocates, including industrial manufacturers at some times, the pragmatic response to the "necessary" employment of mothers in the urban-industrial economy was the public provision of affordable supervision for their children. The logic of California's farm economy led in a different direction. Agribusiness owners counted on the labor of all hands, and very low wages meant that farm worker families also relied on the earning power of every family member. As a Federal Interagency Committee on Migrant Labor recognized and deplored in 1947, children frequently figured in this equation as added laborers and wage earners.[135] In California, at least through the 1930s and likely well beyond, compulsory education laws were little enforced for farm workers' children. Even where schools did exist for children of migrant workers, their daily and yearly schedules might be shaped to accommodate the crops rather than child education.[136] "Why don't school age children help in the cotton fields?" questioned F. Presley Abshire (R-Sonoma), a state senator and farmer, after testimony in 1954 at a hearing describing the value of the sole Child Care Center in the state for farm workers' children.[137]

The federal government had made some provisions for the care of children in farm labor camps during the Depression and into the early 1940s, but the money ended about the time that the World War II funding for child care programs began; few wartime centers served rural areas. Immediately after the war some national and state attention to the need for child care among farm workers did help to produce the rural Fresno County center that Sen. Abshire apparently found of questionable worth. The Fresno center remained open in its first year only during the fall-to-winter harvest season and operated in a building provided by the Calflax ranch. Fresno County also became one of a handful of counties that levied a small Child Care Center tax to provide additional operating funds for the center. The company-provided building, county tax revenue, parents' fees, state aid, and a grant from the Rosenberg Foundation helped to establish and maintain the center. The evident concerted effort needed to launch this rather modest endeavor in the care of farm workers' children would not be repeated in other California locations for more than a decade.[138]

That officials and the public in rural areas did not unanimously agree on the importance of education for farm workers' children complicated the public provision of child care in rural areas. The restrictive legislation enacted in 1949 asserted that local communities should support any needed Child Care Centers with their own revenues. Clearing the way for the state to exit the program, this law included provisions that allowed local school districts to include child care in the regular school budget and levy taxes for its support, as the Westside District in Fresno County subsequently did. This action, however, as well as the decision to seek state approval for a Child Care Center, ultimately rested with local school districts, and some of these showed little interest in providing services of any kind to farm workers or their children. "As might be expected, we are dealing here with a [school] board that reflects the thinking of landowners in a rural community, who are not easily excited about another tax-supported service," a worker for the California Migrant Ministry explained in 1962. Writing to urge state officials to compel local action on child care centers, she continued: "It may be 'ideal', or 'proper' to have the initiative come from the local area—but I submit this is precisely why most areas do not effectively extend community services among their least-vocal, most-powerless sectors. . . . I am terribly concerned that we are not 'moving' in an instance where the workers themselves express a desire, and a willingness to help plan."[139] By the early 1960s organizing efforts among farmworkers, led by Cesar Chavez, began to challenge the century-long dominance of California's big agribusiness operators and brought renewed national and statewide attention to the miserable work and living conditions of farm workers' families. The United Farm Workers, which grew out of these organizing efforts, signed up entire families by necessity. And the many married women, mothers and workers, who actively joined the movement help to explain the UFW's sponsorship of day care and other services.[140] Although support for them remained limited, in 1964 state lawmakers approved legislation that for the first time in more than a decade allowed a modest expansion of rural Child Care Centers.[141]

During the 1940s and 1950s the building of new Child Care Centers in rural California had been further complicated by the seasonal nature of farm work and the lack of any capital building funds. The state child care program served, with few exceptions, the children of employed parents only. Unless she quickly became reemployed, a parent who for any reason lost her job could also lose access to child care. This posed a real problem for farm workers who harvested seasonal crops. When the Education Department received a request in 1948 for information about establishing a Child Care Center in rural Vista, California, the state's Child Care Center supervisor, John Weber, responded that this "would be most difficult to initiate inasmuch as the Legislature amended the last bill to exclude seasonal crop workers for the very reason that it was most difficult to maintain and operate a child care center program for only a part of any one year. The resulting expenses would be terrific for setting up such a program and then not using it to the fullest extent."[142] The prospect of rural Child Care Centers, as Weber later noted, was also hampered because the State Department of Education had no money to build new facilities (meaning that local communities had to be willing to fund the necessary housing), and because the state legislature barred approval of any new child care center if its operation would reduce funding to one that already existed. Both provisions tended to favor already established centers. When Governor Warren informally sought information in early 1950 about the possibility of starting child care centers in the agricultural districts of the San Joaquin Valley, the state's superintendent of public instruction, Roy Simpson, responded negatively. Even if a local school district requested a center, Simpson noted, "without additional funds it would be impossible to approve the establishment of additional centers anywhere in the state."[143]

The rural-urban split provided a serious postwar challenge to child care advocates throughout their effort to gain permanency for the program. The legislation that provided for the end of all state funds in 1949 pointedly maintained the outdated reconversion rationale for the centers. Child care advocates eked out an eight-month continuance of state funding in 1950, but this new legislation laid further administrative groundwork for turning over the centers to local counties and school districts. For advocates of the Child Care Centers, the loss of state funding was tantamount to loss of the program. Local school districts were already strapped, and many school superintendents and boards were not at all convinced of the merit of the child care program. County support also seemed unlikely and specifically carried with it the suggestion that county public welfare agencies become involved in the program—an idea denounced by both Child Care Center workers and the California Parents Association for Child Care Centers.

The Return of a Wartime Rationale for Child Care

While the rural-urban split was a predictable challenge for child care advocates, the advent in 1950 of the Korean conflict and its attendant defense production needs would seem to have offered a positive opportunity for new program growth. But the Korean conflict failed to produce any federal funds for child care and produced only superficial sympathy among state legislators for the needs of defense workers. The war brought manufacturers back into active child care advocacy and also renewed support from veterans', civic, labor, and social welfare organizations. These groups unsuccessfully insisted on the urgent and widespread need for child care services to war workers and families of servicemen.[144] Some Child Care Center supporters may have felt uncertain about how to use the war in lobbying for a continuing program. Having spent years fighting to maintain a peacetime program with state funds, they were loath to allow redefinition of the program as a wartime contingency that relied on federal funds.

Just before the deployment of U.S. troops in Korea, the California legislature approved a second interim committee, this one under the auspices of a social welfare rather than education committee, to determine if there was a continuing need for child care centers. By the time this committee opened its investigation in mid-1950 wartime contingencies had returned to the child care debate. Because it had maintained many of the Child Care Centers created during World War II, California appeared better positioned to handle the presumed upsurge in the employment of mothers with young children. When the new armed forces mobilization arrived, however, budget austerity at the statehouse had forced some Child Care Centers to operate below maximum capacity, and many could not stay open for the full six-day workweek required of war workers. Regardless of the size of their facility, without more money to hire additional teachers these centers could not accept any new children into their programs. Further, the legislature's means test, which as we have seen disqualified middle-income families, effectively barred access to the Child Care Centers for most war workers and many servicemen's wives.[145] A survey of northern Child Care Center operations in early September 1950 reported daily applications from wives of recently activated servicemen and from women accepting work in war industries. Nearly all had to be turned away because their incomes exceeded the means test maximum. Reports from San Diego and Los Angeles confirmed this problem.[146] The Assembly's Interim Committee accurately summarized the situation: "Many parents already utilizing the centers have had incomes increased because of longer working hours or other factors in industry. This has resulted in making them ineligible under the means test. Many other applicants entering war industry have been turned away on an income basis. The total income from earnings of mothers and their allotments from servicemen husbands has necessitated rejection of applications on an income basis."[147]

The experience of Mr. and Mrs. J. C. Vieira and their young son offers a concrete illustration of one of these new wartime dilemmas. The Vieiras enrolled their child in the Compton public center before the outbreak of the Korean conflict. At the time their combined incomes stood under the $275 monthly maximum. However, a routine six-month application review, completed after Mr. Vieira's recall to active duty in August 1950, showed that his newly promised serviceman's salary put the couple's earnings over the established income limit. Mrs. Vieira detailed the problem in a letter to Governor Earl Warren: "My husband was called into the Army this past month & now the school informs me, that they can't care for my son much longer as a bill hasn't been passed to care for service men children. . . . Sir, I have to work to meet our expences & and my husband won't be making to much money that I may stay home & care for [our son]. We are willing to pay the nursery as much as we possibly can. But we can't afford the high price of a private nursery. Our child is doing so well in this school & he is in good hands, that gives my husband & I a great relief to know."[148] Mrs. Vieira closed by calling for legislation that would permit any child of a serviceman to enroll in the state child care program. This letter drew only a perfunctory response from the governor's office while a letter in November from her husband overseas garnered more attention but little satisfaction. Through extraordinary efforts by the local admitting teacher the Vieiras received some assurances that their child would not be immediately removed from the Child Care Center; but Mrs. Vieira's request that all servicemen's families with working wives be given access to Child Care Centers would not be granted.[149]

When it released its report in January 1951, the Assembly Interim Committee described itself as "particularly sympathetic" to the needs of families like the Vieiras but implied that perhaps some mere administrative readjustments might allow access to public child care for such truly deserving cases. As a counterpoint to this wartime need, the committee asserted that "the primary purpose of the [state Child Care Center program] is to enable low income families to continue being self-supporting through employment of the sole parent or both parents." This justified a peacetime program, but the committee report still avoided an outright statement in favor of permanency.[150] With regard to war-related child care services, the committee, drawing on the example of World War II, saw the federal government as the proper source of support for child care services. The committee sent a res-

olution seeking federal aid to each of California's congressional representatives and advised state legislators that "exemption from the means test for
families engaged in defense work would be difficult to administer and
would create additional demand for use of centers that the centers cannot
meet." Reassuring state lawmakers that they did not need to act on the issue
of access for defense workers, the committee report suggested that federal
funds might be forthcoming if labor shortages necessitated the massive recruitment of women.[151]

But the call for federal funding of child care during the Korean war remained unanswered, and the manner in which state legislators adjusted the
admission calculus for California Child Care Centers in 1951 continued to
bar access to the program for most defense workers and many families of
servicemen. The conservative response to calls for increased wartime funding of child care illustrates the powerful hold of the Cold War's faith in domestic containment. In California, even as women became a more accepted
and indeed sought-after part of the workforce, a conservative gender ideology contradictorily insisted on their full-time presence in the home.[152]
Nonetheless, the relative ease with which state lawmakers agreed to again
temporarily extend state funding for child care, this time from February 15,
1951, through the end of the fiscal year, June 30, 1951, no doubt stemmed
from the availability of a war rationale. In June 1951, after again narrowly es-
caping death in a Senate Finance Committee dominated by rural legislators, California's child care program won its longest extension of life to date:
two years. The new law included the first extensive revision of the state's
Child Care Center program since 1947, as legislators approved a new state
funding formula and a raft of new admission procedures and requirements.[153]
Bucking the recommendation of their own study committee, state legislators voted to again exempt workers in "essential industry" and retained other
categories of exemptions, including nurses and teachers. The new law even
provided the first moderate increase in four years in the income levels incorporated into the means test.[154]

"Essential industry" represented a much broader range of employment
than simply aircraft or shipyard work directly related to the production of
war materiel. The blanket inclusion of this large group of workers, without
regard to income, would have substantially reversed the effect of the legislative restrictions imposed in 1947 that increasingly limited access to Child
Care Centers to low-income families alone. Instead it would have allowed
a broad new group of middle-income families to use the service for the first
time. Granting access to such a potentially large new category of families

would certainly have increased pressure on Sacramento, and likely Washington, to provide funds for expanding the program.

For Child Care Center advocates, however, the problem was that what the legislators promised in one sentence they nullified in another. The new law made increased fees mandatory for all families and specified that any family belonging to an exempt group would nevertheless need to pay the prohibitively high full cost of the service. Instead of dramatically increasing the number of child care center users, the new law proved more limiting than its predecessor. During fiscal year 1950–51 families in exempt categories accounted for a full 21 percent of the centers' enrollment. Only eight months into the succeeding fiscal year, and despite the inclusion of a significant new exempt category, that number had declined to 8.9 percent of all child care families. In a further indication that the child care program remained unavailable to defense workers, a report in 1952 found that a "major portion of unused capacity is in centers located in areas carrying on large defense production."[155]

Since 1947 child care administrators had applied fees on a sliding scale for all parents. Families who earned slightly more than the maximum were still eligible to use the centers but as a member of an exempt category paid slightly more than those who fell within the income limit. Only a few parents in the very highest income ranges paid fees approaching full cost of the service. The new system meant that a family earning $300 a month with a child enrolled in preschool would pay about $22 of its income for child care; by contrast, a family earning $301—just over the income maximum—owed about $68 for identical care. Exempt families with more then one child faced double or triple these prohibitive costs. Parents and child care center administrators tried to change this inequity, but full-cost fees remained permanently in effect for most exempt groups. In 1953, however, with the backing of the State Education Department, state legislators agreed to a more progressive income eligibility scale for exempt day care users who were also single parents.[156]

Instead of broadening the base of Child Care Center enrollment, the Korean War simply allowed state legislators to prolong their delay in finding a peacetime rationale for publicly subsidized Child Care Centers. The law enacted in 1951 stated that the legislature's policy was "to continue to provide until June 30, 1953, a means for meeting an emergency, existing in certain communities in the State, created by the employment of women with children, due to the increased drafting of men in the armed forces, and the extended operations increase in industries, as a result of the troubled and unsettled world conditions."[157] Postponing the inevitable, legislators latched onto the Korean War as a renewed legitimization of the state Child Care Centers, even as their own policies continued to place the centers off limits to many service-connected families and defense workers.

The California Parents Association for Child Care Centers and to a lesser degree its education supporters showed ambivalence about seeking federal funding of expanded child care services during the Korean War, and this was precisely because they sought a permanent peacetime rationale for a state-supported child care program. Remembering the difficult battle fought to gain recognition of some state responsibility after V-J Day, they weren't eager to repeat that effort. "The program should not lose its identity as a State function," the executive board of the CPACCC warned in early 1951. Fred Luke, president of the CPACCC, explained further: "We agree that federal subsidy will be required to expand the program to care for defense workers; we are anxious, however, that the program not be called again a 'war emergency,' and that the program remain identified as a state function, not a national function."[158]

As the 1950s opened, the lack of a permanent peacetime rationale imperiled the long-term survival of California's state child care program. Regardless of any new war demands, the Parents Association and other day care advocates in California believed that their core mission should be to preserve what they had already won. Unlike in the months immediately following World War II (when day care activists practiced a dual strategy of pressuring both Washington and Sacramento for funding), during the Korean War California's most loyal Child Care Center supporters kept their attention focused on their home state and on finding a permanent peacetime rationale.[159]

Productive Citizenship as a Peacetime Rationale for Public Child Care

The idea that a publicly funded child care service might provide a policy alternative to the Aid to Dependent Children program had been around for some years; as the status of California's Child Care Centers looked increasingly desperate, this justification for their peacetime continuation took center stage. From the time of the first postwar legislative battles, parents and their supporters stressed that a state-subsidized child care program allowed families to remain financially self-supporting rather than "relief burdens." Aside from emphasizing the supposed moral superiority of work to the acceptance of relief, this argument played to a common wisdom that a child care program would reduce costs, especially that of Aid to Dependent Children, by ensuring that "deserving women" could remain in the workforce.

In 1950 day care advocates formally packaged the argument that Child Care Centers were a less costly alternative to ADC and presented this as a fiscal reality. Should the Child Care Centers cease to operate, program advocates estimated that the public relief bill for single-parent Child Care Center families alone would be as high as $7.75 million annually. Meanwhile, they pointed out, the state spent about $5 million on the entire child care program each year.[160] Ignoring the fact that federal funds helped to offset the cost of the ADC program to the state treasury—meaning the ADC and child care numbers weren't exactly comparable—California child care advocates simply cited these figures to assert that Child Care Centers were the cheaper public policy alternative. Making the case for the fiscal superiority of day care was considered an important political step to shore up conservative support for a child care program. By contrast, in the District of Columbia comparisons of the costs of day care funding and ADC recognized the federal offset, making it impossible to argue that day care was the less expensive alternative. Indeed one California analyst (who apparently supported the child care cause) privately calculated that if the child care program closed and as a result half of all child care families sought relief through ADC the fiscal cost to California would remain the same; it might even be reduced, he noted, since federal funds were available for the ADC program. Because of this, the analyst suggested that program supporters should not rely on cost savings as their argument for child care but instead should stress the income that families can gain through employment and the "taxes they pay—wealth they pro[duce]."[161]

Lawrence Arnstein, a former businessman and longtime public health activist who had been involved in the effort to continue the child care program at least since the close of World War II, and who had helped to bring important conservative credentials to the child care cause, adopted this advice and passed it along to Child Care Center workers and parents. While Arnstein continued to assert that Child Care Centers were a less costly program than ADC, he also argued that the "productive" earning power of child care parents—between $28 and $30 million in annual combined wages—gave significant fuel to California's economy. As "productive citizens," child care parents were "taxpayers not taxeaters."[162] Explicitly contrasting the long-established public policy of Aid to Dependent Children with the much newer idea of publicly subsidized child care, the productive citizenship argument now declared the latter policy not only fiscally and morally superior but an economic boon as well.[163] Parents combined references to the older rationales with this new positive economic argument. "It is American, most basically American, in my opinion, that one assume responsibility for himself insofar as he is able," testified Betty Bachman, legislative chair of the CPACCC, in 1954. A parent who retained access to the child care centers because her occupation was schoolteaching, Bachman argued: "The California Child Care Center program is primarily designed for those citizens who occupy a marginal position in our economy . . . we feel [it] has rendered a most valuable service to the State in helping to maintain these families as producing units in their economy. . . . We are contributors to our society and proud that we are able to be."[164]

The productive citizenship rationale allowed mothers to move their claim to legitimate workforce participation beyond private domestic concerns. Claiming their importance to the state economy, parents both linked their wage earning to the "official economy" and suggested a peacetime reason for publicly supported child care. Broadening women's right to be in the workplace remained critical to this justification. In the immediate postwar debate, supporters of the Child Care Centers sought to undergird the argument of private need for the employment of mothers by stressing industrialization as a natural, inevitable, and overall positive event that resulted in a greater number of women wage-earners. By the early 1950s the "productive citizenship" rationale for Child Care Centers emphasized a new official-economic reason for women's employment: the essential role of "womanpower" in the state's peacetime economy. Focusing on the "official-economic" reasons that mothers worked gave female employment both an air of inevitability and a positive role in the economic health of the state. This no doubt proved less threatening to state lawmakers who voted to support the child care program than any argument premised on a change in the role of mothers.[165]

Politicians' greater acquiescence in mothers' presence in the workforce, and their willingness to fund day care, did not mean that they agreed with parents on the reason for public continuance of a child care service. If state legislators (and some day care advocates) focused on the productive contributions of "womanpower" to explain the importance of public support for child care, this singular economic focus—defining "productivity" as participation in the market economy and according to the number of dollars earned—did not fully encompass how Child Care Centers' parents defined "productive citizenship." Seeking to recast the understanding of both paid work and motherhood, parents claimed their status as productive citizens based on not only the economic but also the social contributions that they believed they made to society. Inscribing her letter to Governor Warren in 1950 with the notation "Housewife, Mother, Secretary," one child care mother gave notice of how she understood her multiple productive roles in society.[166]

As productive citizens, parents also took pride in maintaining "autonomous households." They measured their "productive" value to the community by their ability to shape their own and their family's futures, which they saw as an important feature and indication of full American citizenship.[167] For Addie Stangeland, a job at Douglas Aircraft during World War II finally granted her the opportunity to support her home as she wished. A divorced mother with two children, she had found work as a seamstress before the war, but low wages forced her to send her children to an orphanage. Asked to summarize her work experience as a southern California war worker, she responded, "Those were my best years, really. They were my most productive because I had responsibilities to meet and Douglas' wages helped me to meet them. I could give my children more and I did by making more. So, I think, really, when it comes right down to it, those Douglas years were about the happiest, the most productive."[168] The kind of social and economic productivity that Stangeland describes as enabled by her wage earning is repeatedly echoed in the letters and statements of parents who used the postwar Child Care Center program in California.

"I am now working and I feel proud that I can keep my family together and my children are given all the love and security they so desperately need," one Child Care Center mother wrote.[169] In a letter written in 1950, another sole-support mother urged Governor Warren's strong support for Child Care Centers by arguing, "I am proud of the fact, that, alone I can care for & support my children myself, but if the Centers are abolished, I will be more than in a quandary. My salary is not adequate for private schooling, so I shall have to appeal to the *State* for aid. Not only will I lose pride in myself, but I will become a problem to others. There are many women in the same position as myself, and to abolish these Centers will cause inconvenience and grief to many, and an additional expense to the state."[170] Praising the governor as an "extremely able administrator" with the "best interests of your state and your state's citizens at heart," a parent activist from Stockton insisted, "Do not ignore the requests of this relatively small group who ask only to be able to hold their heads up and still provide the best possible for our future citizens."[171]

Finally, the testimony in 1950 of Rosa Lee Clements, a representative of CPACCC, suggests how access to the child care service allowed mothers to argue from a position of independence and self-support and how this position brought crucial strength to their call for a continuation of the Child Care Centers: "In our day, I believe that all possible encouragement should be given to the citizens of the State to be independent, self-supporting, cohesive family units; the State should encourage people to be independent; it should not encourage people to further dependence on the State's welfare funds. Certainly the Child Care Centers are sound social support to fundamentally independent units; with intelligent social support, such as Child Care Centers, these families can give their children the security they need to develop into useful members of a democratic society."[172] The use of a child care service importantly allowed California mothers to make their case as productive citizens; at the same time, engaging in productive citizenship gave them the right to claim public provision of child care as a social right.[173]

Unlike turn-of-the-century maternalist reformers who frequently sought public policy changes on behalf of other women and children, working mothers who used the Child Care Centers sought a public service for themselves. They did not appeal to an idealized motherhood but called for a particular public service based on their own experience, as wage earners and homemakers, and they argued on their own behalf. Mothers especially (as opposed to fathers whose children were enrolled in the centers) drove the call for publicly provided child care because they were disproportionately represented as Child Care Center parents and because societal prescription dictated that childrearing was their responsibility. The mid-twentieth-century call for publicly provided child care in California also differed from earlier maternalist campaigns because it occurred several decades after the achievement of women's suffrage. Child Care Center mothers made their demand both as taxpayers and as voting citizens. The sense of entitlement might have rubbed some politicians the wrong way. A list of "Do's" and "Don'ts" prepared in 1954 advised parents writing to state lawmakers regarding the child care program: "Don't begin on the righteous note of 'as a citizen and taxpayer.'"[174]

Many parents also used their position as productive citizens to demand a service that gave them the opportunity to fully join in the postwar era's booming consumer economy. "Since the right of a family to improve its standard of living is an accepted tradition in American society, this necessarily includes the right of a woman with dependent children to contribute toward a family goal," the Los Angeles Parents Council insisted in 1946.[175] Writing to Governor Warren four years later, a father whose child attended a Child Care Center argued, "The need for extra-parental child care is not a temporary situation. It is a positive means of raising the standards of California by helping parents give their children the advantages every child needs. State supported child care centers are a vital part of the lives of many of us."[176] The predominantly working-class families who had access to the state Child Care Centers also imbibed the era's consumerism and rising expectations of living standards. Preparing for the effort to renew child care authorization and funding in 1955, a Legislative Bulletin advised Child Care Center workers to initiate a writing campaign but to *screen letters carefully* . . . Cars, T.V., electric refrigerators, etc., given as reasons for mothers working are 'taboo'" (emphasis in original).[177]

From "Lean" Years to Permanency

"This is a lean year and we need to stand together," a bulletin of the Parents Association advised in March 1954. Although the Child Care Centers weathered the difficult years of the early 1950s, the combination of a restrictive means test, decreasing state funding, and prohibitive fees put the program through hard times. Despite inflation, the state money allocated to school districts operating Child Care Centers dropped precipitously: from $5.6 to $3.9 million between 1949 and 1954. In the same period, average yearly enrollment declined statewide from about thirteen thousand to just below eleven thousand. In 1955 the coalition of child care supporters, driven especially by parents and educators, would redouble its efforts to win permanent standing for the program.[178]

As early as December 1950 Governor Warren had finally suggested the need for a permanent Child Care Center program, but Warren left the governor's mansion in 1953 after receiving appointment as the Chief Justice of the U.S. Supreme Court. Advocates of permanent Child Care Centers held his successor, Goodwin Knight (R), to his early commitment of support for the program. Like Warren, the State Education Department, which had for several years studiously avoided either killing the program or giving it a hearty endorsement, finally also granted its blessing to a continuing program in late 1950. The department put its lobbying muscle to work by sponsoring its own child care legislation in 1953. All of these developments seemed auspicious for the program's permanent survival, but the legislature remained intransigent.[179]

Still clinging to an outdated Korean War rationale for the program, the legislature in 1954 appointed a third interim committee, again under the social welfare aegis, to study the need for a continuing Child Care Center program. For advocates of a state-funded program, the composition of the committee could not have been more unpromising. The state senators au-

DON'T LET THIS LIGHT FAIL

This cartoon by Leo Thiele accompanied an editorial in the Los Angeles
Mirror and Daily News in March 1955 supporting continued state
funding of California Child Care Centers.

thorized to lead the investigation represented overwhelmingly rural areas
and none had a Child Care Center currently operating in their home counties.[180] Predictably, despite receiving overwhelming testimonial support in
favor of a continued state-funded program administered by the Education
Department, the Senate committee drew the opposite conclusion from its
investigation in 1954. In their report committee members insisted that if any
publicly funded child care program existed it should be the responsibility of

local communities. "The present program, wherein 86 percent of all child care centers are located in four counties, should not be continued with state funds. We believe communities desiring this type of service should finance the operation from parent fees and local tax revenues."[181] Coalescing in defense of the program, child care advocates overcame this negative beginning to the legislative campaign of 1955 and in the end won the most liberal child care legislation in years. Advocates had to settle for a third two-year extension of the program, but in the meantime they won increased dollars and new funding sources for the program, a slightly liberalized means test for two-parent families, and a modified fee schedule for some single parents, among other revisions to the law.[182]

The all-out campaign fell only a hair's breadth short of achieving permanent authorization for the program, and although the legislature did not revisit the outdated wartime rationale, the signals that Child Care Center advocates received gave them much greater confidence that the program had a permanent peacetime future.[183] Two years later, with apparently little fanfare, the legislature changed its policy statement on Child Care Centers and made them a permanent fixture in the State Education Department budget. "The policy of the Legislature," they now explained, "is to continue Child Care Centers to provide care and supervision of children necessitated by the employment of women with children." Governor Knight signed the permanent authorizing legislation into law on June 22, 1957.[184] Although funds for the Child Care Center budgets would need approval each year, the permanent authorization gave the program a significant advantage. Further, its long incubation developed the bureaucratic notion of the program. Just one year after permanent authorization was granted, a state legislative analyst, Alan Post, revived the notion that the child care program should be funded solely at the county and local levels; his idea appears to have garnered little attention from lawmakers. With the program on a permanent footing, child care advocates, especially early childhood educators, turned their attention more fully to matters of professionalization, and along with parents they continued to press for new categories of "exempt" child care users, a more progressive scaling of program fees, and higher income limits in general.[185]

Republicans dominated California politics for much of the first sixty years of the twentieth century. During the postwar Child Care Center struggle, moderate Republicans in the state's neo-Progressive tradition would bring crucial legislative know-how and muscle to the effort to maintain the program. A shift in political winds as the 1960s neared brought many new Democrats to Sacramento. The Democratic change at the statehouse, and

in 1961 in the White House, would portend big changes for publicly provided child care generally and the fate of California's Child Care Center
program more specifically.

At the height of World War II California's federally supported child care
program enrolled more than 25,000 children; when the state assumed primary funding for the program in March 1946 enrollment had declined to a
little more than half of that. Fifteen years later, having undergone expansion and contraction during its long temporary status, California's permanently authorized peacetime child care service had arrived back at its early
postwar size and enrolled some thirteen thousand children.

The state's child care program originated out of a wartime contingency
and offered an affordable and convenient service designed for wage-earning
mothers. Federal lawmakers funded the program because they believed that
full-time participation of mothers with young children in the labor force
would be necessary to win World War II. After the war had been won, California parents, education professionals, and social welfare advocates organized to save their state's substantial program, and they helped to win a critical extension of federal funds by appealing to the plight of servicemen's
wives whose husbands remained overseas. Once the war became more re-
mote, Californians who sought to make publicly provided child care permanent statewide struggled to defend and explain the presence of mothers
in the paid workforce. As in other jurisdictions, state lawmakers most readily understood that some women worked for wages because of private family needs. But within California's neo-Progressive political context and in a
booming postwar economy, a substantial number of lawmakers also came
to concede that mothers earned wages for other than domestic reasons.
They believed that "official economic" concerns also helped to explain the
presence of mothers in the workforce.

State policymakers continued for many years to formally justify continued state support of child care with reference to war or postwar reconversion needs. At the same time, the administrative policies that they dictated
in annual child care legislation suggested a separate reason for the program's
continued existence. If state policymakers increasingly accepted the presence of mothers in the workforce as inevitable, they nonetheless maintained faith in the superiority of full-time maternal care of children. Loath
to assume the costs of child care in any case, they redefined the program to
ensure its availability primarily to very low-income families.

Fiscal conservatism always remained an important consideration, but the development and administration of a legislatively defined means test in the California program also demonstrates a common postwar perception that any publicly supported child care program did not properly serve all citizens. Even as lawmakers began to accept official-economy explanations of women's presence in the labor force, they still insisted that a permanent, publicly funded program should only be available to families with certifiable private need. Thus, although Californians granted a much broader acceptance to the idea of mothers as wage earners, state lawmakers did not translate this acceptance into public support for a widely accessible child care program.

By the 1950s day care supporters advanced their claims for permanent public support of the state program by arguing as "productive citizens" that a policy of publicly provided child care was both cost effective and a source of economic strength for California. Because it emphasized the key contributions of "womanpower" to the state economy, the productive citizenship rationale uniquely allowed mothers to argue for publicly provided child care from the status of a publicly valued wage earner. Parents, especially mothers, understood productive citizenship as the combination of the economic and social contributions that they made to society, while many supporters and most lawmakers understood this argument in more purely economic terms.

Unlike their counterparts in Cleveland and the District of Columbia, the early childhood educators who worked in California's child care program emerged as important and key advocates for maintaining the program. Drawing from their roots in the nursery school movement, early childhood educators would be important figures in the effort to define women's wage earning as an "official economic" phenomenon, instead of a private domestic concern that might require public intervention in limited cases. This notion, like the idea of early childhood education itself, suggested that day care was a universal need. Child care workers, who claimed a professional identity as educators, argued that wherever young children were cared for, education occurred; they insisted that their knowledge of child development made them both ideal child care workers and administrators.

In the 1960s a new set of political realities would give educators the chance to further press the importance of early childhood education for young children. The growing popularity of preschool programs allowed California's early childhood educators to successfully redefine the legislated mission of the state child care service from "provision of care and supervision" to "provision of educational supervision." The education professionals further succeeded in removing the word "care" from the program alto-

gether by rechristening the state child care service "Children's Centers."
The upsurge in support for the education of young children did not however mark a strengthening of the idea that publicly provided child care
might serve all classes of families. A combination of factors, including a narrow understanding of the relative merits of day care and ADC, the rise of "compensatory" education theory, and a dramatic increase in the visibility and
presence of commercial child care facilities, combined to ensure that state-
supported child care would be extended only to selected "needy" families.

In California federal funding for day care and compensatory education
reignited the jurisdictional battle between state education and welfare departments over the child care center program, and it gave a new and decided advantage to welfare. Drowned out in the substantial reformulation
of program goals by federal policymakers, social work and education professionals would be parents' earlier claims to publicly subsidized child care as
a service that enabled them to be productive citizens.

I was really torn up on it because for one thing, I wanted to stay home with the baby; two, I wanted to help Josh get through [school]; three, I really enjoyed that job.
—Betty Boggs, former "Rosie the Riveter"

FIVE

Responding to the Increased Employment of Mothers

From the Rise of Commercial Child Care to the Enactment of Early Welfare Reform, 1950–1965

Recalling her decision in 1955 to continue working after the birth of her first child, Betty Boggs described conflicting needs and desires. A teenager when she worked as the proverbial riveter in an aircraft factory in southern California, by the 1950s Boggs had settled into a laboratory job with Sylvania Electronic. She remembered that her desire to help her husband finish his engineering degree finally led her to return to work soon after her son's birth. At her job she earned a promotion to supervisor, but finding a "baby-sitter" to care for her infant "was a chore." Boggs used five caregivers in two years. "I was paying ten dollars a week at that time for child care [and the] care wasn't good. . . . The woman she wanted the money . . . you just didn't want any old body." By the time her son turned two and she gave birth to a second child, Boggs quit work. "I don't think at that time there were any of the . . . pre-school sort of thing, which would have really worked out nice."[1]

Betty Boggs's story captures the contradictions and dilemmas that faced many middle-class white mothers in the 1950s. In deciding whether to work she weighed her own desire to care for her child—an inclination strongly confirmed by the era's approval of female domesticity—against her wish to stay with a job that she enjoyed and that validated a contrary popular message that stressed individual achievement and self-fulfillment for women. Many women in this position drew on yet a third ideal to justify their decisions to work: the American dream. Like Betty Boggs they explained their presence in the workforce as a way to help their families achieve the kind of successful consumer lifestyle that became a stereotype of the 1950s.

Between the end of the 1940s and the beginning of the 1960s a significant shift in popular (and policymakers') attitudes occurred regarding the paid employment of mothers. Previously considered fully and properly occupied with unpaid child-rearing and housekeeping tasks, mothers were officially defined as "unemployable." In the two decades after World War II, however, a steady rise in the number of mothers who worked for wages called this policy assumption into question. It helped to force a reassessment of the notion that any mother, regardless of her income, should have the opportunity to devote her full-time efforts to caring for her children in her own home. This ideal lay at the core of the Aid to Dependent Children program. The intent of this program, which offered cash grants to very poor women, was to enable these women to keep and raise their own children in their own homes. (It had simply been assumed that women without dire economic need would "choose" this "occupation.")

As long as cash grants to poor mothers remained the preferred policy, advocates of public child care funding for working mothers remained at a serious disadvantage. This was true even though administrative contingencies (including discrimination and limited state and local funding) meant that even with ADC a large number of poor mothers necessarily worked to support themselves and their families. But the long-standing workforce presence of these mothers, who were typically members of racial minority groups and divorced or separated women, did not disturb the assumption that all mothers should be at home. Since economic need presumably drove these women to work, the most avid supporters of the ADC ideal simply saw them as evidence that more public aid should be available. In the postwar era, however, an increasing number of married, middle-class women entered the workforce. And their presence, popularly understood as the result of a choice rather than a need, introduced new questions about the place of mothers in society and the related question of public funding for child care.

In debating child care funding in the 1950s and early 1960s, federal policymakers sought both to rationalize women's participation in the workforce and to chart an appropriate public policy response. At the same time, a general lack of funds to support public child care during the 1950s, coupled with the employment of more middle-class mothers, encouraged the growth of child care as a business and consequently spawned a renewed social welfare emphasis on the regulation of child care services. Throughout the 1950s and early 1960s, federal policymakers held fast to the conviction that child care should be primarily a private concern. This was true in 1954 when Congress enacted a tax deduction for child care and remained so when the Public Welfare Amendments of 1962 resulted in the first appropriation of federal day care funding since the close of World War II.

In other ways, however, the early 1960s represented a significant break from past child care policy.[2] That change was linked to a loss of faith in the central assumption of ADC. The debate surrounding enactment of the Public Welfare Amendments of 1962 clearly called into question the appropriateness of cash grants intended to enable poor women to be full-time homemakers and mothers. Both liberal and conservative policymakers suggested that this program might simply be producing subsequent generations of families dependent on federal cash aid. The reform legislation that emerged promoted a host of social services to accompany cash aid and ensure family "rehabilitation," and it was in this context that publicly provided child care received its first federal dollars since the end of World War II.[3]

The Occupation of Motherhood and the Child Care Tax Deduction

"When a man marries, no one expects him to cease being a commuter and to become a farmer because it would be good for the children—though it might. But when a woman marries her occupation becomes an auxiliary activity."[4] Historian David Potter, who made this observation in the early 1960s, used the word "occupation" to describe women's paid work outside the home, but he might just as well have attached the label to their work within the home. Formerly the processors of homegrown food and clothing, women in late industrial America, Potter wrote, had become consumers "in a society where consumption is an increasingly important economic function." According to Potter, "the responsibilities of the consumer are no mean task. To handle them successfully, a person must be something of a dietitian, a judge of the quality of many goods, a successful planner, a skillful decorator, and a budget manager. The business of converting a monthly sum of money into a physical basis for a pleasant life involves a real art, and it might be counted as a major activity even if there were not children to rear and meals to prepare."[5] In this formulation, the economic duties of the housewife apparently reside fully in the art of market transactions: better consuming. The economic realm excluded "children to rear and meals to prepare" tasks, which women as housewives, their domestics, or slaves had been performing long before the first factory began producing consumer goods.

Economist Nancy Folbre writes that the nineteenth-century "moral elevation of the home was accompanied by the economic devaluation of the work performed there." In short, economists of that era resolved an older dilemma about the productive value of "services" by treating unpaid household labor as moral and altruistic rather than economic and self-interested. In the new schema the division between productive and unproductive labor mirrored the difference between work done in the marketplace (economic) and work done in the home (domestic). American domestic experts from the antebellum Catherine Beecher to her early-twentieth-century home economist counterparts had sought to demonstrate that the attendant duties of keeping house—cooking and cleaning—could be specified as tasks and should be well managed.[6] The enormous success of the Children's Bureau's guide to raising children, *Infant Care* (1914), preempted in the postwar by Dr. Benjamin Spock's popular *Common Sense Guide to Baby Care* (1946), also suggested that caring for children involved acquiring job skills and knowledge.[7] The term "homemaking" was however meant to convey more than the ability to efficiently perform a series of tasks, and by the 1950s a new language of psychology had imbued the occupation with added responsibilities. Motherhood and homemaking called for emotional commitment from women; even to suggest a connection to the market economy sullied their image as quintessentially uncorrupted by self-interest. By definition, then, motherhood would be an unsalaried vocation.[8]

A mother's entrance into the labor market raised the question of her commitment to this primary career in the home even as it brought the economic aspects of women's home labor to the fore. In 1948 the Bureau of Labor Statistics (BLS) acknowledged that there were monetary costs associated with women leaving home to work but described most of these related to the job outside the home rather than to the replacement of the unpaid work that women regularly performed inside the home. Explaining why it had chosen to devise a standard city worker budget around a model family composed of "an employed father, a housewife not gainfully employed, and two children under 15,"[9] Ewan Clague, commissioner of the BLS, commented: "The manner of living and the expenditures would both be significantly different if the mother were assumed to be employed. For example, a working woman would likely spend more for clothes, transportation, household operation, and meals away from home than is allowed in the budget for the woman of the family."[10] Although the survey clearly counted on the unpaid labor of housewives in determining budget needs, it may have assumed that women would continue to perform many or all of these duties even if they entered the paid workforce.

The cost of meals and laundry are calculated in the BLS budget of the city worker's family as the dollar value of food items, added to the price of major household appliances: "the gas or electric cook stove, the mechanical refrigerator, and the washing machine." The "mother, as homemaker," the survey continues, "not only prepares the family meals but also performs the heavier household tasks, such as cleaning and the laundry of household linens and clothing. . . . Since there is usually no paid household help, the house is ordinarily equipped as a workplace with essential facilities for carrying out these tasks without undue physical strain." This gave the house as the shop floor of the solitary unpaid mother explicit description.[11]

Although the model family used in the survey had two school-age children, "a boy 13 years of age . . . and a girl 8," the detailed discussion of the family's "manner of living" did not describe any of the unpaid child care duties that their presence entailed. Presumably, the "not gainfully employed" mother saw the children off to school, met them afterward, and supervised their activities entirely during the months-long annual summer vacation. This work existed so far outside the official economic realm, however, that there was apparently not a need to describe how it happened or to attach any costs to it.[12] In the early 1950s a movement to amend the tax code and allow a working mother to deduct from her income the amount of money paid for housekeeping and child care would challenge this separation.[13]

Representative Kenneth Keating (R-N.Y.) introduced the first such proposal for a tax deduction in 1947. Several years later he explained that he had suggested the legislation after receiving letters and talking with "wage-earning women who were forced to employ someone to look after their home and children while they were working." He continued, "I was impressed with the argument that they should be able to deduct these expenses in the same way a businessman can deduct the ordinary expenses incidental to the conduct of his business."[14] On Capitol Hill the idea received little attention at first, but by the congressional session of 1949–50 three more House members introduced similar legislation.[15] In 1950 the Congress of Industrial Organizations (CIO) passed a resolution favoring a tax deduction for child care expenses, and in December of that year Lillian Hatcher of the United Auto Workers Women's Department endorsed the tax deduction at a meeting of the Women's Bureau Labor Advisory Committee. Citing the interest of trade union women in the possible tax code change, the Women's Bureau inquired about the impetus for this legislation in letters to three members of Congress who had formally proposed a deduction for child care expenses in the legislative session of 1951–52. The bureau's query "as to whether [prior] interest in this bill has been expressed by women's or civic groups" brought a unanimous no from the lawmakers.[16]

The members did, however, cite support from individual constituents for the proposed child care tax deduction. Representative Keating indicated that he had some "25 or 30 individual letters from women expressing deep interest in this legislation." Representative J. Caleb Boggs (R-Del.) could find only six letters on the topic received by his office, all supportive and "all but one of them . . . from women who are working and are thereby required to pay private nursery schools or others considerable amounts of money to permit their absence from home during the work day." The office of Rep. Edna Kelly (D-N.Y.), the most recent member proposing a deduction, reported "very little expression of interest" from individuals.[17] One possible reason for the small but growing interest in this legislation appears in a letter sent to the Women's Bureau in April 1951 from a professional librarian and mother of a three-year-old. Pointing out first that she could not deduct the hundred dollars that she spent monthly on child care, even while a business owner could deduct any "necessary business expense," the writer added: "It does seem that a change should be made this year because of the additional social security tax on household employees."[18] In 1950 Congress had revamped the Social Security Act and for the first time extended coverage to some domestic workers. The new law required that individuals regularly employing private household help pay benefits into the Social Security system.[19] By 1952 the child care tax deduction, now seen as an issue of tax fairness for women, had broadened its base of support. Significantly, the Internal Revenue Commissioner's office began to feel pressure to suggest a tax deduction for child care expenses, and the proposal also received attention in the popular press. In 1953 the ability to deduct child care costs had become such a hot topic that by the time the House Ways and Means Committee convened tax code revision hearings in June no fewer than thirty related legislative proposals had already been introduced in that year.[20]

The growing popularity of a deduction for child care tax expenses brought into question the whole notion of unpaid motherhood; the logic of the proposals directly challenged the idea that work done inside the home had no market value. If a mother paying a housekeeper or nursery school had a tax relief claim comparable to that of a businessman who paid a secretary or hired a night watchman—to use two examples given in the record—could work done inside the home still be considered entirely outside the productive economy? The business deduction analogy, in fact, contradicted the tax agency's official understanding of the nature of unpaid (and paid) labor inside the home.[21] In 1939 a tax appeals court rejected Henry and Lillie Wright Smith's claim that the wages they paid a nanny to care for their young child while they both worked were a legitimate deduction from their taxable income. The Smiths noted that business owners could deduct from their taxable income any cost judged necessary for them to earn income; they argued that the wages paid their nanny were an essential and necessary cost enabling Lillie Smith to earn an income. The tax court did not agree.[22]

Instead, the court compared the rendering of household services to a worker's need to wear clothes when he left the house or to see a doctor when he was sick. Clothes and medical costs were not deductible as business expenses, the court argued, and neither were the similarly "personal" and "private" tasks of housekeeping and childrearing. The court stated, "We are not prepared to say that the care of children, like similar aspects of family and household life, is other than a personal concern. The wife's services as custodian of the home and protector of its children are ordinarily rendered without monetary compensation. There results no taxable income from performance of this service and the correlative expenditure is personal and not susceptible of deduction." Even if a wife chose to hire someone to perform "her domestic function" this did not "deprive the same work performed by others of its personal character nor furnish a reason why its cost should be treated as an offset in the guise of a deductible item."[23]

The court's reasoning fit easily within long social and legal traditions that bound women to the home and its unpaid labor, but it sounded at odds with a resurgent and broadening postwar definition of liberal individual rights.[24] The syndicated columnist Sylvia Porter described the inability of the nation's many working mothers to "deduct the expense of domestic help 'ordinary and necessary' in the production of her income" as "grossly unfair," "clearly an injustice," and "painfully unrealistic."[25] Even the author of the opinion in Smith had to admit that when it came to deciding what were "necessary" business expenses, "the line is not always an easy one to draw." Supporters of the tax deduction for child care were quick to recognize the available populist rhetoric. "Can anyone really go on record as voting that the 'business' expense of a working mother—which arises from her concern to be self-supporting, at the same time keep her home together and her children well and happy—is not deductible; while the cost of a membership in a couple of country clubs may be?" asked Rep. Sam Yorty (D-Calif.) of Los Angeles.[26]

For supporters of the child care tax deduction a basic problem with the tax fairness argument was its presumption that mothers could rightfully be earning wages when the occupation of motherhood in fact required full-time commitment to a prescribed, unsalaried vocation. Representative Kenneth Roberts (D-Ala.) noted that one of the "serious objections" to his legislation that would have granted a tax deduction for the child care expenses of working mothers came " from those who say that to encourage mothers to work is an attack on the sanctity of motherhood and the generally accepted idea that her place is in the home."[27] A delegate who opposed the tax deduction at the UAW convention in 1953 echoed this traditionalist concern: "The old American way of life of the husband being the breadwinner and the woman staying home taking care of the children and the home seems to be passé," he lamented.[28]

Increasingly it seemed that traditional gender obligations clashed with the imperatives of an expanding, consumer-driven market economy. By the early 1950s the Census Bureau reported that the "income of husband-and-wife families in which the wife was a paid worker was considerably higher, on the average, than that of those in which the wife did not have a paid job or did only unpaid work on the family farm or in the family business."[29] By 1953, as public and congressional debate on the child care tax deduction reached a high point, close to one-third of married women who lived with their husbands and had school-age children engaged in paid labor. Married women who lived with their husbands and were the mothers of preschoolers were a great deal less likely to work for wages: between 15 and 16 percent were in the labor force that year. Still, the labor force participation rate of mothers of young children showed a significant increase in only the preceding five years and seemed incomparably removed from the much lower rates that prevailed in 1940.[30]

The House Ways and Means Committee opened hearings in June 1953 that were aimed at accomplishing the first major tax overhaul in decades. That the rewrite would happen under Dwight Eisenhower, the first Republican president elected since Herbert Hoover, gave the tax bill added significance for members on both sides of the aisle. The hearings would stretch over two months as the Ways and Means Committee heard more than five hundred witnesses discuss forty major tax topics—from stock options and deferred compensation plans to deduction of medical and dental expenses.[31] Discussion of the child care tax deduction came on the first day of testimony. All thirteen witnesses who spoke on the topic strongly supported a revision of the tax law to include a deduction for child care expenses. Most, in fact, were members of the House of Representatives who had introduced specific proposals themselves. Additional testimony came from nurses and unionized office workers; finally, two individual working women traveled to Capitol Hill from nearby suburbs in Maryland and Virginia to urge creation of the child care tax deduction.[32]

As the argument had developed in the press it seemed to be a simple matter of justice. Businessmen could deduct necessary expenses; working mothers could not. An editorial in *Redbook* in February 1953 declared, "with full indignation, that it's the absolute responsibility of President Eisenhower and the Congress to change the tax laws so the working wife isn't penalized for working."[33] But a difficulty with this reasoning quickly emerged in the hearing record, just as it had in debate outside the hearing room: a businessman didn't have to justify earning income, whereas a working mother did. To claim an expense as business-related and therefore deductible a businessman simply needed to show the expense as necessary to his ability to earn income. The first task of the working mother, and of those who spoke in her behalf, was not to show that the wages she paid for child care were an expense necessary for her to earn an income; it was instead to explain why a mother would be earning income at all.[34]

The incongruity of a wage-earning mother stemmed from the idea that motherhood required a single-minded, altruistic devotion to family and children. To suggest another possibility, and especially to make the mother an economic actor, tarred her as merely self-interested—manifestly unmotherly. It seems clear from the letters and actions of the working mothers who were day care activists in Cleveland, the District of Columbia, and California that many women saw affordable, accessible child care as in their own best interest. Yet displaying self-interest in a child care service in a nondeferential manner, or one unmediated by family concerns, did not generally win these women political support. Although self-interested action seemed an appropriate, indeed essential characteristic for fathers and men, because it demonstrated their rationality, for women self-interest remained somewhat unseemly; for mothers of young children, especially, it would be seen as more selfish than rational.[35]

Accordingly, while a number of witnesses backed up their call for "tax fairness" by citing seemingly extravagant or tangential expenses that business could deduct—lavish entertainment or a suite at the Waldorf, for instance—nearly everyone spent a much greater amount of time explaining why a mother earned an income. Most stressed that mothers did not choose paid work over unpaid housework, but rather that economic necessity brought mothers to the labor force; a few speakers additionally noted that the economy or a particular industry needed women workers. In either case a mother did not make the decision to work based on her own conception of self-interest (whatever that may have been) but only in the interest of her family, children, community, or the country as a whole. Further, setting the legislation apart from the idea that it might enhance a mother's ability to choose work, many witnesses argued for the child care tax deduction as a way for government to prevent juvenile delinquency and support families.[36]

Representative Edna Kelly led off the testimony, noting that her legislative proposal limited eligibility for the deduction to widows and widowers, who she believed were the "first line of duty." Allowing these taxpayers a child care tax deduction would not only be an act of "justice" but also "a matter to help protect the children" and "a measure to protect the family."[37] Her colleague Rep. Leonor Sullivan (D-Mo.), who like Kelly had been widowed while her children were still young, argued somewhat more expansively for women's place in the workforce. She noted that many women with children already worked, asserted that economic need brought them to the workplace, and added, "under our present economic system we need these women workers."[38] Representative Kenneth Roberts, whose bill appears to have received the widest public attention, stated that about a quarter of the nineteen million women in the work force had children under the age of eighteen and asserted, "these women do not work because they prefer to do so. They work because of necessity. They work because they have been left the head of their family and need the money in order to eat or they work to supplement their husband's small earnings." The great national demand for nurses and teachers, he further noted, explained why women were in the workforce and gave them a purpose. The legislation, he concluded, "did not inten[d] to encourage mothers to work who do not need to do so." Rather, he noted, "its purpose is to apply the same principle to the individual wage earner as is applied to business generally."[39]

Rep. Noah Mason (R-Ill.) emerged as the committee's conservative point man on this issue. He saw the justice in granting some deduction for widows and widowers and possibly for other sole parents, but where a husband worked, his wife's entrance into paid labor translated immediately into an unwarranted act of self-interest and even greed on the part of a mother: "I know of dozens of instances in my own little town where the mother learned she could earn money during World War II and now insists upon doing it." Several witnesses later, he expanded on his distaste for the two-earner family by raising the "fur coat" flag.[40] Across the nation, critics of working mothers bandied about claims that trivialized women's paid labor by insisting that women sought paid work merely to buy luxuries for themselves; a fur coat seemed to come to many minds first. Mason's preachment suggests that at bottom, the seemingly ubiquitous complaint about fur coats represented an objection to the idea that a woman might by her own wages fulfill a personal desire, and to a concomitant belief that to do so represented a violation of selfless motherhood. "A married lady insists upon working so that she can buy a $750 fur coat because her husband cannot afford it. He is working; he is earning what we would call a good living, but she cannot afford these luxuries and she wants these luxuries and therefore she goes to work and earns for herself enough to get these luxuries, and she neglects her children or hires someone who is not capable of handling them and is letting them run the streets and thus bringing about juvenile delinquency?"[41] Although the experts had reached conflicting findings on the matter, Mason repeatedly stressed his belief that juvenile delinquency always and necessarily resulted when a self-interested mother left the home for the workplace.[42]

For Rep. Mason the major public policy dilemma was much the same as it had been for Congress in its debate over publicly funded child care in Washington, and as it continued to be for the state legislature in California: how to draw a line between the women who were compelled to work and those who simply wanted to work. Within this reasoning, those compelled to work might be considered a proper object of public concern and thus merit some government assistance; but the members of the second group were potential "abusers" of the system. When Rep. Arthur Klein (D-N.Y.) presented testimony on the necessity for many wives in his working-class district to earn wages in addition to their husbands, Rep. Mason interrupted to patiently explain the difficulty as he saw it. "Our problem, sir, is to draw a line between those women who have to work, are compelled to work because their husbands do not earn enough, or because they are unable to earn money or incapable of earning it, and those women who want to work to earn extra money to buy things they want that their husbands cannot afford to buy for them. Where shall we draw the line? That is the only question in my mind as to our problem." Representative Klein quickly conceded that "some of these women might decide they do not like housework and want to get a job." He suggested that a means test might be a possible way out of the dilemma and emphasized his agreement with Mason that only women who entered the workforce through economic need should be eligible for the tax deduction.[43]

If one applies to men the dichotomy of work engaged in out of choice versus work engaged in because of economic need, it quickly becomes clear that the dichotomy is rooted in gender assumptions and obligations. The great majority of fathers had no more choice about going out to earn wages than they did about putting clothes on in the morning (to use the tax court's analogy). Nonetheless, when pressed, most witnesses conceded with Mason that a distinction between mothers who earned wages because of economic need and those who did so because they wanted to do so represented a critical dividing line for the tax deduction policy. Financially secure and confident in her right to pursue a professional career, Nancy Henderson would be an exception. Henderson, who introduced herself as a "housewife" and "working mother," argued that any maximum income level used to determine eligibility for the deduction would discriminate against professionally trained high-income mothers. "If such an income tax deduction is accepted in principle, it should be universally applied. Because a woman has been able to acquire an education and has pursued a career along with her family, she should not be penalized because of her capability and ambition and the fact that she is earning a salary of $6,000 or more." Under tough questioning from Rep. Mason, Henderson remained unbending.[44]

Henderson insisted on granting to a young married female professional a "personal decision" with regard to taking on (in Mason's words) "the dual obligation and responsibility of raising a family, keeping a home, and holding on to her career." What about in an economic depression, he continued, "then would you say she should have the right to her career as well as her married privileges?" Henderson thought that whoever was the better worker should keep the job. When Mason grandly referred to the "thousand, if not millions" of married women who "neglected" their families to go out and earn money, only to spend it on themselves, Henderson acknowledged a division between need and choice but did not agree with the policy implications that Mason and others drew from it. It seemed to her that most women did work out of economic necessity, but this was no reason to think that professional women shouldn't be allowed to work: "I work out of choice," she asserted.[45]

The House Ways and Means Committee concluded its tax hearings in mid-August and announced that rewriting the "antiquated" tax code would be its "first order of business" in the coming year. Drawing on the committee's work, the Treasury Department proposed twenty-five specific revisions to the tax code, including a limited deduction for child care expenses. And in his State of the Union address in January 1954, President Eisenhower stressed that his administration wanted to reduce "tax inequities" for "small taxpayers," "reduce restraints on the growth of small business," and "encour-

age initiative enterprise and production." The postwar agenda of an expanding economy encouraged by fiscal policy remained on course.[46]

But if Democrats and Republicans agreed on the objective, how to get
there was a different story. Almost immediately Democrats derided the administration's tax plan as a scheme that benefited businesses and the wealthy
while leaving most taxpayers without any relief. The 875-page proposed tax
bill released by the House Ways and Means Committee in March was opposed by the committee's Democrats as giving a "mere pittance of relief to
the average taxpayer and substantial relief to larger businesses." Democrats
in both the House and the Senate would unsuccessfully press for an amendment to increase the personal tax exemption for every taxpayer, while seeking at the same time to derail provisions designed to reduce taxes on certain
business investments and on dividend income. Within this partisan drama
the child care tax deduction figured as a way for the administration and the
Republicans to insist that their tax plan did include breaks for the "small
taxpayers," while Democrats and their allies saw the provision as an inadequate (and not necessarily important) bone tossed to a few.[47]

In any case the child care deduction proposed by the House Ways and
Means Committee, and subsequently passed by the full House in March
1954, provided a much smaller deduction for child care expense than had
been envisioned by many of the members of Congress who introduced legislation on the topic (see table 5). Under the House plan, a maximum deduction of $600 a year would be available to certain sole-support parents
who provided for a child less than ten years of age.[48] By comparison, the
thirty legislative proposals introduced in the prior year had been more likely
to include no limit for the deduction or to set it somewhere between $1,500
and $2,000 annually; most of the bills had allowed a deduction for the costs
of care for children through fifteen years of age; and although some proposals limited eligibility to a sole-support parent, close to two-thirds would have
offered the deduction for child care costs to employed mothers or taxpayers
generally.[49]

In subsequent Senate hearings on the tax proposal, Sen. Russell Long
(D-La.) pointed out that the proposed tax code changes would continue to
allow a businessman to deduct the full costs of expenses related to earning
income while granting widows a much more limited ability to do so. Initially the Treasury Department defended the circumscribed nature of the
child care tax deduction by arguing that to offer at least some relief would
be an improvement on the current law, which allowed no deduction for
child care expenses at all. Besides, they suggested, expanding the deduction
further would be too costly. Long continued to press the issue. How would

Table 5. Major Provisions of Twenty-Nine Child Care Tax Deduction Bills Introduced in Congress, January–June 1953, with Number of Bills to Which Each Provision Applies (Listed in Descending Order of Frequency)

Eligible Class	Maximum Annual Income	Maximum Annual Amount Deductible (adjusted gross income per taxpayer unless otherwise indicated)	Age of Child
Taxpayer (11)	No income limit (14)	$2,000–$2,500[a] (8)	Under 16 (22)
Employed mother (8)	$6,000, plus $500 for each child for	$1,300–$1,800[b] (8)	Under 14 (2)
Widow, widower, legally divorced, or separated[c] (5)	whom expenses deducted (6)[d]	No maximum (5)	Under 12 (2)
Widow, widower (3)	Deduction phased out after $5,000 or $7,500 (4)	Full cost up to certain maximum adjusted gross income ($5,000 or $7,500), then phased out (4)	Not specified or not clear (2) Under 6 (1)
Widow, legally divorced or separated (2)	$3,600–$4,500 (household) (2)	Deduction cannot exceed income (3)	
	$5,000, plus $600 for each child for whom expenses deducted (1)	$1,800 or 75% of adjusted gross income (1)	
	$6,000 (family), plus $500 for each child for whom expenses deducted (1)		
	$5,000 (family), plus $600 for each child for whom expenses deducted (1)		

Source: Adapted from "Provisions for Income Tax Deductions for Child Care and House-keeping Services" in Legislation Introduced in 83d Congress (1953), box 20, General Correspondence 1948–53, Records of the U.S. Women's Bureau, National Archives.

[a] Seven bills limited weekly maximum deduction to $40.

[b] Two bills limited maximum weekly deduction to $25 or $30.

[c] One proposal did not specify legal status but simply required that claimant not live with spouse; a separate bill extended eligibility to wives whose husbands were enlisted and serving abroad.

[d] One of these proposals dealt with gross income.

the Treasury Department react to "a proposal to permit working mothers to deduct that same expense of hiring a baby sitter, even though . . . they are married and their husbands are able to work?" he asked. Explaining the department's opposition to this notion, Treasury Secretary George Humphrey stated: "The Ways and Means Committee held long hearings on that and many of the child-care organizations and many of the churches and a great many people came in and objected to it. The Ways and Means Committee selected this as the proper way to do it."[50] It's not clear what objections Humphrey is talking about here. Although it's possible or even likely that the House Ways and Means Committee received some correspondence from those opposed to the tax deduction for child care, none of these letters, if there were any, made it into the hearing record. Neither does the printed record of the hearing include testimony from churches or child care organizations—pro or con—regarding the child care deduction. With the single exception of the American Federation of Labor, every one of the approximately twenty-five statements made before the House Ways and Means Committee, or submitted for the record, advocated a deduction for child care expenses in the rewritten tax code.[51]

When Sen. Long said he didn't care who disliked the idea and that he needed to know what the objections were, Humphrey replied: "The child-delinquency cases. There are great arguments that the mother ought to be at home looking after her children where there is a wage earner in the family." Long suggested that a mother might be working to help her children go to college or "become better citizens." And he finally succeeded in forcing Humphrey to concede that the child care deduction was "every bit as much of a legitimate expense on the part of a mother who feels that she must work, even though she is married, as it is on behalf of a businessman who has to hire that night watchman."[52] Long's adamant questioning on the hearing record more likely represented political posturing designed to make administration witnesses uncomfortable rather than serious consideration of the idea that the child care tax deduction should be broadened. And while the Senate acted to provide slightly less rigid eligibility requirements than had earlier been approved by the House—most significantly by allowing low- to middle-income two-earner families to claim some tax relief—it left in place the low cap on expenses that could be deducted.

When President Eisenhower signed the revised tax code into law in August 1954, eligible working parents could deduct up to $600 in actual child care expenses. To qualify, the expense had to have been for care of a child under the age of twelve years and used to enable the taxpayer to earn income. Sole-support mothers and widowers were eligible regardless of their

income level; married two-earner couples could qualify for the full deduction amount if they filed a joint return and earned less than $4,500 annually
(or about 84 percent of the national median income for two-earner families
in 1954).[53] In the first year of the tax benefit's existence about 230,000 taxpayers claimed a little over $73 million in tax deductions for money spent
on child care. About three-quarters of the child care deductions claimed in
that year were made by individuals or families with adjusted gross incomes
of less than $5,000.[54]

Working Mothers, Commercial Opportunity, and State Regulation

The dependent care tax deduction offered limited federal support for the
purchase of nonmaternal child care, and for decades to come it represented
the largest government "expenditure" (understood as revenue lost to the
treasury) for child care costs. By making this tax code adjustment, federal
lawmakers tacitly supported the use of paid, private child care arrangements
over direct public provision or subsidy of child care. Congress rejected the
latter option in 1945–46, when it ultimately ceased funding the network of
child care centers opened during World War II, and again in 1950–51 during the Korean War, when appropriators refused to allow spending on child
care for homefront defense workers.

In succeeding years an increasing number of mothers joined the paid
workforce and a small but growing number of private, for-profit child care
centers emerged to meet the consequent need for expanded child care services. Although reluctant to change their understanding of nonmaternal
child care as a temporary charity that should be offered only in limited circumstances, and long disdainful of proprietary child care services, social
welfare workers were forced to respond to these new circumstances. In the
absence of tax dollars or adequate charity funds to directly provide a sufficient quantity of child care, they began to promote licensing and regulations as a way to improve commercial child care services. By consulting
with, training, and licensing the growing class of child care entrepreneurs
they hoped, at least, to ensure the quality of the services offered. Some commercial child care providers understood what they could gain from the improved status that grew out of staff training and facility licensing, but at the
same time they resisted bureaucratic intervention in their business planning. Claiming status as private business entrepreneurs offering child care
services (rather than moral guardians who were voluntarily providing char-

ity), they ultimately helped to shape state and local child care standards as well as the meanings of nonmaternal child care provision. ·

The number of working mothers with children under the age of six rose from 1.2 million in 1948 to 2 million in 1955 and reached 3.1 million in 1965. Employment of mothers with school-age children (only) also rose sharply, from close to 2 million in 1948 to just under 5 million in 1965.[55] When the Korean War ended in 1953, the Census Bureau reported that the "working wife" had become "a characteristic feature of the American economy."[56] The vastly increased number of mothers in the workplace meant that the issue of arranging child care for young children, which during peacetime had been largely marginalized as a problem of the unfortunate poor and of sole-support mothers, became an issue of concern for a much broader group of families. A 1958 Census Bureau survey of the child care arrangements of full-time working women with children under twelve found that the great majority (82 percent) of these children lived in two-parent households. Unpaid care inside the home, provided usually by siblings, fathers, or grandmothers, remained the most common child care arrangement for working mothers. At the same time, care outside the child's home, whether in a group facility or (more frequently) at a caretaker's home, totaled close to 22 percent of all arrangements made; anywhere from a quarter to as many as one-third of the families regularly paid for child care.[57]

In response to the increasingly common employment of mothers, at least some private "charity" day care agencies may have begun to broaden their understanding of who should be served—particularly to include families where mothers worked to help pay mortgages, improve their children's educational opportunities, or to in some other way enhance their families' economic standing. But in general these traditional providers of outside-the-home care had limited capacity and continued to question their role in serving the expanding number of working mothers seeking class mobility or personal satisfaction in work.[58] At the same time, direct government provision or subsidy of paid child care remained virtually nonexistent. A 1960 study by the Children's Bureau of day care facilities, including a limited number of individual "family day care" homes, found that only 7.1 percent of all licensed facilities in the nation were supported with public tax dollars. Further, the report noted that if California's unusually large number of public centers were removed from the mix, the proportion of taxpayer-supported services would have dropped to 1.3 percent. Within this near total public service vacuum a few individuals began to see a market for child care provision. Indeed the same report found that about two-thirds of all licensed facilities were proprietary and commercial.[59]

The facilities survey gave national numbers to a reality that local social welfare workers had recognized at least a decade earlier. With the number of employed mothers increasing, demand for child care in communities grew, and without money to boost public provision of child care, some social welfare workers came to hope that through government regulation and education commercial child care could become an important community resource. Regulation of day care centers had been an early-twentieth-century campaign of the day nursery movement. The few laws enacted were judged marginally effective at best, and the effort dissipated even as public and private social workers continued to view for-profit day care services with disdain.[60] Reporting on a decline in private nonprofit and public child care facilities after World War II, a state welfare worker in Iowa depicted for-profit child care sites as seemingly irredeemable: "In Des Moines a notorious operator of three places has sent a steady stream of disillusioned mothers forth to seek the services of the juvenile court or of licensed placing agencies. Sickening stories of neglect, drinking, and degeneracy are told by those who do not stay. In several instances, women who had worked in war-time nurseries and had first hand knowledge of the need for continued service, opened up independent services on 'shoe string' support. Several were definitely bad. The women did not offer good care on their own responsibility largely because of inadequate housing and personal instability."[61] A joint publication of federal agencies in 1953, concerned with planning child care services for working mothers, used less Dickensian language but showed obvious distaste for the "rapid spread" of child care services as "business ventures" that charged "exorbitant fees" and provided "substandard care." While antipathy to commercial provision of child care endured, the practical realities of postwar America demanded new responses. Social service regulators and some of their private allies began to see both a duty to improve standards and the possibility that commercial services might provide acceptable care.[62]

A renewed campaign to ensure better child care through licensing and standards developed in the 1950s. By 1952 the Children's Bureau would seek specific federal funds to provide "program materials" and other assistance to state public health and social welfare agencies that were involved with licensing or otherwise designing regulations for child care facilities. Federal appropriators denied this request, but the campaign to improve and expand child care through education and regulation moved forward despite the lack of federal fiscal support.[63] Between 1950 and 1957 legislatures in twenty-one states established or revised day care licensing laws. The sharp rise in licensing legislation even more dramatically produced a welter of new standards for day care operators. Over the same seven-year period, thirty-two state departments charged with licensing child care facilities issued standards or regulations concerning group day care.[64]

The upsurge in licensing, aimed primarily at commercial providers, reflected a realization that even if publicly funded and philanthropic centers existed, they could not meet the total demand for care.[65] In 1955 a representative of the Welfare Council of Metropolitan Chicago noted that "by far the largest number of children in Chicago are served by commercial nurseries." While some of these remained of poor quality, many had improved, and, he continued, "we are certainly less plagued by sub-standard services than we were prior to the licensing law some four years ago."[66] A representative of Boston United Community Services believed that education about the elements of a good child care program also represented an important way to improve standards at commercial centers. The group had already seen an "improved concept of day care" through wide distribution of a pamphlet they had produced on the subject, and they planned to work with state regulators to "further the formation of courses for commercial day care operators and their staffs" and "develop model [licensing] legislation."[67]

Commercial operators began to organize in this period, and some evidence suggests that state social welfare departments helped to foster them as part of an effort to improve care standards at for-profit centers. In 1952 group care proprietors in Dallas were a part of a local child welfare planning committee. At the proprietors' request the committee (including state public and private welfare agencies) planned a two-day institute covering topics such as "interpretation of child care, adequate standards, good programming, [and] administrative and operating techniques." A longer-term objective of the planning committee was "to develop a permanent organization of commercial operators who could continue to exchange ideas and knowledge, and perhaps be the means of attracting other interested and qualified women into the operation of child-care centers or homes."[68] Indeed the Texas Licensed Child Care Association, with members in Fort Worth, Houston, Dallas, and Austin, came together by 1953 and would help to rewrite state licensing regulations for the industry.[69] In California two groups of private day care operators (one in the north and one in the south) also organized in the early 1950s. The southern group, eventually named the Pre-School Association, formed after a licensing agent for the welfare department suggested that private operators meet to "discuss and find solutions to common problems." Like its northern counterpart, the Private Nursery School Association of Northern California, the Pre-School Association of Southern California helped to improve and police the standards of other proprietors in the interest of the whole group. It grew into a "generally effective" lobby in Sacramento for "legislation favorable to the private owner's interests." By the 1960s both groups were operating statewide and to varying degrees opposed state child care legislation promoted by supporters of California's public Child Care Centers.[70]

Indeed, the advent of much more broadly accepted and somewhat improved commercial care helped to divide group day care users between those who paid full cost and those whose children attended public and private, voluntary centers and who usually paid a partial fee or no fee at all. This new division of group care users reinforced existing distinctions that assigned separate meanings to the nonmaternal care of young children according to a family's ability to buy a certain kind of child care arrangement. Wealthy women had rarely been condemned for hiring nannies and nursemaids to care for their children. Especially by the 1950s, professional women who privately arranged for their children's care while they pursued a career might similarly escape condemnation. Commercial group care facilities potentially lowered the cost of nonmaternal child care for additional two-earner families with more moderate incomes, and at the same time allowed them to make private arrangements for their children's care while they worked. Further, operating as a form of private enterprise in the official economy, commercial and proprietary centers could potentially establish a status distinct from that of older private, charity-based day nurseries.[71]

Social welfare literature continued to describe day care as an unfortunate necessity for "abnormal" families unable to otherwise provide proper care for their children. But even for social workers this did not prevent an early separation between "unfortunate" patrons of public and private, voluntary care facilities and the new class of child care consumers using the best commercial services. Further, many private operators cast off the social welfare stigma by naming their service a "preschool" or "nursery school" rather than a day care center.[72] A report in the early 1950s from Dallas, where the vast majority of more than 3,500 children using day care were in commercial centers or private homes that charged a fee, found current facilities inadequate to the need. The state public welfare department saw "little prospect" that the community would support more public centers, and even if Dallas residents did help support more voluntary centers, this could never be expected to meet more than the "most pressing needs." The agency concluded, "Private facilities will be required for those who can pay for them and this calls for an increased number of well-equipped and licensed commercial centers."[73]

In the long run, organizations of commercial operators helped to solidify the difference between public and private, voluntary day care users on the one hand and those who enrolled in commercial centers on the other. The existence across California of a public child care program limited primarily to lower-income and sole-support families appeared to encourage (rather than impede) the development of commercial centers. From 1951 to 1961 the number of child care facilities licensed by the California State Department of Social Welfare increased by approximately 60 percent. And from its earliest days, the California Pre-School Association, representing primarily private owners in southern California, sought to stake out the territory of commercial providers rather than that of publicly subsidized child care. The private operators were especially unhappy that publicly subsidized centers continued to enroll a small number of "exempt" families served by the state's publicly subsidized centers.[74]

"Exempt" families were allowed to use California's child care service, regardless of their income level, because they worked in occupations considered essential to the community welfare or the national defense. After mid-1951 these families were required to pay the full cost of care if they enrolled their child in a state-supported center, and their numbers declined substantially. Insisting, contrary to the advocates of the state child care program, that good commercial options were now available, the Pre-School Association believed that no person able to pay the full cost of group care should be enrolled in a center that received public funding.[75] Testifying at a state legislative committee hearing on the California program in 1954, a representative of the Pre-School Association accused parents who were exempt from the means test of "burdening the tax structure." He asserted that "tax-subsidized facilities should be confined in their enrollments to the children of needy working parents, without exception."[76] A few years later the Private Nursery School Association of Northern California took a similar stand on state-subsidized child care, requesting that the law be changed to make "only those in need" eligible to attend state-subsidized child care centers, and calling for the elimination of the sliding scale system of fee payment.[77] In short, private operators believed that allowing exempt families to have access to publicly supported centers transgressed their right to market commercial child care to middle-income families, and at least the Pre-School Association had no qualms about portraying the families as an undue "tax burden," even though they paid a full-cost fee.

The state Senate committee seemed convinced by the private operators' argument. In their report to the full legislature in 1955, the committee members backed up their call for an end to all state funding for the child care program with the claim that commercial child care facilities of high quality were widely available, affordable alternatives to a public program. Additionally, they turned the spotlight on eligibility and admission procedures at the publicly supported centers, suggesting that sometimes lax administration allowed parents who could adequately pay for the service elsewhere to use the state program.[78]

From the early 1960s on, private care operators would help to define and limit who could and could not receive care and education in California's newly authorized "compensatory education" program; additionally, although it studiously proclaimed that it was not opposed to the state's child care program, the private group openly worked against any increases in the number of public child care centers. When federal money brought expansion in any case, private operators successfully insisted that new centers be located exclusively in low-income neighborhoods.[79] Although in later decades some commercial operators began to see federal money as a tool for expanding their businesses, they objected to government regulation of their businesses and to spending public money in ways that they believed would unnecessarily raise teachers' salaries and set other unreasonable operating standards. Like the National Association of Child Care Management (an industry group that was a force in federal day care legislation in the 1980s), members of the California Pre-School Association collectively used their status as entrepreneurs in the official economy to insist that licensing standards remain reasonable from their point of view. When the State Department of Social Welfare sought to write more stringent staff standards "in the role of a latter-day Paul Revere [the Pre-School Association] sent out the alarm to members that free enterprise in group care was in danger." Members responded, "eloquently presenting their case" to the State Department of Social Welfare with a "barrage of letters, telegrams and testimony at public hearings."[80]

A lengthy battle over child care regulations in Ohio also presaged later friction around this issue between federal administrators and organized commercial care providers. Although Ohio did have a licensing law, by the early 1950s private and public social workers were complaining that it had no enforcement teeth. These advocates of statewide regulations sought to replace a patchwork of unevenly enforced municipal codes with state-enforced standards that covered both for-profit and nonprofit operators. For nearly three decades they would be stymied by the active resistance to regulation of proprietary day care operators. The Committee on Day Care Planning, a part of the Cleveland Welfare Federation's Children's Council, was organized (or reactivated) in 1955 after a ruling by the state attorney general that cast doubt on the legal authority of the State Department of Public

Welfare to enforce licensing standards.[81] The Cleveland day care group, citing as undesirable the growth in commercial child care services, sought to enhance municipal regulation of child care centers and also joined state lobbying efforts to gain legislative authority for enforceable state day care standards. The lobbying appeared to have paid off in 1959 when the Ohio state legislature approved H.B. 896, described in the Cleveland committee's meeting minutes as "authoriz[ing] the State Department of Welfare to establish responsible rules and regulations for children's agencies and institutions [that] would have the force of law." Drafting of state standards began shortly, and the department produced final regulations in December 1961.[82]

As it happened, the years spent lobbying for and drafting the child care rules far exceeded the length of time they remained in effect. Shortly after their release, Helen Baughman, owner-operator of Aunt Helen's Merry Day Nursery in Cuyahoga Falls, and thirty other nursery and child-care operators from Cleveland, Columbus, Cincinnati, Akron, Dayton, and other Ohio cities challenged the regulation in the Franklin County Common Pleas Court. The proprietary child care operators charged that the state Department of Public Welfare did not have the authority to make rules and regulations covering the field of private day care nurseries, that in adopting the rules the department had not complied with state laws concerning procedures for adopting new regulations, and finally that the rules were "discriminatory [and] vague" and constituted "an invasion of privacy and a taking of property without due process of law." The court agreed with the private operators in June 1962 when it found that the State Department of Public Welfare's rulemaking power was limited to "beneficial and correctional institutions" and that day care centers were neither of these. It also ruled that the department's method of adopting the child care rules did not comply with Ohio's Administrative Procedures Act and that the private operators had been adversely affected by the child care rules. In upholding the decision, a state appellate court focused much of its decision on the failure of the department to follow the Administrative Procedures Act. But it also stated its agreement with the lower court's finding of harm to the private day care operators and noted that some "operators or their representatives" expressed the view that "the rules might well operate so adversely as to put them out of business."[83]

Although some of Ohio's child care centers would become subject to state rules in the later 1960s, efforts by advocates to obtain enforceable and uniform rules that applied equally to all child care centers in the state would not succeed for more than two decades. In the interim there would be further challenges by proprietary operators to the rulemaking authority of the State Department of Public Welfare so that enforceable standards applicable to all Ohio child care centers ultimately were not adopted until the middle 1980s.[84]

Fostering Public Child Care Support within Welfare Reform

After the defeat of federal child care support during the Korean War years and a subsequent rush of day care licensing and regulatory reforms at the state level, social work activists began again to seek federal money for the provision of child care. By the early 1960s their goal merged with the energetic efforts of the newly elected administration of John F. Kennedy to reform the nation's primary program of support for poor mothers and their children: the Aid to Dependent Children (ADC) program, or "welfare." Enacted in 1935 as a part of the landmark Social Security Act, ADC built on the framework of state mother's pension programs, which had been created largely in the name of providing support for the young children of widowed mothers. In principle if not necessarily in practice, this support was intended to allow these "deserving" mothers the opportunity to stay at home full-time and raise their children, rather than earn wages to support their family. But in the decades since their rapid establishment (first at the state level and then, in 1935, with federal subsidy), both public support for these cash grants and professional confidence in their effectiveness eroded.[85]

In the first place, the typical population served by the program shifted relatively quickly from the early "deserving" target population of widows with young children to a politically less sympathetic group: unmarried, divorced, and otherwise separated mothers. This change resulted both from an increased number of divorced, separated, and unmarried mothers and from legislative changes. The amendments to the Social Security Act enacted in 1939 created a new "survivor's insurance" benefit for widows and their children. Compared to ADC, this program provided far more generous benefits, with no means test, to families whose deceased fathers had worked in covered jobs. Even with a likely administrative bias toward aiding widows, as early as 1948 thirty-seven of the forty-eight states, along with the District of Columbia, reported that among families receiving ADC, the most common status of the father was estranged, deserted, "not married to mother," and divorced.[86] By 1961 only 7.7 percent of ADC families were eligible for the program because the father had died, compared to 67.2 percent because of the father's absence from the home (divorced, separated, deserted, not married to mother, imprisoned, or "other reason").[87]

In addition to this shift in the kind of families served, the postwar period also saw a large increase in the absolute number of people receiving ADC. Between 1946 and 1961 the number of recipients rose from 885,000 to more than 3.5 million. Again, aside from demographic changes (population growth and possibly the migration of African American families from the South to northern states that were more likely to provide aid), the increase is in part explained by legislative changes that broadened program eligibility. Among a number of changes, the most significant came in 1950 when Congress agreed to subsidize state ADC payments intended to support the mother, instead of restricting this subsidy to aid offered solely on behalf of her children.[88]

In 1956 Congress amended the purpose of the original ADC program—providing financial assistance to needy dependent children—to add promoting "maximum self-support and personal independence consistent with the maintenance of continuing parental care and protection." Preparing to enact reforms that would build on this significant change in the program's orientation, in 1958 Congress established two advisory boards to study the federal public (cash) welfare and child welfare programs. The reports with recommended changes were submitted to Congress in 1960 just as two high-profile news stories—one in Louisiana and the other in Newburgh, New York—thrust the administration of welfare into the headlines and further encouraged a reformed federal welfare system.

In Louisiana the state legislature passed a new "suitable home" restriction, as a result of which nearly one-quarter of the state's ADC cases—including 22,501 children—became ineligible for cash aid in August 1960. The new state law provided that no assistance would be permitted for "any person who is living with his or her mother if the mother has had an illegitimate child after a check has been received from the Welfare Department unless and until proof satisfactory to the parish board of the Public Welfare has been presented showing that the mother has ceased illicit relationships and is maintaining a suitable home."[89] Child welfare advocates were especially dismayed that Louisiana's policy apparently overlooked the assumed right of all children to receive aid based on their own needs alone. Adding insult, further investigation revealed that other states had "quietly adopted" policies similar to that of Louisiana and that no federal policy absolutely forbade the practice.[90]

Responding to the controversy, in early 1961 Arthur Fleming, the soon-to-retire secretary of the U.S. Department of Health, Education and Welfare, notified states that as of July 1, 1961, if a child otherwise eligible for ADC was denied aid because of a determination that the home was "unsuitable," the state would be out of compliance with federal policy and thus unable to claim any federal subsidy for its ADC program. The regulation stated that assistance to the child must be continued "during the time efforts are being made to either improve the home conditions or to make arrangements for the child elsewhere." That is, a state could not simply relieve itself of all responsibility for children it deemed to be living in "unsuitable" homes: federal regulation now tied significant responsibilities to such a determination. Services to "improve" the home would be required, or the child would need to be removed from the home (a process requiring a court order and further obligating the state's child welfare system to assume full-time custody of the children). The practical, and intended, effect of the new rule was to deny states the right to end benefits to children simply because they were born out of wedlock.[91]

Congress quickly sought to mute the effect of the new regulation by granting states a temporary reprieve from any federal financial penalty for noncompliance with the new regulation. Later, as part of the Public Welfare Amendments of 1962, Congress provided that a state could not be financially penalized for failing to provide ADC to an eligible child so long as the state, by law, made some other cash aid provision for the eligible child (such as providing the child with local "general assistance"). Federal lawmakers also sought to cushion any financial repercussions to the states by offering to subsidize foster care costs for children who were removed from homes that had been receiving ADC benefits—provided that the court order permitting the removal included a finding that remaining in the home was "contrary to the welfare" of the child.[92]

When it was enacted, Louisiana's "suitable home" law had a disproportionate effect on African American cash aid recipients and was understood as an attack on their civil rights. Outside the black community, the immediate focus remained on the children who had lost benefits rather than the unmarried mothers who cared for them, and these children garnered significant sympathy. By contrast, the efforts to cut public assistance costs in Newburgh, New York, a small, formerly industrial city, had explicitly racial overtones and drew even broader public attention. The city manager, Joseph Mitchell, sought to place the blame for its declining fortunes on the growth of its African American population and more particularly on their use of welfare benefits. Claiming that blacks moved into Newburgh to get aid, in June 1961 Mitchell issued a thirteen-point welfare reform proposal designed to curtail access to ADC benefits. His proposals included mandatory work for able-bodied male recipients, a three-month limit on aid within any one year, the denial of aid to mothers who bore out-of-wedlock children after they received aid, and a "variety of harassments to discourage relief applications." Most of Mitchell's proposals were ultimately deemed too harsh and were disallowed by state and federal administrators; and his statistics concerning the amount of welfare offered to African Americans in Newburgh were found to be inaccurate. But his tale of rising welfare costs linked to "unwanted migrants and unwed moms" found a receptive audience nationally and endured.[93]

Offered in the context of these news headlines and public attitudes, the Kennedy administration's proposals for welfare reform promised "relief from relief" and were specifically designed to make the Aid to Dependent Children program more "palatable."[94] As adopted by Congress, the Public Welfare Amendments of 1962 offered substantial federal support to the recently added goal of maximum self-support and personal independence for adult aid recipients. New provisions committed the federal treasury to provide $3 out of every $4 that a state spent on "rehabilitation" services for ADC recipient parents and caretakers (that is, services deemed necessary for a family to be self-supporting); it also allowed states to use this generous funding match to provide the same services for individuals in families deemed "at risk" of becoming public assistance recipients. The new law promised some federal subsidy for community work and training projects that states could choose to establish for the employment of adult ADC recipients. Further, it required states to provide child care services, if needed, for any work-program trainee and to deduct "any expenses reasonably attributable" to earning income before determining a family's eligibility for ADC. Finally, the new law separately authorized expanded funds for state and local child welfare services, redefined child welfare services to include day care for children of working mothers, allocated a certain portion of funds provided for child welfare to meet child day care needs, and called for coordinating child welfare services with services made available to children eligible for ADC.[95]

Child care became an explicit part of the Public Welfare Amendments of 1962 primarily through the lobbying efforts of social work activists. In the local and state postwar child care debates described earlier in this book, some advocates of publicly supported child care had suggested that child care was morally and fiscally superior to offering cash welfare through the ADC. Others who joined the debate pointedly suggested that taxpayer-funded child care contradicted what they understood as the primary purpose of the federal ADC program: providing for the full-time care of a child in the home by his or her mother. But for the social work activists who championed child care funding in 1962, neither of these positions may have been as important as the political reality: that the federal legislation to amend the ADC and child welfare programs generally provided an expedient legislative vehicle, almost certain to pass, with which to link their cause.

By 1956 Elinor Guggenheimer, a wealthy, well-connected civic activist, veteran of New York city and state postwar child care battles, and member of the Child Welfare League of America's Day Care Committee, had begun to formulate a strategy for raising the issue of day care to national prominence. Guggenheimer met with other professionals interested in child care provisions at a social work conference in 1957 and established the Inter-City Committee for Day Care (ICC). Organizing as a network of child welfare professionals, ICC members brought a different set of skills to their effort than those initially available to the grassroots organizations of day care users in Cleveland, the District of Columbia, and California. The group displayed both political savvy and access in its first three years, as it persuaded federal agencies to conduct research on day care, helped to craft day care legislation that was introduced in the U.S. Congress, and mobilized contacts nationwide to give day care greater prominence at the important White House Conference on Children and Youth in 1960. That same year, the group formally incorporated as the National Committee for the Day Care of Children (NCDCC) and inspired a national conference on day care cosponsored by the Women's Bureau and Children's Bureau.[96]

In August 1961 the National Committee for the Day Care of Children led more than thirty day care activists from eight states to Washington to lobby for day care funding. Representing primarily community day care associations and including some public welfare officials, they visited members of Congress and new political appointees in the Kennedy administration. They found a receptive audience in Abraham Ribicoff, the new Secretary of Health, Education, and Welfare. Ribicoff told the day care supporters that he had begun "taking a new look" at the nation's welfare system and understood that day care could be an asset: "Suppose we have work-relief programs. How can we put women to work if there is no place to put their children? We can't even send a woman to a school for job training if there is no place to put the children. The only way to work ourselves out of a third generation on relief is to have a place for the children to be well cared for while the mother works." Indicating his willingness to include day care in the administration's planned reform proposals, the secretary asked the committee's representatives to send their child care ideas to a committee of social welfare experts appointed by the administration that was reviewing possible legislative changes to the welfare law, primarily the Aid to Dependent Children (ADC) program.[97]

In the document that it sent to the Kennedy administration's Ad Hoc

Committee on Public Welfare, the National Committee on the Day Care of Children argued that federal day care funding would address the "growing picture of child neglect"; care for the children of working mothers topped an extensive list of circumstances in which day care was needed. The NCDCC noted the substantial and growing number of working mothers who, it argued, had become an essential part of the nation's workforce, and it cited a 1958 Census Bureau survey of child care arrangements, which found that some 400,000 children under the age of twelve had no care or supervision—even though their mothers worked full time. Other groups cited as having a specific need for services included children of migrant workers, those on military installations or living in areas affected by the defense economy, handicapped children, children from "broken or otherwise disturbed homes," children living in cities, and "deprived" children. In addition, afterschool and extended-school programs were needed for school-age children, while children under the age of three needed greater access to family day care. In summarizing its argument for federal funding, the NCDCC stated, "Mothers must be given a choice or helped by our social agencies to make the choice between such alternatives as—Aid to Dependent Children, full-time placement of their children [in foster care], or working in support of their families while still providing good care for their children." To allow this choice, day care programs that were safe and that stimulated intellectual, emotional, and physical growth in children were essential, the group continued. The NCDCC document suggested a first-year grant of $25 million to encourage program activity and set minimum standards.[98]

The Kennedy administration ultimately proposed one-fifth that amount, $5 million, for the first year of the legislation (fiscal year 1963) and $10 million in subsequent years—provided that Congress appropriated a minimum amount of funds for child welfare services overall.[99] In a manner consistent with its call to reserve a certain amount of child welfare funds for day care funding and following the NCDCC lead in promoting day care services as a solution to child neglect, the administration's bill redefined child welfare services to give explicit mention of "protecting and promoting the welfare of children of working mothers." Previously described in the law as being for the "protection and care of homeless, dependent, and neglected children, and children in danger of becoming delinquent," the longer definition proposed by the administration provided that child welfare services were "designed to supplement, or substitute for, parental care and supervision." Other listed purposes of child welfare services included "preventing or remedying, or assisting in the solution of problems which may result in, the neglect, abuse, exploitation, or delinquency of children," "protecting and caring for homeless, dependent, or neglected children," and "otherwise protecting and promoting the welfare of children, including the strengthening of their own homes where possible or, where needed, the provision of adequate care of children away from their homes in foster family homes or day-care or other child-care facilities."[100]

Despite Secretary Ribicoff's earlier explicit linking of day care with the administration's goal of "rehabilitating" ADC recipients and providing "relief from relief," the administration's legislative proposal made only one direct reference to day care services for aid recipients. It stated that "appropriate arrangements for the care and protection of the dependent child" must be made for ADC recipients who participated in federally supported "community work and training programs." Although the legislation newly allowed states to use federal funds for this purpose, establishing work training programs for ADC recipients was optional for states. Further, because Congress in 1961 had authorized payment of ADC to families where a father was unemployed, the training funds were often justified with reference to the presence of an identifiable group of "employable" (male) aid recipients.[101]

At the same time, however, all the administration's day care proposals were organized in the proposed legislation under the heading "Improvements in Services to Prevent or Reduce Dependency," and congressional discussion of the bill made absolutely clear that federally funded day care services should first be available to ADC families. The small amount of federal funding offered, a maximum of $10 million, guaranteed that at best an estimated ten thousand to fifteen thousand children could be served with this money.[102] Alone this would seem to have ensured continuation of a long-standing practice in social welfare of resolving a scarcity of day care funding by offering services to only those deemed most needy by case workers. Congress however chose to make certain that ADC recipients would receive priority for day care funding by adopting several amendments to the administration's day care proposals.

Although the day care proposals were a relatively small part of the bill, representing less than 2 percent of the total bill's projected first-year costs, the issue of federal day care funding received disproportionate attention in the hearing record. The House Ways and Means Committee took the majority of this testimony. At least ten witnesses who appeared before the committee, including Secretary Ribicoff, referred to the day care provisions of the bill, and two statements on the day care provisions were also made a part of the House hearing record. Owing no doubt to the lobbying efforts of the NCDCC, the Ways and Means Committee received more than forty letters supporting federal day care funding, which were also added to the hearing record. The letters came from fifteen states and were written by nursery school teachers, day care center staff and directors, social welfare advocates, and officials in public welfare departments. Reflecting a fundamental difference from the earlier campaigns for public child care funding in Cleveland, the District of Columbia, and California—where mothers who used day care were the primary correspondents and offered lengthy defenses of a publicly funded service—in this campaign only one single-paragraph letter came from a group of parents whose children attended a day care center in New York City.[103]

Most of those who testified in favor of the day care funds emphasized the growing number of working mothers in the country. Defending his administration's proposal to provide federal funds for day care, Secretary Ribicoff testified, "One of the most significant social changes in this century is the great increase in the number of married women in the labor force." He continued by noting, "About 3 million mothers with children under the age of 6 are now working, and 5 million mothers with children over the age of 6. Yet, the development of adequate day-care services has stood relatively still." Ellen Winston, speaking as past president of the American Public Welfare Association, asserted that "working mothers have taken their place as a prominent and indispensable part of the social and economic scene of this country." Noting the apparently inexorable rise in employed mothers, Joseph Reid, executive director of the Child Welfare League of America, concluded that "day care is an essential public utility."

But even as they justified federal day care funding with reference to a general expansion in the employment of mothers—fueled, as Secretary Ribicoff noted, by an increase in employment among married women—most of these day care funding advocates also described the use of this federal day care funds for a much more narrow group of women. Secretary Ribicoff illustrated the need for federal funding by quoting an Illinois study showing a lack of day care services for ADC recipients who worked or sought work. Ellen Winston, who emphasized that "the development of day-care facilities should not be promoted as a means for exerting pressure on ADC mothers to take employment," nonetheless found the service in accord with the "rehabilitation concept of ADC" and sought their use to "facilitate employment when it is in the best interest of the family." Joseph Reid described day care as a way to avoid full-time foster care placement of children among the very poor.

Alone among those witnesses who testified in favor of day care funding, Elinor Guggenheimer of the NCDCC did not appeal to the growing number of working mothers as a justification for new federal day care funding. Instead, most of her testimony focused on children: the NCDCC believed good day care services for children to be "one of the major solutions" to the "devastating problem of child neglect," Guggenheimer told the committee, and when she mentioned parents it was almost exclusively in the context of ADC. She began her testimony with a discussion of day care's "rehabilitative" possibilities for ADC adult recipients: "We are deeply convinced that rehabilitative and preventive programs are urgently needed. This country has many examples of families who have been on public assistance for two and even three generations. The patterns of dependency will never be broken unless children are exposed to at least one wage earner in the family." Continuing in this tone, Guggenheimer stated that the NCDCC favored "mothers staying home with young children" but also knew that "public assistance levels are low," and, she argued, this was "depressing and demoralizing" for those families. "There are mothers who should be allowed to choose work, if the community could guarantee that their children would not be neglected."[104]

The idea of women choosing to work—a recurring theme in the NCDCC arguments for day care—ran counter to decades of social welfare wisdom that explained and justified women's participation in the labor force as an economic necessity. As promoted by the Children's Bureau, the ADC program had been about allowing a mother to "choose" full-time homemaking despite the economic loss of a male breadwinner. The NCDCC argument turned this notion on its head and suggested that women might choose work but to do so needed day care services. Like the Children's Bureau, which had never hidden its belief that the correct choice was full-time homemaking, the NCDCC seemed also to suggest a correct choice. Although Guggenheimer noted the NCDCC's preference that mothers of young children should stay at home, between the "depressing and demoralizing" dependence on ADC and the "rehabilitative" possibilities of day care, which accompanied work, the correct choice, at least for an ADC recipient, is hard to miss.[105]

As it happened, that mothers might choose work over homemaking was precisely the concern of several vocal opponents of federal day care funding. Here too, however, when this "choice" was applied to mothers who received ADC, the concern faded or disappeared. A pediatrician from Mobile, Alabama, who wrote to his congressman in opposition to federal day care funds asserted, "Basic love and security will not be learned by the young child in the day care center but with the mother at home." At the same time he conceded that "maybe those mothers on relief rolls need some assistance through a day care center but the majority of working mothers of pre-school-age children should be in the home."[106]

The most politically potent opponent of the administration's day care proposals was Monsignor Raymond Gallagher, secretary of the National Conference of Catholic Charities.[107] As he expressed his concerns before the House Ways and Means Committee the heart of the matter was the scope of the proposal. Laying aside the minuscule funding offered (which he did not discuss), Gallagher objected to the lack of limits in the proposed bill. Specifically, the legislation provided that federal funds were to assist states in providing "care and protection of children whose parents are, for part of the day, working or seeking work, or otherwise absent from the home or unable for other reasons to provide parental supervision." While Gallagher could agree with funding day care to meet a specific "necessity or a therapeutic objective"—for instance, he believed that for "rehabilitative" purposes "day-care opportunities should be made available to the children of families now on relief rolls" to enable mothers to find work—the proposed language appeared to make the day care needs of any working mother a concern of the public purse.

Again, Gallagher did not focus on any fiscal concerns that this might raise: rather, his concerns were ideological. "Who is to say that millions more mothers are absolutely necessary for the labor market? Putting it another way, who is to say that the United States can endure a blow to family life of this proportion where indiscriminate recruitment of mothers of small children for industry continues without giving evidence of having thought through to the very ultimate the effect that this has on family life generally." For Gallagher, continued increases in the employment of mothers should not be taken as a given. Rather, the effect of mothers' widespread employment should be seriously examined for the harms that it had done or might do to the nation.[108]

But despite his sweeping objection to the employment of mothers of young children, Gallagher indicated his willingness for the poorest of families to receive federally funded day care services. Indeed, after the House Ways and Means Committee amended the legislation to incorporate limitations on how states could use the day care funds he endorsed the measure.[109] According to Bernard Greenblatt, who in 1965 interviewed key players in the day care debate of 1962, there was general agreement among the advocates that federal day care funds should be targeted to meet specific needs, although not everyone thought that receipt of cash aid should be the only test of eligibility. The Children's Bureau, which would be called on to approve a state's day care service plan but had apparently been out of the loop in the original administration proposal, helped to shape the limitations on the use of federal grants for day care.[110]

Explaining the day care proposals generally, the House Ways and Means Committee Report on the Public Welfare Amendments first cited the rise in employment among mothers of young children and then went on to note the importance of economic necessity as a reason for this employment, for both married and sole-support mothers. The committee explained the new language that it had added as a way to see that "the most urgent needs for expanding and improving day-care services will be met first." To accomplish this, the committee proposed requiring a state to make certain assurances before receiving federal day care funds. The mechanics of these requirements, which included a determination of need for services (with priority to certain low-income or other families) and a finding that day care was in the best interest of the mother and the child, ensured that a caseworker rather than the mother or parents would determine a family's need for day care. Finally, "to encourage the development of well-rounded day care programs of high quality," the House legislation added to the administration's requirement that states fully involve the resources of public education and health agencies in planning for day care by providing for the establishment of a committee to advise the state on the general policy involved in providing day care. Composed of representatives of both public and private social welfare agencies, as well as other professional and civic groups with an interest in day care, this committee was to make certain that interested private parties would have an opportunity to shape the state's public day care policy.[111]

On March 15 the Ways and Means Committee version of the Public Welfare Amendments of 1962 easily cleared the full House of Representatives by a vote of 319 to 69, and the bill moved to the Senate, where the Finance Committee would began considering it in May. The day care proposals were the subject of far less testimony before the Senate committee, but they remained contentious. When Secretary Ribicoff testified in favor of the House-amended day care proposals he received extended questioning on the issue, which appeared to have been intended to test the strength of the limitations. In addition, a representative of the Illinois Chamber of Commerce testified in opposition to federal day care funding (arguing that day care was a state funding concern). And while Gallagher of the National Conference on Catholic Charities now endorsed the day care proposals, although he wished for a more clear statement tying eligibility to financial need, a statement submitted by the New York State Catholic Welfare Committee gave notice of its continued staunch opposition. Insisting that it was not opposed to day care as a social welfare service to the needy, the committee argued that no study demonstrated the efficacy of day care for ADC recipients specifically. In place of the federal day care funds proposed to be available for all states, the New York committee urged a one-year pilot project that would offer subsidized day care in a few selected areas and would be used to study "how, if at all, day care can be of use to aid parents of children in financial need to strengthen the family life."[112] The Senate committee ultimately salved concerns about federal subsidy of families without financial need by adding an explicit instruction that any family who met the state-defined need for day care yet was able to pay some or all of the day care cost would need to be charged whatever amount they could pay.[113]

Although the welfare legislation had moved from introduction to passage by the full House in six weeks, the Senate acted more slowly. Hearings were delayed for nearly two months, after which the bill did not reach the full Senate floor for another six weeks. Seeking to shore up wavering support among some senators, the National Committee for Day Care of Children organized a parade of day care enrollees in Colorado and instigated a letter and telegram campaign from constituents in New Hampshire. After two weeks of floor debate and numerous amendments, the full Senate passed the welfare reform legislation on July 17. When he signed the bill into law on July 25, 1962, President Kennedy called it the most far-reaching revision of the public welfare program since its enactment in 1935. "This measure," he explained, "embodies a new approach—stressing services in addition to support, rehabilitation instead of relief, and training for useful work instead of prolonged dependency."[114]

In recognition of the new focus on services to the entire family, the Public Welfare Amendments renamed the ADC program Aid to Families with Dependent Children (AFDC). The legislation marked the first time since the end of World War II that lawmakers had set aside federal funds in support of day care. The dollars eventually provided were limited—just under $16 million in the four years that the set-aside was in place—but the provisions proved important in drawing attention, planning, and support from public agencies to day care.[115] "States are making herculean efforts to establish and expand their day care programs," the Children's Bureau reported in January 1964. In the first year that the set-aside day care funds were available (1963) thirty-one states submitted plans to use those funds, which were limited by congressional appropriators to $800,000 for any one state; in the following year forty-three states sought their share of the appropriation. Noting that "need exceeds funds available," the Children's Bureau listed the primary use of these funds as support of personnel to improve state licensing of facilities, give consultation to child care center staff, and work with the federally required state multidisciplinary advisory committee on day care.

Indeed, as compiled by the Children's Bureau, "personnel services" were the largest cost item in the states' budgets for day care services in 1963. The next-largest line items were "cooperative projects" (which apparently dealt with planning between welfare, health, and education agencies) and "day care of children." By comparison, the state day care budgets in 1964 showed a far greater amount to be spent for day care of children than for cooperative projects, although personnel costs continued to rank highest.[116]

The reintroduction of federal day care funds through state welfare agencies indeed provided new opportunities at the state and local levels, but expanded child care services did not necessarily follow immediately. As with the provision of day care funds during World War II, local and in this instance state efforts to secure new services were key; supporters of increased day care services confronted officials who were indifferent or perhaps even hostile to the expansion of day care for working mothers, and to gain access to funds they needed to master a maze of state and federal bureaucratic details. In the District of Columbia, for example, officials moved quickly to establish a public advisory board enabling the city to obtain federal day care funds. These funds were almost immediately used to provide care for 132 children in AFDC families whose mothers were enrolled in job training programs. The city's unelected leaders, however, resisted expanding the day care program to serve low-income working mothers—including those who had recently secured a job through the training program—even as day care activists pointed out that without a continued day care subsidy few of these trained mothers could be expected to succeed.[117]

The city's own pilot job training program, established in April 1961 and intended "to rehabilitate recipients of aid to dependent children in an effort to make them self-supporting by teaching them skills," had already illustrated this reality. The program, which provided housing, child care, and other services during the training period, was considered successful in preparing mothers for employment and was also able to find them public housing. The scarcity, cost, and location of child care, however, posed a more difficult problem. There were no publicly subsidized facilities in the District of Columbia, and space was not often available at the city's private nonprofit centers (which had declined in number from six to four between 1955 and 1960). And like the city's commercial centers, many of the nonprofit centers were not located in parts of the city convenient for the use of public housing tenants. Further, the cost of private commercial care in the city ranged between $900 and $1,200 a year, but "the best [annual] salary the pioneer [job training] center has been able to secure for their workers . . . has averaged about $2,000." Under pressure from local activists and federal lawmakers, and on the verge of a turnover in the District's leadership, local officials eventually expanded services to more children of working mothers. But several years would elapse before this was accomplished.[118]

In California the reintroduction of federal dollars for day care revived turf tensions between the state social welfare and education departments. The federal requirement that the new money must be administered by public welfare agencies (as part of child welfare services) greatly increased the significance of social welfare administrators in determining priorities for child care spending. California's public Child Care Centers had always been under the administration of the Education Department, and this added to their uniqueness in the nation. In the initial postwar era, the idea of moving the child care program's administration to the state welfare department was generally defeated on practical terms. Pro-education forces argued that the state's Social Welfare Department did not have the same resources or experience to administer the child care program while the Education Department, by virtue of having already run the wartime program, had both. But by the early 1960s the tremendous growth in commercial child care centers meant that the state's Social Welfare Department now also had a substantial presence in the delivery of child care in the state. By 1960 full-day child care programs licensed by the State Department of Social Welfare were running in more than 530 facilities statewide; in contrast, public centers administered by the Department of Education were in about 230 facilities.[119]

Working within the already established administrative framework, and in anticipation of federal day care funds, the state departments of social welfare and education quickly reached an agreement. It provided that Social Welfare, after determining that a particular child was eligible for services, would use federal dollars to pay the Education Department a specified per hour rate for the child's participation in a Child Care Center. Plans were separately made to use the federal funds set aside for day care by the Public Welfare Amendments to build five child care centers in rural communities. In the end the new federal money did not materialize as quickly, or as generously, as expected, and only one of the rural centers was established. And by 1966, four years after the federal set-aside of day care funds began, 438 of the 8,794 families served in the Child Care Center program were AFDC recipients. This was a significant increase over the 230 families receiving cash aid and served by the Child Care Center program in 1962, but it still represented less than 5 percent of all families in the program.[120]

Back in Washington, the Senate Finance Committee successfully sought an increase in overall federal child welfare funds as part of the Social Security Amendments of 1965, but the committee also deleted the set-aside for day care. "Experience has shown that earmarking is no longer necessary in order to stimulate the initiation and expansion of day care services in the states," the committee stated, because day care has "now been recognized as an integral part of child welfare services." Although states could continue to use any child welfare funds for day care (as long as they also met the day care plan requirements regarding priority for services, establishment of an advisory board, and other items spelled out in the amendments of 1962), there would be no special pot of child welfare money dedicated solely for day care. Effective January 1, 1966, the federal day care set-aside ceased to exist.[121]

But even had the set-aside remained in the law, it likely would soon have been overshadowed by the federal child care subsidy contained in a separate part of the Public Welfare Amendments. As it turned out, the federal effort to encourage states to "rehabilitate" families and promote their independence from cash aid became a far more lucrative source of child care funds for the states. As described earlier, the Public Welfare Amendments pledged the federal government to guarantee $3 out of every $4 that a state spent on certain services to AFDC recipients and those considered "likely" or "potential" recipients. Whereas the total amount of earmarked day care funding made available through the child welfare account amounted to less than $16 million over four years (1963–66), money spent for child day care under the AFDC program, once "discovered" by state administrators, would far outstrip this earlier spending. Although federal regulators may initially have limited use of the matching funds to the provision of "compensatory education" for eligible children, this would soon change. In 1970 alone, states drew an estimated $114 million in federal matching funds to provide day care to AFDC mothers who were at work or in training and to other low-income mothers. By contrast, out of the federal child welfare funds appropriated that year, states spent an estimated $3 million on day care.[122]

Again, California provides a ready example of the importance of the federal matching funds for services. At a meeting in 1965 attended by state policymakers concerned with enhancing California's child care finances, a social welfare administrator identified the federal matching funds in the Public Welfare Amendments, as yet largely untapped, as a "pot of gold." After two intense years of state lawmaking designed to maximize the use of this and other newly available federal funds (linked to early childhood education initiatives and the war on poverty), the state dramatically expanded its child care program. Beginning in 1967 and using money primarily available under the AFDC program, California's child care program nearly doubled its capacity. In 1965 the state legislature amended the law to rename the program Children's Centers and to include "instruction," along with care, as a purpose of the program. Even with this change, and despite the fact that the program remained under the administration of the Education Department, by 1974 about 87 percent of the children served in the state's Children's Centers had been determined eligible for the service by state social welfare workers.[123]

Social welfare eligibility rested on current or former receipt of AFDC, participation of the child's parent in the federal work training program for AFDC recipients, or a determination by the social worker that the family was a "potential" AFDC recipient. The shift from eligibility based solely on income limits prescribed in state law and applied by child care program staff likely did not significantly increase the number of sole-support families that used the centers. That figure had been increasing at least since 1950, and as early as 1966—just before the major expansion of AFDC-related funding for Children's Centers—more than 86 percent of the children using the program were from single-parent families. Although the low monthly incomes of AFDC recipients probably reduced the overall average income of program participants, the effect may not have been dramatic. Again, the survey data in 1966 showed an average monthly income of more than $285 for families receiving AFDC and using the Children's Centers, while the average monthly income of all families supported by one parent was a little more than $364 and about a third of all such families reported monthly income between $300 and $363. Although the program had been trumpeted as a service to "taxpayers not taxeaters"—a claim implicitly disparaging toward cash welfare, and one increasingly muddied by the presence of AFDC recipients among the program's users—the most fundamental change experienced by California's Children's Centers was that access to the service rested increasingly with social welfare caseworkers. Instead of being a good option available to independent but low-income families who needed to make inexpensive child care arrangements, the program had been reconfigured as a prescribed therapy for rehabilitating dependent families.[124]

Lawmakers debating the need for federal financing of child care in the long decade stretching from the end of the Korean conflict (1953) to the initiation of the domestic War on Poverty (1965) generally maintained the view that provision of child care was a private and local matter; at the same time, they laid the groundwork for new federal responsibilities in the field. Repeatedly cited as a reason for public action, in the end the increasing number of married mothers entering the labor force provided more context for action than justification for having the program in the first place. In fact, in the general absence of both public finances and widespread activism by day care users, for much of the decade state social welfare regulators and private commercial operators defined the child care field overall. Federal policy responded in a more limited manner and was primarily intended to enable sole-support mothers to pay for and obtain child care, both public and private, and to "rehabilitate" families by enabling work or training among recipients of cash aid.

In 1954 Congress revised the federal tax code to provide a limited tax break for working parents who paid for child care. The new tax policy essentially recognized child care as an "expense" of any mother who chose to enter the workforce, but it was targeted to serve primarily single-parent families and two-parent families with low to moderate incomes. Congress took this action—providing a small subsidy for the private arrangement of non-maternal child care—at the same time that a growing number of commercial centers signaled the possibility that child care would become a new field of private enterprise.

Collectively, for-profit centers offered outside-the-home care to more families from a greater variety of incomes than had historically been feasible under nonprofit auspices. The dramatic expansion in these private commercial centers was encouraged by the dearth of publicly supported child care in a period when a rapidly rising number of mothers engaged in paid labor. Seeking to improve standards but with little money available for the purpose, state social service regulators and their allies successfully sought legislation that granted licensing authority for centers operated within approved standards. Licensing gave commercial operators a level of respectability that they had not previously held. Finally, the emergence of private associations of child care proprietors helped to ensure the full consideration of market issues in the drafting of child care licensing standards and to solidify an enduring definition of publicly subsidized child care as a provision only for the very poor. Private owners sought to ensure their business interests by insisting that they should play a role in writing the regulations and that publicly supported child care must not compete with them for paying customers.

In 1962, as a result of a general reform of public and child welfare measures, Congress appropriated the first direct federal funds for child care services since the close of World War II. As in 1954, advocates of day care funding frequently cited the increased employment of mothers as a reason for the federal government to act. But also as in 1954, and in keeping with the view of child care economics advanced by commercial operators, federal lawmakers offered much more selective child care aid. On the one hand, the Public Welfare Amendments of 1962 redefined child welfare services, traditionally offered to prevent the neglect and abuse of children, to include day care for working mothers. Funds offered were limited, and with the growing acceptance of wage earning by mothers, it was increasingly difficult to accept the premise of the funding: that the children of working mothers were by default victims of neglect and thus subject to public intervention. In contrast to the limited funds made available under the child welfare rationale, far more child care funding resulted from lawmakers' desire to "rehabilitate" families and reduce dependence on government benefits. In this context day care services were intended to enable AFDC recipients to work or engage in training programs, and could also be used by families deemed "potential" AFDC recipients.

The only way to work ourselves out of a third generation on relief is to have a place for the children to be well cared for while the mother works.—Abraham Ribicoff, secretary, U.S. Department of Health, Education and Welfare, August 5, 1961

The majority of families using the Child Care Centers are sole-parent, and we hold our heads high because we chose to be self-supporting rather than take the easier route of Aid to Families with Dependent Children. Many of us have been at one time or still are within the 'poverty group.' We do NOT consider ourselves welfare cases.—Margaret Pignatelli, president, California Parents' Association for Child Care Centers, to President Lyndon Johnson, March 29, 1965

EPILOGUE

The two decades after World War II were a period of tremendous opportunity for child care but almost no social provision resulted. In the political debates that surrounded child care funding in the first two decades after World War II, it's possible to locate an emerging consensus on women's wage earning and child care. Both would ideally remain private issues. Mothers who were able to combine wage earning and childrearing by purchasing child care services in the private market began to feel lesser public condemnation of their work. While they remained fully obligated to childrearing, a shift in public opinion granted them some opportunity to engage in wage work. At the same time, for poor mothers who were not financially able to privately purchase child care, it became increasingly acceptable to argue that the proper public policy should be to promote work, not to provide cash aid. This shift in opinion would have far-reaching implications for child care policy.

In 2000 the federal government and states spent more than $9 billion to provide child care for low-income families, primarily for those receiving or formerly receiving cash assistance; in 1995 the roughly comparable figure was $3 billion.[1] The central reason for this dramatic increase in child care spending for low-income and very poor families was the enactment in 1996 of a radical welfare reform law that linked eligibility for federal cash aid to participation in the workforce. Repealing the Aid to Families with Dependent Children program, in which less stringent work requirements had been developed by earlier reforms, the new law established the Temporary Assistance for Needy Families (TANF) block grant, and it fully embraced work as the cure for "welfare dependency." When Congress began to debate renewal of the TANF block grant in 2002, there was a broad consensus among policymakers on the merits of work for mothers who received cash welfare. The question was not whether these women should work but how much; at the same time the question was not whether we should fund child care (for low-income women) but to what extent.

The assumption that mothers with young children are employable represents a sea change from the attitudes of policymakers in the early postwar period. A recurring theme of this book has been the need for mothers who sought continued public support of child care services to explain *why* they worked. As much as possible, these mothers drew attention to the way wage work enabled them to maintain independent households—support and care for their children, buy food and consumer goods, even pay a mortgage. Contrasting themselves to mothers who received cash welfare, working-class day care users from Cleveland, the District of Columbia, and California cited the economic and social productivity of their wage earning as a way to claim independent citizenship and, with this status, the *right* to public provision of child care.

No citizenship right to social provisions that recognized and supported the contributions of both wage work and mother work grew out of these disparate state and local calls for public financing of child care in the early postwar period. Lawmakers instead focused on the perceived "unproductivity" of mothers who used welfare grants to be full-time mothers; and today, most public child care spending is conflated with welfare reform.

Source Abbreviations

CBR	Records of the U.S. Children's Bureau, boxes 115–18, Central Files, Record Group 102, National Archives
CPACCC	California Parents Association for Child Care Centers
CSA	California State Archives
DCCP	Mothers Day Care Committee, unprocessed papers, Western Reserve Historical Society, Cleveland
DCR	Records of the Government of the District of Columbia, Record Group 351, National Archives
EWP	Earl Warren Papers, California State Archives, Sacramento
FCPP	Federation for Community Planning Papers, Western Reserve Historical Society, Cleveland
FWA	Federal Works Agency
FWAR	Records of the Federal Works Agency, Record Group 162, National Archives
HGDP	Helen Gahagan Douglas Papers, Carl Albert Congressional Research and Studies Center, Congressional Archives, University of Oklahoma, Norman
HSTP	Harry S. Truman Papers, Harry S. Truman Library, Independence, Mo.
HWP	Harry S. Wender Papers, Historical Society of Washington, Washington, D.C.
JWP	Papers of John Weber, Archives of Pacific Oaks College, Pasadena, Calif.

NAACP	National Association for the Advancement of Colored People
SDCR	Committee on the District, Records of the U.S. Senate, Record Group 46, National Archives
SDE	State Department of Education
SDEP	State Department of Education Papers, California State Archives, Sacramento
TSMP	Papers of Theresa S. Mahler, Archives of Pacific Oaks College, Pasadena, Calif.
WBR	Records of the U.S. Women's Bureau, Record Group 86, National Archives

Note: Correspondents whose letters are unpublished are identified only by their initials.

Introduction

1. For example, see Kerber, Kessler-Harris, and Sklar, *U.S. History as Women's History*; for an international perspective, see Koven and Michel, *Mothers of a New World*.

2. Marshall, "Citizenship and Social Class"; Rogers M. Smith, "'One United People.'" Smith argues that American citizenship drew from classical liberalism, classical republicanism, and a set of ethnocultural traditions he terms "Americanism." I am referring here specifically to his discussion of the impact of classical liberalism on the shape of American citizenship.

3. For a survey of the expansive list of denials, qualifications, and exceptions to the universal ideal of U.S. citizenship see Kerber, "The Meanings of Citizenship."

4. Mink, "The Lady and the Tramp"; Kerber, *Women of the Republic*; Kerber, "A Constitutional Right to Be Treated Like American Ladies."

5. Fraser and Gordon, "A Genealogy of *Dependency*"; Montgomery, *Citizen Worker*, 15–25; Welter, "The Cult of True Womanhood"; Kessler-Harris, *Out to Work*, 49–51.

6. Fraser and Gordon, "A Genealogy of *Dependency*," 314–19; Martha May, "Bread before Roses."

7. Folbre, "The Unproductive Housewife," 464–65.

8. Jacqueline Jones, *Labor of Love, Labor of Sorrow*, 160–231; Boris, "When Work Is Slavery."

9. Flexner, *A Century of Struggle*. Regarding the contours and meaning of maternalism see Koven and Michel, *Mothers of a New World*; Ladd-Taylor, *Mother-Work*; and Kornbluh, "The New Literature on Gender and the Welfare State."

10. Kessler-Harris, *A Woman's Wage*, 31–32; Cott, *The Grounding of Modern Feminism*, 29–30.

11. Willrich, "Home Slackers"; Gordon, *Pitied but Not Entitled*; Coontz, *The Way We Never Were*, 133–40; Barbara Nelson, "The Origins of the Two-Channel Welfare State"; Pateman, "The Patriarchal Welfare State."

12. Fraser, "Struggle over Needs."

13. Coontz, *The Way We Never Were*, 125–33; Lagemann, "Education to 1877"; Cott, "Giving Character to Our Whole Civil Polity."

14. Goodwyn, *The Populist Moment*; Trachtenberg, *The Incorporation of America*; Montgomery, *Beyond Equality*; Hall, "Laissez-Faire Constitutionalism and Liberty in the Late Nineteenth Century"; Dawley, *Struggles For Justice*.

15. Boris, "When Work Is Slavery," 37–38. Goodwin, *Gender and the Politics of Welfare Reform*, 162–64. See also DeForest, Rubin, and Wynia with the assistance of Lauve and Shaw, *Legislative History of the Aid to Dependent Children Program*.

16. For largely celebratory accounts of events before and after World War II see Evans, *Born for Liberty*; Garrison, "Our Skirts Gave Them Courage"; and Swerdlow, "Ladies' Day at the Capitol."

17. I am grateful to Vicki Ruiz for helping me clarify my thinking on this argument by suggesting the term "productive citizenship."

18. Rose, *A Mother's Job*, 5.

19. Michel, *Children's Interests, Mothers' Rights*, 118–49; Riley, "Caring for Rosie's Children."

20. The phrase "dissident citizenship" is from Sparks, "Dissident Citizenship." See also Fraser, "Struggle over Needs," 203.

21. Michel, *Children's Interests, Mothers' Rights*, 192–235.

22. Natalie Fousekis most fully describes child care workers' use of centers as bases of activism. See her dissertation, "Fighting for Our Children."

Chapter 1

1. Mrs. L. M. Stone [pseud.], Dallas, to President Franklin Roosevelt, the White House, ca. February 1945, CBR.

2. Waller, "The Coming War on Women." Distributed as a part of Sunday papers in major metropolitan areas across the nation, *This Week* had a circulation of approximately 6.4 million in 1945.

3. Waller, "The Coming War on Women," 5.

4. Alice Scott Nutt, assistant to the director, Social Service Division, U.S. Children's Bureau, to Mrs. L. M. Stone (pseud.), Dallas, March 13, 1945, CBR.

5. The term "official economy" and its definition are drawn from Fraser, "Struggle over Needs," 206.

6. Michel, "American Women and the Discourse of the Democratic Family in World War II," 154–67; Elaine Tyler May, *Homeward Bound*.

7. Kessler-Harris, *In Pursuit of Equity*, provides an important survey of U.S. women's economic citizenship in the twentieth century.

8. Kerber, "Separate Spheres, Female Worlds, Woman's Place," 3. See also Pateman, "The Patriarchal Welfare State," 236–37; Cott, "Giving Character to Our Whole Civil Polity."

9. I use the term "labor liberals," as usefully suggested by Eileen Boris, to describe politicians and others who continued to seek some structural reforms of society in

the postwar period. They are distinguished (briefly) from liberals who espoused the "New Deal liberalism," which was increasingly oriented toward individual rights, as described by Alan Brinkley in *The End of Reform*.

10. *American Women in the Postwar World*.

11. Ibid., 26–30.

12. Ibid., 11–13. The CIO's Political Action Committee formed an important lobby for "full employment" in the postwar period. See Alan Brinkley, *The End of Reform*, 260. For an overview of the CIO's full employment ideal see "The Answer Is Full Employment."

13. *American Women in the Postwar World*, 17–18.

14. Ibid., 3–7.

15. Ibid., 31–33; Berch, *Radical by Design*.

16. Class, "Public Policy and Working Mothers."

17. Hawes's analysis resonates with the current thinking of the sociologists Orloff, "Gender and the Social Rights of Citizenship," and O'Connor, "Gender, Class and Citizenship in the Comparative Analysis of Welfare State Regimes." Her suggestions also recall reformers' campaigns from the nineteenth and early twentieth centuries, which aimed to incorporate nurseries, cafeterias, and other services into the spatial design of homes and neighborhoods. See Hayden, *The Grand Domestic Revolution*, and Gilman, *Women and Economics*.

18. *American Women in the Postwar World*, 31–33.

19. Alan Brinkley, *The End of Reform*, 260–62.

20. Sec. 2(b) of the Full Employment Act, as printed in the record of hearings before the U.S. Senate Committee on Banking and Currency, *The Full Employment Act of 1945*, 6.

21. The draft legislation does not name the sex of the housekeepers, but as the text discussion makes clear, "housewives" were the people whom the bill's sponsors had in mind.

22. *The Full Employment Act of 1945*, 1–53. The meaning of "right to work" was widely debated but in this discussion dealt in some way with an individual's entitlement (inherent or granted) to "remunerative labor" or at least to the *opportunity* for such labor. Except when using direct quotes, I have generally substituted the phrase "right to paid work." This is to emphasize, first, that the debate was not about a right to engage in unpaid work—such as childrearing—and second, to distinguish this discussion from the meaning of "right to work" that came into use after passage of the anti-labor Taft-Hartley Act of 1947. In the much narrower and far less obvious Taft-Hartley meaning, "right to work" as a labor policy term came to mean the absence of a closed union shop.

23. Senator Murdock raised the question of exempting students as well as housewives. *The Full Employment Act of 1945*, 19.

24. *The Full Employment Act of 1945*, 19.

25. Ibid., 19–20.

26. Ibid., 29. See also Kessler-Harris, *In Pursuit of Equity*, 19–20, 61–63.

27. I noted just a handful of direct references made to the housekeeping exemp-

tion in the lengthy Senate hearing record. All references were brief and none were by organized women's groups.

28. Women's groups who either testified or submitted statements generally supportive of the Full Employment Act of 1945, none of whom raised questions about the housekeeping exception, included the National Council of Jewish Women, 941–42; the National Social Studies Committee of the American Association of University Women, 1161–63; and a group of veterans' wives who used the acronym WIVES, 1177–78. A letter from the president of the General Federation of Women's Clubs was less enthusiastic about the act, but the reticence was unrelated to the housekeeping exception, 1058. Unions representing a majority or proportionately significant group of women workers also did not raise objections to the housekeeping exemption. Testimony and statements came from the International Ladies' Garment Workers Union, 1059–60; the United Textile Workers, 1108; the United Office and Professional Workers, 967–68; the United Electrical Workers, 963–66; and the American Federation of State County and Municipal Employees, 1241–42. (All page references are to *The Full Employment Act of 1945*.)

29. *The Full Employment Act of 1945*, 747–753. Although this cannot be said of its gender discourse, in other ways the YWCA statement was progressive. It devoted specific attention to the need to ensure jobs for African American women (and men) as well as for white women, and it implied broad possibilities for postwar public works projects. For more on the YWCA, and especially its efforts to promote racial integration and equality, see Lynn, "Gender and Progressive Politics."

30. Alan Brinkley, *The End of Reform*, 260–64; *The Full Employment Act of 1945*, 6–9. See also Wasem, "No More Depressions."

31. U.S. Congress, House, Conference Report, *Declaring A National Policy on Employment, Production, and Purchasing Power, and for Other Purposes*, 1–2; *Congressional Quarterly Almanac* (1946) 2:71–73; Weir, "The Federal Government and Unemployment." The advisory panel became the Council of Economic Advisors. Although this group would indeed be very important for government fiscal planning, its role had been imagined much more grandly in the earlier proposed legislation.

32. *Declaring a National Policy on Employment, Production, and Purchasing Power, and for Other Purposes*, 1–2.

33. *The Full Employment Act of 1945*, 29.

34. U.S. Congress, Senate, Committee on Banking and Currency, *Assuring Full Employment in a Free Competitive Economy*, 32–33; *Declaring a National Policy on Employment, Production, and Purchasing Power, and for Other Purposes*, 5–7.

35. Alan Brinkley, *The End of Reform*, 263–64.

36. U.S. Women's Bureau, *Employment of Women in the Early Postwar Period*.

37. Milkman, *Gender at Work*, 116. Kesselman, *Fleeting Opportunities*, 103.

38. "Remember Rosie the Riveter? She's Back on the Home Front Now," *Washington Post*, March 10, 1946. See also Kessler-Harris, *Out to Work*, 297.

39. Reskin and Hartmann, *Women's Work, Men's Work*, 37–44.

40. President's Committee on Civil Rights, *To Secure These Rights*, 55–56; Anderson, *Wartime Women*, 30–64, "Postwar and Postscript."

41. U.S. Women's Bureau, *Employment of Women in the Early Postwar Period*, summary page and 13; Milkman, *Gender at Work*, 117; Tobias and Anderson, "What Really Happened to Rosie the Riveter?," 11; Deslippe, *"Rights, Not Roses,"* 73–75, 79, 94–96.

42. "Women Want Jobs—but Not the Kind Offered by USES," *Cleveland Press*, May 29, 1946; "Claims Women Refuse Many Proffered Jobs," *Cleveland Press*, November 15, 1945.

43. "Hope for Getting Maid Is Brighter, But Cost Is High," *Cleveland Plain Dealer*, October 16, 1945.

44. "17 Women to Get Certificates as Domestics," *Cleveland Press*, July 17, 1946.

45. Tobias and Anderson, "What Really Happened to Rosie the Riveter?" 25–26; see also "Job Limitation Law Again Covers Women," *Cleveland Press*, December 15, 1945.

46. Baer, *The Chains of Protection*; Lehrer, *Origins of Protective Labor Legislation for Women, 1905–1925*.

47. Elizabeth Baker, *Protective Labor Legislation with Special Reference to Women in the State of New York*, 77. Before 1900 one state court (Massachusetts) had upheld state protective labor legislation specifically for women while another (Illinois) had repealed such a law—arguing that sex alone didn't justify special protection. According to Baker, a 1900 case in Pennsylvania is the first instance where a court relied on the idea of women's "physical inferiority" and "potential motherhood" to uphold a state labor law for women alone.

48. *Muller v. Oregon*, 28 S.Ct. Rpt. 324 (1907). This case was argued on January 15, 1908, and decided February 24, 1908. See also Elaine Johnson, "Protective Legislation and Women's Work"; Kessler-Harris, *Out to Work*, 180–214; Elizabeth Baker, *Protective Labor Legislation*, 150–64.

49. Hall, "Paternalistic Sexism and Liberty to Contract, 1873–1923." The *Muller* opinion noted that it was not intended to set aside the Court's recent decision in *Lochner v. New York*, 198 U.S. 4 (1905), which relied on freedom-of-contract principles to declare unconstitutional a New York law that set limits on the number of hours that bakers (men) could work.

50. Key New Deal legislation with major impact on the employment contract included the Fair Labor Standards Act of 1938, the Social Security Act of 1935, and the National Labor Relations Act of 1935. Each of these laws had significant gaps in coverage—especially with respect to domestic and agricultural workers and workers in small, intrastate businesses.

51. In 1898, recognizing particular hazards of the job, the Court let stand a Utah law restricting the number of hours that miners could be asked to work, *Holden v. Hardy*, 169 U.S. 366 (1898). In 1916 the Supreme Court went further when it upheld an Oregon law that limited the number of hours for employees in factories, mines, and mills, *Bunting v. Oregon*, 37 S. Ct. Rpt. 435 (1916). Workmen's compensation laws passed in forty-two states by 1920 granted some disability and death benefits to primarily white male workers who dominated the heavy industry workforce. Barbara Nelson, "The Origins of the Two-Channel Welfare State," 123–51.

52. Kelly, Harbison, and Belz, *The American Constitution*, 490.

53. The notion of "motherwork" is derived from Boris, "When Work Is Slavery."

54. Mathews, *Cases and Materials on the Employment Relation and Protective Labor Legislation*, 120–23; Baer, *The Chains of Protection*, 111–21. See also Marat Moore, *Women in the Mines*.

55. Gabin, *Feminism and the Labor Movement*, 154–55.

56. Kennedy and Orescanin, "Protective Labor Legislation in Indiana"; Schatz, *The Electrical Workers*, 158–60; Gabin, *Feminism and the Labor Movement*, 158, 191–201; Elizabeth Baker, *Protective Labor Legislation with Special Reference to Women in the State of New York*, 175–93; AFL-CIO Research Department, "Summary of Responses by AFL-CIO National Unions and State Bodies to Women's Commission Questionnaire on Protective Labor Legislation for Women," November 26, 1962, folder 3, box 17, UAW Women's Department papers, Merrill-Palmer Institute, Kresge Historical Library Collection, Archives of Labor and Urban Affairs, Wayne State University, Detroit; President's Commission on the Status of Women, "Report of the Committee on Protective Labor Legislation"; Dorothy Sue Cobble, "Dishing It Out," 94–98.

57. Laughlin, *Women's Work and Public Policy*, 40; Cobble, "Recapturing Working Class Feminism," 61–68; Leopold, "Federal Equal Pay Legislation."

58. Laughlin, *Women's Work and Public Policy*, 8–9.

59. Ibid., 40. Kossoudji and Dresser, "Working Class Rosies"; Deslippe, *"Rights, Not Roses,"* 11–66.

60. Ross, "Sex Discrimination and 'Protective' Labor Legislation," 6; Kessler-Harris, *Out to Work*, 187–88.

61. U.S. Women's Bureau, *Employed Mothers and Child Care*, 36.

62. Ibid., 78.

63. Ibid., 44.

64. Ibid., 62.

65. Ibid., 36; see also 56.

66. Ibid., 44.

67. Ibid., 46.

68. The best overall history of child care in the United States, including the formation of the National Federation of Day Nurseries and its preference for private child care solutions, is told in Michel, *Children's Interests, Mothers' Rights*. See also Rose, *A Mother's Job*; Durst, "Day Nurseries and Wage-Earning Mothers in the United States, 1890–1930."

69. Michel, "The Limits of Maternalism." See also Cahan, *Past Caring*, 21–23, 25–28; Greenblatt, *Responsibility for Child Care*, 37–39.

70. Cahan, *Past Caring*, 21–28; Rose, *A Mother's Job*, 158–61.

71. Beatty, *Preschool Education in America*, 132–68; Michel, *Children's Interests, Mothers' Rights*, 113–20; Cahan, *Past Caring*, 29–32; Greenblatt, *Responsibility for Child Care*, 42–45; Rose, *A Mother's Job*, 106–11.

72. California Legislature, *Technical Staff Report to the Joint Committee on Preschool and Primary Training* (hereafter cited as *Technical Staff Report*), table 44a, p. 286. The figures cited are from the FWA. The agency described as a "unit" each group of children supervised separately under the leadership of a head teacher; in this book the word "center" replaces the word "unit." (See also table 1.)

73. Funding authorization through Title II of the National Defense Housing Act of 1940, which provided for defense public works and was commonly called the Lanham Act, was specifically requested by the FWA.

74. Riley, "Caring for Rosie's Children," 395–423.

75. U.S. Congress, House, Committee on Appropriations, *Second Deficiency Appropriation Bill for 1945*, 631; U.S. Congress, House, Committee on Appropriations, *Hearing on the First Supplemental Surplus Appropriation Rescission Bill, 1946*, 435. A "project" referred to any number of day care centers sponsored by a single community or applicant.

76. Tobias and Anderson, "What Really Happened to Rosie the Riveter?"; Mary G. Moon, assistant commissioner for war public services, FWA, to Henry J. Sullivan, division engineer, Bureau of Community Facilities, FWA, Washington, May 12, 1945, Central Files, 1941–49, FWAR; "Mothers of 7600 Children Provide Child Care Facts," Emergency Child Care Committee, Welfare Council of Metropolitan Los Angeles, folder 4b, box 17, HGDP.

77. California Legislature, *Technical Staff Report*, table 44a, p. 286.

78. U.S. Children's Bureau, "Status of Day Care Programs for Children," October 31, 1950 (mimeograph), box 815, container 33, FCPP.

79. U.S. Children's Bureau. "Licensed Day Care Facilities for Children," preliminary report prepared by Seth Low, October 1960, in U.S. Congress, House, Committee on Ways and Means, *Public Welfare Amendments of 1962*, 189–217 and table 15. The report noted that twenty-nine of these fifty-two centers were in Texas. In addition to these stateside centers, the report noted that an additional sixteen public centers operated in Puerto Rico. Data were obtained through questionnaires sent to all fifty states, the District of Columbia, and Puerto Rico. Every jurisdiction replied.

80. U.S. Women's Bureau, *Women Workers in Ten War Production Areas and Their Postwar Employment Plans*; Milkman, *Gender at Work*, 99–127. See also O'Farrell and Kornbluh, *Rocking the Boat*, 167–68.

81. U.S. Bureau of the Census, *Historical Statistics of the United States: Colonial Times to 1970*, series D-36, 131–32. The highest wartime rate of female labor force participation was 36.3 percent, reached in 1944; by 1956 this figure too was surpassed as the proportion of women in the workforce reached 36.9 percent.

82. U.S. Children's Bureau, *Children of Working Mothers*, 3–6; U.S. Bureau of the Census, *Historical Statistics of the United States*, series B-20, D-60, pp. 51, 133.

83. Fraser, "Struggle over Needs," 204–9; Sparks, "Dissident Citizenship."

84. California Legislature, *Technical Staff Report*, table 44b, p. 286; Riley, "Caring for Rosie's Children," 409–15.

85. For an indication of the early breadth and intensity of the protests see National Committee on Group Care of Children, "Community Planning on Group Care of Children," bulletins 1 (December 1945) and 2 (January 1946), CBR. For a discussion of activism by women in Philadelphia see Rose, "A *Mother's Job*," 181–94. Michel reviews activism in New York in *Children's Interests, Mothers' Rights*, 193–202. Activism in Cleveland, the District of Columbia, and California is given detailed discussion in chapters 2, 3, and 4 of this book; regarding the California day care activism

see also Fousekis, "Fighting for Our Children." There is an anecdotal reference to Washington state activism in Schroedel, *Alone in a Crowd*, 41–50.

86. California Legislature, *Technical Staff Report*, tables 44b, 44c, 46, pp. 283–304 (quote at 284).

87. Ibid., table 46. National Committee on Group Care of Children, "Community Planning on Group Care of Children," bulletin 2, p. 5.

88. V. L. M., Owensboro, Ky., to Katherine Lenroot, chief, Children's Bureau, Washington, March 6, 1946, CBR.

89. The National Committee on Group Day Care of Children was formed in November 1945 as a temporary body and included social welfare and early childhood representatives. The committee produced several bulletins and was a kind of information clearinghouse regarding community protest, planning, and continuance of child care centers.

90. National Committee on Group Care of Children, "Community Planning on Group Care of Children," bulletin 1, December 1945, 3, CBR; Katherine Lenroot, chief, U.S. Children's Bureau, Washington, to V. L. M., Owensboro, Ky., March 27, 1946, CBR; M. E. Fretwell, executive secretary, West Point Welfare Association, West Point, Ga., to Katherine Lenroot, August 2, 1946, CBR; and Oscar Ewing, administrator, Federal Security Agency, to Alexander J. Resa, Concannon Dillon & Snook, Chicago, November 4, 1948, CBR. The federal legislators exempted Puerto Rico from the restriction on using school lunch money for child care centers and nursery schools.

91. Spencer Huffman, president, Baltimore County Association on Pre-School Education, to Catherine [*sic*] Lenroot, August 5, 1947, U.S. Children's Bureau, CBR.

92. Rosalind G. Bates and Mollie Malone, legislative chairmen, Los Angeles Business Women's Council, to Roy E. Simpson, superintendent, California Department of Education, Sacramento, May 4, 1948, and Frank Wright, associate superintendent of public instruction, Sacramento, to Dr. Rosalind G. Bates, May 10, 1948, F3640:1140, both in Records Relating to the State Board of Education, Child Care Centers and Day Nurseries, EWP; Rosalind Bates to Los Angeles City Council, June 2, 1948 (with accompanying petition bearing about six hundred signatures), Los Angeles City Archives.

93. Mildred Arnold, director, Social Service Division, Children's Bureau, Washington, to Hazel Minor McCreery, Jefferson School, Flint, Mich., December 10, 1946, and Mildred Arnold to Celvah Rosenthal, New York, March 12, 1947, both in CBR; "Some Statistics about the Child Day Care Centers Based on Five Months Operation under the Board of Public Welfare," folder "Nursery Schools," tray: SEN 80A-F6 118, 80th Cong., SDCR.

94. The New York state legislature did vote a small amount of funds to continue some child care centers for migrant workers.

95. New York City had not been deemed "war-impacted" and so was ineligible for federal wartime funds under the Lanham Act. However, a large wartime child care program was funded with parents' fees and state and city dollars. For more on the

New York program see Goldsmith, *Better Day Care for the Young Child,* 12–24; Michel, *Children's Interests, Mothers' Rights,* chapter 6; "Annual Report of the President," Child Care Center Parents' Association of New York, Inc., May 24, 1948, CBR; Greenblatt, *Responsibility for Child Care,* 127–28, 155 n. 4.

96. Orville Crays, child welfare consultant, U.S. Children's Bureau, Boston, to I. Evelyn Smith, consultant on foster care, U.S. Children's Bureau, Washington, May 1947 (with attached report of A. M. Forman, February 20, 1947), CBR; Mary K. Prendergast, assistant supervisor in education, Dept. of Education, Massachusetts, to I. Evelyn Smith, February 26, 1948, CBR.

97. "Community Facilities of Seattle, Wash.," Dorothy Frost, field reporter, September 11, 1952, box 11, General Correspondence, 1948–53; Mrs. Louise Kiskaddon, supervisor, Seattle Public School's Nurseries, notes from interview by Elsie Wolfe, field reporter, Women's Bureau, March 7, 1951, box 5, General Correspondence, 1948–53, WBR.

98. For more information about the District of Columbia, see chapter 3. Information about the Detroit centers is primarily gleaned from letters and news clips that don't always agree on the exact number of centers operating. It is clear that their number declined steadily from as many as sixty-five federally subsidized child care centers during the war to just three in 1957 when all public funding ceased. Also administration of the Detroit centers transferred from city education to city welfare auspices by July 1946. See limited information in Gertrude Kelly, secretary, Women's Committee, Local 174, United Auto Workers, Detroit, to Helen Gahagan Douglas, February 7, 1946, folder 4a, box 17, HGDP; Interoffice memo, I. Evelyn Smith to Bessie Trout and Mildred Arnold, U.S. Children's Bureau, October 2, 1945, CBR; and I. Evelyn Smith to Dorothy Waite, July 25, 1946, CBR. "Status of Day Care Programs for Children," October 31, 1950, box 815, container 33, FCPP; State of Michigan, Dept. of Social Welfare, *Directory of Nursery Schools and Day Care Centers,* February 1948, and *Directory of Nursery Schools and Day Care Centers,* September 1952, Lansing, folder 1, box 65, Merrill-Palmer Institute, Kresge Historical Library Collection, Archives of Labor and Urban Affairs, Wayne State University, Detroit; Mildred Jeffrey, UAW, to Mary V. Beck, Detroit Common Council, March 11, 1957, folder 16, box 28, Mildred Jeffrey Collection, UAW Research Department, Merrill-Palmer Institute, Kresge Historical Library Collection, Archives of Labor and Urban Affairs, Wayne State University, Detroit.

99. For more information about California, see chapter 4. Regarding the success achieved by an active group of public day care users in Philadelphia, see Rose, *A Mother's Job,* 361–64.

Chapter 2

1. The epigraph is from a Cleveland Day Care Committee press release, [n.d.] ca. September 1945. My thanks to Bernice Zahm for sharing a copy of this press release with me from her personal files.

2. FWA press release, "Drastic Administrative Changes under the Lanham Act," August 19, 1945, and instruction sent to all division engineers, August 14, 1945, Of-

ficial Files, HSTP; Major General Philip B. Fleming, administrator, FWA, to Judge Samuel Rosenman, White House, October 2, 1945, box 1, correspondence of the administrator with the White House, 1942–49, FWAR. See also W. H. Cheney, division engineer, Bureau of Community Facilities, FWA, Berkeley, Calif., to George Field, commissioner, Bureau of Community Facilities, FWA, Washington, August 4, 1945, with "Minutes of Division No. 7 Meeting," July 23, 1945, Central Files, 1941–49, FWAR; and "Minutes of State Day Care Committee," Detroit, July 24, 1945, CBR.

3. Women's Bureau, *Planning Services for Children of Employed Mothers*, 7–10. No federally subsidized wartime child care centers operated in the state of New Mexico.

4. Fleming to Rosenman, October 2, 1945, box 1, correspondence of the administrator with the White House, 1942–49, FWAR; "Child Care Projects, August 31, 1945—State of Ohio," Records Relating to Child Care, 1943–46, FWAR. Before and during the war Greater Cleveland also housed eight privately supported centers: three by churches and five by the Cleveland Day Nursery Association. These programs cared for about five hundred children while the federally subsidized centers served an additional fifteen hundred.

5. Brooklyn Acres Day Care Center meeting minutes, August 26, 1945, and "Day Care Committee of Woodhill Community Center meeting minutes, August 27, 1945, DCCP; I. Evelyn Smith, consultant, foster care, Social Service Division, Children's Bureau, Washington, to Mrs. Leon M. Ginsberg, Baltimore, CBR. See also numerous newspaper reports on the day care issue in the *Cleveland Plain Dealer* and *Cleveland Press*, August and September 1945.

6. No title, n.d. "This is a copy of the letters I sent air mail-special delivery," DCCP. On September 8, 1945, Eleanor Roosevelt wrote about the need for continued federal support of day care centers in her nationally syndicated column *My Day*. She noted receiving many letters and referenced a list of reasons to keep the centers open that was sent to her by a Philadelphia woman.

7. *Congressional Record* 91 (1945): 8657. U.S. Congress, House, Committee on Appropriations, *Hearing on the First Supplemental Surplus Appropriation Rescission Bill*, 1946, 424. Bessie Trout to Miss Wood, February 6, 1946, interoffice memo, U.S. Children's Bureau, regarding information received from Hazel Gabbard of the U.S. Office of Education, CBR.

8. Representative Helen Gahagan Douglas (D-Calif.) requested that the FWA make this tally and she had the findings published in the *Congressional Record* 91 (1945): A3998–A4002. The FWA tally included letters mailed directly to the agency and those routed through the White House and other government offices to the agency. As of September 19, 1945, it had received 2,267 letters, postcards, and wires, and petitions signed by 3,647 individuals. It would continue to receive thousands of letters.

9. Kessler-Harris, *Out to Work*, 294–95; Evans, *Born for Liberty*, 224; Anderson, *Wartime Women*, 84–88, 122–46. Some advocates of increased female labor force participation had called for publicly supported child care centers as well as cafeterias and laundries. See Anthony, *Out of the Kitchen into the War*.

10. C. F., Cleveland, to Katherine Lenroot, chief, U.S. Children's Bureau, August 26, 1945, CBR.

11. *Congressional Record* 91 (1945): A4000. Letters regarding the child care program are in the HSTP; the Truman presidential library holds some 144 letters and telegrams—received at the White House during the month of October 1945—from individuals and private groups who supported continued federal funds for day care. (In addition several senators, mayors, and other politicians wrote to the president in this month.) The letters came from twenty-eight states and the District of Columbia.

12. S. B., Cleveland, n.d. [ca. October 10, 1945] to President Harry Truman, HSTP.

13. J. H., Oakland, Calif., October 6, 1945, to President Harry Truman; and E. L., Washington, October 12, 1945, to President Harry Truman, HSTP.

14. M. H., Ogden, Utah, October 18, 1945, to President Harry Truman; and A. K., Chicago, October 6, 1945, to President Harry Truman, HSTP.

15. R. G., Chicago, October 5, 1945, to President Harry Truman, HSTP.

16. "Statement by Mrs. Florence Kerr, Director of FWA War Public Services, with regard to the Federal Works Agency's child care program," n.d. [ca. 1943], Records Relating to Child Care in World War II, 1943–46, FWAR.

17. Maj. Gen. Philip B. Fleming, administrator, FWA, Washington, to Judge Samuel I. Rosenman, [filed] September 3, 1945, HSTP; Sonya Michel, *Children's Interests, Mothers' Rights*, 127–28, 132–35; Anderson, *Wartime Women*, 122–46. See also Straub, "United States Government Policy toward Civilian Women during World War II."

18. Fleming to Rosenman, September 3, 1945, HSTP. Rep. Frank Havenner (D-Calif.) to President Truman, October 3, 1945, HSTP. "Telephone Conversation between Senator LaFollette of Wisconsin and General Fleming," September 14, 1945, and "Telephone Conversation between Mr. George MacMillan Secretary to Senator Thomas of Utah and General Fleming," September 19, 1945, Correspondence of General Philip Fleming, 1942–49, FWAR.

19. Michel, *Children's Interests, Mothers' Rights*, chapter 4; Dratch, "The Politics of Child Care in the 1940s." The Children's Bureau, which during the war remained a part of the Department of Labor, was allied with the Office of Education (a part of the independent Federal Security Agency) in its effort to administer and define the wartime child care program.

20. For the Children's Bureau view of the wartime child care program, its administration, and appropriate postwar action on child care see Katherine Lenroot, chief, Children's Bureau, to Secretary [of Labor Frances Perkins], August 31, 1945, CBR. For an early review of the controversy, as understood by the FWA, see Alan Johnstone, general counsel, FWA, to James F. Byrnes, White House, Washington, July 19, 1943, with attached "Memorandum," General Counsel's Files, FWAR; Anderson, *Wartime Women*, 129–43.

21. On the significance of professionalized social work in the definition of day care programs as "therapeutic" see Michel, *Children's Interests, Mothers' Rights*, 109–12.

22. U.S. Women's Bureau, *Planning Services for Children of Employed Mothers*, 9–10.

23. "Day Care Needs in Cuyahoga County—June 1947," Federation for Community Planning, folder 815, container 33, FCPP. Two-thirds of the funding for the forty Cuyahoga County centers came from the federal government as authorized by the Lanham Act. The remaining one-third came primarily from parents' fees. The program was administered jointly through the Emergency Child Care Committee for the Cleveland Board of Education and the Welfare Federation. Additional federal money, used for case work consulting, came from U.S. Children's Bureau funds and was administered by the Division of Social Administration, Ohio State Department of Public Welfare.

24. "Telephone Conversation between Mr. George MacMillan, Secretary to Senator Thomas of Utah and General Fleming," September 19, 1945, correspondence of Gen. Philip Fleming, 1942–49, FWAR.

25. Lenroot, "Current National Developments and Problems in Public-Welfare Services for Children"; Lenroot, "Planning Services for Children to Supplement the Home and School"; "Children's Bureau Chief Cites Need for Long Range Day Care Program with 'Welfare of Children First,'" March 1, 1946, CBR; Michel, *Children's Interests, Mothers' Rights*, chapters 4, 5.

26. Howard Hopkirk, executive director, Child Welfare League of America, to President Harry Truman, September 28, 1945, and untitled notes labeled "SOUTHALL, Miss Maycie K.," n.d., HSTP.

27. Copy of letter from Howard Hopkirk to President Harry Truman, September 18, 1945, with attached "An Inventory of Day Care," CBR.

28. Lola Petit, national corresponding secretary, [D.C.] Parents Committee for Child Care, to Mildred Chomos, secretary, [Cleveland] Day Care Committee, September 24, 1945, DCCP. See also Rose, *A Mother's Job*, 189–90.

29. Samuel I. Rosenman, White House, to Maj. Gen. Philip B. Fleming, administrator, FWA, Washington, August 24, 1945, HSTP; Press release, August 27, 1945, Correspondence of administrator with the White House, 1942–49, FWAR; "Child Care Projects for Which Federal Assistance under the Lanham Act Was Being Provided as of August 31, 1945," Records Relating to Child Care, 1943–46, FWAR.

30. Belle Likover, interview by author, transcribed tape recording, Shaker Heights, Ohio, June 4 and 6, 1996. Bella Tract Likover remarried during the course of the day care struggle. A war widow whose husband, Joseph Tracht, died on Leyte in early 1945, she appears first in news stories as Bella Tracht and after her remarriage in 1946 as Bella Likover. Today she spells her name Belle. I refer to her throughout the text and footnotes with the name she used at the time she is quoted. See also "2,000 to Meet to Push Child Care," *Cleveland Plain Dealer*, September 23, 1945, and "Cleveland Woman to Join D.C. Child Care Plea," *Washington Star*, September 24, 1945. Representatives of Cleveland's Emergency Child Care Committee (ECCC) had also traveled to Washington to press for continued child care funding. See "Washington Will Hear City's Day Care Fund Pleas Today," *Cleveland Plain Dealer*, September 5, 1945, and "Bulletin from Emergency Child Care Com-

mittee Regarding Current Day Care Situation," September 15, 1945, folder 803, container 32, FCPP.

31. "For the Day Care Centers," *Cleveland Press*, August 28, 1945. See also "Child Care Centers," *Cleveland Plain Dealer*, August 29, 1945.

32. "An Emergency Resolution Memorializing the Congress of the United States to Take Immediate Action," effective September 12, 1945, City Council archives, Cleveland City Hall. The resolution drew heavily on language used in a press release of the Cleveland Day Care Committee.

33. Regarding the hoped-for national conference see Mina Billmyer, vice chairman, Day Care Committee (form letter), to Helen Gahagan Douglas, September 20, 1945, folder 4a, box 17, HGDP, and Elsie Bond, New York Committee on Child Care, Development and Protection, to Mina Billmyer, October 1, 1945, DCCP.

34. "Day Care Committee Program, Keep Them in Good Hands," October 4, 1945, DCCP. Glenna B. Johnson, supervisor, case work, Emergency Child Care, Cleveland, to Bessie Trout, Children's Bureau, Washington, October 6, 1945, CBR; "500 Mothers Plead for Child Centers; Truman Acts," *Cleveland Plain Dealer*, October 5, 1945. For more on Rep. Doyle's child care program advocacy, see chapter 4. The Day Care Committee's apparent first choice for keynote speaker was Rep. Helen Gahagan Douglas (D-Calif.). See B. S. Zahm, program chairman, Day Care Committee, to Rep. Helen Gahagan Douglas, September 17, 1945, folder 4a, box 17, HGDP.

35. "Day Care Committee Program, Keep Them in Good Hands," DCCP. Rep. Frances Payne Bolton was the only U.S. representative from the Cleveland area not on the list of supporters. U.S. Sens. Harold Burton and Robert Taft of Ohio also were not listed. Senator Taft strongly opposed continued federal funding; Sen. Burton had written to President Truman citing pressure to continue day care support from constituents (especially in Cleveland). See Sen. Harold Burton to President Truman, September 27, 1945, HSTP, and Sen. Burton to Mrs. O'Connell, September 8, 1945, DCCP.

36. Bernice Zahm to Governor Frank Lausche, September 24, 1945, DCCP; "Lausche: No Funds for Child Centers," *Cleveland Press*, August 31, 1945. Regarding Lausche's conservatism see Buckley, "My Secret Right-Wing Conspiracy."

37. Mrs. B. S. Zahm to Father Murphy, September 22, 1945, DCCP. In 1945 the Catholic Charities in Cleveland helped to fund and administer ten child welfare programs (including a day nursery, orphanages, and foster care). In addition to heading Catholic Charities, Father Murphy also served on the board of trustees of the Welfare Federation.

38. Press release dated October 5, 1945, with attached letter to congressional leaders requesting continued funding of child care, October 4, 1945, box 4, Records Relating to Child Care in World War II, FWAR; Fleming to Rosenman, October 2, 1945, box 1, correspondence of the administrator with the White House, 1942–49, FWAR.

39. *Hearing on the First Supplemental Surplus Appropriation Rescission Bill, 1946*, 943–45. The district parents' group and California lawmakers appeared before the committee on October 4, 5, and 9, 1945.

40. Ibid., 946, 950–51. For more on the significance of California and the California congressmembers in the extension of federal funding see chapter 4.

41. *Hearing on the First Supplemental Surplus Appropriation Rescission Bill, 1946*, 947. Fleming to Rosenman, October 2, 1945, box 1, correspondence of the administrator with the White House, 1942–49, FWAR. The final legislation granted less than $6 million in total and was incorporated in a large appropriation bill, which did not clear all the legislative hurdles until December. However, by late October the FWA had been assured that it would have the money for child care.

42. California Legislature, *Technical Staff Report*, 286; actual percentage (37.3) extrapolated from table 44a.

43. Bessie Trout to Miss Wood, February 6, 1946, CBR.

44. Lipsitz, *Rainbow at Midnight*.

45. Women's postwar exodus from wartime work has been portrayed as ranging from voluntary to forced. Campbell, *Women at War with America*; Evans, *Born for Liberty*, 228–62; Elaine Tyler May, *Homeward Bound*; Honey, *Creating Rosie the Riveter*; Rupp, *Mobilizing Women For War*; Tobias and Anderson, "What Really Happened to Rosie the Riveter?"; and Kesselman, *Fleeting Opportunities*. There are a growing number of studies that critique the dominance of the domestic-bound image of women in the postwar years. See Meyerowitz, *Not June Cleaver*; Deslippe, "*Rights Not Roses*"; Kaledin, *Mothers and More*; Ware, "American Women in the 1950s."

46. U.S. Women's Bureau, *Women Workers in Ten War Production Areas*, 2–5, 8–9. See also Milkman, *Gender at Work*, 102–4; Anderson, *Wartime Women*, 5–6. Women left low-paying service jobs to take up war production work with such relish that the Women's Bureau developed a bulletin about war workers—tellingly produced about African American women—that emphasized the value of civilian labor to the war production. Women's Bureau, *Negro Women War Workers*. See also the oral history of Tina Hill in Gluck, *Rosie the Riveter Revisited*.

47. Milkman, *Gender at Work*, 99–152; Deslippe, "*Rights Not Roses*," 67–113; Kossoudji and Dresser, "Working Class Rosies"; Gabin, *Feminism in the Labor Movement*, chapter 3.

48. Milkman, *Gender at Work*, 100.

49. Ohio State Employment Services figures cited in "Day Care Needs in Cuyahoga County, June 1947," 15, folder 815, container 33, FCPP.

50. Minutes of Emergency Child Care Committee meeting, December 7, 1945, report from Belle Tracht, folder 803, container 32, FCPP.

51. This justification of women's wage-work through much of the nineteenth and twentieth centuries has been conditioned by their family responsibilities. Kessler-Harris, *Out to Work*, 318.

52. U.S. Women's Bureau, *Women Workers in Ten War Production Areas*, 19.

53. Ruiz, *Cannery Women, Cannery Lives*; Clark-Lewis "'This Work Had an End': African-American Domestic Workers in Washington, D.C., 1910–1940"; Blewett, "The Sexual Division of Labor and the Artisan Tradition in Early Industrial Capitalism"; Milkman, *Women, Work and Protest*; Devra Weber, "*Raiz Fuerte*." With the notable exception of Blewett's essay, these case studies present women's activism

around their families as a radical or reforming consciousness. Drawn from the experiences of working-class as opposed to middle- and upper-class women, these findings conflict somewhat with an earlier argument, Degler, *At Odds*, which suggests that attention to family needs is incompatible with women's autonomy.

54. Rose, *A Mother's Job*, 190–94; Sapiro, "The Gender Basis of American Social Policy," 41–48.

55. The St. John's statement, August 31, 1945 (made on behalf of forty mothers), appears in the record of June 1946 hearings regarding the Maternal and Child Welfare Act. See U.S. Congress, Senate, Committee on Education and Labor, *Hearings on Maternal and Child Welfare*, 284–86. It's impossible to say exactly why one statement was chosen over another. Aside from discomfort with the language, the St. John's statement may have been rejected for coalition-building purposes. The members of the Day Care Committee used their statement of principles to organize broad support (as evidenced by their many appeals for supporters to sign their statement regarding day care before the mass meeting of October 4, 1945). The Cleveland social worker Glenna Johnson gave a more pragmatic but also plausible reason for rejection of the St. John's statement when she wrote to the Children's Bureau that it "was not adopted by the general group as they thought it was too long for a statement of general principles." (The full statement ran slightly more than two pages, double-spaced.) Glenna B. Johnson to Bessie Trout, Children's Bureau, Washington, October 6, 1945, CBR.

56. "Glenna Beach Johnson," *Who's Who of American Women*, 7th ed., 1972–73 (Wilmette, Ill.: Marquis Who's Who, 1971). Johnson's biography lists her as the executive director of the Women's International League for Peace and Freedom in 1968 and as a member of the ACLU, CORE, and the NAACP.

57. Glenna Johnson, "What Mothers Think about Day Care," 104.

58. Fraser, "Struggle over Needs," 207–8, 219–21.

59. "Constitution and By-Laws of Parents Day Care Association," n.d. [ca. November 1945], DCCP.

60. Glenna Johnson to Bessie Trout, September 14, 1945, CBR.

61. "Report on Future Program for Day Care of Children—from the Emergency Child Care Committee to the Children's Council [of the Welfare Federation]," October 12, 1945, folder 803, container 32, FCPP. On the whole, the report itself seems to take a more conservative tone than what members of the committee expressed both to newspapers and in the minutes of some committee meetings. This final report was also more conservative than a preliminary report prepared by the ECCC in August 1945. For instance, the earlier report included this statement: "The committee also recognizes that, in a democracy, the right to work is the right of every individual." This is a recognition decidedly not included in the October report of the ECCC. See "Progress Report of Committee on Future Program to the Emergency Child Care Committee," August 31, 1945, folder 803, container 32, FCPP.

62. "Report on Future Program for Day Care of Children," October 12, 1945, folder 803, container 32, FCPP.

63. In 1945 the *Catholic Universe Bulletin* (Cleveland) had 52,824 subscribers. See *Ayer & Sons Directory of Newspapers and Periodicals*, 1945, 709. Circulation grew to

74,807 by 1949. Each year there were "well-organized" subscription drives and "reading the newspaper was presented as the duty of any well-informed Catholic person." Information regarding readership, subscription drives, and the 1949 subscription rate received in personal communication of Chris Krosel, Archives of the Diocese of Cleveland, to author, n.d. [ca. September 30, 1996]. For more about the significance of the *Catholic Universe Bulletin* see Van Tassel and Grabowski, *The Encyclopedia of Cleveland History*, s.v. "Catholic Universe Bulletin."

64. See, for example, "Family Wage Seen Key to Working Women Problem," September 14, 1945, and "Pope Defends Women Workers, Again Asks 'Family Pay,'" August 24, 1945, in *Catholic Universe Bulletin*.

65. Martha May, "Bread before Roses"; Kessler-Harris, *Out to Work*, 68.

66. "'Mother's in Industry': America's No. 1 Foolishness," *Catholic Universe Bulletin*, September 21, 1945.

67. Pope Pius XII's message to women, *Catholic Universe Bulletin*, October 26, 1945. See also "Pope Calls for Women's Crusade to Save Society," *Catholic Universe Bulletin*, October 26, 1945.

68. Van Tassel and Grabowski, *The Encyclopedia of Cleveland History*, s.v. "Child Care"; B. S. Zahm to Father Murphy, September 22, 1945, DCCP. See also Bishop Edward Hoban, Cleveland Diocese, to the Clergy and Faithful of Cuyahoga and Summit Counties, October 16, 1946 (urging support of the Community Fund drive); and Bishop Edward Hoban, Cleveland Diocese, to the Clergy of Cuyahoga County and the City of Cleveland, October 30, 1946 (urging voters' support of community service levies), diocesan letters, archives, Diocese of Cleveland.

69. Father Albert J. Murphy to Rt. Rev. Msgr. R. M. Wagner, Cincinnati, January 31, 1940, and February 5, 1940, and Agnes K. Quinlan, executive secretary, Catholic Welfare Division of the Diocese of Columbus to Rt. Rev. Msgr. A. J. Murphy, March 5, 1946, and March 14, 1946 (with attachments), Catholic Charities Corp., archives, Diocese of Cleveland.

70. U.S. Congress, Senate, Committee on Education and Labor, *Hearings on Maternal and Child Welfare*, 9.

71. Coontz, *The Way We Never Were*, 125–33; Gordon, "Putting Children First."

72. "Minutes, Subcommittee on Long-Range Planning for Day Care for Children," November 29, 1945, folder 44, container 2, FCPP.

73. "Day Care Centers Saved for Month," *Cleveland Plain Dealer*, February 22, 1946; Telephone conversation with Bernice Zahm, Sherman Oaks, Calif., September 15, 1997; "Mothers Hit Hall Loss, Charge Bias to Schools," *Cleveland News*, September 20, 1945.

74. "Mothers to Seek State Funds to Continue Day-Care Centers," *Cleveland Plain Dealer*, August 30, 1945; "Reports Truman Backs Day Care," *Cleveland Plain Dealer*, August 31, 1945; "Lausche: No Funds for Child Centers," *Cleveland Press*, August 31, 1945; "Governor Weighs State Aid for Child Day Care Centers," *Cleveland Press*, October 23, 1945; "Bulletin from the Emergency Child Care Committee: Statement on Planning Continuing Program for Day Care of Children After March 1, 1946," February 21, 1946, folder 803, container 32, FCPP.

75. "Consolidated Statement Summarizing Receipts," February 11, 1946, *Official*

Journal of the County Commissioners, Cuyahoga County Archives, Cleveland; Van Tassel and Grabowski, *The Encyclopedia of Cleveland History*, s.v. "Child Care."

76. Ohio, *General Code, Annotated* (1952 series), sections 3070-1 to 3070-36.

77. Ohio, *Opinions of the Attorney General*, March 2, 1946, no. 769.

78. John Grabowski, Introduction to *Cleveland: The Making of a City*, 2d ed.; Van Tassel and Grabowski, *The Encyclopedia of Cleveland History*, xlvii–xlix; David D. Van Tassel, Introduction to *Cleveland: A Tradition of Reform*.

79. "Bulletin from the Emergency Child Care Committee: Statement on Planning Continuing Program for Day Care of Children after March 1, 1946," February 21, 1946, folder 803, container 32, FCPP; "Minutes of Committee on Long-Range Planning for Day Care for Children," March 12, 1946, folder 44, container 2, FCPP; "City Will Not Be Day Care Banker," *Cleveland Plain Dealer*, February 14, 1946; "Sweeny Meets with Mayor on Day Care," *Cleveland Press*, February 20, 1946. The County Child Welfare board was founded in 1930 with Sweeny as an avid proponent. He became the board's first and, until the postwar day care struggle, only chair. See "Lausche's First Three Cabinet Choices All Are Graduates of County Service," *Cleveland News*, November 10, 1941, and "Joseph T. Sweeny Dies, Rites Friday," *Cleveland Press*, September 17, 1946.

80. "Police Awaiting Day Care Protest: Full Load Out of Question for City, Sweeny Says," *Cleveland Plain Dealer*, February 21, 1946.

81. Sparks, "Dissident Citizenship."

82. This account of the sit-in is drawn largely from two detailed press stories. See "Mothers Invade City Hall: Child Care Will Go On," *Cleveland Press*, February 21, 1946, and "Day Care Centers Saved for Month: Mothers Win Temporary Victory at City Hall," *Cleveland Plain Dealer*, February 22, 1946.

83. "Mothers Invade City Hall: Child Care Will Go On," *Cleveland Press*, February 21, 1946, and "Day Care Centers Saved for Month: Mothers Win Temporary Victory at City Hall," *Cleveland Plain Dealer*, February 22, 1946.

84. "An Emergency Ordinance," City Council papers, Archives at City Hall, Cleveland (numerous telegrams in support of day care funding are also in the City Council papers at Record File no. 488-46); "20,000 Allotted to Child Day Care: Mothers Hear Council Extend Service to March 31," *Cleveland Plain Dealer*, February 26, 1946.

85. "Day Care Centers Saved for Month: Mothers Win Temporary Victory at City Hall," *Cleveland Plain Dealer*, February 22, 1946; "'Kicked Around' Sweeny Quits Child Welfare Post in Care Center Battle," *Cleveland News*, May 13, 1946. See also Edward D. Lynde, executive secretary, Cleveland Welfare Federation, to Joseph Sweeny, city finance director, Cleveland, February 15, 1946; "Minutes of Committee on Long-Range Planning for Day Care for Children," March 12, 1946, folder 44, container 2, FCPP; "Minutes, Emergency Child Care Committee," March 15, 1946, folder 803, container 32, FCPP.

86. Edward D. Lynde, executive secretary, Cleveland Welfare Federation, to Joseph Sweeny, city finance director, Cleveland, February 15, 1946; "Minutes of Committee on Long-Range Planning for Day Care for Children," March 12, 1946, folder 44, container 2, FCPP; "Minutes, Emergency Child Care Committee,"

March 15, 1946, folder 803, container 32, FCPP. The Welfare Federation through its Planning Committee pressed for a thirty-day city funding reprieve to allow time for analysis of need. Its behind-the-scenes phone, meeting, and letter-writing negotiations were no doubt critical. At the same time it seems virtually certain that without the Parents Day Care Association (PDCA) City Hall demonstration, the city's top officials would have let the day care program lapse. Interestingly, the minutes of neither the Planning Committee nor the Emergency Child Care Committee immediately after the public demonstration in February refer to the crucial PDCA action. Reading these documents unsupplemented by local newspapers gives the impression that only formal negotiations produced the city funding reprieve.

87. Mary M. Aikin, acting general chairman, "Women Workers Face the Future," Cleveland, to Mayor Thomas Burke, Cleveland, February 28, 1946; A. E. Stevenson, secretary, Cleveland Industrial Union Council, to unidentified correspondent with attached "Resolution Adopted by the Cleveland Industrial Union Council—February 27, 1946," February 28, 1946, DCCP.

88. "Urge Permanent Aid in Child Care: Social and Religious Leaders Ask City-Council Help," *Cleveland Plain Dealer*, April 12, 1946; "Urge County to Take Over Day Centers," *Cleveland Press*, April 12, 1946. The Emergency Child Care Committee folded with the end of federal funding. See "Minutes, Emergency Child Care Committee," March 15, 1946, folder 803, container 32, FCPP.

89. "An Emergency Ordinance to Amend Section 1 of Ordinance No. 552-46, passed February 25, 1946," and "An Emergency Ordinance Authorizing the Director of Finance to Make Available the sum of $20,000," City Council papers, City Hall Archives, Cleveland; "An Emergency Ordinance Authorizing the Director of Finance to Make Available the Sum of $10,000," exhibit C of "Petition," May 15, 1946, Cuyahoga County Courthouse, Common Pleas, no. 564259.

90. Belle Likover, interview by author.

91. A. E. Stevenson, secretary, Cleveland Industrial Union Council, to unidentified correspondent with attached "Resolution Adopted by the Cleveland Industrial Union Council—February 27, 1946," February 28, 1946, DCCP.

92. "Before March 10," *Cleveland Press*, February 2, 1946.

93. Margaret J. Banfield, "Says State Child Care Like 'Another Germany,'" letter to the editor, *Cleveland Press*, September 1, 1945.

94. "Mothers Map Mass Meeting to Save Child Care Centers," *Cleveland Plain Dealer*, August 28, 1945. According to Belle Likover, even though the committees nominally chose inclusive names, fathers were at war and therefore did not participate in committee activities.

95. "Governor Weighs State Aid for Child Day Care Centers," *Cleveland Press*, October 23, 1945.

96. "Day Care Centers Saved for Month," *Cleveland Plain Dealer*, February 22, 1946.

97. "Sees Petty Troubles as Danger to Homes," *Catholic Universe Bulletin*, May 17, 1946, and "Diocesan Institute on Catholic Family Life," program, May 10, 1946, diocesan letters, archives, Diocese of Cleveland. In his address, Crawley also touched on the importance of a woman's housekeeping duties. "If the wife is a lazy or incom-

petent housekeeper, there is no home to maintain. To be a good housekeeper is within the realm of every wife and mother."

98. "'Kicked Around' Sweeny Quits Child Welfare Post in Care Center Battle," *Cleveland News*, May 13, 1946.

99. Ibid.; "Day Care Group Plans New Protest," *Cleveland Press*, May 11, 1946.

100. "Children Lobby for Day Care," *Cleveland Press*, May 13, 1946.

101. Ibid.; "We Can't Even Tell It to Sweeny," DCCP; "Mothers Await Day Care Reply: Burke Weighs Plea to Save Program; Tax Need Cited," *Cleveland Plain Dealer*, May 14, 1946; Belle Likover, interview by author.

102. "Mothers Await Day Care Reply," *Cleveland Plain Dealer*, May 14, 1946; "'Kicked Around' Sweeny Quits Child Welfare Post in Care Center Battle," *Cleveland News*, May 13, 1946. Regarding Sweeny's resignation the *News* reported: "Sweeny's action is a direct result of the battle waged between Greater Cleveland working mothers and city and county officials over operation of child day care centers."

103. "Mayo Hits Day Care Stalling, Urges Speedy Finance Plan," *Cleveland Press*, May 14, 1946.

104. Department of Public Relations, Welfare Federation, "Day Care Centers" (press release), May 13, 1946, folder 64, container 3, FCPP. See also Edward D. Lynde, executive secretary, Welfare Federation, to Mayor Thomas Burke, Cleveland, May 15, 1946, folder 44, container 2, FCPP.

105. "Child Care Centers," *Cleveland Plain Dealer*, May 14, 1946.

106. "Should We Pay for Child Day Care?" *Saturday Town Meeting*, in *Cleveland News*, May 18, 1946.

107. Ibid.

108. Ibid.

109. William Chafe, *The American Woman*, 190–91.

110. "Should We Pay for Child Care?" *Cleveland News*, May 18, 1946.

111. Elaine Tyler May, *Homeward Bound*, 16–36. See also Michel, "American Women and the Discourse of the Democratic Family in World War II."

112. "Should We Pay for Child Day Care?" *Cleveland News*, May 18, 1946.

113. "Reader Response to Town Meeting—Continuation of Day Care Centers Favored by Majority of Those Voting," *Cleveland News*, May 23, 1946 (letter from Mrs. W. K. Northrup in May 23, 1946, column), and "Reader Response to Town Meeting—Majority of Those Voting Want Day Care Centers Continued," *Cleveland News*, May 24, 1946.

114. Court of Common Pleas of Ohio, Cuyahoga County, no. 564259, Cleveland. All information about Patrick T. Ferrie gleaned from multiple volumes of the *Cleveland City Directory* and from county tax records at the Cuyahoga County Archives, Cleveland.

115. Belle Likover, interview by author. Augustus Parker is no longer living, and, according to Likover, neither are any other city council members from that time. Lee Howley died in 1983. As of 1996 his papers had not been donated to any archive. Some city law department records from the 1940s remain in storage in the City Hall subbasement but are unprocessed. The position of the Cleveland Catholic Diocese

on women's place has previously been discussed. Beyond their common Catholic faith, I could find little that might link Ferrie with Lee Howley or Joseph Sweeny. Ferrie retired from his job (with an office at City Hall) before Sweeny and Howley began working there. In a slight but possible connection, Ferrie did have well over forty years of service at the city fire department, where Howley's father and grandfather had both been employed as well.

116. County treasurer tax records, 1943, 1944, 1945, Cuyahoga County Archives, Cleveland; "Finance Chief Sweeny Cuts City Tax Debt 20 Millions," *Cleveland News*, June 6, 1946.

117. Scharf, "The Women's Movement in Cleveland from 1850."

118. "Burke Seeks Cost-Sharing Day Care Plan," *Cleveland Press*, May 15, 1946; "Suit Seeks to Cut Child Care Funds: Action on Day Centers Expected since March 1," *Cleveland Plain Dealer*, May 16, 1946.

119. Court of Common Pleas, no. 564259.

120. Mr. Nekvasil to Mr. Gregory, Welfare Federation, folder 44, container 2, June 4, 1946, FCPP. This document summarizes the events of the trial, as observed by Mr. Nekvasil, on the morning of June 3, 1946. Mr. Nekvasil did not return for the afternoon session of the trial and I was unable to find any other documentation of the oral arguments.

121. Court of Common Pleas, no. 564259.

122. Mr. Nekvasil to Mr. Gregory, June 4, 1946, folder 44, container 2, FCPP.

123. Ibid.; Court of Common Pleas, no. 564259.

124. "Sweeny Hits Proposed Child Day Care Plan," *Cleveland Press*, June 22, 1946. Regarding the origins of the proposed plan and details of the same or a similar plan see "Day Care Meeting," minutes, June 3, 1946, and untitled document with handwritten notation "rec'd 6/20/46," both in folder 44, container 2, FCPP. See also "Citizens Group Proposes 12-Point Day Care Plan," *Cleveland News*, May 27, 1946.

125. "An Emergency Ordinance Authorizing the Director of Finance to Make Available the Sum of $10,000.00 for the Purpose of Operating Day Care Centers in the City of Cleveland for a Period Not Later Than June 30, 1946," City Council papers, City Hall archives, Cleveland.

126. *Ferrie v. Sweeny*, 72 N.E. 2d 128.

127. "Brief of Amicus Curiae in Support of Defendants' Position," Court of Common Pleas, no. 564259. The *Cleveland News* ran a four-part series about the need for more recreation spending: "City Needs 90 More Playspots as Bulwark to Curb Crimes and Juvenile Delinquency," May 20, 1946; "Overlapping Agencies of City Spread $1,500,000 Too Thin," May 21, 1946; "City Prepares to Put All Recreation Facilities in Hands of a Single Board," May 22, 1946; and "Neglected West Side Area Points Up City's Need for More Playgrounds," May 23, 1946. Even as its funding of day care centers came under legal scrutiny, the city of Cleveland moved to broaden its recreation program. In late May 1946 Mayor Thomas Burke appointed the school board president Norma Wulff, who had earlier criticized the day care center program, and the city's law director Lee Howley as key members of a committee established to improve and better coordinate services of the city's recreation program.

128. "Court Rules against City Aid for Day Care," *Cleveland Press*, June 26, 1946;

"Use of County Foster Homes Suggested to Save Day Care," *Cleveland Plain Dealer*, June 27, 1946.

129. "Day Care Meeting," June 3, 1946, folder 44, container 2, FCPP; "Surplus Dog Funds Urged for Day Care: Mothers Ask Action as Centers Near Closing Date," *Cleveland Press*, June 28, 1946; "Consolidated Statement Summarizing Receipts," February 11, 1946, *Official Journal of the County Commissioners*, Cuyahoga County Archives, Cleveland.

130. "Mall Lawns Serve as Day Care Center," *Cleveland Press*, July 1, 1946. "Youngsters Romp on Lawn of City Hall as Mothers Fight for Day Care Centers," *Cleveland News*, July 1, 1946; "Mall to Be Child Center All Week Mothers Decide," *Cleveland Plain Dealer*, July 2, 1946; "Only One Day Care Center Remains to Aid Mothers," *Cleveland Press*, July 3, 1946.

131. "Dean Mayo Group, Mothers Seek to Save Day Care," *Cleveland Press*, June 27, 1946; "Use of County Foster Homes Suggested to Save Day Care," *Cleveland Plain Dealer*, June 27, 1946; "Day Care 'March' on Hall Forecast," *Cleveland Plain Dealer*, June 28, 1946; "Mall to Be Child Center All Week, Mothers Decide," *Cleveland Plain* Dealer, July 2, 1946; *Cleveland News*, July 2, 1946.

132. Mina Billmyer, secretary, Parents Day Care Association, Cleveland, to "Dear Parent" [form letter], July 12, 1946, DCCP.

133. "Juvenile Day Care Centers, Inc.," August 13, 1946, DCCP; Paul R. Cherney, child welfare consultant, Cleveland, to Martha Wood, director of field services, Children's Bureau, Washington, regarding "Correspondence with the Parents Day Care Association," CBR; "Seek $50,000 Fund for Day Care Centers," *Cleveland Press*, August 23, 1946.

134. "Resolution Accepting Resignation of Joseph T. Sweeny as Member of the County Child Welfare Board," September 3, 1946, and "Resolution Appointing Edward J. Crawley as a Member of the County Child Welfare Board to Fill the Unexpired Term of Joseph T. Sweeny," *Official Journal of the Cuyahoga County Commissioners*, Cuyahoga County Archives, Cleveland. Just a few weeks later, on September 16, 1946, Sweeny unexpectedly died of a stroke. He was widely eulogized for his financial acumen and his charitable service to the community. The City Council, the County Child Welfare Board, and the Catholic Charities Corporation Board of Trustees were among the institutions that praised his service to the community. The Catholic Charities Board of Trustees, of which Sweeny had been a member from 1934 until his death, noted that he was a "devout Catholic and a devoted husband and father." It continued, "Upon the firm foundation of his practical Catholicity he carried on his work as a public servant in such a manner as to evoke the warm approbation of everyone and he found time to use his splendid talents in the cause of humanity by very active participation in the works of charitable causes." Minutes, regular meeting, Board of Trustees, Catholic Charities Corporation of Cleveland, October 20, 1946, archives, Diocese of Cleveland.

135. "Day Care Meeting," June 3, folder 44, container 2, FCPP; *Ferrie v. Sweeny*, 72 N.E. 2d 128; "Memorandum of Plaintiff," Cuyahoga Court of Common Pleas, no. 564259.

136. Ohio, *Opinions of the Attorney General*, January 31, 1947, no. 1537, 1947; and

Ohio, *Opinions of the Attorney General*, March 2, 1946, no. 769, 1946. Cuyahoga County commissioners themselves had requested the March 1946 opinion from the attorney general and by their carefully drawn questions helped to shape his initial and most conservative opinion. In his January 1947 opinion the attorney general acknowledged this, saying: "The conclusion at which I arrived in [March 1946] was necessarily limited to the questions specifically enumerated in the request which gave rise to the opinion."

137. Paul R. Cherney, child welfare consultant, Cleveland, to Martha Wood, director of field services, Children's Bureau, Washington, regarding "Correspondence with the Parents Day Care Association," CBR.

138. Edward J. Crawley, chairman, Advisory Committee on Day Care to Child Welfare Board, Cuyahoga County, Ohio, to Malcolm Vilas, chairman, Child Welfare Board, Cuyahoga County, Ohio, with attached "Day Care Needs in Cuyahoga County—June 1947," October 10, 1947, folder 815, container 33, FCPP.

139. Kirscher, "History of Day Care in Ohio, 1920–1970," 79; Van Tassel and Grabowski, *The Encyclopedia of Cleveland History*, s.v. "Child Care."

140. See Horowitz, "Rethinking Betty Friedan and *The Feminine Mystique*."

Chapter 3

1. Even in wartime, then, there were severe limits to this public approval of wage-earning mothers. See Anderson, *Wartime Women*, 122–46; Straub, "United States Government Policy toward Civilian Women during World War II."

2. Child Care Projects for August 31, 1945—District of Columbia, Records Relating to Child Care, 1943–45, FWAR. See also "48 Child Care Centers in DC Area May Be Closed by FWA Plan," *Washington Star*, August 19, 1945; "Mothers Ask Continuation of Nursery Aid," *Washington Star*, August 24, 1945; D. V. Auld, director, War Public Works Project, Washington, to "The Engineer Commissioner," February 8, 1946, folder "Board of Public Welfare," box 22, accession no. 65A-1987, DCR.

3. Vivian McMahill, letter to the editor, *Washington Post*, August 26, 1945.

4. Vivian McMahill, letter to the editor, *Washington Star*, August 25, 1945.

5. "Parents Meet Today with School Board on Child Care Centers," *Washington Star*, August 27, 1945.

6. "Parents Push Fight to Retain Nursery Schools," *Washington Star*, August 24, 1945; "Working Mothers Organize to Keep Child Care Centers Open," *Washington Post*, September 12, 1945; "Parents Meet Today with School Board on Child Care Centers," *Washington Star*, August 27, 1945; "Mothers Ask Truman for Child-Care Funds Until Congress Acts," *Washington Star*, August 29, 1945; "Working Mothers to Urge Support of Child Care," *Washington Post*, September 2, 1945; "Commissioners Grant Child Care Hearing," *Washington Star*, September 5, 1945; "D.C. Nurseries Extended to October 27," *Washington Star*, September 6, 1945; "Social Group to Back FWA Child Care Aid," *Washington Post*, September 6, 1945; "Child Care Unit Plans New Plea to Fleming; Mothers Complain Commissioner Mason Is 'Indifferent,'" *Washington Star*, September 7, 1945; "Fleming Quoted as Urging End of

Care Centers," *Washington Star*, September 17, 1945; "District Mothers Find House Group Favors Child Care Extension," *Washington Star*, September 23, 1945. This partial listing of newspaper stories that focused on the group's early activities suggests the range of activities that the group initiated on behalf of the day care centers. Because I was regrettably unable to locate papers specifically belonging to the Parents' Committee, I have relied on newspaper accounts, congressional hearing transcripts, a few scattered personal papers, and (for later years) several oral histories to reconstruct the group's activities,

7. Bledsoe, "A Study of the Status of Group Day Care in the District of Columbia," 33–34. For newspaper references to specific community groups that supported the Parents' Committee see, "Parents Push Fight to Retain Nursery Schools," *Washington Star*, August 24, 1945; "Committee of Mothers Denies Child Care Centers are Charity," *Washington Star*, August 25, 1945; "CIO Office Workers Aid Child Care Centers," *Washington Afro-American*, September 1, 1945; "Citizens' Meeting Seeks to Continue Child Day Care," *Washington Post*, September 5, 1945; "Social Group to Back FWA Child Care Aid," *Washington Post*, September 6, 1945; "House Group to Discuss Child Care," *Washington Post*, September 14, 1945.

8. "Overhasty," *Washington Post*, August 26, 1945.

9. "Committee of Mothers Denies Child Care Centers Are Charity," *Washington Star*, August 25, 1945.

10. Peter Edson, "Baby Sitter," *Washington Daily News*, August 29, 1945.

11. "The Nursery Centers," *Washington Star*, August 24, 1945; "Too Abrupt an End," *Washington Star*, August 31, 1945.

12. "Child Care Projects, August 31, 1945," Records Relating to Child Care, 1943–46, FWAR.

13. Lola G. Pettit, national corresponding secretary, Parents' Committee for Child Care, District of Columbia, to Mildred Chomos, Day Care Committee, Cleveland, September 24, 1945, unprocessed papers, DCCP. "District Mothers Find House Group Favors Child Care Extension," *Washington Star*, September 23, 1945.

14. George H. Field, commissioner, FWA, to Mr. Henry J. Sullivan, division engineer, Bureau of Community Facilities, FWA, Washington, October 6, 1945, and Mary Moon, assistant commissioner for war public services, FWA, to Mr. Laurence A. Gillett, division engineer, Bureau of Community Facilities, FWA, New York, October 12, 1945, CBR.

15. "Washington Is Your City," Voteless D.C. League of Women Voters, 1949, folder "League of Women Voters," tray 185, SEN 81A-F5, 81st Cong., SDCR.

16. David Brinkley, *Washington Goes to War*, 75–76; Bargeron, "The Mayor of Washington."

17. "Washington Is Your City," Voteless D.C. League of Women Voters, 1949, folder "League of Women Voters," tray 185, SEN 81A-F5, 81st Cong., SDCR.

18. Bargeron, "The Mayor of Washington."

19. Rep. George Mahon (D-Tex.) to John Russell Young, president, D.C. Board of Commissioners, January 29, 1946, and Young to Mahon, January 31, 1946, both in folder M, box 8; accession no. 65A-1987, commissioners' office, DCR.

20. "Child Care Unit Plans New Plea to Fleming; Mothers Complain Commissioner Mason Is 'Indifferent,'" *Washington Star*, September 7, 1945.

21. "D.C. Child Care Center Fund to Be Rejected," *Washington Star*, February 12, 1946; "D.C. Day Care Parley Hopelessly Snarled by Funds Question," *Washington Star*, February 28, 1946; "Temporary Closing of Nursery Schools Ordered by Board," *Washington Star*, March 2, 1946.

22. Six centers located in buildings owned by the National Capital Housing Authority and two in buildings owned by the District continued to be available. "Officials Order Service Halted At 22 Nurseries: Centers Must Close Pending Formation of Corporation," *Washington Star*, March 1, 1946; "Mothers Provide Stop-Gap for 22 Nurseries," *Washington Times-Herald*, March 1, 1946; "Child Care Muddled," *Washington Daily News*, March 2, 1946; "Mothers Seek New Locations for Nurseries," *Washington Star*, March 3, 1946; "Day Care Provided for 150 Children in Churches and Homes," *Washington Star*, March 5, 1946; "Religious Groups Join Drive to Raise Cash for Nurseries," *Washington Times Herald*, March 5, 1946; "Mothers Seek Day Care Aid for Children," *Washington Post*, March 5, 1946; "Health Conditions Hit in Makeshift Church Nursery Centers," *Washington Star*, March 8, 1946. See also Bledsoe, "A Study of the Status of Group Day Care in the District of Columbia," 35.

23. "Day Care Centers Due to Return to Schools," *Washington Post*, April 12, 1946; "Sharpe Acts to Speed Opening of Nurseries as Mothers March," *Washington Star*, April 12, 1946; "Nurseries Reopening in 14 Schools Delayed for Another Week," *Washington Star*, April 13, 1946; "Day Nursery Proposal of Mothers Rejected by Commissioners," *Washington Star*, April 19, 1946; "Care Centers Reopening Is Delayed," *Washington Post*, April 24, 1946.

24. John Russell Young, president, Board of Commissioners, District of Columbia, to Mrs. Mary L. Hunt, chairman, Mothers' [sic] Committee on Day Care Centers, February 21, 1946, HWP. See also Bledsoe, "A Study of the Status of Group Day Care in the District of Columbia," 34–35.

25. Harry Wender to Board of Commissioners, District Building, March 1, 1946, and "Certificate of Incorporation of Child Day Care Centers of the District of Columbia, Inc.," March 6, 1946, HWP. "Public Appeal Made by Mothers for Funds to Run Day Nurseries," *Washington Star*, February 27, 1946. "Action on Day Care Awaits Opinion by Corporation Counsel," *Washington Star*, March 7, 1946. See also Bledsoe, "A Study of the Status of Group Day Care in the District of Columbia," 34–35.

26. Herbert Wilett, Jr., executive director, Community War Fund, to Rev. Francis W. McPeek, campaign director, CDCC, March 19, 1946, and G. M. Thornett, secretary, D.C. Board of Commissioners, to Harry Wender, March 26, 1946, both in HWP; "Mothers Corporation for Child Care Gets Tentative Approval," *Washington Star*, March 27, 1946; "District Backs Mothers Plan for Child Care," *Washington Post*, March 27, 1946; "Child Care Plan of Mothers Gets District Approval," *Washington Star*, April 25, 1946; "8 Care Centers Open Again in D.C. Schools," *Washington Post*, April 30, 1946.

27. "D.C. Child Care Centers Fund to Be Rejected," *Washington Star*, February 12, 1946; "Mason Fears Day Care Centers May Tend to Break Up Homes," *Washington Star*, May 12, 1944.

28. Green, *A Secret City*; Jaffe and Sherwood, *Dream City*.

29. "Preliminary Report of Committee Activities through June 15, 1950," District of Columbia Committee, Midcentury White House Conference on Children and Youth, p. 4, box 8, Acc. 65A-1987 (unprocessed), commissioners' office, DCR. The low rates of assistance meant that relatively few people in the city got any aid at all; it did not mean that in dollar figures the District's assistance ranked lowest in the country.

30. National Committee on Segregation in the Nation's Capital, *Segregation in Washington*; Green, *A Secret City*; U.S. Bureau of the Census, *Census of the Population: 1950*, vol. II, part 9, *District of Columbia*, tables 32–32a.

31. National Committee on Segregation in the Nation's Capital, *Segregation in Washington*, chapter 10; "The Job Colorline in the Nation's Capital," 6–14, n.d. [ca. 1943], folder 1462, box 78-66, NAACP-DC Branch papers, Moorland-Spingarn Research Center, Howard University.

32. National Committee on Segregation in the Nation's Capital, *Segregation in Washington*, chapter 10; "The Job Colorline in the Nation's Capital," 31–35, n.d. [ca. 1943], folder 1462, box 78-66, NAACP-DC Branch papers, Moorland-Spingarn Research Center, Howard University; Green, *A Secret City*, 315–16; National Committee on Segregation in the Nation's Capital, *Segregation in Washington*, 56.

33. Green, *A Secret City*, 258–60; David Brinkley, *Washington Goes to War*, 250–51; "The Job Colorline in the Nation's Capital," 5–6, n.d. [ca. 1943], folder 1462, box 78-66, NAACP-DC Branch papers, Moorland-Spingarn Research Center, Howard University.

34. Green, *A Secret City*, 242, 315–19; "The Job Colorline in the Nation's Capital," 20–30, n.d. [ca. 1943], folder 1462, box 78-66, NAACP-DC Branch papers, Moorland-Spingarn Research Center, Howard University; National Committee on Segregation in the Nation's Capital, *Segregation in Washington*, 5.

35. U.S. Bureau of the Census, *Census of the Population: 1950*, vol. II, part 9, *District of Columbia*, table 28a (see also table 2 in text).

36. "Names of Parents Using the District Day Care Centers and the Positions They Hold," folder S 3258, box 14, SEN81A-E5, 81st Cong., SDCR. Of a total of 212 parents (of whom twelve appear to have male first names), 78 worked for government agencies and their specific occupation is not listed. The remaining 134 parents—66 white and 68 black—worked in the private sector. Among the black workers 42, or 61.8 percent, gave "domestic" as their occupation; among the white workers only 2, or 3 percent, gave "domestic" as their occupation.

37. Regarding the District's inadequate child welfare institutions see U.S. Congress, House, Committee on the District of Columbia, *Hearing on Need for Child Care Revision*, May 8, 1945. At this hearing, members of the General Federation of Women's Clubs, D.C., describe truly deplorable sanitary conditions and a badly deteriorated physical plant. They save some of their strongest criticism for the lack of resources that sometimes forced black and white girls to share living space; the club-

women insisted that any improvement plan must uphold the D.C. Board of Public Welfare's stated policy of segregation.

38. Women's Bureau, *Employed Mothers and Child Care*, 18.

39. U.S. Congress, House, Committee on the District of Columbia, *Continuing a System of Nurseries and Nursery Schools*, 1949; "Child Day Care Centers— Narrative Report," January 12, 1950, and "Child Day Care Centers," n.d. [ca. October 1949], both in folder S 3258, box 14, SEN 81A-E5, 81st Cong., SDCR. In March 1949 the Board of Public Welfare reported there were forty-five eligible black families waiting to use the centers compared to seven white families. The disparity in January 1950 had declined somewhat, with fifty black families on the waiting list and twelve white families.

40. "Parents Protest Plan to Close Nursing Centers," *Washington Star*, August 22, 1945; "Mothers Ask Continuation of Nursery Aid," *Washington Post*, August 24, 1945; "Religious Groups Join Drive to Raise Cash for Nurseries," *Washington Times-Herald*, March 5, 1946; "Gigantic Task Ahead for Them," *Washington Afro-American*, March 16, 1946; "Mass Meeting Called by Mothers Seeking to Reopen Nurseries," *Washington Star*, March 17, 1946. The Washington Federation of Churches, which integrated its membership in the mid-1930s, gave strong support to the day care cause. The major city neighborhood organizations were split by race, with the Federation of Citizens Associations representing white neighborhood groups and the Federation of Civic Associations representing black groups. Of these two umbrella groups only the Federation of Civic Associations came out in support of the day care centers; however a number of member associations of the white Federation of Citizens Associations passed resolutions in support of the day care centers. Local chapters of the General Federation of Women's Clubs and the American Association of University Women were whites-only groups. The GFWC chapter had ardently segregationist members in leadership positions; in 1950 the chapter voted against support of the centers but no member bothered to testify for the group on the issue then or in previous years. (See "End Day Care Centers Club Federation Urges," *Washington Post*, April 25, 1950.) The issue of segregation in the late 1940s consumed the D.C. chapter of AAUW after a narrow majority of its members voted to deny membership to Mary Church Terrell, a long-time black female activist and D.C. resident. Amidst the race debate, which eventually led to the expulsion of the segregationist D.C. chapter from the national AAUW, day care appears not to have gained the local chapter's attention. (See papers of the AAUW-DC at the Historical Society of Washington.)

41. Flora O. Calhoun, interview by author, transcribed tape recording, Washington, May 23, 1997.

42. Ellen Adamson Andruzzi, telephone interview by author, transcribed tape recording, June 7 and 13, 1997.

43. "Child Care Centers Hearing Slated by House Committee," *Washington Post*, February 20, 1946; U.S. Congress, House, Committee on Appropriations, *First Supplemental Surplus Appropriation Rescission Bill*, 1946, 943–45.

44. U.S. Congress, House, Committee on the District of Columbia, *Child Care Centers*, 3–4.

45. Ibid., 3–6.

46. Ibid., 8–12. Median families incomes are from 1949. See U.S. Bureau of Census, *Census of the Population: 1950*, vol. II, part 9, *District of Columbia*, tables 32, 32a (again, I have used the word "black" where the census report used "non-white"; for an explanation see table 2 in text); Bargeron, "The Mayor of Washington." See also miscellaneous items (including unset text) in Guy Mason, biographical clippings file, *Washington Star*, Washingtoniana Division, Martin Luther King Jr. Public Library, Washington, D.C.

47. U.S. Congress, House, Committee on the District of Columbia, *Child Care Centers*, 11–12.

48. U.S. Congress, House, Committee on Appropriations, *District of Columbia Appropriation Bill for 1947*, 1069.

49. Ibid., 1070.

50. Ibid., 1070–71.

51. "Dr. Gannon Discusses Problem of Day Nursery Maintenance," *Washington Star*, February 2, 1946. See also "Education Board Members Urge Starting Children in School at 3," *Washington Star*, January 31, 1946; "D.C. Day Care Centers Urged for Children as Young as 2," *Washington Post*, February 1, 1946.

52. See, for example, House of Representatives floor debate on funding day care, *Congressional Record* 92 (1946): 4928–4930.

53. U.S. Congress, House, Committee on Appropriations, *District of Columbia Appropriation Bill for 1947*, 1071.

54. Harvey, *The Fifties: A Women's Oral History*; Rupp and Taylor, *Survival in the Doldrums*.

55. U.S. Congress, House, Committee on the District of Columbia, *Child Care Centers*, 31.

56. Council of Social Agencies of the District of Columbia and Vicinity, "Report of the Social Survey: Children's Services, Public and Private," November 1946, Washingtoniana Division, Martin Luther King Jr. Public Library, Washington, D.C., 70–75. A survey in February 1946 of nonprofit and commercial, licensed, full-day nursery care in the District revealed a capacity to care for 596 children at 25 centers (16 served whites, 9 served blacks). Most centers had no vacancies, especially the seven nonprofits, most of which received Community Chest subsidies and so were able to offer care on a sliding scale. For the rest of the centers fees ranged from $22 to $50 a month. The survey reported that families with an annual income of $3,000 or less would find it difficult to pay for day care services.

57. U.S. Congress, House, Committee on the District of Columbia, *Child Care Centers*, 47. See also Mrs. A. S., District of Columbia, to President Harry Truman, October 4, 1945, HSTP. "If a Domestic Worker, Be a Good One, Says League," *Washington Afro-American*, October 6, 1945.

58. U.S. Congress, House, Committee on the District of Columbia, *Child Care Centers*, 53–54. See also "Day Center Close May Send Child Back to Orphanage," *Washington Post*, February 21, 1946.

59. Addams quoted in Michel, "The Limits of Maternalism," 291.

60. Gordon, *Pitied but Not Entitled*, 37–64; Cahan, *Past Caring*, 21–28; Michel,

"The Limits of Maternalism," 277–320; DeForest, Rubin, and Wynia with Lauve and Shaw, *Legislative History of the A.D.C. Program.*

61. Gordon, *Pitied but Not Entitled*, 287–306; "D.C. Child Care Centers Fund to Be Rejected, *Washington Star*, February 12, 1946; "Child Center Continuance Turned Down," *Washington Post*, February 13, 1946. Commissioner Mason later denied suggesting, contrary to newspaper reports in both the *Star* and the *Post*, that women should seek ADC rather then public day care. Neither newspaper retracted its story, and the statement seems consistent with Mason's views. By this point, however, whether he'd said it or not, the suggestion that women turn to ADC had received wide community discussion.

62. Law, "Women, Work, Welfare, and the Preservation of Patriarchy," 1257–58; Goodwin, *Gender and the Politics of Welfare Reform*, 6, 157–81.

63. "Working Mothers Hit Mason's Suggestion They Go on Relief," *Washington Star*, February 14, 1946; Mrs. Mary Hunt, chairman, Parents' Committee for Child Care, to editor, *Washington Post*, February 20, 1946.

64. "Desperate Mother" to editor, *Washington Star*, February 19, 1946.

65. Sapiro, "The Gender Basis of American Social Policy"; Meyerowitz, "Beyond the Feminine Mystique."

66. U.S. Congress, House, Committee on the District of Columbia, *Child Care Centers*, 22–25.

67. Thomas E. Mattingly, M.D., to editor, *Washington Star*, February 18, 1946.

68. Bledsoe, "A Study of the Status of Group Day Care in the District of Columbia," 63–64.

69. "Closing of Nursery Schools Makes Mother Plead for a Man," *Washington Post*, February 16, 1946; U.S. Congress, House, Committee on the District of Columbia, *Child Care Centers*, 45–46.

70. "Closing of Nursery Schools Makes Mother Plead for a Man," *Washington Post*, February 16, 1946.

71. Ibid.; "Husband-Hunting Divorcee Waits in Vain for 'Six Suitors,'" *Washington Post*, February 17, 1946.

72. U.S. Congress, House, Committee on the District of Columbia, *Child Care Centers*, 45–46.

73. U.S. Congress, House, Committee on the District of Columbia, *H.R. 3208*, 28–36.

74. An analysis of day care users who responded to a survey sponsored by the Parents' Committee found that 173, or more than 61 percent of all those surveyed, had reported working to supplement their husband's (or family) incomes. Of this number, 48 said that they were supplementing their husband's service allotment, five did not indicate their husband's military status, and the remaining 120 women reported their husbands were living at home and employed. Approximately 72 percent of these non-sole-support women reported household incomes of $3,500 or less—meaning two incomes placed them basically at or below the median white household income level for the District ($3,400). Calculations based on Bledsoe, "A Study of the Status of Group Day Care in the District of Columbia," 52 table VII.

75. U.S. Congress, Senate, Committee on the District of Columbia, *H.R. 5933*,

35–38. For biographical information regarding Rosina Tucker see Salem, *African American Women*, 520–21; and Mabunda and Phelps, *Contemporary Black Biography*, 209–12.

76. U.S. Congress, Senate, Committee on the District of Columbia, *H.R.* 5933, 35–38.

77. *Congressional Record* 92 (1946): 4928–30, 7883, 8198–99, 8207. Gladys Cook, president, Child Day Care Centers of Washington, D.C., to Citizens Organizations Interested in the Day Care Centers for Children, May 27, 1948. See also *H.R.* 5933.

78. *Congressional Record* 92 (1946): 9074–80. See also Pearson, "Washington Merry-Go-Round," *Washington Post*, July 25, 1946; "D.C. Day Care Funds Slashed by $94,000," *Washington Post*, July 18, 1946; "Conferees Cut Day-Care Fund to $250,000," *Washington Star*, July 18, 1946.

79. For opposition by the commissioner and Board of Public Welfare see John Russell Young, president, Board of Commissioners, D.C., to C. Douglas Buck, chairman, Committee on the District of Columbia; U.S. Senate, March 27, 1947, folder S 751, box 4, SEN 80A-E6, 80th Cong., SDCR; Minutes of the Agency Services Committee meeting, January 17, 1947, box 11, Records Relating to Charitable and Reformatory Institutions, Records of the Board of Public Welfare, Minutes 1926–53, DCR; Ray L. Huff, director of public welfare, to Miss Gladys H. Cook, president, Child Day Care Centers, January, 30, 1947, HWP.

80. "Day Care Bill Passes Senate, but Truman's Action Is Uncertain," *Washington Star*, July 3, 1946; U.S. Congress, House, Committee on the District of Columbia, *Child Care Centers*, 11; "A Preliminary Six-Year Plan for Post-War Washington," prepared by Brigadier General Gordon R. Young, engineer commissioner, June 1946, XIV: Special Items, "Child Care Centers," folder 1311, box 78-58, NAACP-DC branch Papers, Moorland-Spingarn Research Center, Howard University.

81. U.S. Congress, House, Committee on the District of Columbia, *H.R.* 3208, 18–20.

82. U.S. Bureau of Labor Statistics, *Workers' Budgets in the United States*, 27, 30, table 6. For June 1947, the BLS estimated the annual budget for a four-person family in Washington at $3,458. A two-person family was expected to need 65 percent of this budget ($2,248 a year) and a three-person family 84 percent ($2,905 a year).

83. U.S. Congress, Senate, Committee on the District of Columbia, *Nurseries and Nursery Schools*, 26–28; "Child Day Care Centers," n.d. [ca. late 1949 or early 1950], folder S 3258, box 14, SEN81A-E5, 81st Cong., SDCR. The maximum income level of $1,200 was the cutoff point for a family of four. Presumably smaller families would need to have a still lower annual income. District of Columbia Committee, Midcentury White House Conference on Children and Youth, "Preliminary Report of Committee Activities Through June 15, 1950," box 8, Commissioner Young, commissioners' office, accession no. 65A-1987, DCR. This report reviewed the low levels of assistance granted by the city, contrasted to other locations, and observed that the "figures seem to indicate that there is some unreality in terms of needs or requirements for assistance, even when the District's high average income is taken into account."

84. Regarding community and day care user support see testimony in U.S. Congress, Senate, Committee on the District of Columbia, *Nurseries and Nursery Schools* and U.S. Congress, House, Committee on the District of Columbia, *H.R. 3208*. See also letters to Senate Committee on the District of Columbia, folder S 751, box 4, SEN80A-E6, 80th Cong., SDCR.

85. Andruzzi, interview by author.

86. Ibid.; U.S. Congress, Senate, Committee on the District of Columbia, *Nurseries and Nursery Schools*, 194–98. Ellen Andruzzi, legislative chairman, Parents' Committee, Washington, D.C., to Sen. Capper, Senate District Committee, April 19, 1947, folder S 751, box 4, SEN 80A-E6, 80th Congress, SDCR.

87. U.S. Congress, Senate, Committee on the District of Columbia, *Nurseries and Nursery Schools*, 64–65.

88. Ibid.

89. U.S. Congress, Senate, Committee on Appropriations, *District of Columbia Appropriation Bill for 1948*, 94–97

90. Constance Severn, phone interview by author, transcribed tape recording, May 17, 1997.

91. U.S. Congress, House, Committee on the District of Columbia, *H.R. 3208*, 44–45.

92. U.S. Congress, Senate, Committee on the District of Columbia, *H.R. 5808*, 25–33; U.S. Congress, House, Committee on the District of Columbia, *H.R. 5808*; Eliot, "Nursery Schools Fifty Years Ago."

93. Andruzzi, interview by author; Calhoun, interview by author.

94. Coontz, *The Way We Never Were*, 128–40; Steinfels, *Who's Minding the Children*, 50–51; Durst, "Day Nurseries and Wage-Earning Mothers in the United States, 1890–1930," 10–62.

95. Cahan, *Past Caring*, 28–29; Durst, "Day Nurseries and Wage-Earning Mothers in the United States," 49–50; Malone, "A Study of Day Care Methods Adopted by Mothers Rejected from District Day Nurseries under Provisions of Public Law 237" (see especially Malone's comments regarding "Family L"); Public Law 514, chapter 582, 79th Cong., 2d sess.; "Administrative Order 2.20/1: Revised Scale of Fees and Handicaps, August 26, 1946," HWP.

96. "Administrative Order 2.20/1—Revised Scale of Fees and Handicaps."

97. Ibid.

98. Ibid.

99. U.S. Congress, Senate, Committee on the District of Columbia, *Nurseries and Nursery Schools*, 1947; U.S. Congress, House, Committee on the District of Columbia, *H.R. 3208*.

100. Malone, "A Study of Day Care Methods Adopted by Mothers Rejected from District Day Nurseries," 4–5.

101. Ibid. Malone surveyed 26 of the 107 families ruled ineligible after the stricter requirements were implemented in July 1947.

102. On the other hand, Elizabeth Rose noted a postwar increase in the number of two-earner families whose children were enrolled at public day care centers in

Philadelphia. At the same time she found a more dramatic upsurge in attendance by children from two-earner households at the city's privately funded centers. See Rose, *A Mother's Job,* 198–99.

103. U.S. Congress, House, Committee on the District of Columbia, *H.R.* 5805, 22; U.S. Congress, House, Committee on the District of Columbia, *Child Day Care Centers,* 9–11. Of 767 total rejections an estimated 450 were based on income, 250 on a child's failure to meet the minmum age of two years, 40 on failure to meet the federally mandated one-year residency or relationship requirement, and 27 on "other" reasons.

104. "Committee of Mothers Denies Child Care Centers Are Charity," *Washington Star,* August 25, 1945; U.S. Congress, House, Committee on the District of Columbia, *H.R.* 5808, 22–23; U.S. Congress, House, Committee on the District of Columbia, *Continuing a System of Nurseries and Nursery Schools,* 1949, p. 2; U.S. Congress, House, Committee on the District of Columbia, *Continuing a System of Nurseries and Nursery Schools,* 1950, p. 2.

105. "Child Day Care Centers," n.d. [ca. late 1949 or early 1950], folder S 3258, box 14, SEN81A-E5, 81st Cong., SDCR; "Day Care, Dec. 1950" [handwritten label on Senate District Committee stationery] and "Names of Parents Using the District Day Care Centers and the Positions They Hold," December 1950, both in folder S 3258, box 14, SEN 81A-E5, 81st Congress, SDCR.

106. Andruzzi, interview by author.

107. U.S. Congress, House, Committee on the District of Columbia, *H.R.* 5808: *Executive Session.* Senator John Cooper had earlier suggested that perhaps the program emphasized quality *too* much since the basic goal was custodial care; cost had to be cut somewhere. U.S. Congress, Senate, Committee on the District of Columbia, *Nurseries and Nursery Schools,* 153–54.

108. See U.S. Congress, Senate, Committee on the District of Columbia, *H.R.* 5808; U.S. Congress, House, Committee on the District of Columbia, *H.R.* 5808.

109. U.S. Congess, Senate, Committee on the District of Columbia, *Continuation of Child Day Care Centers in the District,* 4–11; "Margaret Chase Smith Is Dead at 97," *New York Times,* May 30, 1995.

110. U.S. Congress, Senate, Committee on the District of Columbia, *Continuation of Child Day Care Centers in the District,* 37–40.

111. Ibid., 61–62.

112. Palmer, "Housewife and Household Worker"; Clark-Lewis, "'This Work Had an End'"; Glenn, "From Servitude to Service Work."

113. U.S. Congress, Senate, Committee on the District of Columbia, *Continuation of Child Day Care Centers in the District,* 90–95.

114. Ibid.

115. "Day Care Center Funds Restored by Senate Unit," *Washington Star,* May 9, 1949; James R. Kirkland, counsel, Committee on the District of Columbia, U.S. Senate, to D.C. Board of Commissioners, May 11, 1949, James Kirkland to Sen. Matthew N. Neely, chairman, Senate District Committee, October 31, 1949, and "Report on Day Care Centers Operated by the District of Columbia," November 10, 1949, all in folder S 3258, box 14, SEN 81A-E5, 81st Cong., SDCR.

116. "Report on Day Care Centers Operated by the District of Columbia," folder S 3258, box 14, SEN 81A-E5, SDCR.

117. G. M. Thornett, secretary, Board of Commissioners, D.C., to Mr. Edgar Morris, chairman, Board of Public Welfare, November 17, 1949, and John Russell Young, president, Board of Commissioners, D.C., to Robert H. Mollohan, clerk, Senate Committee on the District, January 3, 1950, both in folder S 3258, box 14, SEN 81A-E5, SDCR; "Churches Study Plan to Run D.C. Child Centers," *Washington Star*, December 18, 1949.

118. John Russell Young to Robert H. Mollohan, January 27, 1950, folder S 3258, box 14, SEN 81A-E5, 81st Congress, Senate, Record Group 46, National Archives.

119. J. George Stewart, minority clerk, Committee on the District of Columbia, U.S. Senate, to Sen. Margaret Chase Smith, February 1, 1950, and Gerhard P. Van Arkel, counsel, Senate District Committee, to Rabbi Norman Gerstenfeld, with attached proposed draft letter for Gerstenfeld to send to Commissioner John Russell Young, April 3, 1950, folder S 3258, box 14, SEN 81A-E5, SDCR; "New Effort to Continue Day Care Centers Here Slated after Parley," *Washington Star*, February 15, 1950; "District May Pay Bill, Let Churches Conduct Child Care Centers," *Washington Star*, February 19, 1950.

120. "Day Care Center Bill Awaits Action of Senate," *Washington Star*, April 28, 1950; "Child Day Care Bill Goes to House after Passage by Senate," May 13, 1950; "Day Care Bill Is Debated at House Hearing," *Washington Star*, June 1, 1950; U.S. Congress, House, Committee on the District of Columbia, *Continuing a System of Nurseries and Nursery Schools*, 1950. See also U.S. Congress, House, Committee on the District of Columbia, *S. 3258*, and U.S. Congress, House, Committee on the District of Columbia, *Executive Session*, March 25, 1949.

121. "Senate to Wage Fight for Permanent Child Day Care Centers," *Washington Star*, June 28, 1950; U.S. Congress, House, Conference Report, *District of Columbia Day Care Nurseries and Nursery Schools*. See also Sen. Lester C. Hunt, chairman of the conference, to John Russell Young, June 29, 1950, folder S 3258, box 14, SEN 81A-E5, SDCR.

122. "Supplemental Appropriations for FY Ending June 30, 1951 and Other Purposes" (Public Law 843, 81st Cong., 2d sess.), approved September 27, 1950; "False Economy Seen in House Move to Cut Day Care Center Fund," *Washington Star*, September 2, 1950; "House Fight Due in Effort to Save Child Care Plan: Conferees Find Day Center Too Knotty a Problem," *Washington Star*, September 17, 1950; "D.C. Child Care Program Extended until End of Year," *Washington Star*, September 21, 1950.

123. "Day Care Centers Closing This Week," *Washington Post*, December 18, 1950; "Day Care Center Closings Pose Problem for Mothers of 300," *Washington Star*, December 23, 1950; "Commissioners Ask Fund to Operate Day-Care Centers," *Washington Star*, December 26, 1950; "Congress Gets Plea for $50,000 to Run Day Care Centers," *Washington Star*, January 22, 1951. See also Irene S. Raine, Washington, to Gerhard Van Arkle, counsel, Senate District Committee, December 7, 1950, with attached copy of letter from Irene Raine, chairman, Parents Committee, Washington, D.C., to President Harry Truman, White House, folder S3258, box 14, SEN 81A-E5, SDCR.

124. "Mothers Ask $50,000 Fund for Day Care Centers," *Washington Star*, February 2, 1951; "Southeast Day Care Center Is Cleared of Equipment," February 25, 1951.

125. "Shea Reports Closing of Day Care Centers Caused Little Hardship," *Washington Star*, April 5, 1951; U.S. Congress, House, Committee on Appropriations, *Third Supplemental Appropriation Bill, 1951*, 2. See also "Day Care Fund Reported Cut from D.C. Bill," *Washington Star*, March 14, 1951; "Day Care Centers Future in Doubt, West Reports," *Washington Star*, March 23, 1951; "Hunt to Ask New Funds for Day Care Centers," *Washington Star*, March 31, 1951.

126. "Child Day Care Center Bill Waits Truman Signature," *Washington Star*, September 23, 1950.

127. *Congressional Quarterly Almanac* 7 (1951): 184–90.

128. Truman issued an executive order on October 4, 1951, formally transferring most authority over recreation and day care centers to the FSA (to which Congress had already given some duties). In addition to recent housing legislation, between 1946 and 1950 Congress had enacted major legislation and granted funding in three areas directly under the purview of FSA, all of which were repeated in the community facilities provision of the Maybank bill. See U.S. Congress, House, Committee on Banking and Currency, *Defense Housing and Community Facilities Act*, 95–112.

129. U.S. Congress, House, Committee on Banking and Currency, *Defense Housing and Community Facilities Act*, 100–101; U.S. Congress, Senate, Committee on Banking and Currency, *Defense Housing Act*, 96.

130. Data on community day care needs were gathered in 1951 and 1952. See investigative reports and summaries in boxes 10–11, General Correspondence, 1948–53, WBR. The information was not published until January 1953. See Women's Bureau, *Employed Mothers and Child Care*. Regarding the political status of the Women's Bureau in the early postwar period see Laughlin, *Women's Work and Public Policy*, 33–38.

131. Lindemeyer, "*A Right to Childhood*," 249–61.

132. Helen Clausen, Bureau of Boarding Homes and Institutions, State Department of Social Welfare, to Lucile Kennedy, chief, Division of Child Welfare, SDSW, Sacramento, F3752:1564, Division of Chief's Files, Child Care: Conferences and Workshops, 1950–51, Division of Public School Administration, SDEP; I. Evelyn Smith, "While Mothers Work at Defense Jobs," 125–26, 135.

133. See testimony of Eric Lindman, Office of Education, in U.S. Congress, Senate, Committee on Banking and Currency, *Defense Housing Act*, 106–7.

134. Other nongovernment agency testimony that called attention to the need for day care came from representatives of the National Federation of Settlements and Neighborhood Centers and the American Association of Social Workers. (Both witnesses focused first and primarily on the need for more and better housing.) A staff member of the Association for Childhood Education, International, gave sole focus to day care and noted that she spoke also on behalf of the American Home Economics Association, the National Consumers League, the National Council of Jewish Women, and the United Council of Church Women. See U.S. Congress, House, Committee on Banking and Currency, *Defense Housing and Communty Facilities*

Act, 195–200, 303–6, 385–89. See also letters regarding day care in U.S. Congress, Senate, Committee on Banking and Currency, *Defense Housing Act*, 542, and U.S. Congress, House, *Defense Housing and Community Facilities Act*, 413–14.

135. U.S. Congress, Senate, Committee on Banking and Currency, *Defense Housing Act*, 238, 243.

136. Ibid. See also Fahy's testimony in U.S. Congress, House, Committee on Banking and Currency, *Defense Housing and Community Facilities Act*, 229–34.

137. U.S. Congress, Senate, Committee on Banking and Currency, *Defense Housing Act*, 351. See also O'Grady's testimony in U.S. Congress, House, Committee on Banking and Currency, *Defense Housing and Community Facilities Act*, 297–306.

138. *Congressional Quarterly Almanac* 7 (1951): 162, 184. The authorization for funding ran two years, and the FSA did seek full funding (for items unrelated to day care) in the next appropriations cycle. The agency instead received about $4 million again. See *Congressional Quarterly Almanac* 8 (1952): 117.

139. U.S. Congress, House, Committee on Appropriations, *Second Supplemental Appropriation Bill, 1952*, 6. Although a committee report is not technically binding on federal agencies, explicit language denying funding for a certain program is nearly impossible to ignore. Each year agency officials must justify their budget requests for all programs; flouting a spending limitation in a report in one year can mean jeopardizing the entire agency budget in the following year.

140. U.S. Congress, House, Committee on Appropriations, *(Report on) Second Supplemental Appropriation Bill for 1952*, 136–37.

141. Ibid., 139.

142. U.S. Congress, House, Committee on Appropriations, *Second Supplemental Appropriation Bill for 1952*, 6.

143. U.S. Congress, House, Committee on Appropriations, *(Report on) Second Supplemental Appropriation Bill for 1952*, 139. The agency asked for $1.5 million for day care operations and $300,000 for construction. By contrast, in fiscal year 1950 California spent more than $4.5 million on its state child care program.

144. U.S. Congress, House, Committee on Appropriations, *Third Supplemental Appropriation Bill, 1952*, 348; U.S. Congress, Senate, Committee on Appropriations, *Third Supplemental Appropriation Bill, 1952*, 165–69.

145. *Congressional Quarterly Almanac* 8 (1952): 117.

146. *Congressional Record* 92 (1946): 9074–80. See also Pearson, "Washington Merry-Go-Round," *Washington Post*, July 25, 1946; "Conferees Cut Day-Care Fund to $250,000," *Washington Star*, July 18, 1946. At the Senate appropriations hearing in 1951, Sen. Robert Kerr (D-Okla.) said that the House appropriations committee action showed "fact blindness" and suggested that the representatives' stated reasons for denying funds to child care were disingenuous. His fellow senators seemed little impressed by his protest. See U.S. Congress, Senate, Committee on Appropriations, *Second Supplemental Appropriation Bill for 1952*, 249–53.

147. United Community Services, Family and Child Welfare Section, "Report of Committee on Child Dependency," September 1955, folder 3-421, box 188, Department of Public Welfare, General Files, DCR.

Chapter 4

1. Betty Bachman, legislative chairman, California Parents Association for Child Care Centers (CPACCC), to "Mr. Chairman, Members of the Committee, and Mr. Ohlosson" [Senate Interim Committee on Social Welfare, California], n.d. [ca. October 1954], box 4, TSMP.

2. The state child care program initiated in California was formally titled Child Care Centers.

3. California State Department of Education, *Child Care Centers by School Districts*, 2; California Legislature, *Technical Staff Report*, 291; California State Department of Education, *Report of Child Care Centers Administered and Operated by California School Districts*, March 1949, 6–7, 9; California Senate Interim Committee on Social Welfare, *Report on the Child Care Center Program*, 25; California Legislative Analyst, "The Child Care Program: State of California," October 23, 1958, 8–10, 22, box 4, TSMP; Ronald W. Cox, associate superintendent of public instruction, State Department of Education, Sacramento, to Hon. Carlos Bee, chairman, Special Education Subcommittee, Assembly Interim Committee on Education, September 18, 1962, 5, copy in California State Library, Sacramento.

4. Fousekis, "Fighting for Our Children," 103–4, 119–20, 131–32.

5. Putnam, "The Progressive Legacy in California," 249–50. See also White, *It's Your Misfortune and None of My Own*, 574–611.

6. White, *It's Your Misfortune and None of My Own*, 498–502, 513–17; Putnam, "The Progressive Legacy," 258; U.S. Bureau of the Census, *Census of the Population: 1960*, vol. 1, part 6, *California*, "Graphic Summary," chart 1 and table 1.

7. The Welfare Planning Council of Metropolitan Los Angeles seemed especially cheerful about the future. See, for example, Welfare Planning Council, Los Angeles Region, Research Department, *Background for Planning* (Los Angeles, 1955). For a dyspeptic view of postwar suburbanization in southern California, which nonetheless demonstrates the efforts of white Angelenos to shape an "ideal" future for themselves, see Mike Davis, *City of Quartz*, 153–219. See also Leonard, "Years of Hope, Days of Fear."

8. U.S. Bureau of the Census, *Census of the Population: 1960*, vol. 1, part 6, *California*, tables 53, 54, 59 (percentages extrapolated from data given in these tables); U.S. Women's Bureau, *Employed Mothers and Child Care*, 79–80.

9. Fraser, "Struggle over Needs," 204–7.

10. Ibid.

11. As of August 31, 1945, 49 percent of the mothers who enrolled their children in California's wartime child care program were the wives of servicemen or their widows. "Child Care Projects, August 31, 1945: California, Records Relating to Child Care, 1943–45," FWAR.

12. For a longer description of the servicemen's wife rationale see chapter 2 above.

13. As of September 19, 1945, 838 California residents had signed petitions, which had been received at the FWA; the agency had also received 1,485 letters, wires, and postcards from the California correspondents. *Congressional Record* 91 (1945): A4000.

14. Mrs. Marvin G. Ronk, Los Angeles, to Rep. Helen Gahagan Douglas, August 27, 1945; Mrs. G. R. Meadows, Los Angeles, to Rep. Helen Gahagan Douglas, August 20, 1945; Mrs. Beatrice Kinman, Los Angeles, to Rep. Helen Gahagan Douglas, August 20, 1945. Letters transcribed in *Congressional Record* 91 (1945): A3999. See also approximately seventy additional letters, most of them written by southern California mothers who used the wartime child care service and all of them asking for the program's continuation, in folders 4a and 4b, box 17, HGDP.

15. *Congressional Record* 91 (1945): 8554, 8657. U.S. Congress, House, Committee on Appropriations, *First Supplemental Surplus Appropriation Rescission Bill, 1946*, 939–40.

16. "Telephone Conversation between Congressman Doyle of California and General Fleming," September 5, 1945, box 4, Correspondence of General Fleming, 1942–49, FWAR; Rep. Clyde Doyle to President Harry Truman, September 28, 1945, with attached copy of H.R. 4204, HSTP.

17. Concerns regarding the end of child care funding expressed on the House floor by Reps. Doyle (Long Beach) and Douglas (Los Angeles) were echoed by Reps. Richard Welch (San Francisco), Gordon McDonough (Los Angeles), J. Leroy Johnson (Vallejo), Frank Havenner (San Francisco), and Ned Healy (Los Angeles). A few representatives from other states spoke on the issue as well. One representative each from Wisconsin, Oregon, North Carolina, and Michigan also gave statements in support of child care funding for the record. I did not find any Senate floor discussion on this issue. *Congressional Record* 91 (1945): 8554–55, 8657, 9337, 9502, A700, A1010, A3929, A3998–A4002, A4015, A4025, A4026, A4076–77, A4080–81, A4154–57, A4194–95, A4290–91.

18. The California representatives were joined by representatives from Oregon and Washington in their meeting with the FWA, but they were the only state delegation to appear before the hearing committee. See testimony of Reps. Healy, Doyle, Welch, McDonough, Jerry Voorhis (San Dimas), Douglas, and Ellis E. Patterson (Los Angeles), all of California, in U.S. Congress, House, Committee on Appropriations, *First Supplemental Surplus Appropriation Rescission Bill, 1946*, 195, 939–40, 945–53.

19. "Rep. Clyde Doyle Dies at 75; Active in Anti-Red Activities," *New York Times*, March 15, 1963, and "Rep. Doyle Dies in Washington; Rites Pending," *Los Angeles Times*, March 15, 1963. See also Scobie, *Center Stage*. A third California representative, Ned Healy, was a liberal who represented his Los Angeles district for only one term. During this time he sponsored the first child care center bill for the District of Columbia, which defined the program as educational and sought to give it permanent status with universal access.

20. Governor Earl Warren, Sacramento, to President Harry S. Truman, Washington, September 12, 1945, HSTP.

21. U.S. Congress, House, Committee on Appropriations, *First Supplemental Surplus Appropriation Rescission Bill, 1946*, 948, 953–55. Jess Dorsey, California state senator, to Rep. Helen Gahagan Douglas, September 17, 1945, folder 4b, box, 17, HGDP.

22. Truman to Warren, September 27, 1945, HSTP (the FWA drafted Truman's response to Warren).

23. Prescott, Milich, and Jones, *The "Politics" of Day Care*, 6–7; California State Department of Education, *Child Care Centers by School District*, iii, 1; Summary of statement by Dr. Bernard Lonsdale, consultant in elementary education, Child Care Conference, 1950, folder VII-3, box 2, JWP.

24. California State Department of Education, *Child Care Centers by School Districts*, 1–5; Prescott, Milich, and Jones, *The "Politics" of Day Care*, 6–7.

25. Mary H. Isham, regional supervisor, War Public Services, FWA, Berkeley, to Florence Kerr, assistant to the administrator, FWA, Washington, January 25, 1944, with attached correspondence of Child Care Coordinating Committee for Women in Industry, George D. Nickel, executive secretary, Los Angeles, January 17, 1944, Phillip M. Connelly, secretary, Los Angeles CIO Council (telegram), January 25, 1944, to Major General Philip Fleming, FWA, Washington; see also Fleming to Connelly, January 31, 1944, all in boxes 74–75, Central Files, 1941–49, FWAR; Child Care Coordinating Committee for Women in Industry, "Importance of Child Care Programs to the Aircraft Industry," March 1945, folder 4, box 21, HGDP.

26. Feldman, *Portrait of a Gentle Man*, 1–28, 31–34; Frances Lomas Feldman, interview by author, transcribed tape recording, July 21 and 28, 1997, Pasadena, Calif.

27. Anderson, *Wartime Women*, 133–41; Stewart, "Preschools and Politics," 72; California Department of Education, *Child Care Centers by School District*, 23.

28. California Department of Education, *Child Care Centers by School District*, iii; Child Care Coordinating Committee for Women in Industry, "Need for Lanham Act Fund for Child Care in Southern California," January 17, 1944, Central Files, 1941–49, FWAR. See also Anderson, *Wartime Women*, 133–41.

29. "Parents Act in Nursery School Crisis," *Los Angeles Times*, August 24, 1945; Beach Vasey, Los Angeles, to Governor Earl Warren, August 29, 1945, F3640:8460–65, W. T. Sweigert Special Files, 1945–46, EWP; Fousekis, "Fighting for Our Children," 80–81.

30. Beach Vasey to Governor Warren, August 17, 1945, and Vasey to Warren, August 29, 1945, F3640:8460–65, W. T. Sweigert Special Files, 1945–46, EWP; Elizabeth Farago, "Emergency Care of Children" (press release), ANE Southern California, spring 1945, folder 35, box 4 outsize, HGDP; Ernest E. Debs, oral history interview by Carlos Vásquez, 1987 (UCLA Oral History Program for the California State Archives, State Government Oral History Program), transcript, 69. A part of California's unique political landscape in this period (and again a heritage of the nonpartisan philosophy of the Progressive period) was the frequency with which politicians were elected on the ticket of both major parties. A candidate filed for his own party nomination but could also seek nomination from the opposing party. Thus the party status of both Hawkins and Debs was reported by California's *Assembly Journal* as D-R. The men were Democrats (listed first) who also filed for and won nomination on the Republican ticket in their districts. For more on cross filing see Putnam, "The Progressive Legacy," 257.

31. Fousekis, "Fighting for Our Children," 83–85.

32. Beach Vasey to Gov. Warren, August 29, 1945, F3640:8460–65, W. T. Sweigert Special Files, 1945–46, EWP.

33. Reese, "Maternalism and Political Mobilization," 573; Beach Vasey to Gover-

nor Warren, August, 17, 1945, and Vasey to Warren, Los Angeles, August 29, 1945, F3640:8460–65, W. T. Sweigert Special Files, 1945–46, EWP.

34. Marjorie Rowe, executive secretary, Parents' Council, Los Angeles, to Rep. Helen Gahagan Douglas, September 17, 1945, transcribed and reprinted in *Congressional Record* 91(1945): A3998; Prescott, Milich, and Jones, *The "Politics" of Day Care*, 7.

35. "Tenney Alters Stand on Child Care Centers," *Los Angeles Times*, September 10, 1945; Pritchard, "California Un-American Activities Investigations."

36. Pollack, "Schools That Save Families"; Ernest Geddes to Gov. Earl Warren, July 1, 1949, chapter 780, Governor's Chaptered Bill Files, 1949, CSA; Geddes, "California Assemblyman," 128, 194, 198–99, 211. Geddes's papers were not preserved. His several references to child care in the 1976 oral history seem particularly significant since the topic was not raised by the interviewer. Geddes tells his child care "conversion" story in a slightly different way in this oral history, but not inconsistently with his recollections to *Nation's Business* in 1952. See also Prescott, Milich, and Jones, *The "Politics" of Day Care*, 19. Other sources regarding Geddes's visit to the Baldwin Park center and his importance to California's child care program include Stewart, "Preschools and Politics," 91; and Arnstein, *Community Service in California Public Health and Social Welfare*, 126–27.

37. Marjorie Rowe to Helen Gahagan Douglas, September, 17, 1945, transcribed and reproduced in *Congressional Record* 91 (1945): A3998.

38. "Continuation of Centers for Child Care Urged," *Los Angeles Times*, September 26, 1945; Reese, "Maternalism and Political Mobilization," 573–74. The newspaper reported about two hundred in the audience; Reese, "Maternalism and Political Mobilization," pegs the attendance at more than three hundred.

39. Letter to Governor Warren from H. C. M., Los Angeles, January 19, 1946, F3640:8738–52, Proposed Legislation, Child Care Centers, 1946–47, EWP.

40. "Extended Care of Children at Schools Praised," Reader's Editorials, *Los Angeles Times*, September 3, 1945.

41. H. P., Hollywood, to President Harry Truman, October 9, 1945, HSTP. (Identical letter, H. P. to Helen Gahagan Douglas, folder 4b, box 17, HGDP.)

42. Ruth MacFarland, executive secretary, ECCC, Welfare Council of Metropolitan Los Angeles, to Howell H. Barnes, director, War Mobilization Office, Los Angeles, September 21, 1945, folder 4b, box 17, HGDP.

43. Beach Vasey to Governor Warren, November 20, 1945, F3640:8460–65, W. T. Sweigert Special Files, EWP; Reese, "Maternalism and Political Mobilization," 574–75. See also Fousekis, "Fighting for Our Children," 71 n. 2, 143.

44. "Message of Governor Earl Warren," California State Legislature, Extraordinary Session, January 7, 1946, F3640:8460–65, W. T. Sweigert Special Files, EWP.

45. Beach Vasey to Gov. Warren, February 19, 1946, and February 20, 1946, in chapters 34 and 35, Governor's Chaptered Bill Files, 1946 First Extraordinary Session, CSA; Putnam, "The Progressive Legacy," 258; "Press Release: Los Angeles County Newspapers," Sacramento, February 20, F3640:1140, Records Relating to the State Board of Education, Child Care Centers and Day Nurseries, EWP.

46. Cahan, *Past Caring*, 21–28; "Planning Services for Children to Supplement

the Home and School," 145–46; Johnson, "Day Care: An Essential in Peacetime Economy," 9–10. Linda Gordon has traced the history of "casework" and its importance to the social work profession as well as its role in helping to solidify rationales for particular rather than universal claims to public support. See Gordon, *Pitied but Not Entitled*, 102–8, 162–64, 175–81, 272–78.

47. Stewart, "Preschools and Politics," 72–73; Prescott, Milich, and Jones, *The "Politics" of Day Care*, 73. See also Feldman interview by author.

48. Letter to I. Evelyn Smith, consultant, U.S. Children's Bureau, Washington, from John R. Weber, supervisor, Child Care Centers, Los Angeles, December 5, 1947, CBR.

49. Charles Wollenberg, SDSW, Sacramento, to Governor Earl Warren, chapter 4, Governor's Chaptered Bill Files, 1948 Regular Session, CSA.

50. Wollenberg's immediate successor was Charles Schottland (a former employee of the U.S. Children's Bureau) who was in turn followed by J. M. Wedmeyer. Neither Schottland nor Wedmeyer appears to have been hostile to the program. Other than Wollenberg's comment cited above, I did not find significant evidence of SDSW efforts on behalf of, or against, the program throughout the first decade and a half following World War II.

51. Gordon, *Pitied but Not Entitled*, 255–85. See also Hobson, "Feminist Strategies and Gendered Discourse in Welfare States," 389–99. For most of the period discussed in this chapter, the California program through which federal Aid to Dependent Children benefits were administered was called Aid to Needy Children. To avoid confusion for readers, I refer to it throughout this chapter as Aid to Dependent Children or ADC.

52. Michel, *Children's Interests, Mothers' Rights*, 83–87.

53. Phadke, "Licensing of Child Care in California, 1911–1961," 40–61, 97, 103; Prescott, Milich, and Jones, *The "Politics" of Day Care*, 57–59. In 1913 a predecessor agency of the SDSW had been among the first in the nation to gain regulatory authority over some group child care institutions.

54. California State Department of Education, *Child Care Centers by School District*, 5–7. It was also important that some top bureaucrats at the State Education Department avidly believed in the program's value. See Stewart, "Preschools and Politics," 73, 110–113.

55. California Legislature, *Technical Staff Report*, 137, 145; Prescott, Milich, and Jones, *The "Politics" of Day Care*, 74–75; Stewart, "Preschools and Politics," 91–94; Bierman, "The Influence of Pressure Groups on Child Care Center Legislation in California," 46–51; Fousekis, "Fighting for Our Children," 84–86.

56. California Legislature, *Technical Staff Report*, 21; National Education Association, Research Division, "Child-Care Centers, Nursery Schools, and Kindergartens," September 1946, folder 7-3, box 7, Rosalie M. Blau Collection, Urban Archives, California State University, Northridge; Frank, "The Beginnings of Child Development and Family Life Education in the Twentieth Century," 4; Eliot, "Nursery Schools Fifty Years Ago"; Stewart, "Preschools and Politics," 43–53.

57. U.S. Congress, Senate, Committee on the District of Columbia, *H.R. 5933*,

62–70; "Education Board Opposes Bill for Day-Care Units," *Washington Star*, May 2, 1946; "Subcommittee Adds Millions for Schools; School Board Rejects Control of Nurseries," *Washington Post*, May 2, 1946.

58. California Legislature, *Technical Staff Report*, 21, 115–22.

59. Ibid., 137.

60. See comments of Docia Zavitkovsky and Roslie Blau in Bothman, "Reflections of the Pioneers on the Early History of the Santa Monica Children's Centers and Changing Child-Rearing Philosophies," 15–16; California Legislature, *Technical Staff Report*, 145, 391–92; Prescott, Milich, and Jones, *The "Politics" of Day Care*, 74.

61. Beatty, *Preschool Education in America*, 132–36; Cahan, *Past Caring*, 30–32. See also Greenblatt, *Responsibility for Child Care*, 41–75.

62. California Legislature, *Technical Staff Report*, 147.

63. "Day Care in Today's Community," n.d. [likely 1957], folder IV-3, box 1, JWP.

64. In all of California there were only five non-school applicants for wartime financial aid through the Lanham Act. California Department of Education, *California Program for the Care of Children of Working Parents*; California Department of Education, *Child Care Centers by School District*, 2–4; Ronald Cox, "Legislation for Child Care from the Point of View of the Department of Education," October 20, 1956, 2–3, TSMP; Grubb and Lazerson, "Child Care, Government Financing, and the Public Schools."

65. Fousekis, "Fighting for Our Children," 133–38; Stewart, "Preschools and Politics," 89–90; Reese, "Maternalism and Political Mobilization," 574; Bothman, "Reflections of the Pioneers," 14–15; John R. Weber, supervisor, Child Care Centers, Los Angeles, to I. Evelyn Smith, consultant, U.S. Children's Bureau, Washington, December 5, 1947, CBR.

66. Stewart, "Preschools and Politics," 27–29; Prescott, Milich, and Jones, *The "Politics" of Day Care*, 5; Committee on Community Chest Day Nurseries, Child Welfare Division and Welfare Planning Council, Los Angeles Region, Research Department, "Use of Day Nurseries: A Study of Utilization of Four Chest Supported Day Nurseries in the Los Angeles Area," Special Report Series no. 38 (Welfare Planning Council, Los Angeles, January 1954).

67. Halper, "Recollections of Los Angeles Children's Centers' Early Days," 6–18. See also Scales, "A Study of the Development of the Los Angeles Unified School District Children's Centers," 26–28; A Nursery School Teacher, "The Pages of Nursery School History," printed in ANE of Southern California, news release, Spring 1945, folder 35, box 4 outsize, HGDP; Irene T. Heineman, assistant superintendent, California State Department of Education, to Florence Kerr, assistant to the administrator and director, War Public Services, FWA, Sacramento, December 7, 1944, Central Files, 1941–49, FWAR.

68. Stewart, "Preschools and Politics," 32–42; Beatty, *Preschool Education in America*, 92–100; Raftery, "Los Angeles Clubwomen and Progressive Reform," 147–53; Gullett, "Feminism, Politics, and Voluntary Groups"; Prescott, Milich, and Jones, *The "Politics" of Day Care*, 70, 73; California Legislature, *Technical Staff Report*, 17, 21–25.

69. Putnam, "The Progressive Legacy in California," 249. See also California Legislature, *Technical Staff Report*.

70. California Legislature, *Technical Staff Report*, 11.

71. CPACCC, "Interim Newsletter to Child Care Center Friends and Parents," n.d.[forwarded to State Department of Education, received August 29, 1949], F3752:1562, Child Care Division Chief's Files, Division of Public School Administration, SDEP; "Welcome to the Child Care Centers" [booklet], n.d., and copies of annual CPACCC convention bulletins in Pamphlets etc., 1948–62, box 5, TSMP. Regarding educators, child care center workers, and the California Committee for Child Care see "California Committee For Child Care," n.d., F3640:10837–49, Legislative Files, Proposed Legislation, General, Child Care Centers, 1948–49, EWP; John Weber, Los Angeles, SDE, to I. Evelyn Smith, Children's Bureau, Washington, December 5, 1947, CBR; "Minutes of the Joint Legislative Committees of the Associations for Nursery Education, Northern and Southern California," February 27, 1949, Fresno, Calif., box 4, TSMP; John R. Weber, supervisor, Child Care Centers, SDE, Los Angeles, to Ronald W. Cox, SDE, Sacramento, October 18, 1950, with attached "The 1949–50 State Child Care Conference," folder 45, box 3, Rosalie M. Blau Collection, Urban Archives, California State University, Northridge. See also Natalie Fousekis, "Fighting for Our Children," 133–42, 180–239. Fousekis collected several oral histories that provide illuminating biographical details regarding the California child care activists Mary Young and Theresa Mahler and a behind-the scenes look at child care advocates' organization.

72. Fousekis, "Fighting for Our Children," 96–105, 114–20, 184–85; Arnstein, *Community Service*, 111–33; Feldman, *Portrait of a Gentle Man*, 32–34; Feldman interview by author; Bierman, "Influence of Pressure Groups," 42–62g.

73. Regarding opposition from the Catholic Church, which had largely disappeared by the early 1950s, see Arnstein, *Community Service*, 115–17; Feldman, *Portrait of a Gentle Man*, 33–34; Feldman interview by author; and Bierman, "Influence of Pressure Groups," 36–40. Regarding private operator opposition see testimony of Paul E. Greene, chairman, Counseling Committee, Preschool Association of Southern California, in California Senate Interim Committee on Social Welfare, *Report on the Child Care Center Program*, 55. See also "Message from Mary Young, Legislative Chairman," April 4, 1961," box 4, TSMP.

74. Petition prepared by Los Angeles Parents' Council for Child Care Centers, signed and submitted, American Legion Post 516, Los Angeles, to Governor Earl Warren, December 28, 1946, F3640:1140, Records Relating to the State Board of Education, Child Care Centers and Day Nurseries, EWP.

75. Anna Marie Anderson, Federation of Parents for Child Care Centers, Whittier, Calif., to Sen. W. P. Rich, Marysville, Calif., February 21, 1947, F3640:8738–52, Proposed Legislation, Child Care Centers, 1946–47, EWP.

76. F. C. D., Los Angeles, to Governor Earl Warren, December 12, 1946, F3640:8738–52, Proposed Legislation, Child Care Centers, 1946–47, EWP.

77. Mrs. L. N. C., Los Angeles, to Governor Earl Warren, December 10, 1946, F3640:8738–52, Proposed Legislation, Child Care Centers, 1946–47, EWP.

78. Mrs. S. B. Jr., Reseda, to Governor Earl Warren, November 27, 1946, F3640:8738–52, Proposed Legislation, Child Care Centers, 1946–47, EWP.

79. California Legislature, *Technical Staff Report*, 141. Monsignor Thomas O'Dwyer, who represented a variety of Catholic social welfare concerns in Los Angeles, was a prominent day care foe and frequent committee witness. For a description of his work and Catholic opposition see comments by George D. Nickel in Frances Feldman, *Portrait of a Gentle Man*, 33–34, and Feldman interview by author.

80. Directors of Catholic Social Service and Education Rt. Rev. Thomas O'Dwyer, Los Angeles, Rt. Rev. William Flanagan, San Francisco, Rt. Rev. Thomas McNamara, San Diego, V. Rev. Raymond O'Flaherty, Los Angeles, Rev. Patrick Hannon, Fresno, Rev. Harry Markham, Sacramento, V. Rev. Patrick Dignan, Los Angeles, V. Rev. James Dowling, Fresno, Rt. Rev. James T. O'Dowd, San Francisco, Rev. Franklin Hurd, San Diego, Rev. Raymond Renwald, Sacramento, to the Members of the California Legislature, n.d [copy of letter likely first circulated in March 1948], box 4, TSMP.

81. California Legislature, *Technical Staff Report*, 145.

82. Ibid., 11, 37–39. The labor force statistics were drawn from a survey in April 1944 that covered San Diego and the Los Angeles and San Francisco Bay areas.

83. Ibid.; Fraser, "Struggle over Needs," 204–7.

84. Cahan, *Past Caring*, 30–32; Beatty, *Preschool Education in America*, 132–68.

85. *A Brief Inquiry into the Need for a Child Care Program in California*, prepared by Educators and Parents Groups in California, December 1948, 4–5, TSMP.

86. The phrase "domestic containment" is from May, *Homeward Bound*.

87. California State Department of Education, *Report of Child Care Centers*, 6. Enrollment stood at 13,533 in March 1946 (when the state assumed major funding responsibility) and climbed to 15,765 by September.

88. Emergency Child Care Committee, "Mothers of 7600 Children Provide Child Care Facts," Welfare Council of Metropolitan Los Angeles, folder 4b, box 17, HGDP; Research Department, "Facts Concerning Child Care Centers in Los Angeles County," Welfare Council of Metropolitan Los Angeles, January 1946, 6–7, Item no. 26168, City Council, 1945–48, Los Angeles City Archives.

89. California State Department of Education, Child Care Bulletin no. 4, September 30, 1946, box 4, TSMP; Eleanor Rorick, secretary, Executive Board, Parents' Council for Child Care Centers, Los Angeles, to Roy Simpson, Superintendent of Public Instruction, SDE, November 18, 1946, F3640:1140, Records Relating to the State Board of Education, Child Care Centers and Day Nurseries, EWP.

90. Because of program overhead costs only reductions in program size large enough to lower the number of centers operating would have made a difference to the bottom line. Enrollment at the centers in December 1946 had declined to 11,104 (from the September peak of 15,765). The steep decrease was partly seasonal, with December typically showing the lowest enrollment figures for any given year. In the first half of 1947 enrollment stayed at around 12,000.

91. California State Department of Education, *Report of Child Care Centers*, 5; "Meeting of Special Committee to Determine Eligibility for Admission to Child

Care Centers," March 30, 1946, folder II-1, box 1, JWP. Regarding the size of the Los Angeles County waiting list in the last quarter of 1946 see California Legislature, *Technical Staff Report*, 440–42.

92. Geddes, *California Assemblyman*, 48–50. Geddes's child care legislation of 1947 largely mirrored the recommendations made by the legislature's Interim Committee on Preschool Training. The *Technical Staff Report* had not explicitly proposed an income test. Several months later, however, when the legislators released their recommendation they proposed specific maximum income levels and a sliding scale of fees. Regarding the Interim Committee's recommendations and the legislative options in 1947 see Lynette Messer, "Legislative Review," March 1947, box 4, TSMP.

93. Chang, "Comparative Study of Child Day Care Centers in Los Angeles, California and Canton, China," 84–86.

94. California Legislature, *Technical Staff Report*, 153. Regarding admission standards considered ideal by the U.S. Children's Bureau and social workers see "New Bases for Eligibility in New York City Day Care Centers," 73; Alice T. Dashiell, "Trends in Day Care," 53–56.

95. A *Brief Inquiry into the Need for a Child Care Program in California*, prepared by Educators and Parents Groups in California, December 1948, 17, TSMP.

96. Comment of Rhoda Kellogg, supervisor of the wartime program in Vallejo, Calif., quoted in Stewart, "Preschools and Politics," 74–75.

97. "Child Care Centers Southern Section Meeting, Minutes," June 27, 1947, F3752:1563, Child Care Division Chief's Files, Division of Public School Administration, SDEP.

98. "Rules and Regulations (Revised) Established by the Superintendent of Public Instruction Relating to the Expenditure of State Funds for Children in Child Care Centers," in California Legislature, *Technical Staff Report*, 433–35. These revised regulations were quite similar to temporary standards released just days after Governor Warren signed the 1946 legislation into law. See California State Department of Education, Child Care Bulletin no. 1, February 25, 1946, box 4, TSMP.

99. California Legislature, *Technical Staff Report*, 440–42.

100. For descriptions of the long history of *de jure* and *de facto* segregation in California public schools see Wollenberg, *All Deliberate Speed*, and González, *Chicano Education in the Era of Segregation*.

101. Welfare Council of Metropolitan Los Angeles, *News*, March 1950, 5. The survey was conducted in 1948 by researchers at the University of California, Berkeley. Their study found that 17 percent of the children attending Los Angeles County Child Care Centers were "Negro, Mexican, [or] Oriental." In 1949 this percentage had budged upward to 18 percent. In 1949 the survey found nearly 32 percent of the children enrolled at public Child Care Centers in Los Angeles *city* were from these same racial and ethnic groups. The Welfare Council noted that other than the public centers, child care facilities for these groups are "especially inadequate."

102. Dorothy G. Briggs, Los Angeles, to Rep. Helen Gahagan Douglas, August 29, 1945, transcribed and reproduced in *Congressional Record* 91 (1945): A3999.

103. Mrs. W. L., Los Angeles, to Governor Earl Warren, December 13, 1946, F3640:8738–52, "Proposed Legislation, Child Care Centers, 1946–47," EWP.

104. D. L. M., Millbrae, Calif., to Governor Earl Warren, January 4, 1951, F3640:12947, Legislative Files, Proposed Legislation, General, Child Care Centers, 1949–51, EWP.

105. Chang, "Comparative Study of Child Day Care Centers," 125–35.

106. Prescott, Milich, and Jones, The "Politics" of Day Care, 28; Stewart, "Preschool and Politics," 88; Bierman, "The Influence of Pressure Groups," 3; Welfare Council of Metropolitan Los Angeles, News, March 1950, 5; News, March 1951, 3; News, June 1954, 6; Feldman interview by author. Prescott, Milich, and Jones report strong concern about the anti-discrimination regulation among some private operators who feared losing enrollment if they integrated their businesses.

107. Parents' Council for Child Care Centers, Los Angeles (telegrams), to Governor Earl Warren, November 2, 1946, and November 13, 1946; Eleanor Rorick, Executive Board, Parents' Council for Child Care Centers, Los Angeles, to Roy Simpson, superintendent of public instruction, SDE, November 18, 1946, F3640:1140, "Records Relating to the State Board of Education, Child Care Centers and Day Nurseries," EWP.

108. Mrs. Doris Day Scott, president, San Francisco Child Care Council, to Walter E. Dexter, superintendent of public instruction, SDE, April 1, 1946, box 1, folder II-1, JWP.

109. Mr. & Mrs. D. G. F., Los Angeles, to Governor Earl Warren, December 2, 1946, F3640:1140, "Records Relating to the State Board of Education Child Care Centers and Day Nurseries," EWP.

110. Anna Maria Anderson, Federation of Parents for Child Care Centers, Whittier, Calif., to State Sen. W. P. Rich, Marysville, Calif., February 21, 1947, F3640:8738–52, Proposed Legislation, Child Care Centers, 1946–47, EWP.

111. L. B., Oakland, Calif., to Governor Earl Warren, August 15, 1950, F3640:1141, "Records Relating to the State Board of Education, Child Care Centers and Day Nurseries," EWP.

112. Some testimony given in 1946 and excerpted in the Technical Staff Report, along with later documents, indicates that not all parents, or parents' groups, disagreed with the idea of a means test, but other testimony in the same report and additional letters to Governor Warren demonstrate many opposed limiting access in this way.

113. The final legislation in 1947 was A.B. 1781 (signed June 27) and A.B. 1782 (signed June 28): see chapter 956, 1947 Regular Session, Governor's Chaptered Bill Files, CSA. For single- and two-parent families with more children, the legislature stipulated that the total monthly income per each family member could not exceed $60. This meant, for instance, that a single parent with three children could have a maximum yearly income of $2,880, and a two-parent family with three children could have a maximum yearly income of $3,600. This progressive income scale contrasts to the entirely flat yearly income limit of $2,600 (regardless of family size) imposed by the U.S. Congress in 1947 at the District of Columbia's public centers.

114. U.S. Bureau of the Census, *Census of the Population: 1950*, vol. II, part 5, California, table 3; "Report of Committee on Administration of the Means Test," in California Legislature, *Technical Staff Report*, 435–36. See also "Special Committee on Financial Needs in Child Care Centers," March 1946, and "Suggested Monthly Family Budgets based on Heller Foundation Wage-Earner Level," March 26, 1946, box 4, TSMP. "Meeting of Special Committee to Determine Eligibility for Admission to Child Care Centers," March 30, 1946, folder II-1, box 1, JWP.

115. *A Brief Inquiry into the Need for a Child Care Program in California*, 17.

116. Francis Feldman gave a vivid description of a discriminatorily applied uniform budget. She recalled that when she joined the Los Angeles County Department of Public Welfare in 1943 "they had a standard [public assistance] budget but they gave 20 percent less to the black family and another five percent off of that to the Hispanic family—because everybody 'knew' that they only ate beans and stuff like that." After she and several colleagues protested, the policy was changed. Feldman interview by author.

117. Educators had chosen the wage-earner level to establish their guidelines for admission to public child care. See "Suggested Monthly Family Budgets Based on Heller Foundation Wage-Earner Level," March 1946, box 4, TSMP. Regarding standard budget calculations consciously based on the ideal of the female homemaker and male breadwinner see discussion in chapter 5 of U.S. Bureau of Labor Statistics, "City Workers' Budgets."

118. Wartime wage and price controls were lifted in 1946; prices rose sharply over the next several years, dropped off some from 1948 to 1949, advanced rapidly in 1950 and 1951 (with the advent of U.S. involvement in the Korean War), and stabilized between 1952 and 1955. For the rest of the decade the Consumer Price Index rose 1 to 2 percent annually. *Congress and the Nation, 1945–1964*, 339–40.

119. California State Department of Education, *Report of Child Care Centers*, 6, 8.

120. California Assembly, *Report on Child Care Center Operations under Geddes-Kraft*, 9–10, copy in California State Library, Sacramento.

121. California Legislature, *Technical Staff Report*, 41–42; California Assembly, *Report on Child Care Center Operations under Geddes-Kraft*, and Ronald Cox, SDE, to Honorable Carlos Bee, appendix C, table I, both in California State Library, Sacramento.

122. California Assembly, *Second Report of the Assembly Interim Committee* (Survey conducted by John B. Knight Co., Hollywood, March 1949), excerpted in Bierman, "The Influence of Pressure Groups on Child Care Center Legislation in California," 32–36. The survey questioned close to three thousand people. Respondents were apparently selected to approximate the party affiliation, sex, age (20 years or older), and occupation of all Californians as given in 1948 census data. Additionally, 57.2 percent were homeowners (as opposed to renters) and 29.3 were union members or belonged to a household where the "head of the house" was a union member.

123. California State Department of Education, "Survey of Families Requesting Service or Enrolling Children in Child Care Centers," April 1955. These families were also unable to qualify under any exempt category.

124. I calculated the proportion of two-parent households among all exempt fam-

ilies as 76.9 percent based on data from tables 11 and 12 in California State Department of Education, "Survey of Families Requesting Service or Enrolling Children in Child Care Centers," April 1955. Regarding the percentage of two-parent households among all families see page 6 in the same report.

125. Leighow, "An 'Obligation to Participate,'" 37–56.

126. California State Department of Education, *Report of Child Care Centers*, 6; Bierman, "The Influence of Pressure Groups," 31–36; Stewart, "Preschools and Politics," 116. In late March 1948 Governor Warren's legislative secretary, Beach Vasey, advised: "For a period of months we have been flooded with correspondence from individuals and organizations of all sorts favoring the continued maintenance of child care centers. No attempt has been made even to count all this correspondence, which has been most numerous and prolonged." See Beach Vasey to Governor Warren, March 31, 1948, chapter 4, Governor's Chaptered Bill Files, CSA.

127. California State Department of Education, *Child Care Centers by School District* (wartime percentages extrapolated from table 2 giving center enrollment and locations for fiscal year 1944–45); California State Department of Education, *Report of Child Care Centers* (percentages extrapolated from tables 2 and 3 giving center locations as of January 1949 and enrollment for the period July 1, 1948, to January 31, 1949.

128. Bierman, "The Influence of Pressure Groups," 65–66; U.S. Bureau of the Census, *Census of the Population: 1950*, vol. II, part 5, *California*, table 12. Regarding areas represented and the number of senators and assembly members see listings of members given in the California State Legislature's *Senate Final History* and *Assembly Final History* for each legislative session. There were, of course, a few notable urban opponents to Child Care Centers as well as some rural supporters.

129. Bierman, "The Influence of Pressure Groups," 66–82; Ernest Geddes to Governor Warren, July 1, 1949, chapter 780, Governor's Chaptered Bill Files, 1949, California State Archives. (The "eleventh hour and 59th minute" quote is from Geddes, who was frustrated by his consequent lack of time to counter the restrictive amendments.)

130. Bierman, "The Influence of Pressure Groups," 78–79; California State Department of Education, *Report of Child Care Centers*, 8–9; California Legislature, *Technical Staff Report*, 153. See also California Legislature, Senate, 1955 Regular Session, *Senate Interim Committee on Social Welfare*, 56–57.

131. California Legislature, *First Preliminary Report by the Assembly Interim Committee*, 123–24. The report cited in this document is undated and is presumed to be circa 1950.

132. Ibid. This quote is from a statement of the Tulare Board of Supervisors to the San Joaquin Valley Agricultural Labor Resources Committee. (Also no date given but presumed circa 1950.)

133. *A Brief Inquiry into the Need for a Child Care Program in California*, prepared by Educators and Parents Groups in California, December 1948, 4–5, TSMP; McWilliams, *Factories in the Field*. See also Weber, *Dark Sweat, White Gold*. Rural and urban workers have very comparable needs for workplace protections and basic services, but the response to their organizing attempts have been quite different. Pe-

culiar American myths about farming and rural life have contributed mightily to this fact. See also Hofstadter, *Age of Reform*, 23–130.

134. California State Legislature, *First Preliminary Report by the Assembly Interim Committee*, 124.

135. González, *Chicano Education in the Era of Segregation*, 96–99. Federal Interagency Committee on Migrant Labor, report VII: *Recommendations on the Education of Children of Migrant Workers* [draft copy August 15, 1946, of final 1947 report], box 63, folder 10, HGDP. See also "Council Asks Better Deal for Migrant Workers and Families."

136. González, *Chicano Education in the Era of Segregation*, 102–5. González notes that while the record of education of migrant children in southwestern states was abysmal, California had a record that might be described as merely dismal. As the draft Federal Interagency Committee on Migrant Labor report notes, by 1946 at least California was one of only a handful of states that "specifically recognized the educational needs of children in migratory and transient families." This does not mean however that schooling was granted.

137. "Hearing on Child Care Centers Program: Senate Interim Committee on Social Welfare," n.d. [October 1954], box 4, TSMP. The exchange between Sen. Abshire and the district superintendent in Fresno of the Westside School District, M. P. Gunderson, is not a part of the hearing excerpts printed in the committee's official report, California Senate Interim Committee on Social Welfare, *Report on the Child Care Center Program*. I am relying for this quote on meeting notes taken by Theresa Mahler, director of Child Care Centers for San Francisco.

138. Women's Bureau, *Planning Services for Children of Employed Mothers*, 11–12; California Assembly, *First Preliminary Report by the Assembly Interim Committee*, 123–34; California Legislature, *Report on Child Care Center Operations under Geddes-Kraft*, 8; "Hearing on Child Care Centers Program: Senate Interim Committee on Social Welfare," box 4, TSMP.

139. Mary McFarland, field program supervisor, California Migrant Ministry, to John Weber, SDE, and Dorothy Kurtz, SDSW, May 8, 1962, folder 29, box 39, National Farm Worker Ministry, Merrill-Palmer Institute, Kresge Historical Library Collection, Archives of Labor and Urban Affairs, Wayne State University, Detroit.

140. Daniels, "Cesar Chavez and California Farmworkers," 371–404; Ruiz, *From Out of the Shadows*, 132–35.

141. Limited funds had been authorized earlier, but the legislature added crippling restrictions on when they could be used and essentially funds remained unavailable until the 1964 provision.

142. John Weber, supervisor of child care centers, SDE, to Mrs. Harriet Foote, Vista, Calif., November 10, 1948, F3752:1563, Division of Public School Administration, Division Chief's Files, Child Care, 1947–49, SDEP.

143. Roy Simpson, superintendent of public instruction, SDE, Sacramento, to Governor Earl Warren, January 11, 1950, F3640:12943, Legislative Files, Proposed Legislation, General, Child Care Centers, 1949–51, EWP.

144. Elsie Wolfe, a field investigator for the U.S. Women's Bureau, documented widespread war-related calls for more child care services. See her interview notes

and summary reports from San Francisco, San Diego, and Los Angeles, January and February 1951, box 5, General Correspondence, 1948–63, WBR.

145. Supplemental Statement by CPACCC to Assembly Interim Committee on Social Welfare, October 17, 1950, Los Angeles, box 4, TSMP; Letter to Governor Earl Warren from M. L. Royar, rear admiral, Supply Corps, USN, Commanding Officer, Naval Supply Center, Oakland, Calif., September 1950, F3640:12946, Legislative Files, Proposed Legislation, General, Child Care Centers, 1949–51, EWP; Statement of the Welfare Council of Metropolitan Los Angeles, Child Welfare Division, Child Care Centers Committee, to Assembly Interim Committee on Social Welfare, October 10, 1950, box 4, TSMP.

146. Supplemental Statement, CPACCC to Assembly Interim Committee on Social Welfare, October 17, 1950, box 4, TSMP; California Assembly, *First Preliminary Report by the Assembly Interim Committee*, 122–23.

147. California Assembly, *First Preliminary Report by the Assembly Interim Committee*, 107, 110–11, 122–23; "Survey of Changed Conditions in Child Care Centers," F3640:1141, Records Relating to the State Board of Education, Child Care Centers and Day Nurseries, EWP; Statement of Welfare Council of Metropolitan Los Angeles, Child Welfare Division, before Assembly Interim Committee on Social Welfare, October 10, 1950, box 4, TSMP. (This testimony is excerpted in the printed committee report, 148, but quoted statement is not included.)

148. Mrs. J. C. Vieira, Compton, Calif., to Governor Earl Warren, September 15, 1950, F3640:1141, "Records Relating to the State Board of Education, Child Care Centers and Day Nurseries," EWP.

149. Beach Vasey, legislative secretary, Governor's Office, to Mrs. J. C. Vieira, September 15, 1950; M. F. Small, departmental secretary, Governor's Office, to S/Sgt. Jess C. Vieira, November 28, 1950; Frank M. Wright, associate superintendent of public instruction, SDE, to S/Sgt. Jess C. Vieira, December 5, 1950; J. R. Weber, supervisor, Child Care Centers, SDE, Los Angeles, to Frank M. Wright, December 15, 1950; Ellen Y. Hemming, director, Nursery Schools, Compton City Schools, Compton, Calif., to John R. Weber, December 20, 1950; J. R. Weber, "Eligibility: Vieira case, Compton," to Dr. Frank M. Wright, January 8, 1951. All documents in F3640:1141, Records Relating to the State Board of Education, Child Care Centers and Day Nurseries, EWP.

150. California Assembly, *First Preliminary Report by the Assembly Interim Committee*, 104, 110.

151. Ibid., 111; Resolution of the Assembly Interim Committee on Social Welfare, Relative to Federal Support for Child Care Centers, August 17, 1950, folder 7b, box 64, HGDP.

152. Elaine Tyler May, *Homeward Bound*, 89–91.

153. Chapter 1263, Governor's Chaptered Bill Files, June 1951, CSA.

154. Ibid. See also California Legislature, *Child Care Center Operations under Geddes Kraft*.

155. California Legislature, *Report on Child Care Center Operations under Geddes-Kraft*, 8–9.

156. Ibid., 9, 11, 22. These are hypothetical fees based on a two-parent family, en-

rolling one preschool child for forty-five hours a week. (Defense workers with extended work weeks would have required more hours than this.) Based on hourly fee rates given in California Legislature, *Report on Child Care Center Operations under Geddes-Kraft*, the four-week cost for this family if it made $300 or less would have been no more than 12 cents an hour while the cost for the same family if it made more than $300 would have been 37.5 cents an hour.

157. Legislation quoted in Ronald Cox, "Legislation for Child Care from the Point of View of the Department of Education," October 20, 1956, 8, TSMP.

158. Fred P. Luke, chairman, CPACCC, to Mrs. [Elizabeth] Case, chairman, Legislative Committee, Association for Nursery Education of Northern California, with attachment, n.d.[ca. February 1951], box 4, TSMP.

159. Stewart, "Preschools and Politics," 139–45.

160. Lawrence Arnstein, San Francisco Social Hygiene Association, to Theresa Mahler, director, Child Care Centers, San Francisco, July 12, 1950, box 4, TSMP; Lawrence Arnstein to Frank Wright, SDE, Sacramento (with attached statement), September 5, 1950, F3752:1562, Division Chief's Files, Child Care, 1949–51, Division of Public School Administration, SDEP; Lawrence Arnstein to Mr. Verne Scoggins, Governor's Office, September 6, 1950, F3640:12946, Legislative Files, Proposed Legislation, General, Child Care Centers, 1949–51, EWP.

161. N. R. Holcomb [executive secretary, Assembly Interim Committee on Social Welfare] to Lawrence Arnstein [San Francisco Social Hygiene Association], August 17, 1950, box 4, TSMP.

162. In 1950 and later Arnstein attributed the "taxeater vs. taxpayer" quote—and many quotes with similar meaning—to the recently deceased head of the San Francisco Social Hygiene Committee, Ray Lyman Wilbur. It may be that Arnstein himself penned these words for Wilbur's signature, and that he sought to increase their impact by tirelessly citing them alongside Wilbur's prestigious and conservative credentials. These included being "president emeritus of Stanford" and "conservative friend of Hoover." For Arnstein's description of how he came to actively support the Child Care Centers, see Arnstein, *Community Service*, 111–33.

163. N. R. Holcomb [executive secretary, Assembly Interim Committee on Social Welfare] to Lawrence Arnstein, with attached statement, August 17, 1950, and typed notes regarding phone conversation between Holcomb and Arnstein, August 29, 1950, both in box 4, TSMP.

164. Statement of Betty Bachman, legislative chairman, CPACCC, to "Mr. Chairman, Members of the Committee, and Mr. Ohlosson" [Senate Interim Committee on Social Welfare], n.d. [probably October 1954], box 4, TSMP.

165. Fraser, "Struggle over Needs," 204–7. Nationally, the idea of essential "womanpower" gained prominence throughout the 1950s. See Hartmann, "Women's Employment and the Domestic Ideal in the Early Cold War Years"; Women's Bureau, *The Effective Use of Womanpower*; Michel, *Children's Interests, Mothers' Rights*, 167–69.

166. Mrs. L. L. to Governor Earl Warren, February 26, 1950, F3640:12943, Legislative Files, Proposed Legislation, General, Child Care Centers, 1949–51, EWP.

167. The term "autonomous households" is from Orloff, "Gender and the Social

Rights of Citizenship." See also O'Connor, "Gender, Class and Citizenship in the Comparative Analysis of Welfare State Regimes."

168. Addie Stangeland in "Rosie the Riveter Revisited: Women and the World War II Work Experience," vol. 40 (School of Social and Behavioral Sciences, Oral History Resource Center, California State University, Long Beach), 110.

169. *A Brief Inquiry into the Need for a Child Care Program in California*, prepared by Educators and Parents Groups in California, December 1948, case no. 1, Oakland, 14, TSMP.

170. Mrs. B. D. to Governor Earl Warren, February 23, 1950, F3640:12943, Legislative Files, Proposed Legislation, General, Child Care Centers, 1949–51, EWP.

171. Sylvia Vineyard, CPACCC, Stockton, Calif., to Governor Earl Warren, October 28, 1950, F3640:12946, Legislative Files, Proposed Legislation, General, Child Care Centers, 1949–51, EWP.

172. Mrs. Rosa Lee Clements, second vice-chairman, CPACCC, Statement to the Legislative Interim Committee on Social Welfare, San Francisco, September 7, 1950, F3640:12946, Legislative Files, Proposed Legislation, General, Child Care Centers, 1949–51, EWP.

173. The claiming of social rights by citizens has been closely linked to their status as wage earners and their independence. See Marshall, "Citizenship and Social Class"; Fraser and Gordon, "A Genealogy of *Dependency*"; Kessler-Harris, *In Pursuit of Equity*.

174. "Your Reference for Writing to Your State Legislators," n.d. [probably 1954], box 4, TSMP.

175. Petition prepared by Los Angeles Parents' Council for Child Care Centers, signed and submitted, American Legion Post 516, Los Angeles, to Governor Earl Warren, December 28, 1946, F3640:1140, Records Relating to the State Board of Education, Child Care Centers and Day Nurseries, EWP. A similar petition prepared by the San Diego Parents' Council did not include this rationale for public support of child care. See San Diego Parents' Council for Child Care Center[s] Resolution on Child Care, January 6, 1947, F3640:8738–52, Proposed Legislation, Child Care Centers, 1946–47, EWP.

176. W. S., San Diego, to Governor Earl Warren, December 18, 1950, F3640:12947, Legislative Files, Proposed Legislation, General, Child Care Centers, 1949–51, EWP.

177. Theresa S. Mahler, ANE legislative chair, Northern California, Legislative Bulletin no. 4, March 22, 1955, box 4, TSMP. The Welfare Planning Council of Los Angeles reported in 1955, "During recent years, 'Consumers Price Index' has undergone revisions based on studies of the consumption patterns of actual families in the Los Angeles area. Many new products such as frozen food, television, etc. are now part of the expenditures of the family of moderate income, and the latest Index has recognized these changes." Welfare Planning Council, Los Angeles Region, Research Department, *Background for Planning*, 76. Regarding consumerism generally in the postwar period, see Elaine Tyler May, *Homeward Bound*, 162–82.

178. Betty Bachman, CPACCC, Legislative Bulletin, March 16, 1954, box 1, folder II-2, JWP; California Senate Interim Committee on Social Welfare, *Report on the*

Child Care Center Program, 25; Ronald Cox, SDE, to Hon. Carlos Bee, 1–2. The budget numbers in this table included allocations to school districts only. The State Department of Education also received a small amount of money each year to administer the program.

179. Roy Simpson, superintendent of public instruction, SDE, to Beach Vasey, legislative secretary, Governor's Office, February 15, 1950; John Weber to Frank Wright, December 15, 1950; Roy Simpson, superintendent of public instruction, SDE, to Chester G. Hanson, *Los Angeles Times*, December 28, 1950, F3752:1562, Division of Public School Administration, Division Chief's Files, Child Care, SDEP; Chester Hanson, "Child Care Units Boon to Parents," *Los Angeles Times*, December 26, 1950; Theresa Mahler, ANE legislative chair, Northern California, "Legislative Developments Pertaining to Child Care," February 27, 1953, and March 20, 1953, box 4, TSMP; Vice-president, Northern Area, CPACCC, to Gov. Goodwin J. Knight [typed copy, unsigned], May 15, 1954, box 4, TSMP.

180. Theresa Mahler, chairman, Legislative Report, September 23, 1954, box 4, TSMP. California Senate Interim Committee on Social Welfare, *Report on the Child Care Center Program*, 43–57.

181. California Senate Interim Committee on Social Welfare, *Report on the Child Care Center Program*, 8.

182. Chapter 1194, June 1955, Governor's Chaptered Bill Files, CSA; Summary, Child Care Centers Legislation, 1955 Session, box 4, TSMP.

183. In a telling indication of child care advocates' confidence in the program's future, Theresa Mahler, director of the San Francisco Child Care Center Director and a fixture of child care lobbying efforts, scheduled a two-month vacation in Europe that coincided with the Budget Session meeting of the state legislature in 1956. See Theresa Mahler to Assemblyman Ernest Geddes, Claremont, Calif., February 2, 1956, box 4, TSMP.

184. Mary Young, CPACCC, Legislative Report, June 1957, box 5, TSMP; Ronald W. Cox, "The Child Care Center Program from the Point of View of the Department of Education," presented at meeting of Northern Section, California Child Care Directors and Supervisors Association, Berkeley, Calif., January 8, 1960, box 4, TSMP.

185. Legislative Analyst, "The Child Care Center Program," TSMP. Regarding the focus of child care activists' efforts after achievement of permanency see folders 1958 to 1965, TSMP.

Chapter 5

1. Boggs, "Rosie the Riveter Revisited," 80–81.

2. Federal support for "compensatory" early childhood education through Head Start (1964–65) and the Elementary and Secondary Education Act of 1965 is a second significant and related shift in federal policy affecting support for child care funding. These programs, however, are outside the scope of this book.

3. Mittelstadt, "Dependency as a Problem to Be Solved."

4. Potter, "National Character," 442.

5. Ibid., 438.

6. Folbre, "The Unproductive Housewife," 465–67.

7. Ladd-Taylor, *Mother-Work*; LaRossa, *The Modernization of Fatherhood*, 193–99.

8. Weiss, "Mother, the Invention of Necessity"; Coontz, *The Way We Never Were*, 48–49, 97.

9. Kellogg and Brady, "The City Worker's Family Budget," 3. The BLS went to some pains to explain the reasoning behind this family model. It understood that a much greater variety existed but it needed to hang its budget calculations on a concrete example. See report of the Technical Advisory Committee, in *Workers' Budgets in the United States*, 6–9.

10. Clague, foreword to *Workers' Budgets in the United States*, iv–v.

11. Kellogg and Brady, "The City Worker's Family Budget," 10. See also Hayden, *The Grand Domestic Revolution*, 12–17.

12. Significantly as well, there were no *private* "appliances" for child care work that compared to the washing machine, cook stove, and refrigerator, which were all a part of the "housefurnishings" budget. The family in the late 1940s was still explicitly located in the city—not the suburbs. Community recreation, entertainment, and other services, the survey presumed, "must be easily accessible by public transportation." Kellogg and Brady, "The City Worker's Family Budget," 11.

13. It was generally the working mother who was under discussion, although many of the formal proposals as well as the legislation enacted specified that the tax deduction should be available as well for some fathers (mostly widowers). A deduction extended to a two-earner couple clearly would benefit both a mother and father, yet because of the primacy of male wage-earning and female homemaking the deduction is tagged to the mother's salary.

14. Rep. Kenneth Keating to Frieda Miller, director, Women's Bureau, October 4, 1951, box 20, General Correspondence, 1948–53, WBR. U.S. Congress, House, Committee on Ways and Means, *General Revenue Revision*, 64–65.

15. Rep. Keating reintroduced his legislation for the new Congress and was joined by Rep. J. Caleb Boggs (R-Del.), Rep. Helen Gahagan Douglas (D-Calif.), and Rep. John Saylor (R-Pa.).

16. Frieda Miller, Women's Bureau, Washington, to Katherine Ellickson, CIO Education and Research Department, Washington, October 29, 1951, box 20, General Correspondence, 1948–53, WBR; "Summary of Labor Advisory Committee Meeting," December 8, 1950, and Frieda S. Miller to Hon. Kenneth Keating, September 24, 1951, both in box 14, General Correspondence, 1948–53, WBR.

17. Laura H. Dale to Miss Miller, "Report of interview with Representative Caleb Boggs," September 20, 1951, box 20, General Correspondence, 1948–53, WBR; Kenneth Keating to Frieda Miller, October 4, 1951, box 20, General Correspondence, 1948–53, WBR; memo regarding phone call from Rep. Kelly's office, October 9, 1951; and J. Caleb Boggs to Laura H. Dale, October 11, 1951, box 20, General Correspondence, 1948–53, WBR; "Edna F. Kelly Dies at 91; Longtime Member of Congress," *Washington Post*, December 15, 1997.

18. H. K., Alameda, Calif., to Frieda Miller, April 23, 1951, box 20, General Correspondence, 1948–53, WBR.

19. *Congress and the Nation*, 1233. See also "Draft Statement [of Frieda Miller] on Domestic Service Workers Coverage under OASI," February 23, 1950, and "Section by Section Analysis," Old-Age and Survivors Insurance Amendments of 1953, in box 20, General Correspondence, 1948–53, WBR.

20. Laura H. Dale, Women's Bureau, to Miss Miller and Mrs. Morrison, "Income Tax Deduction," November 13, 1952, and Laura H. Dale to Miss Miller and Mrs. Morrison, "Income Tax Deduction for Child Care, Hearings before the House Ways and Means Committee, June 16, 1953," June 25, 1953, both in box 20, General Correspondence, 1948–53, WBR.

21. Labor physically performed in the home—from domestic work to industrial home work—has typically been devalued. See Boris, *Home to Work*.

22. Smith v. Commissioner of Internal Revenue, 40 B.T.A. 1038.

23. Ibid., 1039; See also McCaffery, *Taxing Women*, 111–14.

24. Alan Brinkley, *The End of Reform*, 10; Rogers M. Smith, "'One United People'"; Meyerowitz, "Beyond the Feminine Mystique."

25. Sylvia Porter, "The Working Wife," n.d. [ca. late 1952 or January 1953], reprinted courtesy of Post Hall Syndicate, Inc., U.S. Women's Bureau, box 20, General Correspondence, 1948–53, WBR.

26. Rep. Samuel W. Yorty, "Working Mothers Merit Tax Relief" (press release), n.d. [ca. February 1953], box 4, TSMP.

27. *Congressional Record* 99 (1953): A1481–A82.

28. UAW-CIO, *Proceedings, Fourteenth Constitutional Convention*, 63–64. The UAW convention delegates did not back the tax deduction. Thanks to Eileen Boris for telling me about this material and providing me with a copy of the relevant proceedings pages.

29. U.S. Bureau of the Census, "Family Income in the United States: 1951," 3–4, and "Family Income in the United States: 1952," 3.

30. U.S. Bureau of the Census, *Historical Statistics*, D 71–74.

31. *Congressional Quarterly Almanac* 9 (1953): 409–11; *Congress and the Nation*, 387–403.

32. U.S. Congess, House, Committee on Ways and Means, *General Revenue Revision*, 25–72. In addition to oral testimony, twelve statements or letters from interested individuals and congress members, as well as business, industry, labor, research, and professional groups, were placed on the record. With the exception of one from the American Federation of Labor (AFL), all supported the proposal. The federation said it sympathized with the goal of the proposals but believed that none of them could truly benefit low-income working women and at the same time avoid "wholesale evasion and abuse." It argued that the best solution would be to raise the personal exemption for all adult taxpayers and lower taxes on the first $2,000 in income.

33. "Tax Laws Unfair to Working Wives," *Redbook*, February 1953, reprinted in *Congressional Record*, 83d Cong., 1st sess., 99 (1953): A578–A79. I realize that I am using the word business*men*. This is the term everywhere in the record. I use it to be

true to that record, and more, to accent the presumption about the sex of an individual employed in business.

34. McCaffery, *Taxing Women*, 112–13.

35. Solinger, "Dependency and Choice"; Coontz, *The Way We Never Were*, 48–49, 97; Potter, "National Character," 442.

36. Mothers could and might be encouraged to seek self-fulfillment through *voluntary* service to the community. Many women did this. See Kaledin, *Mothers and More*; and Ware, "American Women in the 1950s." See also Potter, "National Character," 438–39.

37. U.S. Congress, House, Committee on Ways and Means, *General Revenue Revision*, 26–29.

38. U.S. Congress, House, Committee on Ways and Means, *General Revenue Revision*, 31–33; U.S. Congress, House, Office of the Historian, *Women in Congress*, "Leonor Kretzer Sullivan," 249–50.

39. U.S. Congress, House, Committee on Ways and Means, *General Revenue Revision*, 37–42. Representative Kenneth Roberts noted that he had received letters from all parts of the country in support of the child care tax deduction, and he made a relatively perfunctory request to include a limited number of these letters in the hearing record. Although the committee chair, Daniel Reed (R-N.Y.), at first agreed, Rep. Noah Mason (R-Ill.) objected and Roberts's request was disallowed. Mason said that the number of editorials or letters wouldn't affect the committee's decision and remarked, "direct testimony is the only thing we should consider."

40. U.S. Congress, House, Committee on Ways and Means, *General Revenue Revision*, 27. A Midwest conservative and isolationist, Rep. Mason held views that placed him well right of the Eisenhower administration. See "Mason, Noah Morgan," in *Current Biography* (1957), 357–58.

41. U.S. Congress, House, Committee on Ways and Means, *General Revenue Revision*, 35.

42. Gilbert, *A Cycle of Outrage*; Michel, *Children's Interests, Mothers' Rights*, chapter 5.

43. U.S. Congress, House, Committee on Ways and Means, *General Revenue Revision*, 53.

44. Ibid., 61–63.

45. Ibid., 63.

46. *Congressional Quarterly Almanac* 9 (1953): 411; *Congressional Quarterly Almanac* 10 (1954): 480–81.

47. *Congressional Quarterly Almanac* 10 (1954): 476–89, 482; *Congress and the Nation*, 397–403.

48. The bill specified that the deduction would be available to a working widow, widower, divorced person, or working mother whose husband was incapacitated. If a child was physically or mentally unable to go to school a deduction could be taken for his or her care expenses until the age of sixteen.

49. There were thirty legislative proposals made in the first half of 1953; the summary is drawn from available data that described twenty-nine of these proposals.

50. U.S. Congress, Senate, Committee on Finance, *The Internal Revenue Code of 1954*, 116–17.

51. See U.S. Congress, House, Committee on Ways and Means, *General Revenue Revision*, "Topic 2: Expenses of Child or Dependency Care," 25–72.

52. U.S. Congress, Senate, Committee on Finance, *The Internal Revenue Code of 1954*, 117.

53. *Congressional Quarterly Almanac* 10 (1954): 476; Reeder, "The Child Care Deduction," 46–47; U.S. Bureau of the Census, "Historical Income Tables," ‹http://www.census.gov/hhes/income/histinc/f07.html›. The national gross median income for a two-earner family was $5,336 in 1954. The income limit on the child care deduction was based on *adjusted* gross income and was phased out dollar for dollar at income levels above $4,500. Thus an otherwise eligible two-earner couple with adjusted gross income of $4,900 could deduct up to $200 in child care expenses, and a couple with adjusted gross income of $5,099 could deduct only $1 in expenses.

54. Kusko, "The Federal Child Care Tax Deduction," table 1; McCafferty, *Taxing Women*, 114–19.

55. U.S. Bureau of the Census, *Historical Statistics*, 71–72.

56. U.S. Bureau of the Census, Current Population Reports, *Consumer Income*, no. 12 (1953), 3.

57. U.S. Children's Bureau, *Child Care Arrangements of Full-Time Working Mothers*, 14–17. Data regarding the number of paid child care arrangements were not tabulated. Based on the sum of those who obtained outside-the-home care and those who obtained care from nonrelatives in the home, which approximates one-third of all respondents, I have assumed that from one-quarter to one-third of all mothers paid for their care arrangements. However, this sum may overstate the proportion of paid care, since some outside-the-home care may have been provided by relatives without charge.

58. Rose, *A Mother's Job*, 198–203; Ruderman, "Conceptualizing Needs for Day Care," 18. See also day care philosophies as advanced by private charity groups in Cleveland and Hartford, Conn., in Memorandum, Elizabeth L. Knox, chairman, to members of the Day Care Committee of the Family and Child Welfare Division, Greater Hartford Community Council, Hartford, August 31, 1953, folder "Working Mother," General Correspondence, 1948–53, box 28, WBR; and Children's Council, Committee on Day Care Planning, "A Philosophy of Day Care Services and Needs," March 28, 1960, folder 1055, container 43, FCPP.

59. U.S. Children's Bureau, *Licensed Day Care Facilities for Children*, in U.S. Congress, House, Committee on Ways and Means, *Public Welfare Amendments of 1962: Hearings*, 192–93.

60. Michel, *Children's Interests, Mothers' Rights*, 56–57.

61. Mildred Hunt, Division of Child Welfare, State Department of Social Welfare, Des Moines, Iowa, to Elizabeth Deuel, Child Welfare Consultant, Children's Bureau, Minneapolis, February 12, 1947, CBR. See also "An Inventory of Day Care," enclosed with Howard Hopkirk, executive director, Child Welfare League of America, to President Harry Truman, September 18, 1945, Official Files, HSTP.

62. U.S. Women's Bureau, *Planning Services for Children of Employed Mothers*, 21. See also Greenblatt, *Responsibility for Child Care*, 104–7.

63. U.S. Congress, House, Committee on Appropriations, *Third Supplemental Appropriation Bill, 1952*, 348; U.S. Congress, Senate, Committee on Appropriations, *Third Supplemental Appropriation Bill, 1952*, 165–69.

64. Winifred Moore, *Some Aspects of Day Care Licensing at the State Level*, 8, 13.

65. Ibid. See also Emerson, "Teamwork in Licensing Children's Agencies"; and Lewis, "The Strengths in Day Care Licensing."

66. Marion K. Craine, associate executive secretary, Division on Family and Child Welfare, Welfare Council of Metropolitan Chicago, to C. B. Olmsted, Children's Council, Welfare Federation of Cleveland, November 9, 1955, folder 815, container 33, FCPP.

67. Edward T. Landry, associate, child care, Division on Social Services to Families and Individuals, United Community Services of Metropolitan Boston, to C. Bushnell Olmsted, associate executive secretary, Welfare Federation of Cleveland, December 1, 1955, folder 815, container 33, FCPP.

68. U.S. Women's Bureau, *Employed Mothers and Child Care*, 77–79. See also Dorothy Frost, field investigator, "Community Facilities Survey," Dallas, April 4–28, 1952, box 11, General Correspondence, 1948–53, WBR.

69. Telephone interviews by author with Gene Little, November 24, 1999, and Jean Little, November 29, 1999.

70. The northern and southern groups merged in the late 1980s and are now known as the Professional Association for Childhood Education. "Information of [*sic*] the Formation of Professional Association for Childhood Education," compiled by Doris Dorris, early member and later president of PNSA. Telephone interview by author with Doris Dorris, November 23, 1999; Prescott, Milich, and Jones, *The "Politics" of Day Care*, 43–44. See also Testimony of Mr. Paul E. Green, chairman, Counseling Committee, Preschool Association of Southern California, in California Senate Interim Committee on Social Welfare, *The Child Care Center Program*; and J. Rollin Grant, president, Pre-School Association of California, San Diego, to John Weber, supervisor, California Child Care Centers, December 21, 1962, folder 1963, box 4, TSMP.

71. Youcha, *Minding the Children*, 274. While its ratio of children to adults seemed to provide the possibility of less expensive care, good group care did not always cost less. Especially for families with two or more children, fees could be prohibitive; in some areas, notably the South, where a segregated labor force permitted white women the option of hiring an African American maid at extremely low wages, group care might also be more expensive than care in the home.

72. Ruderman, *Child Care and Working Mothers*, 8, 11–23; Greenblatt, *Responsibility for Child Care*, 101, argues that despite proprietors' claims to the contrary, commercial centers did not make the same "educational progress" in their programs that philanthropic centers did after World War II.

73. U.S. Women's Bureau, *Employed Mothers and Child Care*, 77–79.

74. Prescott, Milich, and Jones, *The "Politics" of Day Care*, 8; Jones and Prescott

with Ellison, *Day Care and Nursery Education in Los Angeles County*, 27–28. (This increase includes full-day and part-day programs.)

75. California Senate Interim Committee on Social Welfare, *The Child Care Center Program*, 55. See also notes regarding testimony of [Jennings] Ledbetter, operator of a private nursery, in "Hearings on Child Care Center Program," October 1954, box 4, TSMP.

76. California Senate Interim Committee on Social Welfare, *The Child Care Center Program*, 55.

77. "Information of [sic] the Formation of Professional Association for Childhood Education," compiled by Doris Dorris.

78. California Senate Interim Committee on Social Welfare, *The Child Care Center Program*, 19–23.

79. Mary Young, legislative chairman, California Parents Association for Child Care Centers (address presented at 13th Annual Conference, CPACCC, Long Beach, Calif., November 11, 1961), box 5, TSMP; "Urgent Message," Mary Young, legislative chairman, California Parents Association for Child Care Centers, April 4, 1961, box 4, TSMP; Pre-School Association of California, "President's Message," *Newsletter* 2 (March 1963): 7, box 4, TSMP; J. Rollin Grant, president, Pre-School Association of California, San Diego, to John Weber, supervisor, California Child Care Centers, Sacramento, December 21, 1962, box 4, TSMP; and Weber to Grant, January 4, 1963, box 4, TSMP.

80. Prescott, Milich, and Jones, *The "Politics" of Day Care*, 44, 46 n. 14, 72; Michel, "The Politics of Child Care in America's Public/Private Welfare State," 845; Jones and Prescott with Ellison, *Day Care and Nursery Education in Los Angeles*, 50–53.

81. Moore, *Some Aspects of Day Care Licensing at the State Level*, 20; Minutes of Committee on Day Care Planning, Children's Council, Welfare Federation of Cleveland, September 7, 1955, folder 1054, container 43, FCPP. I was not able to locate this legal opinion (which is referenced in both of the preceding citations) and it is not clear who or what group prompted a legal opinion on the issue.

82. Minutes of the Committee on Day Care Planning, Children's Council, Welfare Federation of Cleveland, September 7, 1955, October 28, 1956, January 30, 1957, November 20, 1957, and December 1, 1959, folder 1054, container 43, FCPP; *In Re Appeal from Rules and Regulations of the Division of Social Administration Department of Public Welfare*, 195 N.E.2d 112 (1963).

83. *In Re Appeal from Rules and Regulations*, 195 N.E.2d 112.

84. Minutes of the Committee on Day Care Planning, Children's Council, Welfare Federation of Cleveland, March 29, 1964, May 16, 1963, May 21, 1963, and October 26, 1964, folder 1054, FCPP; telephone interview by author with Ron Sams, November 23, 1999. See also *Samkel, Inc. d/b/a Children's Academy et al. v. Kenneth Creasy, Director of Public Welfare, and Department of Public Welfare, State of Ohio*, 1982 Ohio App. LEXIS 15074 (1982); and *Samkel Inc. v. Creasy*, no. 82-1663, S.Ct. of Ohio, November 9, 1983.

85. Mittelstadt, "Dependency as a Problem to be Solved"; Curran, "The Psychology of Poverty"; Gordon, *Pitied but Not Entitled*.

86. Federal Security Agency, *Aid to Dependent Children in a Postwar Year*, 12.

87. U.S. Department of Health, Education and Welfare, Robert H. Mugge, "Aid to Families with Dependent Children," 8. Fathers considered absent from home included those who had never married the mother, had deserted the mother, were divorced, separated, or imprisoned, or were absent for some "other reason."

88. *Congress and the Nation*, 1273–83. U.S. Congress, House, Committee on Ways and Means, *1998 Green Book*, 401.

89. Louisiana Public Welfare Department, *Twenty-Fourth Annual Report*, 5–6.

90. Wickenden and Bell, *Public Welfare*, 1–2.

91. Louisiana Department of Public Welfare, *Twenty-Fourth Annual Report*, 5–6, 11; Wickenden and Bell, *Public Welfare*, 1–2; U.S. Department of Health, Education and Welfare, "Denial of Aid to Dependent Children."

92. P.L. 87-543, Section 107(b); U.S. Congress, House, Committee on Ways and Means, *Public Welfare Amendments of 1962*, 18; U.S. Congress, Senate, Committee on Finance, *Public Welfare Amendments of 1962*, 14.

93. Levenstein, "From Innocent Children to Unwanted Migrants and Unwed Moms," 15–18; Wickenden and Bell, *Public Welfare*, 3 (including quotation). See also Gordon, "Putting Children First."

94. Levenstein, "From Innocent Children to Unwanted Migrants and Unwed Moms"; Greenblatt, *Responsibility for Child Care*, 148, 136–37.

95. Public Welfare Amendments of 1962 (P.L. 87-543).

96. Michel, *Children's Interests, Mothers' Rights*, 196–97, 202, 210–35.

97. "Summary Day Care Meetings Held in Washington, D.C., August 3, 1961," NCDCC, Inc., New York; and U.S. Department of Health, Education and Welfare, "Secretary Ribicoff said today that he had told the National Committee of Day Care . . ." (press release), August 5, 1961, box 2, Docia Zavitkowsky papers, Archives of Pacific Oaks College, Pasadena, Calif.

98. Memo to Ad Hoc Committee on Public Welfare from NCDCC, Inc., August 10, 1961, Docia Zavitkowsky papers, Archives of Pacific Oaks College, Pasadena, Calif.

99. An authorization indicates a sum of money that Congress agrees upon for a specific program or purpose. It serves as a guideline, not a mandate, for congressional appropriators who must ultimately draft legislation that provides specific funding levels for authorized discretionary programs. Appropriators may choose to fund programs at a level different from that authorized, or not fund them at all. The administration bill proposed an authorization of $30 million for all child welfare services in fiscal year 1963 and provided for increases in this authorization to $50 million by fiscal year 1969. It further provided that funds appropriated for child welfare services in excess of $25 million (but not more than $10 million) must be set aside for day care services.

100. H.R. 10032, a bill to extend and improve the public assistance and child welfare services program of the Social Security Act, and for other purposes, as introduced February 1, 1962, by Rep. Wilbur Mills. In other references to day care services, the administration bill also required that federal day care dollars support service in licensed facilities only; and it proposed that state welfare agencies plan-

ning to provide day care services should cooperate with state health and education agencies, so that children in day care would receive the greatest possible access to these additional services.

101. H.R. 10032, introduced February 1, 1962; U.S. Congress, House, Committee on Ways and Means, *Report on Public Welfare Amendments of 1962*, 14–16; U.S. Congress, Senate, Committee on Finance, *Report on Public Welfare Amendments of 1962*, 11–13; U.S. Department of Health, Education and Welfare, Cohen and Ball, "Public Welfare Amendments of 1962," 4.

102. U.S. Congress, House, Committee on Ways and Means, *Public Welfare Amendments of 1962*, 608–9.

103. Ibid., 636, 675–76, 678–97. See also Greenblatt, *Responsibility for Child Care*, 147.

104. U.S. Congress, House, Committee on Ways and Means, *Public Welfare Amendments of 1962*, 169, 416, 426, 439–52, 470. Both Reid and Ellen Winston had been members of the Ad Hoc Public Welfare Committee that advised the administration on public welfare changes needed.

105. See also Solinger, "Dependency and Choice."

106. U.S. Congress, House, Committee on Ways and Means, *Public Welfare Amendments of 1962*, 675.

107. Gallagher had recently taken the NCCC post; previously, as director of youth services for the Cleveland, Ohio, Diocesan Catholic Charities, he had been a member of the Ad Hoc Public Welfare Committee.

108. U.S. Congress, House, Committee on Ways and Means, *Public Welfare Amendments of 1962*, 586–91.

109. U.S. Congress, Senate, Finance Committee, *The Public Assistance Act of 1962*, 386–91.

110. Greenblatt, *Responsibility for Child Care*, 138–44, 149–50.

111. U.S. Congress, House, Committee on Ways and Means, *Report on the Public Welfare Amendments of 1962*, 20–22, 58.

112. U.S. Department of Health, Education and Welfare, Cohen and Ball, "Public Welfare Amendments of 1962," 7; U.S. Congress, Senate, Finance Committee, *The Public Assistance Act of 1962*, 138–53, 254–57, 386–94.

113. U.S. Congress, Senate, Finance Committee, *Report on the Public Welfare Amendments of 1962*, 17, 55.

114. U.S. Department of Health, Education and Welfare, Cohen and Ball, "The Public Welfare Amendments of 1962," 5–10; Greenblatt, *Responsibility for Child Care*, 150–52.

115. "Duncan Leans toward Wider Day Care Plan," *Washington Post*, September 14, 1962; "Day Care Unit Plans Plea for Additional Funds," *Washington Post*, September 27, 1962; "Statement on a Pilot Project toward Development of a Comprehensive Day Care Program," folder 3-472a, box 192, DCR.

116. The maximum amount authorized for those four years totaled $35 million, but lawmakers charged with providing the actual funding consistently provided less money than was allowed. See U.S. Women's Bureau, *Federal Funds for Day Care Projects*, 1.

117. U.S. Department of Health, Education and Welfare, "State Action on the Child Welfare Provisions." See also Goldsmith, *Better Day Care for the Young Child*, 103–7.

118. District of Columbia, Department of Human Resources, *Children, the Resource of the Future*; Nettie Podell Ottenberg to Rep. Martha Griffiths, February 14, 1962, and Nettie Podell Ottenberg to Rep. Wilbur Mills, February 14, 1962, with attached report, "Pioneer Public Welfare Center," in U.S. Congress, House, Committee on Ways and Means, *Public Welfare Amendments of 1962*, 689–91. Regarding the number of private voluntary centers in the District see U.S. Congress, House, Committee on Ways and Means, *Public Welfare Amendments of 1962*, 186–87, and limited records and newsclips, September 1962–June 1963, folders 3-472, 3-472(a), and 3-472(b), box 192, entry 21, DCR.

119. Prescott, Milich, and Jones, *The "Politics" of Day Care*, 58; Jones and Prescott with Ellison, *Day Care and Nursery Education in Los Angeles County*, 3–5.

120. Roy E. Simpson, superintendent of public instruction and director of education, to Carlos Bee, chairman, special education subcommittee, Assembly Interim Committee on Education, Report [on Child Care Centers], September 18, 1962; J. M. Wedemeyer, director, California Department of Social Welfare, Sacramento, to Mr. Winslow Christian, administrator, Health and Welfare Agency, Sacramento, Subject: Child Care Augmentation, June 11, 1963, in F3725:1566, Children's Centers, 1963–65, Division Chief's Files, Division of Public School Administration, SDEP; Roscoe Lyda, director, to all districts and divisions, Subject: Day Care Services, Administrative Memo no. 565, May 5, 1964, folder "DC/PS—Admin/Equip," box 3, Anne Ostomel papers, California Social Welfare Archives, University of Southern California, Los Angeles; and Barbara Joe, California Department of Social Welfare, Health and Welfare Agency, to Rose Cohn, L.A. Area, Frank Howard, Sacramento Area, and Grace Krejci, S.F. Area, Subject: Children's Centers, May 19, 1967, folder DC/PS Papers & Articles, box 3, Anne Ostomel papers, California Social Welfare Archives, University of Southern California, Los Angeles.

121. Social Security Amendments of 1965, P.L. 89-97, title II, part 1, sec. 207–8; U.S. Congress, House, Conference Report, *The Social Security Amendments of 1965*; U.S. Congress, Senate, Committee on Finance, *Social Security Amendments of 1965*, 87–88.

122. U.S. Women's Bureau, *Federal Funds for Day Care Projects*, 1 (see also revised version of same publication, February 1969); U.S. Congress, Senate, Committee on Finance, *Material Related to Child Care Legislation*, 10–11. Regarding initial limitations on the use of funds see comments of Eunice Evans, deputy director, California State Department of Social Welfare, as recorded in J. R. Weber, supervisor, California Children's Centers, to M. B. Sloss, "Subject: A Conference to End All Conferences: A Report of a Joint Meeting Held 3-19-65," March 22, 1965, box 4, TSMP. Subsequent amendments to the Social Security Act, including changes in 1967 that created the federal work training program WIN, played a significant role in broadening and clarifying the use of rehabilitation (AFDC social services) funds for day care purposes. The Social Security Amendments of 1974 (P.L. 93-647) moved this funding for services out of the AFDC program and into a separate "Title XX" of the act.

123. J. R. Weber, supervisor, California Children's Centers, to M. B. Sloss, "Subject: A Conference to End All Conferences: A Report of a Joint Meeting Held 3-19-65," March 22, 1965, box 4, TSMP; J. R. Weber to M. B. Sloss, "Meeting of Senator Teale's Senate Subcommittee on Finance Held Tuesday, 3-23-65," March 25, 1965, box 4, TSMP; and "Report by Theresa S. Mahler, Legislative Chairman, California Children's Centers Directors and Supervisors Association, Summarizing Legislative Activity, [mostly 1965]," box 4, TSMP; California Legislative Analyst, "Publicly Subsidized Child Care Services in California."

124. Barbara Joe, California Department of Social Welfare, Health and Welfare Agency, to Rose Cohn, L.A. Area, Frank Howard, Sacramento Area, and Grace Krejci, S.F. Area, Subject: Children's Centers [attaching Department of Education survey of families using Children's Centers, week of November 14–18, 1966], May 19, 1967, folder "DC/PS Papers & Articles," box 3, Anne Ostomel papers, California Social Welfare Archives, University of Southern California, Los Angeles.

Epilogue

1. Melinda Gish, "Child Care: Funding and Spending Under Federal Block Grants" (Congressional Research Service, Washington), March 19, 2002.

BIBLIOGRAPHY

Archival Collections

Cleveland, Ohio
  Archives of the Diocese of Cleveland
    Catholic Charities Corp. papers
    Edward Hoban papers
  Cleveland City Hall Archives
    City Council papers
  Cuyahoga County Archives
    County tax records
    Official Journal of the County Commissioners
  Western Reserve Historical Society
    Federation for Community Planning
    Mothers Day Care Committee, unprocessed
Detroit, Mich.
  Archives of Labor and Urban Affairs at Wayne State University
    CIO Research and Education Department Collection
    Merrill-Palmer Institute Collection
    National Farm Worker Ministry Collection
    UAW Women's Department Collection
Independence, Mo.
  Harry S. Truman Library
    Harry S. Truman, Official Files
Los Angeles, Calif.
  California Social Welfare Archives at the University of Southern California
    Frances Feldman papers, unprocessed

Anne Ostomel papers

Los Angeles City Archives
    City Council papers
New Brunswick, N.J.
  Archives at Rutgers University
    Mary Norton papers
Norman, Okla.
  Carl Albert Center for Congressional Research and Studies Center,
      Congressional Archives at the University of Oklahoma
    Helen Gahagan Douglas papers
Northridge, Calif.
  University Archives, Urban Archives at California State University
    Rosalie M. Blau papers
Pasadena, Calif.
  Archives of Pacific Oaks College, Pasadena, Calif.
    Theresa Mahler papers
    John Weber papers
    Docia Zavitkovsky papers
Sacramento, Calif.
  California State Archives
    Governor's Chaptered Bill Files
    State Department of Education papers
    Earl Warren papers
Washington, D.C.
  Historical Society of Washington, D.C.
    American Association of University Women, D.C. chapter
    General Federation of Women's Clubs, D.C. chapter
    Harry S. Wender papers
  Mary McLeod Bethune Council House Archives
    National Council of Negro Women papers
  Moorland-Spingarn Research Center at Howard University
    National Association for the Advancement of Colored People, D.C. branch
Washington, D.C., and College Park, Md.
  National Archives
    Children's Bureau, Record Group 102
    District of Columbia government, Record Group 351
    Federal Works Agency, Record Group 162
    U.S. House of Representatives, Record Group 233
    U.S. Senate, Record Group 46
    Women's Bureau, Record Group 86

Oral Interviews

Andruzzi, Ellen Adamson. Telephone interview by author. Transcribed tape
    recording, June 7 and 13, 1997.

Calhoun, Flora O. Interview by author. Transcribed tape recording, Washington, D.C., May 23, 1997.

Dorris, Doris. Telephone interview by author, November 23, 1999.

Feldman, Frances Lomas. Interview by author. Transcribed tape recording, Pasadena, Calif., July 21 and 28, 1997.

Likover, Belle Weiner Tracht. Interview by author. Transcribed tape recording, Shaker Heights, Ohio, June 4 and 6, 1996.

Little, Gene. Telephone interview by author, November 24, 1999.

Little, Jean. Telephone interview by author, November 29, 1999.

Sams, Ron. Telephone interview by author, November 23, 1999.

Severn, Constance. Telephone interview by author. Transcribed tape recording, May 17, 1997.

Zahm, Bernice S. Interview by author. Transcribed tape recording, Sherman Oaks, Calif., April 2, 1997, and telephone interview by author, July 24, 1997.

Oral Histories

Arnstein, Lawrence. *Community Service in California Public Health and Social Welfare*. Interview by Edna T. Daniel, transcript. Regional Oral History Office (formerly Regional Cultural History Project), Bancroft Library, University of California, Berkeley, 1964.

Boggs, Betty. Vol. 3, transcript. In "Rosie the Riveter Revisited: Women and the World War II Work Experience." School of Social and Behavioral Sciences, Oral History Resource Center, California State University, Long Beach.

"An Extended Family Experience: The Co-operative Nursery School Movement of Southern California as Told by Parents, Teachers, and Directors." Eight Interviews by Rose Selsenick, director, Crestwood Hills Co-op, West Los Angeles, transcript. Oral History Program, California State University, Northridge, 1977.

Geddes, Ernest R. *California Assemblyman*. Interview by Enid Douglas, transcript. Oral History Program, Claremont Graduate School, Claremont, Calif., 1976.

Stangeland, Addie. Vol. 40, transcript. In "Rosie the Riveter Revisited: Women and the World War II Work Experience." School of Social and Behavioral Sciences, Oral History Resource Center, California State University, Long Beach, Calif.

Newspapers

1945–46
Catholic Universe Bulletin
Cleveland Plain Dealer
Cleveland Press
Cleveland News
Washington Afro-American

1945–51
  Washington Daily News
  Washington Post
  Washington Star
  Washington Times Herald
Various dates
  Los Angeles Times
  San Francisco Chronicle
  New York Times

Other References

Ayer & Sons Directory of Newspapers and Periodicals, 1945 and 1946
Biographical Directory of the American Congress, 1774–1996. CQ Staff Directories, 1997
Cleveland City Directory, 1880–1947
Congressional Quarterly Almanac, 1945–65
Congressional Record, 1945–65
Current Biography, various dates

Legal Decisions

Ferrie v. Sweeny, 72 N.E. 2d 128 (1945)
In Re Appeal From Rules and Regulations of the Division of Social Administration Department of Public Welfare, 195 N.E. 2d 112 (1963)
Muller v. Oregon, 28 S.Ct. Rpt. 324 (1907)
Smith v. Commissioner of Internal Revenue, 40 B.T.A. 1038

U.S. Congressional Hearing Records and Reports

U.S. Congress. House. Committee on Appropriations. *Third Supplemental Appropriation Bill, 1952: Hearing before the Subcommittee on Independent Offices Appropriations.* 82d Cong., 2d sess., February 1952.
———. *Second Supplemental Appropriation Bill for 1952: Hearing before the Subcommittee on Independent Offices Appropriations.* 82d Cong., 1st sess., September 1951.
———. *Second Supplemental Appropriation Bill, 1952.* Report No. 1110. 82d Cong., 1st Sess., October 8, 1951.
———. *Third Supplemental Appropriation Bill, 1951.* Report No. 298. 82d Cong., 1st sess., April 6, 1951.
———. *District of Columbia Appropriation Bill for 1947: Hearing before the Subcommittee of the Committee on Appropriation.* 79th Cong., 1st sess., February and March 1946.
———. *First Supplemental Surplus Appropriation Rescission Bill, 1946: Hearing before the Subcommittee on Deficiency Appropriations.* 79th Cong., 1st sess., September and October, 1945.

——. *Second Deficiency Appropriation Bill for 1945: Hearing before the Subcommittee on Deficiency Appropriations.* 79th Cong., 1st sess., May and June 1945.

U.S. Congress. House. Committee on Banking and Currency. *Defense Housing and Community Facilities Act: Hearing before the Committee on Banking and Currency.* 82d Cong., 1st sess., January and February 1951.

U.S. Congress. House. Committee on the District of Columbia. *Continuing a System of Nurseries and Nursery Schools in the District of Columbia.* Report no. 2253. 81st Cong., 2d sess., June 15, 1950.

——. *S. 3258: Hearing before the Subcommittee on Health, Education, and Recreation.* 81st Cong., 2d sess. CIS unpublished House hearings, microfiche, (81) HD-T.3, June 1, 1950.

——. *Continuing a System of Nurseries and Nursery Schools for the Day Care of School-Age and under School-Age Children in the District of Columbia through June 30, 1950.* Report no. 397. 81st Cong., 1st sess., April 5, 1949.

——. *Executive Session of the Subcommittee on Health, Education and Recreation.* 81st Cong., 1st sess. CIS unpublished House hearings, microfiche, (81) HD-T.19, March 25, 1949.

——. *Child Care Centers (H.R. 1383): Hearing before the Subcommittee on Health, Education and Recreation.* 81st Cong., 1st sess. (unpublished, typed transcript, folder HR1383, box 2, HR81A-D4, Committee on the District of Columbia, Records of the U.S. House of Representatives, Record Group 233, National Archives, Washington), February 24, 1949.

——. *Child Day Care Centers.* 80th Cong., 2d sess., Committee Print. Washington: Government Printing Office, 1948.

——. *H.R. 5808: Executive Session of the Subcommittee on Health, Education, and Recreation,* 80th Cong., 2d sess. (Unpublished, typed transcript. Folder HR 5808, box 8, HR80A-D3, Committee on the District of Columbia, Records of the U.S. House of Representatives, Record Group 233, National Archives, Washington), April 6, 1948.

——. *H.R. 5808, Continuance of Child Day Care Centers: Hearing before the Subcommittee on Health, Education, and Recreation.* 80th Cong., 2d sess. (Unpublished, typed transcript. Folder HR 5808, box 8, HR80A-D3, Committee on the District of Columbia, Records of the U.S. House of Representatives, Record Group 233, National Archives, Washington), March 24, 1948.

——. *H.R. 3208: Hearing before the Subcommittee on Health, Education, and Recreation.* 80th Cong., 1st sess. (Unpublished, typed transcript. Folder H.R. 3208, box 4, HR80A-D3, Committee on the District of Columbia, Records of the U.S. House of Representatives, Record Group 233, National Archives, Washington), June 1947.

——. *Child Care Centers: Hearings before the Committee on the District of Columbia.* 79th Cong., 2d. sess. CIS unpublished U.S. House Hearings, microfiche, (79) HD-T.120, February 25, 1946.

——. *Need for Child Care Revision: Hearing before the Subcommittee on Public Health.* 79th Cong., 1st sess. CIS unpublished U.S. House hearings, microfiche, (79) HD-T.1, May 8, 1945.

U.S. Congress. House. Committee on Ways and Means. *Public Welfare Amend-ments of 1962: Committee Report Accompanying H.R. 10606*, House Report 1414, 87th Cong., 2d sess., March 10, 1962.

———. *Public Welfare Amendments of 1962: Hearings before the Committee on Ways and Means.* 87th Cong., 2d sess., February 1962.

———. *General Revenue Revision: Hearing before Committee on Ways and Means.* 83d Cong., 1st sess., June and July 1953.

U.S. Congress. House. Conference Report. *Declaring A National Policy on Em-ployment Production, and Purchasing Power, and for Other Purposes.* House Rpt. No. 1520. 79th Cong., 2d sess., February 5, 1946.

U.S. Congress. House. Conference Report. *District of Columbia Day Care Nurs-eries and Nursery Schools.* House Report No. 2374. 81st Cong., 2d sess., June 28, 1950.

U.S. Congress. House. Conference Report. *The Social Security Amendments of 1965,* House Report 682, 89th Cong., 1st sess., July 26, 1965.

U.S. Congress. Senate. Committee on Appropriations. *Third Supplemental Appro-priations Bill, 1952: Hearing before the Subcommittee on Independent Agencies.* 82d Cong., 2d sess., March 1952.

———. *Second Supplemental Appropriation Bill for 1952: Hearing before the Com-mittee on Appropriations.* 82d Cong., 1st sess., October 1951.

———. *District of Columbia Appropriation Bill for 1948: Hearing before the Sub-committee of the Committee on Appropriations.* 80th Cong., 1st sess., July 15–17, 1947.

U.S. Congress. Senate. Committee on Banking and Currency. *Defense Housing Act: Hearing before the Committee on Banking and Currency.* 82d Cong., 1st sess., January and February 1951.

———. *The Full Employment Act of 1945: Hearings before the Subcommittee of the Committee on Banking and Currency.* 79th Cong., 1st sess., July, August, and September 1945.

———. *Report to Accompany S.380: Assuring Full Employment in a Free Competi-tive Economy.* Rpt. No. 583. 79th Cong., 1st sess., September 22, 1945.

U.S. Congress. Senate. Committee on the District of Columbia. *Continuation of Child Day Care Centers in the District: Hearing before the Subcommittee on Public Health, Education and Welfare.* 81st Cong., 1st sess. CIS unpublished Senate hearings, microfiche, (81) SD-T.75, (81) SD-T.76, May 5 and 9, 1949.

———. *H.R. 5808: Hearing before the Public Health Subcommittee.* 80th Cong., 2d sess. CIS unpublished Senate hearings, microfiche, (80) SD-T.44, May 27, 1948.

———. *Nurseries and Nursery Schools: Hearings before the Subcommittee on Public Health, Education and Recreation.* 80th Cong., 1st sess. CIS unpublished Sen-ate hearings, microfiche, (80) SD-T.46, (80) SD-T.47, and (80) SD-T.48, April 29, May 8, and June 7, 1947.

———. *H.R. 5933: Hearing before the Committee on the District of Columbia.* 79th Cong., 2d sess. CIS unpublished Senate hearings, microfiche, (79)SD-T.7, June 10, 1946.

U.S. Congress. Senate. Committee on Education and Labor. *Maternal and Child*

Welfare: Hearing before the Committee on Education and Labor. 79th Cong., 2d sess., June 1946.

U.S. Congress. Senate. Committee on Finance. *Material Related to Child Care Legislation*, 92d Cong., 1st sess., July 23, 1971.

———. *Social Security Amendments of 1965, Report to accompany H.R. 6675*, Senate Report 404, part I, 89th Cong., 1st sess., June 30, 1965.

———. *Public Assistance Act of 1962: Hearing before the Committee on Finance.* 87th Cong., 2d sess., May 1962.

———. *Public Welfare Amendments of 1962: Committee Report on H.R. 10606*, Senate Report 1589,. 87th Cong., 2d sess., June 14, 1962.

———. *The Internal Revenue Code of 1954: Hearings before the Committee on Finance.* 83d Cong., 2d sess., April 1954.

Other Federal and State Government Documents

California Legislature. *Technical Staff Report to the Joint Committee on Preschool and Primary Training.* Sacramento, January 17, 1947.

California Legislature. Assembly. 1952 First Extraordinary Session. *Child Care Center Operations under the Geddes-Kraft Child Care Center Act*, March 1952.

———. "First Preliminary Report by the Assembly Interim Committee on Social Welfare on the Child Care Center Program." *Assembly Journal* (January 9, 1951): 101–54.

California Legislature. Legislative Analyst. "Publicly Subsidized Child Care Services in California." Sacramento, August 23, 1974.

———. "The Child Care Program: State of California." Sacramento, October 23, 1958.

California Legislature. Senate. 1955 Regular Session. *The Child Care Center Program: Report of Senate Interim Committee on Social Welfare.* Sacramento, 1955.

California State Department of Education. *California's Major Public and Private Nonprofit Early Childhood Education Programs.* Division of Compensatory Education Programs, February 1970.

———. "Survey of Families Requesting Service or Enrolling Children in Child Care Centers," April 1955.

———. *Report of Child Care Centers Administered and Operated by California School Districts.* Sacramento, March 1949.

———. *Child Care Centers by School Districts.* Sacramento, December 1945.

———. *California Program for the Care of Children of Working Parents.* Sacramento, August 1943.

District of Columbia, Department of Human Resources. *Children, the Resource of the Future: A Comprehensive Child Care Plan.* Washington, November 1974.

Federal Security Agency, Social Security Administration. *Aid to Dependent Children in a Postwar Year: Characteristics of Families Receiving ADC*, June 1948. Report by Elizabeth Alling and Agnes Leisy. Public Assistance Report No. 17: Washington, June 1950.

Louisiana, Department of Public Welfare. *Twenty-Fourth Annual Report*, July 1, 1960–June 30, 1961.

Ohio. *General Code, Annotated.* 1952 series. Sections 3070-1 to 3070-36.

——. *Opinions of the Attorney General.* No. 1537. January 31, 1947.

——. *Opinions of the Attorney General.* No. 769. March 2, 1946.

President's Committee on Civil Rights. *To Secure These Rights.* Washington: Government Printing Office, 1947.

U.S. Bureau of the Census. *Historical Statistics of the United States: Colonial Times to 1970, Bicentennial Edition.* Washington: Government Printing Office, 1975.

——. "Historical Income Tables: Families, (Table) F-7: Type of Family (All Races) by Median and Mean Income, 1947 to 1999." ‹http://www.census.gov/hhes/income/histinc/f07.html›. June 2002.

——. Current Population Reports: Consumer Income. "Family Income in the United States: 1952." Series P-60. No. 15, April 27, 1954.

——. Current Population Reports: Consumer Income. "Family Income in the United States: 1951." Series P-60. No. 12, June 1953.

——. *U.S. Census of Population: 1960.* Vol. I. *Characteristics of the Population.* Part 6. *California.* Washington: Government Printing Office, 1963.

——. *U.S. Census of Population: 1960.* Vol. I. *Characteristics of the Population.* Part 10. *District of Columbia.* Washington: Government Printing Office, 1963.

——. *U.S. Census of Population: 1950.* Vol. II. *Characteristics of the Population.* Part 5. *California.* Washington: Government Printing Office, 1952.

——. *U.S. Census of Population: 1950.* Vol. II. *Characteristics of the Population.* Part 9. *District of Columbia.* Washington: Government Printing Office, 1952.

U.S. Bureau of Labor Statistics. *Workers' Budgets in the United States: City Families and Single Persons, 1946–1947.* Washington: Government Printing Office, 1948.

U.S. Children's Bureau. "Licensed Day Care Facilities for Children." Preliminary report by Seth Low, October 1960.

——. *Children of Working Mothers.* Report by Elizabeth Herzog. Washington: Government Printing Office, 1960.

——. *Child Care Arrangements of Working Mothers.* Report by Henry C. Lajewski. No. 378. Washington: Government Printing Office, 1959.

U.S. Congress. House. Office of the Historian. *Women in Congress, 1917–1990.* Washington: Government Printing Office, 1991.

U.S. Department of Health, Education and Welfare, Robert H. Mugge. "Aid to Families with Dependent Children: Initial Findings of the 1961 Report on the Characteristics of Recipients." *Social Security Bulletin* (March 1963): 3–15.

——. "Denial of Aid to Dependent Children." *Social Security Bulletin* (July 1961): 19.

——. "State Action on the Child Welfare Provisions." *Welfare in Review* 2, no. 1 (January 1964): 20–25.

——. Wilbur J. Cohen and Robert M. Ball. "Public Welfare Amendments of

1962 and Proposals for Health Insurance for the Aged." *Social Security Bulletin* (October 1962): 3–22.

U.S. Office of Economic Opportunity, Community Action Program. *Head Start Child Development Programs*. Washington: Government Printing Office, n.d. [ca. 1966].

U.S. President. *Public Papers of the Presidents of the United States*, Dwight D. Eisenhower. Washington: Office of the Federal Register, National Archives and Records Administration, 1954.

U.S. Women's Bureau. *The Effective Use of Womanpower*. Report of the Conference, March 10–11, 1955. Washington: Government Printing Office, 1955.

———. *Planning Services for Children of Employed Mothers*. A Report Prepared by a Subcommittee of the Interdepartmental Committee on Children and Youth. Washington: Government Printing Office, May 1953.

———. *Employed Mothers and Child Care*. Bulletin no. 246. Washington: Government Printing Office, 1953.

———. *Employment of Women in the Early Postwar Period: With Background of Prewar and War Data*. Report by Mary Elizabeth Pidgeon, Bulletin no. 211. Washington: Government Printing Office, October 1946.

———. *Federal Funds for Day Care Projects*. Washington: Government Printing Office, 1967.

———. *Women Workers in Ten War Production Areas and Their Postwar Employment Plans*. Bulletin No. 209. Washington: Government Printing Office, 1946.

———. *Negro Women War Workers*. Bulletin No. 205. Washington: Government Printing Office, 1945.

Books, Articles, Dissertations, and Reports

American Women in the Postwar World: A Symposium on the Role Women Will Play in Business and Industry. Prepared by *Newsweek's* Club Bureau. New York, 1944, Folder Writings, 1932–49, box 5, Papers of Mary Norton, Archives at Rutgers University, New Brunswick, N.J.

Amott, Teresa, and Julie Matthaei. *Race, Gender and Work: A Multicultural Economic History of Women in the United States*. Rev. ed. Boston: South End, 1996.

Anderson, Karen. *Wartime Women: Sex Roles, Family Relations, and the Status of Women During World War II*. Westport, Conn.: Greenwood, 1981.

"The Answer Is Full Employment." CIO Political Action Committee Pamphlet-of-the-Month no.4, n.d., folder 17, box 8, series 5, National Council of Negro Women, Mary McLeod Bethune Council House, Washington.

Anthony, Susan B., II. *Out of the Kitchen into the War*. New York: Stephen Daye, 1943.

Baer, Judith. *The Chains of Protection: The Judicial Response to Women's Labor Legislation*. Westport, Conn.: Greenwood, 1978.

Baker, Elizabeth Faulkner. *Protective Labor Legislation with Special Reference to Women in the State of New York*. New York: Columbia University, 1925.

Baker, Paula. "The Domestication of Politics: Women and American Political Society, 1780–1920." *American Historical Review* 89 (June 1984): 620–47.

Bargeron, Carlisle. "The Mayor of Washington." *Nation's Business.* February 1946.

Beatty, Barbara. *Preschool Education in America: The Culture of Young Children from the Colonial Era to the Present.* New Haven: Yale University Press, 1995.

Bell, Winifred. "The 'Rights' of the Poor: Welfare Witch-Hunts in the District of Columbia." *Social Work* (January 1968): 60–67.

Berch, Bettina. *Radical by Design: The Life and Style of Elizabeth Hawes.* New York: Dutton, 1988.

Berry, Mary Frances. *The Politics of Parenthood: Child Care, Women's Rights, and the Myth of the Good Mother.* New York: Penguin, 1994.

Bierman, Beatrice. "The Influence of Pressure Groups on Child Care Center Legislation in California." M.A. thesis, University of California, Berkeley, 1950.

Bledsoe, Patricia. "A Study of the Status of Group Day Care in the District of Columbia with a Presentation of Its Historical Development and an Analysis of the Questionnaires of the Parents' Committee for Child Care." M.S.W. thesis, National Catholic School of Social Work, Catholic University of America, June 1946.

Blewett, Mary. "The Sexual Division of Labor and the Artisan Tradition in Early Industrial Capitalism: The Case of New England Shoemaking, 1780–1860." In *"To Toil the Livelong Day": America's Women at Work, 1780–1980,* ed. Carol Groneman and Mary Beth Norton, 35–46. Ithaca, N.Y.: Cornell University Press, 1987.

Boris, Eileen. "When Work Is Slavery." In *Whose Welfare?* ed. Gwendolyn Mink, 36–55. Ithaca, N.Y.: Cornell University Press, 1999.

———. *Home to Work: Motherhood and the Politics of Industrial Homework in the United States.* New York: Cambridge University Press, 1994.

———. "The Power of Motherhood: Black and White Activist Women Redefine the 'Political.'" In *Mothers of a New World: Maternalist Politics and the Origins of Welfare States,* ed. Seth Koven and Sonya Michel, 213–45. New York: Routledge, 1993.

Bothman, Annette. "Reflections of the Pioneers on the Early History of the Santa Monica Children's Centers and Changing Child-Rearing Philosophies." M.A. thesis, California State University, Northridge, May 1976.

Boydston, Jeanne. "To Earn Her Daily Bread: Housework and Antebellum Working-Class Subsistence." In *Unequal Sisters: A Multicultural Reader in U.S. Women's History,* ed. Vicki L. Ruiz and Ellen Carol DuBois. 2d ed., 44–56. New York: Routledge, 1994.

A Brief Inquiry into the Need for a Child Care Program in California. Prepared by Educators and Parents Groups in California. December 1948.

Brinkley, Alan. *The End of Reform: New Deal Liberalism in Recession and War.* New York: Vintage, 1996.

Brinkley, David. *Washington Goes to War.* New York: Ballantine, 1988.

Buckley, William F., Jr. "My Secret Right-Wing Conspiracy." *New Yorker,* October 21 and 28, 1996.

Cahan, Emily. *Past Caring: A History of U.S. Pre-School Care and Education for the Poor, 1820–1965*. New York: National Center for Children in Poverty, School of Public Health, Columbia University, 1989.

Campbell, D'Ann. *Women at War with America: Private Lives in a Patriotic Era*. Cambridge: Harvard University Press, 1984.

Chafe, William. *The American Woman: Her Changing Social, Economic and Political Roles, 1920–1970*. New York: Oxford University Press, 1982.

Chang, Tse Hua. "Comparative Study of Child Day Care Centers in Los Angeles, California and Canton, China." M.A. thesis, Claremont Graduate School, Claremont, Calif., 1949.

"The Children's Hour: Day-Care Centers Are 'Wunderkinder' on Main and Wall Streets." *Barron's National Business and Financial Weekly*, July 5, 1971.

Ciani, Kyle Emily. "Choosing to Care: Meeting Children's Needs in Detroit and San Diego, 1880–1945." Ph.D. diss., Michigan State University, 1998.

Clague, Ewan. "Foreword." In *Workers' Budgets in the United States: City Families and Single Persons, 1946–1947*. U.S. Bureau of Labor Statistics, Bulletin 927, iii–v. Washington: Government Printing Office, 1948.

Clark-Lewis, Elizabeth. "'This Work Had an End': African-American Domestic Workers in Washington, D.C., 1910–1940." In *"To Toil the Livelong Day": America's Women at Work, 1780–1980*, ed. Carol Groneman and Mary Beth Norton, 196–212. Ithaca, N.Y.: Cornell University Press, 1987.

Class, Norris E. "Public Policy and Working Mothers: An Historical Analysis of the American Experience" (1972). In *The Administrative Regulation of Community Care Facilities with Special Reference to Child Care: A Compilation of Papers by Norris E. Class*. School of Social Work, University of Southern California.

Cobble, Dorothy Sue. "Dishing It Out: Waitresses and the Making of Their Unions in San Francisco, 1900–1941." In *Working People of California*, ed. Daniel Cornford, 85–115. Berkeley: University of California Press, 1995.

———. "Recapturing Working Class Feminism: Union Women in the Postwar Era." In *Not June Cleaver: Women and Gender in Postwar America, 1945–1960*, ed. Joanne Meyerowitz, 57–83. Philadelphia: Temple University Press, 1994.

Committee on the Status of Black Americans, National Research Council. "Black Participation in American Society." In *A Common Destiny: Blacks and American Society*, ed. Gerald David Jaynes and Robin M. Williams Jr. Washington: National Academy Press, 1989.

Congress and the Nation, 1945–1964: A Review of Government and Politics in the Postwar Years. Washington: Congressional Quarterly Service, 1965.

Coontz, Stephanie. *The Way We Never Were: American Families and the Nostalgia Trap*. New York: Basic Books, 1992.

Cott, Nancy F. "Marriage and Women's Citizenship in the United States, 1830–1934." *American Historical Review* 103, no. 5 (December 1998): 1440–74.

———. "Giving Character to Our Whole Civil Polity: Marriage and the Public Order in the Late Nineteenth Century." In *U.S. History as Women's History: New Feminist Essays*, ed. Linda Kerber, Alice Kessler-Harris, and Kathryn Kish Sklar, 107–21. Chapel Hill: University of North Carolina Press, 1995.

——. *The Grounding of Modern Feminism*. New Haven: Yale University Press, 1987.

"Council Asks Better Deal for Migrant Workers and Families." *The Child* 12 (October 1948): 10:172–73.

Curran, Laura. "The Psychology of Poverty: Professional Social Work and Aid to Dependent Children in Postwar America, 1946–1963." *Social Services Review* (September 2002): 365–86.

Daniels, Cletus. "Cesar Chavez and the Unionization of California Farmworkers." In *Working People of California*, ed. Daniel Cornford, 371–404. Berkeley: University of California Press, 1995.

Dashiell, Alice T. "Trends in Day Care." *The Child* 11 (September 1946): 3:53–56.

Davis, Mike. *City of Quartz: Excavating the Future in Los Angeles*. New York: Vintage, 1992.

Dawley, Alan. *Struggles for Justice: Social Responsibility and the Liberal State*. Cambridge: Belknap, 1991.

DeForest, Paul, Leonard Rubin, and Ann Wynia, with the assistance of Linda Lauve and James Dale Shaw. *Legislative History of the Aid to Dependent Children Program*. Legal Action Support Project, Report no. 2. Washington: Bureau of Social Science Research, May 1970.

Degler, Carl. *At Odds: Women and the Family in America from the Revolution to the Present*. Oxford University Press, 1980.

Deslippe, Dennis. *"Rights, Not Roses": Unions and the Rise of Working-Class Feminism, 1945–1980*. Urbana: University of Illinois Press, 2000.

Dratch, Howard. "The Politics of Child Care in the 1940s." *Science and Society* 38 (Summer 1974): 167–204.

Dulles, Foster Rhea, and Melvyn Dubofsky. *Labor in America: A History*. 5th ed. Arlington Heights, Ill.: Harlan Davidson, 1993.

Durst, Anne. "Day Nurseries and Wage-Earning Mothers in the United States, 1890–1930." Ph.D. diss., University of Wisconsin, Madison, 1989.

Eliot, Abigail Adams. "Nursery Schools Fifty Years Ago." *Young Children* 27 (April 1972): 4:209–13.

Emerson, Lola B. "Teamwork in Licensing Children's Agencies." *Children* 3, no. 4 (July–August 1956): 135–38.

Evans, Sara. *Born for Liberty: A History of Women in America*. New York: Free Press, 1989.

Feldman, Frances Lomas. *Portrait of a Gentle Man: George D. Nickel*. George D. Nickel Memorial Monograph Series, no. 1. California Social Welfare Archives. University of Southern California, 1991.

Feldstein, Ruth. "'I Wanted the Whole World to See': Race, Gender, and Constructions of Motherhood in the Death of Emmett Till." In *Not June Cleaver: Women and Gender in Postwar America, 1945–1960*, ed. Joanne Meyerowitz, 263–303. Philadelphia: Temple University Press, 1994.

Finkelstein, Barbara. "Uncle Sam and the Children: A History of Government Involvement in Child Rearing." In *Growing Up in America: Children in Historical Perspective*, ed. N. Ray Hiner and Joseph Hawes, 255–66. Urbana: University of Illinois Press, 1985.

Flexner, Eleanor. *A Century of Struggle: The Woman's Right Movement in the United States.* Cambridge: Belknap, 1975.

Folbre, Nancy. "The Unproductive Housewife: Her Evolution in Nineteenth-Century Economic Thought." *Signs* 16 (1991) 3:463–84.

Frank, Lawrence K. "The Beginnings of Child Development and Family Life Education in the Twentieth Century." *Merrill-Palmer Quarterly* 8, no. 4 (October 1962): 7–28.

Fraser, Nancy. "Struggle over Needs: Outline of a Socialist-Feminist Critical Theory of Late Capitalist Political Culture." In *Women, the State and Welfare,* ed. Linda Gordon, 199–225. Madison: University of Wisconsin Press, 1990.

Fraser, Nancy, and Linda Gordon. "A Genealogy of *Dependency*: Tracing a Keyword of the U.S. Welfare State." *Signs* 19, no. 2 (Winter 1994): 309–36.

Gabin, Nancy. *Feminism and the Labor Movement: Women and the United Auto Workers, 1935–1975.* Ithaca, N.Y.: Cornell University Press, 1990.

Garrison, Dee. "'Our Skirts Gave Them Courage': The Civil Defense Protest Movement in New York City, 1955–1961." In *Not June Cleaver: Women and Gender in Postwar America, 1945–1960,* ed. Joanne Meyerowitz, 201–26. Philadelphia: Temple University Press, 1994.

Gilbert, James. *A Cycle of Outrage: America's Reaction to the Juvenile Delinquent in the 1950s.* New York: Oxford University Press, 1986.

Gilje, Paul A. "Infant Abandonment in Early Nineteenth-Century New York: Three Cases." In *Growing Up in America: Children in Historical Perspective,* ed. N. Ray Hiner and Joseph Hawes, 109–17. Urbana: University of Illinois Press, 1985.

Gilman, Charlotte Perkins. *Women and Economics: A Study of the Economic Relation between Men and Women as a Factor in Social Evolution.* Boston: Small, Maynard, 1898.

Glenn, Evelyn Nakano. "From Servitude to Service Work: Historical Continuities in the Racial Division of Paid Reproductive Labor." In *Unequal Sisters: A Multicultural Reader in U.S. Women's History,* ed. Vicki L. Ruiz and Ellen Carol DuBois. 2d ed., 405–35. New York: Routledge, 1994.

Gluck, Sherna Berger. *Rosie the Riveter Revisited: Women, the War and Social Change.* Boston: Twayne, 1987.

Goldsmith, Cornelia. *Better Day Care for the Young Child through a Merged Governmental and Nongovernmental Effort: The Story of Day Care in New York City.* Washington: National Association for the Education of Young Children, 1972.

González, Gilbert G. *Chicano Education in the Era of Segregation.* Philadelphia: Balch Institute, 1990.

Goodwin, Joanne L. *Gender and the Politics of Welfare Reform: Mothers' Pensions in Chicago, 1911–1929.* Chicago: University of Chicago Press, 1997.

Goodwyn, Lawrence. *The Populist Moment: A Short History of the Agrarian Revolt in America.* New York: Oxford University Press, 1978.

Gordon, Linda. "Putting Children First: Women, Maternalism, and Welfare in the Early Twentieth Century." In *U.S. History as Women's History: New Feminist Essays,* ed. Linda Kerber, Alice Kessler-Harris, and Kathryn Kish Sklar, 63–86. Chapel Hill: University of North Carolina Press, 1995.

———. *Pitied but Not Entitled: Single Mothers and the History of Welfare.* New York: Free Press, 1994.

Grabowski, John. "Introduction." In *Cleveland: The Making of a City*, by William Gannon. 2d ed. Kent, Ohio: Kent State University Press, 1990.

Green, Constance. *A Secret City: A History of Race Relations in the Nation's Capital.* Princeton, N.J.: Princeton University Press, 1967.

Greenblatt, Bernard. *Responsibility for Child Care: The Changing Role of Family and State in Child Development.* San Francisco: Jossey-Bass, 1977.

Groneman, Carol, and Mary Beth Norton, eds. *"To Toil the Livelong Day": America's Women at Work, 1780–1980.* Ithaca, N.Y.: Cornell University Press, 1987.

Grubb, W. Norton, and Marvin Lazerson. "Child Care, Government Financing, and the Public Schools: Lessons from the California Children's Centers." *School Review* 86, no. 1 (November 1977): 5–37.

Gullett, Gayle Ann. "Feminism, Politics, and Voluntary Groups: Organized Womanhood in California, 1886–1896." Ph.D. diss., University of California, Riverside, 1983.

Halberstam, David. *The Fifties.* New York: Villard, 1993.

Hall, Kermit, ed. "Laissez-Faire Constitutionalism and Liberty in the Late Nineteenth Century." In *Major Problems in American Constitutional History.* Vol. 2, *From 1870 to the Present*, 23–79. Lexington, Mass.: D. C. Heath, 1992.

———. "Paternalistic Sexism and Liberty to Contract, 1873–1923." In *Major Problems in American Constitutional History.* Vol. 2, *From 1870 to the Present*, 80–141. Lexington, Mass.: D. C. Heath, 1992.

Halper, Betty Lois. "Recollections of Los Angeles Children's Centers' Early Days." M.A. thesis, California State University, Northridge, January 1977.

Harrison, Cynthia. *On Account of Sex: The Politics of Women's Issues, 1945–1968.* Berkeley: University of California Press, 1988.

Hartmann, Susan. *The Other Feminists: Activists in the Liberal Establishment.* New Haven: Yale University Press, 2000.

———. "Women's Employment and the Domestic Ideal in the Early Cold War Years." In *Not June Cleaver: Women and Gender in Postwar America, 1945–1960*, ed. Joanne Meyerowitz, 84–100. Philadelphia: Temple University Press, 1994.

Harvey, Brett. *The Fifties: A Women's Oral History.* New York: HarperCollins, 1993.

Hayden, Delores. *The Grand Domestic Revolution: A History of Feminist Designs for American Homes, Neighborhoods and Cities.* Cambridge: MIT Press, 1981.

Hewitt, Nancy. "Beyond the Search for Sisterhood: American Women's History in the 1980s." In *Unequal Sisters: A Multicultural Reader in U.S. Women's History*, ed. Ellen DuBois and Vicki L. Ruiz, 1st ed., 1–14. New York: Routledge, 1990.

Hobson, Barbara. "Feminist Strategies and Gendered Discourse in Welfare States: Married Women's Right to Work in the United States and Sweden." In *Mothers of a New World: Maternalist Politics and the Origins of Welfare States*, ed. Seth Koven and Sonya Michel, 396–429. New York: Routledge, 1993.

Hofstadter, Richard. *The Age of Reform: From Bryan to F.D.R.* New York: Vintage, 1955.

Honey, Maureen. *Creating Rosie the Riveter: Class, Gender and Propaganda during World War II*. Amherst: University of Massachusetts Press, 1984.

Horowitz, Daniel. "Rethinking Betty Friedan and *The Feminine Mystique*: Labor Union Radicalism and Feminism in Cold War America." *American Quarterly* 48, no. 1 (March 1996): 1–42.

Jaffe, Harry S., and Tom Sherwood. *Dream City: Race, Power, and the Decline of Washington, D.C.* New York: Simon and Schuster, 1994.

Johnson, Elaine Zahnd. "Protective Legislation and Women's Work: Oregon's Ten-Hour Law and the *Muller* v. *Oregon* Case, 1900–1913." Ph.D. diss., University of Oregon, 1980.

Johnson, Glenna. "What Mothers Think about Day Care." *Child* 10 (January 1946) 7:104.

———. "Day Care: An Essential in Peacetime Economy." *Child Welfare League of America Bulletin* (February 1945): 9–10.

Jones, Betty, and Elizabeth Prescott, with Mary Ellison. *Day Care and Nursery Education in Los Angeles County*. Special Report no. 71. Welfare Planning Council, Los Angeles Region, Research Department, May 1964.

Jones, Jacqueline. *Labor of Love, Labor of Sorrow: Black Women, Work and the Family, from Slavery to the Present*. New York: Vintage, 1986.

Kaledin, Eugenia. *Mothers and More: American Women in the 1950s*. Boston: Twayne, 1984.

Kellogg, Lester S., and Dorothy S. Brady. "The City Worker's Family Budget." In *Workers' Budgets in the United States: City Families and Single Persons, 1946–1947*. U.S. Bureau of Labor Statistics, Bulletin 927, 3–40. Washington: Government Printing Office, 1948.

Kelly, Alfred A., Winfred A. Harbison and Herman Belz, *The American Constitution: Its Origins and Development*. Vol. 2. 7th ed. New York: W. W. Norton, 1991.

Kennedy, Jay, and Daniel Orescanin. "Protective Labor Legislation in Indiana." Bureau of Business Research, Graduate School of Business, Indiana University, 1965.

Kerber, Linda. "The Meanings of Citizenship." *Journal of American History* 84, no. 3 (December 1997): 833–54.

———. "A Constitutional Right to Be Treated like American Ladies: Women and the Obligations of Citizenship." In *U.S. History as Women's History: New Feminist Essays*, ed. Linda Kerber, Alice Kessler-Harris, and Kathryn Kish Sklar, 17–35. Chapel Hill: University of North Carolina Press, 1995.

———. "Separate Spheres, Female Worlds, Woman's Place: The Rhetoric of Women's History." *Journal of American History* 75 (June 1988): 9–39.

———. *Women of the Republic: Intellect and Ideology in Revolutionary America*. Chapel Hill: University of North Carolina Press, 1980.

Kerber, Linda, Alice Kessler-Harris, and Kathryn Kish Sklar. *U.S. History as Women's History: New Feminist Essays*. Chapel Hill: University of North Carolina Press, 1995.

Kesselman, Amy. *Fleeting Opportunities: Women Shipyard Workers in Portland*

and Vancouver during World War II and Reconversion. Albany: State University of New York Press, 1990.

Kessler-Harris, Alice. *In Pursuit of Equity: Women, Men, and the Quest for Economic Citizenship in 20th Century America.* New York: Oxford University Press, 2001.

———. "Designing Old Women and Fools: The Construction of the Social Security Amendments of 1939." In *U.S. History as Women's History: New Feminist Essays,* ed. Linda Kerber, Alice Kessler-Harris and Kathryn Kish Sklar, 87–106. Chapel Hill: University of North Carolina Press, 1995.

———. *A Woman's Wage: Historical Meanings and Social Consequences.* Lexington: University Press of Kentucky, 1990.

———. *Out to Work: A History of Wage-Earning Women in the United States.* New York: Oxford University Press, 1982.

Kirscher, Marilyn Adrran. "History of Day Care in Ohio, 1920–1970." M.A. thesis, Ohio State University, 1974.

Kornbluh, Felicia A. "The New Literature on Gender and the Welfare State: The U.S. Case." *Feminist Studies* 22, no. 1 (Spring 1996): 171–98.

Kossoudji, Sherrie A., and Laura J. Dresser. "Working Class Rosies: Women Industrial Workers during World War II." *Journal of Economic History* 52, no. 2 (June 1992): 431–46.

Koven, Seth, and Sonya Michel. "Womanly Duties: Maternalist Politics and the Origins of Welfare States in France, Germany, Great Britain and the United States, 1880–1920." *American Historical Review* 95 (October 1990): 1076–1108.

Koven, Seth, and Sonya Michel, eds. *Mothers of a New World: Maternalist Politics and the Origins of Welfare States.* New York: Routledge, 1993.

Kusko, Andrea Lee. "The Federal Child Care Tax Deduction." Ph.D. diss., Stanford University, 1979.

Ladd-Taylor, Molly. *Mother-Work: Women, Child Welfare, and the State, 1890–1930.* Urbana: University of Illinois Press, 1994.

Langlois, Janet. *Serving the Children Then and Now: An Oral History of Early Childhood Education and Day Care in Metropolitan Detroit.* Center for Urban Studies and Walter P. Reuther Library, College of Urban, Labor and Metropolitan Affairs, Wayne State University, Detroit, 1989.

LaRossa, Ralph. *The Modernization of Fatherhood: A Social and Political History.* Chicago: University of Chicago Press, 1997.

Laughlin, Kathleen A. *Women's Work and Public Policy: A History of the Women's Bureau, U.S. Department of Labor, 1945–1970.* Boston: Northeastern University Press, 2000.

Law, Sylvia. "Women, Work, Welfare, and the Preservation of Patriarchy." *University of Pennsylvania Law Review* 131, no. 6 (May 1983)6: 1249–1339.

Lehrer, Susan. *Origins of Protective Labor Legislation for Women, 1905–1925.* Albany: State University of New York Press, 1987.

Leighow, Susan Rimby. "An 'Obligation to Participate': Married Nurses' Labor Force Participation in the 1950s." In *Not June Cleaver: Women and Gender in Postwar America, 1945–1960,* ed. Joanne Meyerowitz, 37–56. Philadelphia: Temple University Press, 1994.

Lemann, Nicholas. *The Promised Land: The Great Black Migration and How It Changed America.* New York: Vintage, 1992.

Lenroot, Katherine. "Current National Developments and Problems in Public-Welfare Services for Children." *Child* 9, no. 7 (January 1945): 103–5.

Lens, Sidney. *The Labor Wars: From the Molly Maguires to the Sitdowns.* New York: Doubleday, 1973.

Leonard, Kevin. "Years of Hope, Days of Fear: The Impact of World War II on Race Relations in Los Angeles." Ph.D. diss., University of California, Davis, 1992.

Leopold, Alice K. "Federal Equal Pay Legislation." *Labor Law Journal* 6, no. 1 (January 1955): 7–32.

Levenstein, Lisa. "From Innocent Children to Unwanted Migrants and Unwed Moms: Two Chapters in the Public Discourse on Welfare In the United States, 1960–1961." *Journal of Women's History* 11, no. 4 (Winter 2000): 10–33.

Lewis, Lucille, "The Strengths in Day Care Licensing." *Child Welfare*, June 1959, 10–15.

Lindemeyer, Kriste. *"A Right to Childhood": The U.S. Children's Bureau and Child Welfare, 1912–1946.* Urbana: University of Illinois Press, 1997.

Lipsitz, George. *The Possessive Investment in Whiteness: How White People Profit from Identity Politics.* Philadelphia: Temple University Press, 1998.

———. *Rainbow at Midnight: Labor and Culture in the 1940s.* Rev. ed. Urbana: University of Illinois Press, 1994.

Lynn, Susan. "Gender and Progressive Politics: A Bridge to Social Activism of the 1960s." In *Not June Cleaver: Women and Gender in Postwar America, 1945–1960,* ed. Joanne Meyerowitz, 103–27. Philadelphia: Temple University Press, 1994.

Mabunda, L. Mpho, and Shirelle Phelps, eds. *Contemporary Black Biography: Profiles from the International Black Community.* Vol. 14. Detroit: Gale, 1997.

Malone, Zelma Elizabeth. "A Study of Day Care Methods Adopted by the Mothers Rejected from District Day Nurseries under Provisions of Public Law 237." M.S.W. thesis, National Catholic School of Social Service, Catholic University of America, 1948.

Marshall, T. H. "Citizenship and Social Class." In *Citizenship and Social Class and Other Essays,* 1–85. Cambridge: Cambridge University Press, 1950.

Mathews, Robert E., ed. *Cases and Materials on the Employment Relation and Protective Labor Legislation.* Columbus: Northside Letter Shop, 1954.

May, Elaine Tyler. *Homeward Bound: American Families in the Cold War Era.* New York: Basic Books, 1988.

May, Martha. "The Historical Problem of the Family Wage: The Ford Motor Company and the Five Dollar Day." In *Unequal Sisters: A Multicultural Reader in U.S. Women's History,* ed. Ellen Carol DuBois and Vicki L. Ruiz, 1st ed., 275–91. New York: Routledge, 1990.

———. "Bread before Roses: American Workingmen, Labor Unions and the Family Wage." In *Women, Work and Protest: A Century of U.S. Women's Labor History,* ed. Ruth Milkman, 1–21. Boston: Routledge and Kegan Paul, 1985.

McCaffery, Edward. *Taxing Women.* Chicago: University of Chicago Press, 1997.

McWilliams, Carey. *Factories in the Field: The Story of Migratory Farm Labor in California*. Orig. pubd. 1939. Santa Barbara: Peregrine, 1971.

Mead, Margaret, and Frances Kaplan, eds. *American Women: The Report of the President's Commission and Other Publications of the Commission*. New York: Charles Scribner's Sons, 1965.

Meyerowitz, Joanne. "Beyond the Feminine Mystique: A Reassessment of Postwar Mass Culture." In *Not June Cleaver: Women and Gender in Postwar America, 1945–1960*, ed. Joanne Meyerowitz, 229–62. Philadelphia: Temple University Press, 1994.

Meyerowitz, Joanne, ed. *Not June Cleaver: Women and Gender in Postwar America, 1945–1960*. Philadelphia: Temple University Press, 1994.

Michel, Sonya. *Children's Interests, Mothers' Rights: The Shaping of America's Child Care Policy*. New Haven: Yale University Press, 1999.

———. "The Politics of Child Care in America's Public/Private Welfare State." In *Families in the U.S.: Kinship and Domestic Politics*, ed. Karen V. Hansen and Anita Ilta Garey, 837–48. Philadelphia: Temple University Press, 1998.

———. "The Limits of Maternalism: Policies toward American Wage-Earning Mothers during the Progressive Era." In *Mothers of a New World: Maternalist Politics and the Origins of Welfare States*, ed. Seth Koven and Sonya Michel, 277–320. New York: Routledge, 1993.

———. "American Women and the Discourse of the Democratic Family in World War II." In *Behind the Lines: Gender and the Two World Wars*, ed. Margaret Randolph Higonnet, Jane Jenson, Sonya Michel, and Margaret Collins Weitz, 154–67. New Haven: Yale University Press, 1987.

Milkman, Ruth. *Gender at Work: The Dynamics of Job Segregation by Sex during World War II*. Urbana: University of Illinois Press, 1987.

———, ed. *Women, Work and Protest: A Century of U.S. Women's Labor History*. Boston: Routledge and Kegan Paul, 1985.

Mink, Gwendolyn. *Welfare's End*. Ithaca, N.Y.: Cornell University Press, 1998.

———. "The Lady and the Tramp: Gender, Race, and the Origins of the American Welfare State." In *Women, the State and Welfare*, ed. Linda Gordon, 92–122. Madison: University of Wisconsin Press, 1990.

Mittelstadt, Jennifer. "'Dependency as a Problem to Be Solved': Rehabilitation and the American Liberal Consensus on Welfare in the 1950s." *Social Politics* (Summer 2001): 228–57.

Montgomery, David. *Citizen Worker: The Experience of Workers in the United States with Democracy and the Free Market during the Nineteenth Century*. Cambridge: Cambridge University Press, 1993.

———. *Beyond Equality: Labor and the Radical Republicans, 1862–1872*. New York: Alfred A. Knopf, 1967.

Moore, Marat. *Women in the Mines: Stories of Life and Work*. New York: Twayne, 1996.

Moore, Winifred. *Some Aspects of Day Care Licensing at the State Level*. New York: Child Welfare League of America, October 1957.

Muncy, Robyn. *Creating a Female Dominion in American Reform, 1890–1935*. New York: Oxford University Press, 1991.

National Committee on Segregation in the Nation's Capital. *Segregation in Washington*. Chicago, November 1948.

National Manpower Council. *Work in the Lives of Married Women*. Proceedings of a Conference on Womanpower, October 20–25, 1957. New York: Columbia University Press, 1958.

Nelson, Barbara. "The Origins of the Two-Channel Welfare State: Workmen's Compensation and Mothers' Aid." In *Women, the State and Welfare*, ed. Linda Gordon, 123–51. Madison: University of Wisconsin Press, 1990.

Nelson, Richard and Michael Krashinsky. "Two Major Issues of Public Policy: Public Subsidy and Organization of Supply." In *Public Policy for Day Care of Young Children*, ed. Dennis Young and Richard Nelson, 55–69. Lexington, Mass.: D. C. Heath, 1973.

"New Bases for Eligibility in New York City Day Care Centers." *Child* 12, no. 5 (November 1947): 73.

O'Connor, Julia. "Gender, Class and Citizenship in the Comparative Analysis of Welfare State Regimes: Theoretical and Methodological Issues." *British Journal of Sociology* 44, no. 3 (September 1993): 501–18.

O'Farrell, Brigid, and Joyce Kornbluh, eds. *Rocking the Boat: Union Women's Voices, 1915–1975*. New Brunswick, N.J.: Rutgers University Press, 1996.

Orloff, Ann Shola. "Gender and the Social Rights of Citizenship: The Comparative Analysis of Gender Relations and Welfare States." *American Sociological Review* 58 (June 1993): 303–28.

Palmer, Phyllis. "Housewife and Household Worker: Employer-Employee Relationships in the Home, 1928–1941." In *"To Toil the Livelong Day": America's Women at Work, 1780–1980*, ed. Carol Groneman and Mary Beth Norton, 179–95. Ithaca, N.Y.: Cornell University Press, 1987.

Pateman, Carole. "The Patriarchal Welfare State." In *Democracy and the Welfare State*, ed. Amy Guttman, 231–60. Princeton, N.J.: Princeton University Press, 1988.

Patterson, James. *America's Struggle against Poverty, 1900–1994*. 3d ed. Cambridge: Harvard University Press, 1995.

Phadke, Sindhu Vaman. "Licensing of Child Care in California, 1911–1961." Ph.D. diss., University of Southern California, 1963.

"Planning Services for Children to Supplement the Home and School." *Child* 10 (March 1946): 145–46.

Pollack, Jack Harrison. "Schools That Save Families." *Nation's Business*. September 1952.

Potter, David. "National Character." In *American History and the Social Sciences*, ed. Edward Saveth, 427–45. New York: Free Press of Glencoe, 1964. Article first pubd. as "American Women and the American Character," *Stetson University Bulletin*, January 1962.

Prescott, Elisabeth, Cynthia Milich, and Elizabeth Jones. *The "Politics" of Day Care*. Washington: National Association for the Education of Young Children, 1972.

Pritchard, Robert L. "California Un-American Activities Investigations: Subversions on the Right?" *California Historical Society Quarterly* 49 (December 1970): 309–27.

Putnam, Jackson K. "The Progressive Legacy in California: Fifty Years of Politics, 1917–1967." In *California Progressivism Revisited*, ed. William Deverell and Tom Sitton, 247–68. Berkeley: University of California Press, 1994.

Raferty, Judith. "Los Angeles Clubwomen and Progressive Reform." In *California Progressivism Revisited*, ed. William Deverell and Tom Sitton, 144–74. Berkeley: University of California Press, 1994.

Reeder, Janis Ridenour. "The Child Care Deduction: Issues in Horizontal Equity." Ph.D. diss., University of South Carolina, 1978.

Reese, Ellen. "Maternalism and Political Mobilization: How California's Postwar Child Care Campaign Was Won." *Gender and Society* 10, no. 5 (October 1996): 566–89.

Reskin, Barbara, and Heidi I. Hartmann, eds. *Women's Work, Men's Work: Sex Segregation on the Job*. Committee on Women's Employment and Related Social Issues, National Research Council. Washington: National Academy Press, 1986.

Riley, Susan E. "Caring for Rosie's Children: Child Care, American Women and the Federal Government in the World War II Era." Ph.D. diss., University of California, Berkeley, 1996.

Rose, Elizabeth. *A Mother's Job: The History of Day Care, 1890–1960*. New York: Oxford University Press, 1999.

Ross, Susan Deller. "Sex Discrimination and 'Protective' Labor Legislation." Unpublished MS, May 1, 1970, State Historical Society of Wisconsin.

Ruderman, Florence. *Child Care and Working Mothers: A Study of Arrangements Made for Day Time Care of Children*. New York: Child Welfare League of America, 1968.

———. "Conceptualizing Needs for Day Care: Some Conclusions Drawn from the Child Welfare League Day Care Project." In *Day Care—An Expanding Resource*, 14–24. New York: Child Welfare League of America, 1965.

Ruiz, Vicki. *From Out of the Shadows: Mexican Women in Twentieth Century America*. New York: Oxford University Press, 1998.

———. *Cannery Women, Cannery Lives: Mexican Women, Unionization, and the California Food Processing Industry, 1930–1950*. Albuquerque: University of New Mexico, 1987.

Rupp, Leila. *Mobilizing Women for War: German and American Propaganda, 1939–1945*. Princeton, N.J.: Princeton University Press, 1978.

Rupp, Leila J., and Verta Taylor. *Survival in the Doldrums: The American Women's Rights Movement, 1945 to the 1960s*. New York: Oxford University Press, 1987.

Salem, Dorothy C., ed. *African American Women: A Biographical Dictionary*. New York: Garland, 1993.

Sapiro, Virginia. "The Gender Basis of American Social Policy." In *Women, the State and Welfare*, ed. Linda Gordon, 36–54. Madison: University of Wisconsin Press, 1990.

Scales, Janola T. "A Study of the Development of the Los Angeles Unified School District Children's Centers." Ed.D. diss., Pepperdine University, 1983.

Scharf, Lois. "The Women's Movement in Cleveland from 1850." In *Cleveland: A*

Tradition of Reform, ed. John J. Grabowski and David D. Van Tassel, 68–90. Kent, Ohio: Kent State University Press, 1986.

Schatz, Ronald. *The Electrical Workers: A History of Labor at General Electric and Westinghouse, 1923–1960*. Urbana: University of Illinois Press, 1983.

Schroedel, Jean Reith, ed. *Alone in a Crowd: Women in the Trades Tell Their Stories*. Philadelphia: Temple University Press, 1985.

Scobie, Ingrid Winter. *Center Stage: Helen Gahagan Douglas, a Life*. New Brunswick, N.J.: Rutgers University Press, 1992.

Skocpol, Theda. *Protecting Soldiers and Mothers: The Political Origins of Social Policy in the United States*. Cambridge: Belknap, 1992.

Smith, I. Evelyn. "While Mothers Work at Defense Jobs." *Child* 15, no. 7 (March 1951): 125–26.

Smith, Rogers M. "'One United People': Second-Class Female Citizenship and the American Quest for Community." *Yale Journal of Law and the Humanities* 1 (1989): 229–93.

Solinger, Rickie. "Dependency and Choice: The Two Faces of Eve." In *Whose Welfare?* ed. Gwendolyn Mink, 7–35. Ithaca: N.Y.: Cornell University Press, 1999.

Sparks, Holloway. "Dissident Citizenship: Democratic Theory, Political Courage, and Activist Women." *Hypatia* 12, no. 4 (Fall 1997): 74–110.

Steinfels, Margaret O'Brien. *Who's Minding the Children: The History and Politics of Day Care in America*. New York: Simon and Schuster, 1973.

Stewart, Dorothy Jean. "Preschools and Politics: A History of Early Childhood Education in California." Ed.D. diss., University of California, Berkeley, 1990.

Straub, Eleanor, F. "United States Government Policy toward Civilian Women during World War II." *Prologue*, Winter 1973, 240–54.

Streeter, Sandy. "Earmarks and Limitations in Appropriations Bills." Government Division, Congressional Research Service, Library of Congress, February 11, 1999.

Swerdlow, Amy. "Ladies' Day at the Capitol: Women Strike for Peace Versus HUAC." In *Unequal Sisters: A Multicultural Reader in U.S. Women's History*, ed. Ellen DuBois and Vicki L. Ruiz, 224–37. New York: Routledge, 1990.

Technical Advisory Committee. *Workers' Budgets in the United States: City Families and Single Persons, 1946–1947*. U.S. Bureau of Labor Statistics, Bulletin 927, 6–9. Washington: Government Printing Office.

Tobias, Sheila, and Lisa Anderson. "What Really Happened to Rosie the Riveter? Demobilization and the Female Labor Force, 1944–1947." New York: MSS Modular Publications, 1974.

Trachtenberg, Alan. *The Incorporation of America: Culture and Society in the Gilded Age*. New York: Hill and Wang, 1982.

UAW-CIO. *Proceedings, Fourteenth Constitutional Convention*, Atlantic City, N.J., March 22–27, 1953.

Valk, Anne M. "'Mother Power': The Movement for Welfare Rights in Washington, D.C., 1966–1972." *Journal of Women's History* 11, no. 4 (Winter 2000): 34–58.

Van Tassel, David, D. "Introduction." In *Cleveland: A Tradition of Reform*, ed. John J. Grabowski and David D. Van Tassel, 2–11. Kent, Ohio: Kent State University Press, 1986.

Van Tassel, David, D., and John Grabowski, eds. *The Encyclopedia of Cleveland History*. Bloomington, Ind.: Indiana University Press, 1987.

Waller, Willard. "The Coming War on Women." *This Week*, 18 February 1945, 4–5.

Ware, Susan. "American Women in the 1950s: Nonpartisan Politics and Women's Politicization." In *Women, Politics, and Change*, ed. Louise Tilly and Patricia Gurin, 281–99. New York: Russell Sage Foundation, 1990.

Wasem, Ruth. "No More Depressions: Full Employment and the Employment Act of 1946." Ph.D. diss., University of Michigan, 1990.

Weber, Devra. *Dark Sweat, White Gold: California Farm Workers, Cotton, and the New Deal*. Berkeley: University of California Press, 1994.

———. "*Raiz Fuerte*: Oral History and Mexican Farmworkers." In *Unequal Sisters: A Multicultural Reader in U.S. Women's History*, ed. Vicki L. Ruiz and Ellen Carol DuBois, 395–404. 2d ed. New York: Routledge, 1994.

Weiner, Lynn, ed. "Maternalism as a Paradigm." Symposium in *Journal of Women's History* 5, no. 2 (Fall 1993): 95–131.

Weir, Margaret. "The Federal Government and Unemployment: The Frustration of Policy Innovation from the New Deal to the Great Society." In *The Politics of Social Policy in the United States*, ed. Margaret Weir, Ann Orloff, and Theda Skocpol, 149–97. Princeton, N.J.: Princeton University Press, 1988.

Weiss, Nancy Pottersheim. "Mother, the Invention of Necessity: Dr. Benjamin Spock's Baby and Child Care." In *Growing Up in America: Children in Historical Perspective*, ed. N. Ray Hiner and Joseph Hawes, 283–303. Urbana: University of Illinois Press, 1985.

"Welfare Contrast: While Kennedy Pushes National Buildup, Congress Cracks Down in Capital Itself." *Wall Street Journal*, April 9, 1962.

Welfare Planning Council, Los Angeles Region, Research Department. *Background for Planning*. Los Angeles, 1955.

Welter, Barbara. "The Cult of True Womanhood, 1820–1860." *American Quarterly* 18 (1966): 151–74.

White, Richard. *It's Your Misfortune and None of My Own: A New History of the American West*. Norman: University of Oklahoma Press, 1991.

Wickenden, Elizabeth, and Winifred Bell. *Public Welfare: Time for a Change*. Project on Public Services for Families and Children, Sponsored by the New York School of Social Work. New York: Columbia University, 1961.

Willrich, Michael, "Home Slackers: Men, the State and Welfare in Modern America." *Journal of American History* 87, no. 2 (September 2000): 460–89.

Wollenberg, Charles M. *All Deliberate Speed: Segregation and Exclusion in California Schools, 1855–1975*. Berkeley: University of California Press, 1978.

Wright, Gavin. *Old South, New South: Revolutions in the Southern Economy since the Civil War*. New York: Basic Books, 1986.

Youcha, Geraldine. *Minding the Children: Child Care in America from Colonial Times to the Present*. New York: Scribner, 1995.

National Committee for the Day Care of Children (NCDCC), 224, 225, 226, 227–28, 231. *See also* Inter-City Committee for Day Care

National Committee on Group Day Care of Children, 41, 249 (n. 89)

Nickel, George D., 145, 159

"Official-economic institutions," 5–6, 140

Ohio State Department of Public Welfare, 86, 218, 220

Parents Day Care Association (PDCA, Cleveland), 59, 60, 65, 81, 83–85, 86, 259 (n. 86); City Hall demonstrations, 68–69, 71–72, 74–76

Pre-School Association (California), 215–16, 217, 218

Private Nursery School Association of Northern California, 215, 217

"Productive citizenship," 9, 14, 187–91, 195, 240

Protective labor laws, 6, 30–33, 246 (nn. 47, 51)

Public Welfare Amendments of 1962, 199, 222, 225, 231, 233, 299 (nn. 99, 100); and child care, 223, 226, 229–31, 234–35, 236–37

Raine, Irene, 128

Ribicoff, Abraham, 224, 226, 227, 230

Roosevelt, Eleanor, 47, 251 (n. 6)

School Lunch Act, 42

Smith, Margaret Chase, 1, 6, 124, 127, 134

Social Security Amendments of 1965, 233–34

Sweeny, Joseph T., 64, 67, 68, 74, 79, 80, 81, 258 (n. 79), 262 (n. 134)

Temporary Assistance for Needy Families (TANF), 240

Texas Licensed Child Care Association, 215

Tracht, Bella. *See* Likover, Belle (Bella) Tracht

Truman, Harry S., 54, 56–57

Tucker, Rosina, 112

U.S. Children's Bureau, 19, 35–36, 130, 214, 228; and World War II child care, 51–52, 145, 252 (n. 19); and Korean War, 130, 132–33; and Public Welfare Amendments of 1962, 229, 231

U.S. Women's Bureau, 23, 33–34, 58, 130, 202

Wage work, 3, 6, 24, 30–33

—by mothers, 8–9, 10, 12, 26, 90, 198, 205–8, 239–40; and right to paid labor, 21–23, 24–25, 134, 152; and protective labor laws, 30–33; threatens society, 77–78, 105, 162, 229; public benefits of, 104, 130–32, 162–65, 188, 194, 227

Warren, Earl, 141, 143, 147, 150, 151, 191

Weber, John, 159

Welfare Council of (Metropolitan) Los Angeles, 150, 152, 175

Wender, Harry, 97

Women: and labor force participation, 28–29, 38, 58, 59, 139, 165, 204, 213. *See also* Wage work—by mothers

Women's Bureau. *See* U.S. Women's Bureau

Wright, Frank, 159

Zahm, Bernice, 56, 66